PRAISE FOR
REVOLUTION AND OTHER ...
A POLITICAL READER

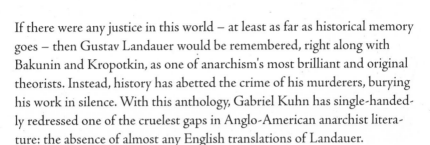

If there were any justice in this world – at least as far as historical memory goes – then Gustav Landauer would be remembered, right along with Bakunin and Kropotkin, as one of anarchism's most brilliant and original theorists. Instead, history has abetted the crime of his murderers, burying his work in silence. With this anthology, Gabriel Kuhn has single-handedly redressed one of the cruelest gaps in Anglo-American anarchist literature: the absence of almost any English translations of Landauer.

> **– Jesse Cohn, author of *Anarchism and the Crisis of Representation: Hermeneutics, Aesthetics, Politics***

Gustav Landauer was, without doubt, one of the brightest intellectual lights within the revolutionary circles of fin de siècle Europe. In this remarkable anthology, Gabriel Kuhn brings together an extensive and splendidly chosen collection of Landauer's most important writings, presenting them for the first time in English translation. With Landauer's ideas coming of age today perhaps more than ever before, Kuhn's work is a valuable and timely piece of scholarship, and one which should be required reading for anyone with an interest in radical social change.

> **– James Horrox, author of *A Living Revolution: Anarchism in the Kibbutz Movement***

Kuhn's meticulously edited book revives not only the "spirit of freedom," as Gustav Landauer put it, necessary for a new society but also the spirited voice of a German Jewish anarchist too long quieted by the lack of English-language translations. Ahead of his time in many ways, Landauer now speaks volumes in this collection of his political writings to the zeitgeist of our own day: revolution from below. His insistence on a communitarian anarchism of the head and heart, of thought and action, rings more relevant than ever too. And if you long, as Landauer did, to "turn your dreams of beauty into a desire for realization," you'll find no better guide than this book – a joy from start to finish.

> **– Cindy Milstein, author of *Anarchism and Its Aspirations* and Institute for Anarchist Studies board member**

This collection of Gustav Landauer's political writings stands as a wonderful achievement. The detailed translations focus on works that have never before been available to an English speaking readership and the ideas contained in these works continue to resonate with contemporary anarchist concerns. Landauer's thought remains a timely and prescient affirmation of an anti-authoritarian tradition that finds value not in dogmatic and hate-fuelled revolutionism, but rather finds inspiration in a soulful humility and a heart-felt compassion in the awareness of the imbrication of self and other.

– Mark Huba, School of Social and Political Sciences, University of Melbourne, Australia

"[E]very Bavarian child at the age of 10 is going to know Walt Whitman by heart." This was the cornerstone of Landauer's educational system as a "people's delegate for culture and education" under the abortive Bavarian Revolution. His beautiful vision of a decentralized, cooperative, and humane society was not extinguished by the brutal hands of the Bolsheviks who stifled his voice in the Workingmen's Internationals or even by the proto-Nazis who assassinated him. His voice, which stirred the kibbutz movement to practical achievement, is now available to English readers who don't want to wait for the supposed "laws of history" to bring about the Socialist Revolution. "Nothing can prevent the united consumers from working for themselves with the aid of mutual credit, from building factories, workshops, houses for themselves, from acquiring land, nothing – if only they have a will and begin."

– Chris Dunlap, Barbary Coast Publishing Collective

GUSTAV LANDAUER

REVOLUTION

AND OTHER WRITINGS
A POLITICAL READER

Edited and Translated by Gabriel Kuhn
Preface by Richard J.F. Day

Revolution and Other Writings: A Political Reader
Edited and translated by Gabriel Kuhn
ISBN: 978-1-60486-054-2
LCCN: 2009901371
This edition copyright ©2010 PM Press
All Rights Reserved

PM Press
PO Box 23912
Oakland, CA 94623
www.pmpress.org

Published in the EU by The Merlin Press Ltd.
6 Crane Street Chambers,
Crane Street,
Pontypool
NP4 6ND,
Wales
www.merlinpress.co.uk
ISBN: 9780850366716

Layout by Daniel Meltzer
Cover art by John Yates

Printed in the USA, on recycled paper

"THE STATE IS A SOCIAL RELATIONSHIP; A CERTAIN way of people relating to one another. It can be destroyed by creating new social relationships; i.e., by people relating to one another differently."
– Gustav Landauer

TABLE OF CONTENTS

৵

Childhood and Youth

Early Anarchism

Through Separation to Community

Revolution

Socialist Hopes

On War and Nationalism

On America

Opinion and Journalism Pieces

Letters

ॐ

Bibliography

Index

PREFACE: LANDAUER TODAY
Richard J.F. Day

THERE'S A CLICHÉ ABOUT WATCHING OUT WHAT YOU ASK FOR, since you may get it in a way that doesn't quite please you. A few years ago, I asked for more of Gustav Landauer's work to be translated into English, and Gabriel Kuhn responded by doing just that. Unlike the cliché scenario, however, I'm very happy with the result. That is, the book you hold in your hand. Since many people will read no further than the first paragraph of this preface, if they read it at all, I want to say right now: buy this book. It's genuinely worth the price.

For those who need a little more convincing, allow me to provide some backup for my opinion. The introduction by Kuhn and Siegbert Wolf does an excellent job of reminding us of the relevance of the life and work of Gustav Landauer in his own time. But what about our time? Why should those of us standing on the ledge between the twentieth and twenty-first centuries be concerned about someone who died so long ago?

It would be too easy, and obviously incorrect, to say that nothing has changed in the last century. Yet, some very important elements of Landauer's context do remain with us today. He was an anarchist living, working, and writing on the margins of an authoritarian state. He was an anti-capitalist activist, a revolutionary who was killed because of who he was, what he believed, and what he did. The state form still seeks total control over our lives, and with new technologies has arguably gone much further in reaching its goal. Corporations still seek the greatest profit over the shortest term for the smallest number of people, while ruining the lives of everyone else and destroying the planet. They, too, seem to be doing better than ever, penetrating deeper, wider, meeting the challenges they face – as always – by mutating and forging ahead.

And us? Well, we are trying, as always, to find places and ways of doing something other, something different, from what the system of states and corporations allows us to do, requires us to do. We protest, we urge reform, we foment revolution. We get occasional good results, here and there, but no one with their eyes open, their ear to the ground, their heart and mind engaged, will deny that we are losing ground, every day, week, month, year... from our vantage point, from that ledge, we see below us what Nietzsche called an abyss. Peak oil, economic meltdown, species decline, including *homo sapiens sapiens*, which despite continuing to increase its population in absolute numbers, is facing an ongoing decline in fertility rates. It's only a matter of time ... the squeamish anti-civilizationists among us, within us, need never overcome our fear of blowing dams. The beast is dying of its own accord, quite simply killing itself.

What, then, as Comrade Lenin and many before him asked, is to be done? I think this is where the work of Gustav Landauer becomes indispensable. The kinds of answers he provided to this question were very much ahead of their time, and have yet to be adequately explored, discussed, and implemented – in any language, as far as I know, but most certainly in English. Unwilling to wait for history to catch up with itself, Landauer called for 'socialism here and now,' for the creation of positive radical alternatives to the dominant order – within, and on the margins of this order. He felt that this was the only way to make the kind of lasting difference that was necessary if things were really going to change, and I agree with him.

The sense of urgency that drove Landauer and his work has only increased since his time, of course, rising now to obsessive-compulsive heights, as can be seen from the kinds of books flying along the conveyor lines of the virtual bookshops these days. Suddenly, it's not only crazy anarchists and indigenous people and Gaian feminists who are talking about the coming destruction of the earth – it's ex-Vice President of the United States Al Gore. It's respectable, mainstream journalists. Everyone is cashing in. The question I'm interested in, is how do we cash out? Or, better yet, how do we leave behind the whole nexus of ideas and practices that give cash its value?

In his answer to this question Landauer was one of the first post-anarchists, inasmuch as he read Nietzsche anarchistically, and through his development of a discursive understanding of the state and capitalism as *states of relations*, rather than 'things.' This is an absolutely crucial insight for, as Karl Marx and Judith Butler have very clearly shown, once we become aware of the fact that we are (re)producing the dominant order through our daily activity, we become able to change our behaviour, and thereby the dominant order itself. Hence the privilege given, by Landauer, to working 'alongside' rather than against the state form, diverting our energies. Here he prefigures the currently hot autonomist marxist concept of prefiguration, although it must be noted that this idea has long been a staple of anarchist theory and practice.

This is the most important answer to the question, Why Landauer, now? Because he provides exactly what we need in order to have some small chance of peering into the abyss and coming up with something to do other than just follow everyone else as they semi-consciously leap into it.

There's another question I want to address, though, which is, Why should we be paying attention to this particular collection of translations? Here I have an abundance of answers, so fecund a proliferation that I will simply list them. For me, perhaps, the greatest strength of this text is the detailed discussion of links between Landauer's life and his writing. When I teach theory, anarchist or otherwise, I always highlight the fact that Gramsci went to prison, got sick, and died, for his ideas. Emma Goldman got 'sent back to Russia' for hers, Walter Benjamin shot himself because he was certain he had missed his last chance to escape the Nazis, people die every day in Oaxaca and Chiapas and Tibet and, yes, even on the lands claimed by the Canadian state, the 'peaceful country' I inhabit – or rather, that inhabits me. The introduction also addresses differing interpretations of Landauer's work in various languages, and its reception and influence around the world. Finally, the extensive bibliography will be of great aid to seasoned Landauer scholars and new explorers alike.

In the texts themselves, the tiny, difficult, often insoluble, problems of translation are treated in a subtle yet straightforward way. The result is a very readable rendering of the German original, a rendering that is perhaps superior to the original, according to some accounts. At the same time, Landauer's delicacy, ferocity, confusion, concision – all of the multiple and contradictory elements that make him who he is, his texts what they are — are preserved. Words, people, and events, that may not be common knowledge in the English-speaking world are accurately identified as such, and footnoted. Overall, this collection is well researched and very tight, in the sense that musicians give to this term. I found myself thinking "Ah, the real thing," that is, activist-oriented theory of the sort that was so common a few generations ago, and is now becoming more common again.

I would like my final words to be some first words from Landauer himself, who is surprisingly good at giving us a laugh, and a timeless, pointed, *anarchist* laugh, at that.

> "I will not hesitate to say the following in all clarity (knowing that I will not receive much appreciation from either side): to some degree, the anarchist politics of assassination only stems from the intentions of a small group amongst them that wants to follow the example of the big political parties. What drives them is vanity — a craving for recognition. What they are trying to say is: 'We are also doing politics. We aren't doing nothing. We are a force to be reckoned with!' These anarchists are not anarchic enough for me." ("Anarchic Thoughts on Anarchism")

Every time I see a twenty-something-year-old male dressed in combat fatigues strutting away from a protest with blood streaming from his head and swearing at the cops, I think of this quote from Gustav Landauer. And I think to myself: All well and good, but who's going to do the dishes, drywall your bedroom, take out the recycling, cook your meals, clean the house, look after the kids and elders, and change your bandages, while you try to get yourself out of jail and then field that short-lived but highly ego-gratifying spate of inquiries from the global media? Here and now, boys, here and now!

EDITOR'S NOTE
Gabriel Kuhn

Paul Avrich has called Gustav Landauer "the most influential German anarchist intellectual of the twentieth century."[1] In the English-speaking world, however, Gustav Landauer has only received limited attention. For decades, almost all of his writings – about a dozen books and pamphlets, as well as hundreds of essays, articles, and letters – remained untranslated. In the 1970s, over fifty years after his death at the hands of reactionary soldiers, a number of scholarly studies about his life and work appeared and his main text, *Aufruf zum Sozialismus*, was published as *For Socialism*. However, few studies or translations of Landauer followed.

Even during his lifetime, Landauer himself bemoaned the lack of foreign translations of his work. In 1910, he addressed the issue in a letter to the famed anarchist historian Max Nettlau.[2] Nettlau, who had elsewhere remarked that Landauer's texts were "not easy to understand, even for German-speakers,"[3] responded by pointing out "the difficulties for translators and foreign readers."[4] Subsequent scholars have shared these sentiments.[5]

The volume presented here attempts to provide a comprehensive collection of Landauer texts covering his political development from its beginnings among radical students, artists, and socialists in late 19th-century Berlin to his death in Munich in 1919.

Roughly, Landauer's writings can be divided into three major categories: "political," "philosophical," and "literary/cultural." This volume focuses on the political. To begin with, this reflects the main interest of both the editor and the publisher. Additionally, many of the English-speakers who have requested Landauer translations in recent years are found in the anarchist community. Furthermore, there seems to be no reason to support the "de-politization" of Landauer's work, which was noted as early as 1920 by Erich Mühsam and as recently as 2008 by Germany's most renowned contemporary Landauer scholar, Siegbert Wolf.[6] Needless to say, there is no reason why this Political Reader cannot be followed by a Philosophical and/or Literary/Cultural Reader should the interest in Landauer persist, or even increase.

The texts collected here intend to **a)** provide a balanced and complete picture of Landauer's political thought, **b)** gather Landauer's best known, most influential, and most characteristic texts, **c)** illustrate Landauer's wide range of interests through a number of unique and original essays and articles, **d)** assemble pieces of particular interest to English-speaking readers, and **e)** allow an insight into Landauer's rich correspondence.

The volume's central text is *Revolution*, a translation of Landauer's 1907 monograph *Die Revolution*, one of his three major works next to *Skepsis und Mystik. Versuche im Anschluss an Mauthners Sprachkritik* [*Skepticism and Mysticism: Essays Inspired by Mauthner's Critique of Language*] (1903) and *Aufruf zum Sozialismus* [*For Socialism*] (1911). *Die Revolution* is a political and philosophical study of history that serves as a bridge from the highly philosophical *Skepsis und Mystik* to the fairly practical *Aufruf zum Sozialismus*. Apart from *Die Revolution*, the volume contains twenty-nine Landauer essays and articles, as well as twelve letters, postcards, and telegrams.

While the selection encompasses all aspects of Landauer's political writing, it is also conscious of the Landauer texts that are already available in English. The book contains only one reprint, "Anarchic Thoughts on Anarchism," which was published (in a slightly different version) in the Fall 2007 issue of *Perspectives on Anarchist Theory*. All other texts appear here in English translation for the first time.

The opening chapters are organized in chronological order, allowing the reader to follow Landauer's political biography: his childhood and youth; his engagement in German anarchist circles in the 1890s; the years of relative seclusion from 1901 to 1908; the subsequent foundation of the Socialist Bund and the resurrection of *Der Sozialist*; his dedicated antimilitaristic struggle during World War I; and finally, the months of the Bavarian Revolution that led to Landauer's death. The Introduction to the volume is structured accordingly. The final three chapters intend to provide additional material: "On America" combines Landauer's most important comments on the continent's political events and developments (Landauer seemed to take a much bigger interest in North America than in Great Britain and Ireland[7]); the "Journalism and Opinion Pieces" provide a glimpse of the remarkably wide range of Landauer's political commentary and of his internationalist orientation;[8] and, finally, the "Letters" document Landauer's correspondence, give some of his beliefs and ideas a more personal voice, and make Landauer the person more tangible (Erich Mühsam: "Shall I speak of Landauer, the man? Of the way he moved, of his personal relationship with others? Read his letters! Read them!"[9]).

Translating Gustav Landauer

As the above quoted comments by Max Nettlau suggest, translating Gustav Landauer poses certain challenges. German has changed a lot in the last one hundred years, and Landauer's style was deemed peculiar and long-winded even in his lifetime.

This volume intends to present Gustav Landauer texts that are readable for a contemporary English-speaking audience, and not only an academic one. When this required rephrasing rather than literal reproduction, I chose the former. Of course, this does not mean that the translations offer a "simplified" Landauer. I am confident that they capture the original, even when I decided against literal renditions of German phrases that hardly make sense to contemporary German-speakers.

One aspect of keeping the texts readable was to rigorously limit the number of untranslated German terms. The handful of German terms that remain are explained in footnotes. Sometimes, the original German terms follow the translation in round brackets. The same goes for German names or essay and book titles. English translations of German names and titles follow in square brackets.

Some of the German terms that need explaining are used so frequently by Landauer that it seems best to offer explanations up front:

Geist − *spirit*: *Geist* is a notoriously difficult German term to translate. "Spirit" is most commonly used in English, and I have adapted to this. However, the philosophical notion of *Geist* − for example in Hegel − lies somewhere between "intellect" and "soul;" as such, it can apply to an individual (in which case it might also be understood as an individual's "essence") as well as to a community, a people, an era, even a place; it defines individual or collective identity beyond its mere physicality (hence the major attacks on the term by materialists). Landauer uses *Geist* much in this sense. In a speech during the Bavarian Revolution, a few months before his death, he offers one of the most concise definitions: "Geist is when knowledge, emotion, and will unite and become an active force."[10] In a less philosophical context, *Geist* can also be a close equivalent to "mind" or "reason." On the few occasions Landauer uses the term in this sense, it has been translated accordingly. "Ghost," another meaning of *Geist*, plays no role in Landauer's usage.

Mitleben – *communality*: *Mitleben* is mainly used in philosophical context. It literally means "living with" and indicates a shared, communal existence. In a stronger ethical sense, it implies the notion that human life is by definition communal since human beings are social beings whose living (*Leben*) is necessarily a "living with" (*Mitleben*). In the few existing Landauer translations, *Mitleben* has most frequently been translated as "communality," which I decided to adopt. Other options include "coexistence," "communal life," or "social life" – though the latter would seem an unfortunate choice as it is the standard translation for Marx's *gesellschaftliches Leben*, and is, apart from its Marxist baggage, a more sociological term than the philosophical (ethical) *Mitleben*.

Verwirklichung – *realization*: The term *Verwirklichung* is central in Landauer's thought. It is translated as "realization." It is important to note, however, that *Verwirklichung* means "realization" in the sense of "to make something real" and not in the sense of "to grasp/understand;" it is a term of *action*, not of intellectual comprehension.

Aufbau – *creation*: *Aufbau* literally means "building up." It is used in a variety of ways. In a physical sense it can function as a general term for scaffolds, stages, etc. In a wider sense, it can be used for anything that is "put together;" depending on the context, possible translations include "assembly," "composition," "structure," etc. In its socio-political sense – Landauer most often uses it in connection with "building" socialism – it stresses the active component of those who build. Hence, due to the lack of a more precise English equivalent, "creation" appears more fitting than the rather technical "establishment" or "formation." (Today, one of Switzerland's most militant socialist groups is called *Aufbau*; there is no direct connection to Gustav Landauer, however.)

Siedlung – *settlement*: *Siedlung* is a key concept in Landauer's vision of socialism. It is the basic communal unit upon which to build a federalist socialist society. It is translated here as "settlement." "Commune" would make a more expressive choice and would also avoid the conservative connotations of "settlement" that mainly derive from its use in colonial contexts. However, "settlement" is the literal translation of *Siedlung* and it was the term that Landauer used at the time. The German term *Kommune* has only been frequently used in the sense of the English "commune" since the 1960s. Its traditional German meaning is "municipality."

Bund – As there is neither a literal nor a standard translation for *Bund* in the sense of individuals "bonding" (*Bund* can also mean "bunch"), several options can be, and have been, used, also in relation to Landauer: "union," "association," "league," "federation," etc. In Landauer's case, the translation mainly concerns the *Sozialistische Bund* that he founded in 1908. In this volume, the term has been left untranslated. Apart from avoiding the difficulty to choose the most fitting English term, the main reason was an etymological connection observed by Siegbert Wolf: Wolf argues that Landauer chose the term *Bund* over other options – like *Föderation* [federation] or *Vereinigung* [association] – because of its relation to *brit*, a Biblical Hebrew word usually translated into English as "covenant." Wolf suggests that Landauer meant to express a union of people beyond mere organizational association: a union built on empathy, solidarity, and justice.[11]

Philister – *philistine*: Landauer makes frequent use of the term *Philister*, popularized as a pejorative for bourgeois scholars by Friedrich Nietzsche. As "philistine" (or "cultural philistine") has been the most common translation of the Nietzschean term, it will be used here too. It must be understood as a term for scholars bereft of soul and spirit, however, not as a term indicating mere lack of education, culture, or taste.

Landauer's language – like that of all German writers at the time, male and female – was marked by an inclusive use of male terms. Given the many problematic implications of a "modern cleaning" of Landauer's language, this has been reproduced in the translations.

All translations by Gabriel Kuhn, except for "Anarchic Thoughts on Anarchism" and "Through Separation to Community" by Gabriel Kuhn and Jesse Cohn.

Acknowledgments

As always, it is impossible to thank everyone who has helped in the publication of this book. The following are a selected few:

Chris Dunlap, who first got me inspired to translate Gustav Landauer during one of my frequent visits to the San Francisco Bay Area in 2003.

Stephen Bender, with whom I shared many laughs while deciphering Landauer texts for the translations of the *Anarchism in Germany and Other Essays* booklet.

Jesse Cohn, whose passion for Gustav Landauer rekindled my interest in Landauer translations in 2006 and gave me the idea for this volume. Jesse has been a dedicated, unfailing, and tremendously helpful support throughout this project.

Richard Day, whose footnote in *Gramsci Is Dead* bemoaning the considerable lack of Gustav Landauer translations turned into extra motivation to see this project through. Richard has generously looked at drafts of the manuscript and has offered priceless editorial advice. I am honored to see his preface included in the book.

Ramsey Kanaan, whose vision and commitment as a publisher, and willingness to go against the economic odds, has made the release of the book possible.

Wolfgang Eckhardt, whose devotion and boundless curiosity as a scholar turns every conversation into a feast of ideas. Many of his editorial suggestions have proven extremely valuable.

Siegbert Wolf, whose expertise in everything Landauer as well as his unfaltering readiness to help cannot be praised enough. He has provided the scholarly backbone to this venture. I am greatly indebted.

James Horrox, Jerry Kaplan, Christian Kayed, and Dimitris Troaditis, who have all provided important information.

Last but not least, Lausanne's Centre International de Recherches sur l'Anarchisme (CIRA) and the wonderful Marianne Enckell, the Amsterdam International Institute of Social History and their extremely accommodating staff, likewise Stockholm's Arbetarrörelsens arkiv and its team, and the Bibliothek der Freien in Berlin, in particular computer wizard Sven-Oliver Buchwald. Without the assistance of projects and institutions like these, independent scholarly research would be near impossible.

1. Paul Avrich, *Anarchist Portraits* (Princeton: Princeton University Press, 1988), 248.

2. *Gustav Landauer. Sein Lebensgang in Briefen* [Gustav Landauer: His Life in Letters], vol. I (Frankfurt am Main: Rütten und Loening, 1929), 313-316.

3. Max Nettlau, Max Nettlau Papers at the IISH, Amsterdam.

4. Max Nettlau, *Geschichte der Anarchie* [The History of Anarchy], vol. V (Vaduz: Topos, 1984), 253-254.

5. Rudolf de Jong, "Gustav Landauer und die internationale anarchistische Bewegung" [Gustav Landauer and the International Anarchist Movement], in Hanna Delf and Gert Mattenklott, *Gustav Landauer im Gespräch* [Gustav Landauer in Discussion] (Tübingen: M. Niemeyer, 1997), 221; Siegbert Wolf, "'Barcelona ist immer noch besser als Wilmersdorf' – Gustav Landauers Blick in die Welt" ['Barcelona Still Beats Wilmersdorf' – Gustav Landauer's Global Perspective], introduction to Gustav Landauer, *Ausgewählte Schriften* [Collected Works], vol. 1: *Internationalismus* (Lich/Hessen: Edition AV, 2008), 31.

6. Erich Mühsam, "Gustav Landauer und die bayrische Revolution" [Gustav Landauer and the Bavarian Revolution], *Der Abend*, August 10, 1920, here quoted from Christoph Knüppel, ed., *"Sei tapfer und wachse dich aus." Gustav Landauer im Dialog mit Erich Mühsam – Briefe und Aufsätze* ["Be Brave, De-

velop, and Mature!" Gustav Landauer and Erich Mühsam – Letters and Essays]
(Lübeck: Erich-Mühsam-Gesellschaft, 2004), 212-214; Siegbert Wolf, "Gesamteinleitung: Erinnerung an Gustav Landauer" [General Introduction: Remembering Gustav Landauer], in Gustav Landauer, *Ausgewählte Schriften*, 1: 13.

7. Landauer only published a handful of reports on political developments in
Great Britain and on British colonial policies in *Der Sozialist*: "Entwicklung
der genossenschaftlichen Produktion in Großbritannien" [The Development of Cooperative Production in Great Britain] (April 1, 1909), "England"
(August 15, 1909), "Australien" (May 15, 1910), "Die englische Ausbeutung-
spolitik in Indien" [The English Politics of Exploitation in India] (May 15,
1910); "Vom Schnee und vom König von England" [Snow and the King of
England] (March 15, 1909) is a parable on human kindness and affection. The
article "From Brooklyn" (May 15, 1910) has little to do with the United States.
It deals with internal conflicts of the German anarchist movement. The title
refers to Johann Most's activities in the U.S.

8. The latter has been documented in the above-mentioned Volume 1, *Inter
nationalismus*, of Landauer's *Ausgewählte Schriften*, edited by Siegbert Wolf.
The volume organizes Landauer texts by country, sixteen altogether, including Albania, Morocco, Palestine, and Serbia. Wolf calls Landauer a "polyglot
scholar" (Siegbert Wolf, "Gesamteinleitung: Erinnerung an Gustav Landauer," 9).

9. Erich Mühsam, "Der revolutionäre Mensch Gustav Landauer" [The Revolutionary Human Being Gustav Landauer], *Fanal*, May 1929, here quoted
from the 1974 edition of Landauer's *Die Revolution* (Berlin: Karin Kramer),
128. All letters are taken from Martin Buber's essential two-volume collection
Gustav Landauers Lebensgang in Briefen. In line with this book's theme, the
focus lies on letters related to political debate. Landauer's letters to Hedwig
Lachmann, his second wife, and Margarethe Faas-Hardegger, with whom he
had a romantic liaison in 1908-1909, are not included. Included are, however,
Landauer's final notes to his daughters.

10. "Der Krieg und die Revolution" [The War and the Revolution], in *Gustav
Landauer und die Revolutionszeit 1918-1919* [Gustav Landauer and the Revolutionary Period of 1918-1919], edited by Ulrich Linse (Berlin: Karin Kramer,
1974), 98.

11. Wolf, "Gesamteinleitung: Erinnerung an Gustav Landauer," 11.

INTRODUCTION
Gabriel Kuhn with Siegbert Wolf

1870-1892: Childhood and Youth

GUSTAV LANDAUER WAS BORN INTO A SECULAR JEWISH family on April 7, 1870, in the Southern German town of Karlsruhe. His parents, Hermann and Rosa, owned a shoe store. Gustav had two older brothers: Friedrich, born in 1866, and Felix, born in 1867. 1868 saw the birth of his cousin Hugo, who later became a successful entrepreneur with liberal leanings, sometimes supporting Gustav financially. The cousins remained close until Gustav's death.

As an adult, Landauer did not maintain close relations to his family. His father died in 1900, his brother Friedrich only one year later. Felix took over the family store. Gustav mentioned his brothers rarely, but apparently tried to visit his mother once every summer.[1] Rosa died in 1932, Felix in 1939.

Little is known about Landauer's youth. It appears that he resisted the career plans laid out by his father, but there are no reports of open rebellion. In his only autobiographical essay, "Twenty-Five Years Ago: On the Jubilee of Wilhelm II," Landauer expresses his frustration with high school and speaks of spending "a lot of time as a youth alone," seeking refuge in "theatre, music, and especially books."

From 1888 to 1892, Landauer studied German and English literature, philosophy, and art history in Heidelberg, Strasbourg, and finally Berlin. With a few interruptions, Berlin remained his home until 1917. The most important acquaintance from his university years was the Czech-Austrian writer and philosopher of language Fritz Mauthner, who had a marked influence on Landauer's intellectual development.

Landauer's birth coincided with the foundation of the modern German nation state. After the victory in the Franco-Prussian War 1870-1871, Prussian prime minister Otto von Bismarck succeeded in uniting the German states and duchies under the emperorship of Kaiser Wilhelm I. This is not without significance. Landauer was certainly a son of the new Germany. The notions of state, nation, and people are central themes in his thought – both generally and in specific relation to German identity.[2] Landauer thereby often distinguishes between the fallacy of the state structure and the promise of nation and people. However, suggesting affiliations with the "völkisch movement," as quite a few of his English commentators have, seems unfortunate.

The noun *Volk*, from which the adjective *völkisch* derives, is the common German term for "(a) people." In the 19th century, *Volk* became politically charged, both in a nationalist way (the *Volk* vs. foreign rulers), and in a socialist (the *Volk* vs. the aristocracy, the royals, the capitalists). In the mid to late 19th century, this was not necessarily perceived as a contradiction. As in anticolonial struggles of the 1960s and '70s, European 19th-century nationalist and socialist struggles often overlapped.

Only within the context of a united and powerful German nation state did the nationalist connotations of *Volk* increasingly feed into xenophobic, racist, and anti-Semitic ideologies. In this context, the völkisch movement emerged as a predominantly bourgeois idealization of "Germanness." It is therefore surprising when Berman and Luke suggest in their introduction to Landauer's *For Socialism* that "the traditional Marxist left ... failed to appropriate the leftist potential of the völkisch movement"[3] – it doesn't seem like there was much to be appropriated. It must rather be considered a logical consequence that, despite a few more moderate voices, the völkisch movement was absorbed by the Nazis in the 1930s.

This, however, had little impact on the socialist embrace of *Volk* – to this day, the German equivalent to Food Not Bombs–type meals is *Volksküche* [people's kitchen]. Hence, there was nothing particular about Landauer being involved in a *Volksbühne* [people's theater], advocating the "Selbstbestimmung des Volkes"[4] [self-determination of the people], or acting as a *Volksbeauftrager* [people's delegate[5]] during the Bavarian Council Republic.[6] Writing about *Volk* must not be confused with being *völkisch*.

Landauer never referenced the völkisch movement positively, even though it was already a notable political force by the 1890s. Landauer never explicitly condemned the völkisch movement either. It appears as if he simply did not take it very seriously. The term rarely appears in his writing.

In summary, it seems misleading to speak of a "völkisch romanticism" in connection with Landauer[7] – especially since the "romantic" label only further suggests an "irrationality" in Landauer's thought that it did not contain. In "Twenty-Five Years Ago," Landauer makes it very clear that overcoming the romantic notions he adhered to as a teenager was a defining moment in his personal and political development. When Landauer later embraced mysticism, there was nothing irrational about this either. *Revolution* and some of the other texts in this volume, in particular "Through Separation to Community," illustrate this convincingly. Neither can the "romantic" label be justified by Landauer's literary interests. In his extensive writings on literature, references to the Romantics are rare. Landauer seemed much more taken by Naturalist drama.[8]

Another historio-political reality that had a decisive impact on the young Gustav Landauer were Bismarck's so-called *Sozialistengesetze* [Socialist Laws], which outlawed socialist organizing in the German Kaiserreich from 1878 to 1890. By default, the laws helped strengthen the U.S. workers' movement: many German socialists emigrated, and at the time of the Haymarket bombing in 1887, the German contingent among the radical workers in the U.S. was the most significant. The majority of the men condemned for the bombing were of German descent.[9]

The years of 1890-1891, after the laws had finally been repealed, proved particularly significant. The *Sozialdemokratische Partei Deutschlands* [Social Democratic Party of Germany] (SPD), emerged from the former *Sozialistische Arbeiterpartei Deutschlands* [Socialist Workers' Party of Germany] (SAPD) at a party convention in Erfurt; it dominated socialist politics in Germany for decades. Right around this time, Landauer moved to Berlin and got involved with a young radical circle of former SAPD members who were denied membership in the newly formed SPD. The circle was known as the *Verein der unabhängigen Sozialisten* [Association of Independent Socialists] or simply the *Jungen* [Young Ones].

Unlike many other radical socialists who turned towards anarchism as disgruntled social democrats – either because they were fed up with reformist party politics or with Marxism (ideologically still firmly in place among Europe's social democrats at the time) – Landauer never had to deal with any social democratic baggage. In "Twenty-Five Years Ago" he states: "I was an anarchist before I was a socialist, and one of the few who had not taken a detour via social democracy."

Landauer never saw the SPD as anything but a fierce political enemy. Only weeks before his death, he declared during a Bavarian Revolution council meeting: "In the entire natural history I know of no more disgusting creature than the Social Democratic Party."[10]

1892-1901: Landauer's early anarchism

Before Landauer became engaged in socialist politics, his worldview was strongly influenced by the philosophers he had read in high school – particularly by Friedrich Nietzsche. Landauer wrote an early novel reflecting this background. *Der Todesprediger* [Preacher of Death], named after a chapter in Friedrich Nietzsche's *Also Sprach Zarathustra* ("Von den Predigern des Todes" [About the Preachers of Death]), was published in 1893 and remains Landauer's longest work of fiction. Some novellas followed later.

Der Todesprediger never gained much critical acclaim, but it is notable for an early libertarian adaptation of Friedrich Nietzsche's philosophy, so characteristic of 1960s and '70s French poststructuralism and of contemporary "postanarchist" theory.[11]

While working on *Der Todesprediger*, Landauer moved within Berlin's young literary and cultural avant-garde, particularly the Friedrichshagener Dichterkreis, a loose circle of free-thinking poets, artists, and intellectuals centered in the Berlin suburb of Friedrichshagen.[12] Soon, though, Landauer grew weary of the aestheticism and social detachment of the young bohemians and became increasingly involved with the *Jungen*. However, he never abandoned his belief in the importance of the cultural struggle. Unsurprisingly, he remained committed to the Neue Freie Volksbühne [New Free People's Theatre] throughout his life.[13] The Neue Freie Volksbühne was a radical offshoot of the Freie Volksbühne [Free People's Theatre], founded in 1890 with the vision of making educational and cultural projects accessible to workers. It was the country's first organization of its kind. Landauer joined in 1891. The Neue Freie Volksbühne separated in 1892. The groups continued to collaborate, however, and in 1914 they opened a common theatre house that exists to this day as the Volksbühne Berlin.[14] Both groups officially reunited in 1919.

It was at the founding assembly of the Neue Freie Volksbühne in Berlin in October 1892 that Landauer met his first wife, the tailor Margarethe (Grete) Leuschner. They were married before the end of the year. Landauer and Leuschner had two daughters: Charlotte Clara, born in 1894, and Marianne, born in 1896. Marianne died only two years later from meningitis.

After the *Jungen* had been banned from the new Social Democratic Party, they founded the journal *Der Sozialist* [The Socialist]. Landauer joined the publishing collective in February 1893. The *Jungen* dissolved as a group soon after, mainly due to increasing tensions between Marxists and anarchists, Landauer being a driving force among the latter. *Der Sozialist* was eventually taken over by the anarchist faction, and Landauer's influence on both form and content increased significantly. From 1895, the journal carried the signifiers "anarchist" and "anarchism" in its subtitle in a number of variations. In his 1895 essay "Anarchismus in Deutschland" [Anarchism in Germany], Landauer declares that "anarchism's lone objective is to end the fight of men against men and to unite humanity so that each individual can unfold his natural potential without obstruction."[15]

Der Sozialist of the 1890s is commonly divided into a "First" *Sozialist*, published from November 1891 to January 1895, and a "Second" *Sozialist*, published as "Neue Folge" [New Series] from August 1895 to December 1899. The interruption of publication in 1895 was caused by increased police surveillance and persecution.

At the end of 1899, the collective folded as a belated result of another split, this time occurring in 1897 between the "proletarian anarchists" (*Arbeiteranarchisten*) and the group around Landauer who moved ever further away from a working class focus. Landauer secured control over the journal, but the rival faction's founding of a new periodical, *Neues Leben* [New Life],[16] weakened *Der Sozialist* drastically. Landauer and his remaining co-editors struggled to keep *Der Sozialist* alive for two years, but were eventually forced to cease publication.

In 1909, Landauer revived *Der Sozialist* as the publishing outlet for the Socialist Bund (*Sozialistischer Bund*).[17] This "Third" *Sozialist* ran until 1915 when both increased repression and economic hardship caused by World War I made further publication impossible. Landauer always intended to revive *Der Sozialist* once again. He mentioned very concrete plans in a letter to Martin Buber at the end of 1918.[18] His untimely death did not allow this to happen.

Der Sozialist was Landauer's defining publishing venture. While he published a selection of books and brochures and plenty of articles for various other papers, at least half of his essays, articles, and translations appeared in *Der Sozialist*. Besides, his influence within the editing collective of the 1890s had been significant, and the "Third" *Sozialist* was basically his own undertaking. As a result, the journal spans – the interruptions notwithstanding – almost twenty-five years of "anarchist-socialist" publishing, to use one of Landauer's favorite terms. No other single project, not even the Socialist Bund, is as inextricably linked to Gustav Landauer the political agitator.

Landauer's rise to the top of the German anarchist circles in the 1890s was rapid. By 1893, when Landauer had barely been active in radical politics for a year, a German police file called him "the most important agitator of the radical revolutionary movement."[19] The same year, Landauer traveled to the Zurich congress of the Second International as an anarchist delegate. The anarchists were expelled from the congress,[20] dominated by German social democrats, and Landauer was accused of being a police informer by the prominent SPD leader August Bebel.[21] After his return to Berlin, Landauer found himself sentenced to almost a year in prison for libelous writing in *Der Sozialist*.

After his release in the summer of 1894,[22] Landauer resumed his work in the *Sozialist* collective. The journal continued to be harassed by the authorities, however, and had to temporarily cease publication in 1895. Landauer was also banned from German universities as a result of his political activism. During the forced *Sozialist* hiatus, Landauer became engaged in the establishment of a workers' consumer cooperative called *Befreiung* [Liberation]. The organization never gained much momentum and disbanded after a few years, but the cooperative idea would stay with Landauer and become a central part of his socialist vision. Similarly, his involvement in an 1896 strike of textile workers in Berlin would leave lasting impressions on the strike as a political means, later frequently evoked by Landauer in the form of an "active general strike" that would supplement the mere refusal of capitalist labor with self-determined work dedicated to the creation of socialism.[23]

In 1896, Landauer was arrested again, this time during a lecture; he was soon released without trial.[24] Once again, he traveled as an anarchist delegate to a Second International congress, this time in London, where the Zurich scenario repeated itself: the anarchists were excluded and responded by organizing their own independent conference. The report prepared by Landauer for the occasion, "Von Zürich bis London. Bericht über die deutsche Arbeiterbewegung an den Londoner Kongress" [From Zurich to London: Report on the German Workers' Movement to the London Congress] became his most translated piece; it appeared in French, Spanish, Italian, Portuguese, and English. The English version was published as a pamphlet under the title "Social Democracy in Germany" by London's Freedom Press in 1896.

As in Zurich, Landauer made a favorable impression on many of the anarchists present, and a speech he gave on the necessity of incorporating the peasantry into the revolutionary struggle drew much attention.[25] As Dutch scholar Rudolf de Jong notes, "Landauer is mentioned prominently in all the reports from the congress, those of anarchists, of anti-anarchists, and of everyone else."[26]

In 1897, most of Landauer's political work outside of *Der Sozialist* went into solidarity campaigns for Spanish anarchists, persecuted, tortured, and killed by the Spanish regime.[27] In February 1897 he stood trial for libel again, this time against a police inspector. Landauer and some of his comrades had exposed said inspector's recruitment of informants from within the radical movement. Landauer was acquitted.[28]

In 1899, coinciding with the end of *Der Sozialist*, Landauer faced yet another libel trial, again involving a police inspector. This time, he received a prison sentence of six months, which he served. Landauer had been active in the defense campaign for Albert Ziethen, a barber and inn keeper, who had been accused of murdering his wife and had been sentenced to life imprisonment. Landauer believed Ziethen innocent and had publicly suggested that he had been framed by a certain police inspector.[29]

Some months prior to his trial, Landauer had fallen in love with the poet and translator Hedwig Lachmann whom he had met at a poetry reading in Berlin. He was soon living with her. In 1903, he divorced Margarethe Leuschner, and he and Lachmann married.[30] They had two daughters: Gudula Susanne, born in 1902; and Brigitte, born in 1906, mother of U.S. film director Mike Nichols (*The Graduate* and others).

Throughout the 1890s, Landauer went on extensive speaking tours in the German-speaking world. In connection with the conferences in Zurich and London he made the acquaintance of many of Europe's best known anarchists: Peter Kropotkin, Max Nettlau, Rudolf Rocker, Errico Malatesta, Louise Michel, and Élisée Reclus, to name but a few. In his numerous articles, Landauer formulated the basis of his "federal-communitarian anarchism,"[31] his "anarchism of the practical creative deed,"[32] and an anarchism that revolves more around "leaving the state"[33] than crushing it. Landauer's anarchism might have been best summarized by his friend and companion Erich Mühsam:

> "Landauer was an anarchist; he called himself an anarchist all his life. However, it would be utterly ridiculous to read his various ideas through the glasses of a specific anarchist branch, to praise or condemn him as an individualist, communist, collectivist, terrorist, or pacifist. First, Landauer, like anyone who is not dogmatically frozen, has gone through developments and changes during the thirty years of his anarchist commitment; second, Landauer never saw anarchism as a politically or organizationally limited doctrine, but as an expression of ordered freedom in thought and action."[34]

Elsewhere, Mühsam mentions one of Gustav Landauer's central convictions; a notion anticipating what would later be celebrated as distinctively "postmodern": "His revolutionary activity was never limited to the fight against state laws and social systems. It concerned all dimensions of life."[35]

Mühsam's view is confirmed by Landauer's distinction between a "social" revolution (which he championed) and a mere "political" revolution (which he accused communists, and most anarchists, of propagating).[36] Landauer began to refer to himself as an "anti-politician" in the late 1890s, with reference to Friedrich Nietzsche's critique of politics in *Ecce Homo*.[37] Landauer evoked the theme throughout his life. Clearly, it is not a demand to retreat from social affairs, but a critique of "formal," "professional," "state" politics. In the 1911 essay "Wer soll anfangen?" [Who Shall Begin?] Landauer writes: "We believe that socialism has no bigger enemy than political power, and that it is socialism's task to establish a social and public order that replaces all such power."[38]

1901-1908: Retreat and Reflection

Ruth Link-Salinger calls the period from 1900 to 1919 the "mature period of Landauer's life."[39] Questions of maturity aside, Landauer certainly went through important changes around the turn of the century. While he did not give up his anarchist and socialist leanings, he framed them in a new philosophical light. This was first characterized by an ever mounting discomfort with over-simplified class analysis, doctrinism, and a light-hearted embrace of violence as a political means. Secondly, Landauer seemed ever more convinced that social change remained unattainable without the "inner" change of the individual.

The fact that most anarchists around him rejected his views only confirmed his sense of increased isolation. A note in Rudolf Rocker's memoirs underlines the position that Landauer held among German anarchists at the time:

> "Gustav Landauer was without doubt the greatest mind among all of Germany's libertarian socialists; it was in a certain sense his curse that, of all places, he had to live and work in Germany. The majority of the era's German anarchists understood him even less than others did; most of them had no idea what a precious gift he was. Landauer remained alone in the circle of people who should have been closest to him..."[40]

Internationally, too, Landauer often felt, in the words of Rudolf de Jong, like a "solitary in the anarchist world."[41] Contrary to his travels in the 1890s, he now avoided the big international anarchist gatherings: he neither attended the International Revolutionary Workers' Congress (later also known as the International Anti-Parliamentary Congress) in Paris in 1900, nor the International Anarchist Congress in Amsterdam in 1907. Even in 1910, by then politically active in Germany again, Landauer writes that he finds "the anarchist movement in all countries extremely dull."[42]

Landauer's retreat and demand for self-reflection must not be misunderstood as an "individualistic" turn, however. Characterizations like "mystical anarchism"[43] are more apt; what Landauer expected individuals to find in the exploration of their "inner being" was no individual essence, but an all-uniting spirit; for Landauer, this was the basis of true communal life. These convictions stemmed as much from the skeptical philosophy of his friend Fritz Mauthner,[44] as from medieval Christian mysticism, most notably from the sermons and scriptures of Meister Eckhart. Although it is most apparent in Landauer's 1903 study *Skepsis und Mystik*, a mystical element characterizes all of Landauer's subsequent work. Thorsten Hinz, author of the outstanding *Mystik und Anarchie. Meister Eckhart und seine Bedeutung im Denken Gustav Landauers* [Mysticism and Anarchy: The Significance of Meister Eckhart in Gustav Landauer's Thought] speaks of a "religiousness without institutions."[45]

In concentrated form, Landauer had articulated his new orientation by 1900, in a talk entitled "Durch Absonderung zur Gemeinschaft." Landauer gave the talk on June 18 at a meeting of the newly founded Neue Gemein-schaft [New Community]. It was published in 1901 in the second issue of the Neue Gemeinschaft's journal *Das Reich der Erfüllung* [The Realm of Fulfillment], and is included in this volume as "Through Separation to Community."[46] It is the key essay addressing Landauer's altered under-standing of political action and social transformation at the turn of the century. It is the most vivid outcome of what Thorsten Hinz calls "a multi-layered life crisis: … philosophical … political … personal."[47] Two years later, the text was almost completely incorporated into *Skepsis und Mystik*.

The Neue Gemeinschaft was a somewhat philosophically ambiguous and politically undefined group led by the brothers Heinrich and Julius Hart. The Hart brothers advocated rural settlements as a means of creat-ing new harmonious communities in tune with the laws of nature and spirit. The ideas appealed to Landauer, not least because the book *Freiland. Ein soziales Zukunftsbild* [Free Land: Image of a Social Future], published by the Hungarian-Austrian economist Theodor Hertzka in 1890, had left a deep impression on him. In *Freiland*, Hertzka had outlined a utopian socialist settlement program in Africa. The book was highly popular in German-speaking socialist circles and different *Freiland* groups emerged throughout the 1890s.[48] The vision of socialist settlements would be cen-tral to the theory of socialism that Landauer formulated some years later.

Landauer knew the Hart brothers and other early Neue Gemeinschaft members from the days of the Friedrichshagener Dichterkreis. Although he did not join the commune that was established in Schlachtensee, a southwestern Berlin suburb, Landauer joined the group with optimism. He left but one year later, unconvinced by the Harts' philosophical sincerity and disillusioned with the escapism they mistook for social transformation. Despite his criticism of the German anarchist movement, Landauer was not ready to forgo the principle of concrete political interference for the lav-ish and self-indulgent events organized by the Neue Gemeinschaft.[49]

Although Landauer's involvement with the group was short, it included encounters that would prove crucial in his biography: first, Landauer met Martin Buber, the renowned Jewish Austrian philosopher, who would become a life-long friend and patron;[50] second, he came upon a young and passionate radical with a curious parallel affection for bohemian lifestyle and anarcho-communist politics: Erich Mühsam. It was in the Neue Gemeinschaft circle, within which neither of them fit, that Landauer and Mühsam first discovered the convictions they shared – they soon left the group together. The Neue Gemeinschaft dissolved in 1904.

Landauer and Mühsam are without doubt Germany's most influential 20th-century anarchists. Rudolf Rocker, the only possible exception, spent most of his life outside the country. In the beginning, Mühsam, the younger and politically less experienced of the two, looked up to Landauer; a teacher-student dynamic long characterized their relationship.[51] However, Mühsam was clearly independent in his ideas and soon equaled Landauer in influence.[52]

Among the most notable differences between the two was Mühsam's openness to party communism, never shared by Landauer.[53] There were also disparities in character: Landauer often appeared to be the philosopher and sage, while Mühsam was notoriously restless and temperamental. The most striking difference, however, related to their personal ethics and ways of life. While Landauer has been called a "conservative revolutionary"[54] – certainly too harsh an assessment, but nonetheless indicative – and only moved in Berlin's bohemian circles briefly as a twenty-year old, Mühsam was a prototype for the anti-bourgeois, libertarian anarchist provocateur stressing the revolutionary potential of "vagabonds," "crooks," the "lumpenproletariat," and "The Fifth Estate," as the title of one of his essays proclaims.[55] While Mühsam immersed himself passionately in debates about free love or the rights of homosexuals, Landauer remained cautious in these respects and always held on to marriage and family as important miniature examples of the communities on which to build a socialist society.[56] Landauer also remained strongly attached to high arts, leading some commentators to speak of a "thoroughly traditionalist conception of art,"[57] while Mühsam was a prolific and progressive "people's" poet and playwright. Nonetheless, suggestions that there was always a "primacy of the aesthetic (over the political)"[58] in Landauer's work are rebuffed by none other than Mühsam himself. He tirelessly defended Landauer as "a strong, fearless spirit, always ready to act,"[59] and objected to "dissolving [Landauer's character] in a sweet brew of bourgeois-ethical love for everyone and everything."[60] In a commemorative essay after Landauer's death, Mühsam states that "it cannot be said clearly enough that Landauer was not a bourgeois, but the opposite: a renewer who always saw social transformation as a requirement for cultural transformation."[61]

From 1901 to 1906, Landauer was absent from radical politics. In 1901 and 1902, he and his new love, Hedwig Lachmann, resided in England, for some months living close to Kropotkin in Bromley. Landauer visited on occasion, and Kropotkin left a strong impression on the young admirer.[62] Landauer began to translate some of Kropotkin's most important works, and eventually published German versions of *Mutual Aid: A Factor of Evolution*, of *Fields, Factories and Workshops*, and of *The Great French Revolution, 1789-1793*. Landauer also socialized with the Cuban-born Catalan anarchist Tárrida del Mármol, with Rudolf Rocker, and with Max Nettlau, all resident in England at the time.

After returning to Berlin, Landauer continued to concentrate on translations. Besides Kropotkin, he translated Oscar Wilde, Walt Whitman, and Rabindranath Tagore, the first Asian Nobel laureate when he received the prize in literature in 1913. Landauer translated some texts by himself, and others with Lachmann. He also published literary essays and, in 1903, *Skepsis und Mystik*.

The closest that Landauer came to political activity during these years was his engagement in the Deutsche Gartenstadt-Gesellschaft [German Garden City Society], an organization inspired by the British Garden City movement and dedicated to socially sensitive urban planning. Landauer did not stay involved for very long, but rekindled his friendship with the brothers Paul and Bernhard Kampffmeyer, friends since the days of the Friedrichshagener Dichterkreis. The Gartenstadt-Gesellschaft disbanded in the 1910s.

To make ends meet, Landauer worked in a Berlin bookstore from 1904 to 1906. In July 1906, he received a letter that would mark another turning point in his life. Martin Buber had been chosen to edit an ambitious publication series, *Die Gesellschaft* [Society], with Frankfurt am Main publisher Rütten und Loening. The series' aim was to present innovative perspectives on all aspects of social life. In his letter to Landauer, Buber came straight to the point: "Dear Landauer, as far as *Die Gesellschaft* goes, this is the situation: the publisher, understandably, wants a book on the highly demanded and intriguing topic of 'revolution.' I cannot think of anyone better suited than you, no matter how hard I try."[63] A year later, *Die Revolution* was published as *Die Gesellschaft* Vol. 13. (Buber published forty volumes in the series, the last ones in 1912.)

Die Revolution is not easy to access. Ruth Link-Salinger calls it "hastily written"[64] and "poorly constructed."[65] It seems hard to disagree. Landauer's inconsistent use of the term "revolution," for example, has confused many readers. In general, Landauer presents "revolution" as a permanent historical struggle for socialism, tied into the renewal of spirit, individuality, and community (in Landauer's mysticism, all one). This philosophical interpretation of revolution is the crux of the book. At the same time, Landauer also employs the term in a much more common manner and refers to individual events of – actual or attempted – radical social transformation as "revolutions." While the context usually reveals the meaning, clearer terminological distinctions would have certainly helped.

The strongest criticism levied against *Die Revolution* is probably Landauer's perception of the Middle Ages, strongly influenced by Peter Kropotkin. Even Landauer adherents call it idealized.[66] Landauer's interpretation of certain historical struggles also seems questionable, for example, when he embraces the reprisals of radical Catholics against moderate 17th-century French kings as "people's uprisings."[67]

However, *Die Revolution* remains one of the most important anarchist analyses of history and revolution and a very unique study. For Siegbert Wolf, it is a "seminal anarchist philosophy of history;"[68] for Rudolf Rocker it is "sparkling" and "a prophet's warning."[69] Erich Mühsam describes the book thus: "On the one hand, *Revolution* proves Landauer's unparalleled capacity in analyzing the problem of revolution scientifically; on the other hand, it proves that he never saw abstraction, science, and critical analysis as anything but means to strengthen what really counts: namely, to prepare, to instigate, and to call people to creative action."[70] *Die Revolution* also contains the most cohesive summary of Landauer's understanding of utopia, one of the most celebrated aspects of his thought.[71] Landauer sees utopia as the driving force behind all revolutionary action. However, revolution being "permanent action"[72] to Landauer, utopia is not some far-away dream that we endlessly chase. In true socialism, it is a force at work in our daily lives.

1908-1914: Socialist Hopes

The publication of *Die Revolution* in 1907 inspired Landauer's return to political agitation and action. In the same year, he published "Dreißig Sozialistische Thesen" [Thirty Socialist Theses],[73] outlining much of what he would formulate at length in the *Aufruf zum Sozialismus* a few years later.

In May 1908, Landauer initiated the Socialist Bund (*Sozialistischer Bund*),[74] with the stated goal of "uniting all humans who are serious about realizing socialism."[75] In "Sätze vom Sozialistischen Bund" [Explanations of the Socialist Bund], Landauer answered the question "How do I become a member of the Socialist Bund?" with: "You look for like-minded people in your social surroundings and form a group with them."[76]

Central to the Bund's idea were the unity of intellectual, artisanal, and artistic work, and the creation of small independent organizations and communities (cooperatives, settlements, etc.) as the basic cells of a new socialist culture and society. The Bund consisted of autonomous groups without central leadership in Germany and Switzerland[77] – in Austria the support of prominent anarchists like Pierre Ramus could not be procured, and Landauer himself was banned from entering the country.[78] Martin Buber and Erich Mühsam were among the Bund's earliest members. At its height, it counted around eight hundred people.

To support the Bund, Landauer revived *Der Sozialist* in 1909, now with the subtitle *Organ des Sozialistischen Bundes* [Journal of the Socialist Bund]. It was published as a bi-weekly. Landauer basically edited it alone, although during the first couple of years he had a strong help in the Swiss syndicalist Margarethe Faas-Hardegger.[79]

Landauer met and fell in love with Faas-Hardegger in the summer of 1908. Given his secluded life with Hedwig Lachmann, he called her a "bridge to the world."[80] Landauer was open about the romantic liaison with his family, with whom he continued to live. The family seemed accepting.[81] His relationship with Faas-Hardegger became remarkably colder in April 1909, when Landauer criticized her harshly for an article questioning the nuclear family and arguing for communal child rearing.[82] Contact ceased completely in 1913.

Apart from longing and passion, Landauer's correspondence with Faas-Hardegger also reveals a character trait that has been described as haughtiness. Landauer was frequently perceived to be self-involved and hard to work with.[83] In June 1909, he answered Faas-Hardegger, who was upset by his repeated criticism: "You call me 'gruesomely harsh?' Well, this has already done you much good."[84]

It has been noted that despite Landauer's commitment to collective action, he excelled most in projects over which he had almost exclusive control, like the Socialist Bund or the "Third" *Sozialist*. In a 1916 letter to Erich Mühsam, Landauer admits, "It has always been difficult for me to adopt and execute the ideas and plans of others."[85] Maybe this explains why Landauer never participated in the establishment of communes or settlements despite his ongoing insistence on their revolutionary importance. Erich Mühsam summarizes this apparent contradiction thus: "Only those who see him as a determined and fearless fighter, kind, soft, and generous in everyday relations, but intolerant, hard, and headstrong to the point of arrogance in important issues, can understand him the way he really was."[86]

Generally, however, Landauer has been described as a gentle, peaceful, considerate person. Characteristic is Augustin Souchy's depiction: "Gustav Landauer's personality fit the images I had after reading his books and essays. His long and slim frame with the fine facial features surrounded by a Christ-like beard, the spirited forehead, and the visionary eyes gazing into a utopian distance gave his appearance a unique appeal."[87]

There are surprisingly few documents that speak of Landauer's personality or the relation to his friends and loved ones in more depth. His letters provide glimpses, but are open to much speculation, and many remain lost. Buber's essential collection only starts in 1899.[88] Landauer's personal notes and diary entries still await proper classification and analysis. Most of Landauer's papers are stored at the International Institute for Social History (IISH) in Amsterdam, with a smaller selection kept at the Jewish National and University Library in Jerusalem.[89]

Landauer's new focus on "socialism" did not indicate a desertion of his anarchist ideals. As Walter Fähnders and Hansgeorg Schmidt-Bergmann point out, "socialism and anarchism are synonyms in Landauer's language."[90] A letter sent by Landauer to Faas-Hardegger in September 1908 seems to confirm this; it concerns the presentation of the *Sozialist*'s editors' collective: "You can choose any of the following: 'Socialist-Anarchists' (my favorite), 'Socialists,' 'Anarchists,' or simply 'Comrades.'"[91] (Faas-Hardegger chose 'Revolutionary Circles,' which was soon dropped from the journal's caption.) Landauer related anarchism and socialism most clearly in the second version of the "Twelve Articles of the Socialist Bund": "Anarchy is just another – due to its negativity and frequent misinterpretation, less useful – name for socialism."[92]

Landauer's renewed activism soon created conflict with old rivals from the Anarchistische Föderation Deutschlands [German Anarchist Federation] (AFD). The AFD was founded in 1903 by the "proletarian anarchist" wing of the 1890s *Sozialist* collective. The group still remained committed to class struggle as the central means for revolution, while Landauer's skepticism about the working class' role as the revolutionary subject had only amplified over the years. The conflict escalated when Landauer refused to advertise *Der freie Arbeiter*, the journal close to the Anarchistische Föderation, in *Der Sozialist* even though *Der freie Arbeiter* had run ads for *Der Sozialist*.[93]

Landauer's view of the proletariat can appear confusing. It is true that he famously notes in *Aufruf zum Sozialismus* that "no social group today would know less than the industrial proletariat what to do in the case of revolution."[94] However, while this expresses frustration with the lethargy of wide parts of the German working class, Landauer is much clearer in his important essay, "Vom freien Arbeitertag," published as "A Free Workers' Council" in this volume: "As far as active social and cultural development is concerned, we cannot expect more from the working class than from other classes; however, things look very different in terms of anger and rejection, of emotion and strength, which are mandatory qualities for effective resistance."[95]

Landauer's criticism of the proletariat always focused on an abstract and idealized notion of it as a privileged revolutionary vanguard; it never implied that he did not take the workers' plight seriously, it never stopped him from engaging in workers' struggles, and it did not mean that he did not acknowledge workers would play a significant role in effective people's uprisings. Landauer always supported workplace activism as long as he did not feel that it was bound to narrow-minded doctrines, Marxist, anarchist, or otherwise. To name but one example, in 1913, he used the means at the disposal of the Socialist Bund to publish the Austrian anarchist Josef Peukert's *Erinnerungen eines Proletariers aus der revolutionären Arbeiterbewegung* [Memories of a Proletarian from the Revolutionary Workers' Movement], and added a passionate preface.[96]

What distinguished Landauer from the "proletarian anarchists" was an idea that was central to his "anarchism-socialism": no one, including the proletariat, is going to be liberated by a merely "external" transformation of political and economic conditions – they will be liberated by "inner" change and by actively engaging in the creation of new forms of communal life.

Landauer constantly rebuked the criticism that the language of *Der Sozialist* was not suited to proletarian readers. In a 1909 letter to Faas-Hardegger, he writes: "The articles in *Der Sozialist* are not at all incomprehensible to the workers; the workers only have to understand that an effort is required to see things as they are."[97] Max Nettlau observed that the implied demands were not always beneficial to Landauer's quest of expanding the Socialist Bund: "It is easy enough to gather the masses around a programme by asking for no more than their votes or contributions, but difficult, if not impossible, to induce – even one man in a thousand – to perform a truly independent act as an individual."[98]

Landauer has often been presented as a righteous but lonely voice in an overall hostile leftist environment. There was certainly truth to this. However, some of the pictures drawn seem exaggerated. There is no doubt that Landauer went through periods of relative isolation, in particular from 1901 to 1906,[99] and, due to his uncompromising antimilitarism, during World War I. At the same time, he was never bereft of respect and support. From him traveling to Zurich and London as an anarchist delegate to Martin Buber commissioning *Die Revolution* to Kurt Eisner calling him to Munich in 1918, there were people who understood and shared his views.

Perhaps ironically, Landauer did not in fact attract any less working class support than his "proletarian" anarchist counterparts. It has often been claimed that Landauer's ideas mainly appealed to libertarian intellectuals. During the Bavarian Revolution, however, there was considerate support for Landauer's vision among workers. As Ulrich Linse points out, in Bavaria "two literary friends of bourgeois background [Landauer and Mühsam] created the possibility for anarchist action, [while] the 'proletarian anarchists' proved to be an isolated and self-centered sect, unable and unwilling to become engaged in any way."[100] After Landauer's death, it was mainly the anarchosyndicalist Freie Arbeiter-Union Deutschlands [Free German Workers' Union] (FAUD) that kept his legacy in Germany alive, and it was Munich's Anarchosyndikalistische Vereinigung [Anarchosyndicalist Alliance] that instigated the erection of a monument at his gravesite in 1925.[101]

Landauer published the most comprehensive summary of his socialist ideas in 1911 with *Aufruf zum Sozialismus*,[102] published in English as *For Socialism* by Telos Press in a translation by Michael J. Parent. Landauer's socialism builds on the following central principles: **a)** inner renewal and unification with the "common spirit;" **b)** direct, immediate action; Erich Mühsam sums this up by suggesting that "the terms 'beginning,' 'realization,' 'action' are more important to the revolutionary Landauer than any scientific pretense...;"[103] in Diego Abad de Santillán's words, Landauer demanded "a revolution from below at every moment;"[104] **c)** communal organization in cooperatives, settlements, etc.[105]

Probably the quintessential and, in the context of a radical history of ideas, most distinctive aspect of Landauer's socialism is the conviction that one has to overcome state and capital by "leaving" rather than "toppling" them.[106] This emphasizes Landauer's notion of socialism as *action*. In 1909, he writes: "Socialism has nothing to do with demanding and waiting; socialism means *doing*."[107]

Landauer counts on the people's ability to create socialist communities according to their needs and abilities. As he explains in "Ein Brief über die anarchistischen Kommunisten" [A Letter About Anarchist Communists]: "The difference between us socialists in the Socialist Bund and the communists is not that we have a different model of a future society. The difference is that we do not have any model. We embrace the future's openness and refuse to determine it. What we want is to realize socialism, doing what we can for its realization *now*."[108]

A number of attributes have been used by scholars to describe Landauer's socialism. Some have focused on the basis of his social vision and have spoken of "cooperative socialism" (*Genossenschafts-Sozialismus*),[109] "community socialism" (*Gemeindesozialismus*),[110] or "agrarian socialism"[111] (in *Aufruf zum Sozialismus* Landauer writes that "the struggle for socialism is a struggle for land; the social question is an agrarian question"[112]). Others have focused on Landauer's advocation of immediate, daily action, coining the term "realization socialism" (*Verwirklichungssozialismus*).[113] Finally, there are those who stress the "utopian" character of Landauer's socialism as opposed to the "scientific" socialism of the Marxists. Most common, however, is the term "cultural socialism" (*Kultursozialismus*). It seems apt considering Landauer's words in the *Aufruf*: "Socialism is a cultural movement, a struggle for the beauty, greatness, and richness of peoples."[114]

1914-1918: War

After the early euphoria related to the Socialist Bund and the resurrection of *Der Sozialist*, the mounting danger of military conflict soon cast long, dark shadows, and the prevention of war became a priority in Landauer's activities.[115] As early as September 1911, he warned of the looming horrors in a talk in Berlin. He also called on German workers to employ an "active general strike" to render war impossible. The talk was later published as "Vom Freien Arbeitertag" and is translated as "A Free Workers' Council" in this volume.

Landauer's legacy as a pacifist is controversial,[116] but together with Hedwig Lachmann he was one of the very few Germans who opposed the war from the beginning. To Landauer and Lachmann's astonishment, even many fellow leftists and anarchists welcomed the war as an opportunity to settle political scores or to bolster whatever abstruse notion of the revolution they had. Some even displayed outright nationalism. The Social Democrats stood almost completely united behind the war, including its "radical" wing, with Karl Liebknecht, later instigator of the Spartacus League and the 1919 Spartacus Uprising, being the only notable exception. Siegbert Wolf writes that, at the outbreak of the war in 1914, "Hedwig Lachmann and Gustav Landauer were barely able to make their antimilitaristic stance comprehensible to friends and acquaintances."[117] For Landauer, the aggressor was always Germany.[118] In 1913, he ends an essay in *Der Sozialist* with the evocative words, "the German people ought to be ashamed!"[119]

Landauer entered a new phase of disappointment and loneliness. This, however, did not stop him from tireless antimilitaristic agitation. The anti-war and anti-nationalism pieces published during this period are ardent warnings against senseless brutality and slaughter, and passionate pleas for the unity of humanity, rather than its division.[120]

In 1913, when the danger of war had become imminent, the Socialist Bund practically ceased to exist. Against all odds, Landauer managed to keep *Der Sozialist* running until the journal's typesetter, Max Müller, was drafted for military service in 1915. The last issue of *Der Sozialist* appeared on March 15. Landauer himself was drafted in May 1915 but declared unfit.

Landauer sought contact with fellow antimilitarists throughout the war. In 1914, he became active in the Forte-Kreis [Forte Circle] in Berlin (named after a planned conference in the Tuscan town of Forte dei

Marmi), a small group of European intellectuals, including Martin Buber, dedicated to transnational understanding. However, when some members professed patriotic sentiments at the war's outbreak, Landauer quickly disassociated himself. The Forte-Kreis disbanded soon after.[121]

In 1915, Landauer met with pacifist German artists and writers in Switzerland, where Hugo Ball, Emmy Hennings, Richard Huelsenbeck, and many other prominent Dadaist and expressionist pacifists lived in exile. The company of these like-minded spirits was balm for Landauer's soul. In Berlin, he joined the Aufbruch [Departure] circle around Ernst Joël, a young Jewish student,[122] and published several essays in the *Aufbruch* journal. Landauer also became active in the Bund Neues Vaterland [New Fatherland Federation], Germany's most influential pacifist organization. Among its early members were Albert Einstein[123] and Kurt Eisner, who would beckon Landauer to come to Munich a few years later.[124] Meanwhile, *Aufruf zum Sozialismus* was banned.

In 1916, Lachmann and Landauer were involved in establishing the Zentralstelle Völkerrecht [Centre for International Law], another pacifist organization.[125] Landauer served as chairman of the Berlin chapter. In 1917, Landauer and Lachmann decided to move to the Lachmann family's home in Krumbach, a small town in the Swabian part of Bavaria.

In February 1918, the war still dragging on, Hedwig Lachmann died unexpectedly of pneumonia. It took Landauer months to recover. He self-published a pamphlet, "Wie Hedwig Lachmann starb" [How Hedwig Lachmann Died], which he distributed to select friends.

1918-1919: Revolution and Landauer's Death

When Germany's crushing defeat in World War I had become certain, the nation was in turmoil. In late October 1918, a couple of weeks before the armistice that officially ended the war was signed on November 11, navy soldiers in Wilhelmshaven rebelled and initiated the German Revolution of 1918-1919 (also known as *Novemberrevolution*). Soldiers' and workers' uprisings erupted all over the country, and on November 9 the Social Democratic Party – in an attempt not to lose credibility with the masses, and against the explicit will of some of its leaders – proclaimed Germany a republic, bringing an end to the German Kaiserreich. However, radicals continued to organize rebellions, demanding a socialist republic based on principles of direct democracy and self-determination, rather than on bourgeois parliamentarianism. *Alle Macht den Räten!* [All Power to the Councils!] became the rallying cry. The Social Democrats soon made use of all available means to suppress the revolts, including the employment of reactionary military forces and Free Corps units.[126] These helped defeat the most threatening of all rebellions, Berlin's Spartacus Uprising in January 1919, murdering the Spartacists' two most prominent figures, Karl Liebknecht and Rosa Luxemburg. At the end of the month, the council republic in Bremen, proclaimed a few weeks earlier, was also crushed by military force.

Bavaria had been declared a republic on November 7, 1918, by Kurt Eisner, leader of the *Unabhängige Sozialdemokratische Partei Deutschlands* [Independent Social Democratic Party of Germany] (USPD). The USPD had been founded in April 1917 by a break-away faction of SPD members opposed to a continuation of the war. This was the beginning of the so-called Bavarian Revolution.[127]

Eisner was a friend of Gustav Landauer and summoned him to Munich for support. In a letter dated November 14, he wrote: "What I want from you is to advance the transformation of souls as a speaker."[128] Landauer, who had just received a call as dramatic adviser to the Düsseldorf Theatre, where he also temporarily edited the journal *Masken*,[129] complied.

Landauer's excitement about the revolutionary developments should not come as a surprise. It was the one hope he had connected with the horrors of World War I; in a letter to Margarete Susman from March 24, 1917, he wrote: "The revolution that has bypassed Germany in former times has to come at some point. Maybe the war is the first phase? Maybe external influences will force Germans to do what they have not been able to do by themselves?"[130]

In Munich, Landauer became a member of several councils established to both implement and protect the revolution.[131] He reunited with Erich Mühsam, who had already moved to Munich in 1909.[132] Many other anarchists and radicals gathered hopefully in Bavaria, among them Ernst Toller, Otto Neurath, Silvio Gesell, and Ret Marut, better known as B. Traven.

The developments experienced a decisive turn when the USPD dramatically lost the republic's first elections on January 12, 1919. A few weeks later, on February 21, Eisner was assassinated by a right-wing student, while on his way to resign as prime minister. Landauer gave the eulogy at his funeral.[133]

Following Eisner's death, the "Majority" Social Democrats (the regular SPD) established a new government with the support of conservative forces. Opposition within the radical circles in Munich was fierce, and on April 7, 1919, the Bavarian Council Republic was proclaimed by anarchists and USPD members. The Communist Party had considered its proclamation untimely. According to Erich Mühsam's personal report on the Bavarian Revolution, *Von Eisner bis Leviné* [From Eisner to Leviné],[134] this rendered the council republic a lost cause from the outset.[135] It was proclaimed nonetheless, apparently not least upon Landauer's insistence on pushing ahead despite the Communists' disassociation.[136] As Mühsam tells the story, it was Landauer and himself who, after a meeting of Munich's Revolutionary Workers' Council (*Revolutionärer Arbeiterrat*) on the evening of April 4, "retreated to an inn to draft the council republic's declaration."[137]

It remains unclear why Landauer, long skeptical of mere "political" revolution, supported the council republic idea in Bavaria with such fervor. Most likely, he believed that the chance to realize his vision of self-determined socialism on a wide scale had finally arrived. He was appointed People's Delegate for Culture and Education.

One week later, on April 13, the SPD government that had fled to the Northern Bavarian town of Bamberg sent military units to Munich. The assault was repelled by the Communist Red Army coming to the council republic's defense. Before the counterrevolutionaries had been driven from Munich, they had been able to arrest several key figures at a late evening meeting, among them Erich Mühsam;[138] the arrested were taken to prisons in Northern Bavaria. Gustav Landauer had only escaped capture because he had left the said meeting early – unknown to anyone at the time, this would prove to be his death sentence.[139]

The Communists now took control of the council republic (historians have called this the beginning of the "Second" Bavarian Council Republic). Landauer, who had begun to outline far-reaching school and theatre reforms during his one week in office,[140] declared his continued support despite ideological reservations.[141] The Communists left Landauer in doubt about his role. On April 16, he wrote in his last, unsent, letter to his daughters: "As far as I am concerned, I am all right staying here, although I am starting to feel rather useless."[142]

Two weeks later the federal SPD government sent troops from Berlin, which united with right-wing Free Corps units outside of Munich; together they repeated the assault against the Spartacists in Berlin and the council republicans in Bremen. Despite fierce resistance by the Red Army, the Bavarian Council Republic was defeated on May 1. Its prominent representatives, including Landauer, were taken into custody.

Landauer was murdered by soldiers the next day. Rudolf Rocker describes the events thus:

> "After the end of the first council republic, which he had dedicated his rich knowledge and abilities to wholeheartedly, Landauer lived with the widow of his good friend Kurt Eisner. He was arrested in her house on the afternoon of May 1. Close friends had urged him to escape a few days earlier. Then it would have still been a fairly easy thing to do. But Landauer decided to stay. Together with other prisoners he was loaded on a truck and taken to the jail in Starnberg. From there he and some others were driven to Stadelheim a day later.[143] On the way he was horribly mistreated by dehumanized military pawns on the orders of their superiors. One of them, Freiherr von Gagern,[144] hit Landauer over the head with a whip handle. This was the signal to kill the defenseless victim. An eyewitness later said that Landauer used his last strength to shout at his murderers: 'Finish me off – to be human!' He was literally kicked to death. When he still showed signs of life, one of the callous torturers shot a bullet in his head. This was the gruesome end of Gustav Landauer – one of Germany's greatest spirits and finest men."[145]

On May 17, Landauer's eldest daughter Charlotte was finally allowed to travel to Munich. Thanks to her persistence, both Landauer's corpse (dumped in a mass grave) and his confiscated manuscripts were released to the family. Landauer was cremated. His urn remained in a columbarium until 1923, when a tombstone was erected at Munich's Waldfriedhof [Forest Cemetery], mainly the result of the efforts of Bavarian anarcho-syndicalists. Landauer's urn was transferred there on May 1. In 1925, a monument for Landauer, financed by a FAUD donation campaign, was added to the gravesite. A planned inauguration ceremony was prohibited by the police.

In 1933, the Nazis destroyed Landauer's grave, including the monument. His urn was sent to Munich's Jüdische Gemeinde [Jewish Community], and remained anonymously in a wall of the Neue Israelitische

Friedhof [New Jewish Cemetery] until the end of World War II. In 1946, Landauer's daughter Gudula initiated the reestablishment of a grave for Landauer, which he today shares with Kurt Eisner in the Neue Israelitische Friedhof; the gravestone is a remnant of the 1925 monument.

Landauer's Legacy

Landauer's legacy can be divided into two periods: an early, immediate influence that lasted until about the mid 1930s; and a Landauer renaissance that – like many other radical renaissances – began with the social uprisings of the late 1960s. The German publishing history of *Die Revolution* illustrates this well: since its first publication in 1907, *Die Revolution* has seen five reprints: in 1919 and 1923 (with the original publisher Rütten und Loening), in 1974 and 1977 (with long-standing anarchist publisher Karin Kramer), and in 2003 (with Unrast).

Landauer's immediate influence in Germany was both intellectual and practical. Apart from his friends and comrades Erich Mühsam, Martin Buber, Rudolf Rocker, and Augustin Souchy, he inspired the thoughts and writings of Walter Benjamin, Ernst Bloch, Hermann Hesse, Paul Celan, and Arnold Zweig. He also left a lasting impression on two of his well-known comrades from the days of the Bavarian Council Republic: Ernst Toller and Ret Marut, a.k.a. B. Traven. Both published essays in Landauer's honor.[146]

On the practical plane, Landauer's influence was strongest among the anarchosyndicalist FAUD, whose most prominent members were Rocker, Souchy, and Helmut Rüdiger. Landauer's texts were also widely read in the German Youth Movement (*Jugendbewegung*),[147] whose political legacy is rather ambiguous.[148] Landauer's ideas also inspired the German commune movement. Bernhard Braun lists the communes Barkenhoff in Lower Saxony (1919-1923) and Blankenburg in Bavaria (1919-1921) as concrete examples.[149] There is also a moving picture from the Düsseldorf commune Freie Erde [Free Earth], founded in 1921: workers diligently paint an inscription on a marble plate with Landauer's countenance: "We settled this fallow land on July 6, 1921, *In the Spirit of Gustav Landauer*, and we have called it 'Free Earth.'" The Freie Erde existed until 1923.

Thanks to remarkable efforts by Martin Buber, many of Landauer's writings were published posthumously in the 1920s. Buber edited the two-volume *Briefe aus der Französischen Revolution* [Letters from the French Revolution] (1919), selected, translated, and introduced by Landauer; Landauer's Shakespeare lectures, *Shakespeare. Dargestellt in Vorträgen* [Sh. Presented in Lectures], also in two volumes (1920); two essay collections, *Der werdende Mensch. Aufsätze über Leben und Schrifttum* [The Becoming Human: Essays on Life and Literature] (1921) and *Beginnen. Aufsätze über Sozialismus* [Beginning: Essays on Socialism] (1924); and, together with Ina Britschgi-Schimmer, *Gustav Landauer. Sein Lebensgang in Briefen* [Gustav Landauer: His Life in Letters], an extensive two-volume selection of Landauer letters (1929).

It took until the 1960s for new publications by and about Landauer to appear, with the sole exception of the precious booklet *Worte der Würdigung* [Words of Appreciation]; published in 1951, it includes essays in Landauer's honor by Erich Mühsam, Rudolf Rocker, Helmut Rüdiger, and Diego Abad de Santillán. Buber also dedicated a chapter to Landauer in his acclaimed 1949 *Paths to Utopia*, one of the main reasons Landauer did not disappear from consciousness altogether, in particular internationally.[150]

Outside of Germany, Landauer's most notable early influence was on the Kibbutz movement.[151] In a 1920 Landauer special issue of the socialist Zionist Hapoel Hatzair journal *Die Arbeit* [Labor], the preface states: "This issue is dedicated to the memory of Gustav Landauer. It shall express the high esteem in which we hold him... Gustav Landauer was an awakener for us; he has transformed our lives, and he has given our Zionism – which he never mentioned by name – a new meaning, a new intensity, a new direction."[152] The issue also includes a talk that Landauer gave on "Judaism and Socialism" at the opening of Berlin's Jüdische Volksheim [Jewish People's Home], on May 18, 1916.

Whether Landauer would have felt comfortable with such praise remains guesswork.[153] He did give a talk about "Judaism and Socialism"[154] to the Zionistischen Ortsgruppe West-Berlin [Zionist Group West-Berlin] in 1912 (one of his first public reflections on Judaism), but never shared clear thoughts on the Zionist movement. In November 1916, he "agrees in all basic points" with an article on Zionism by his good friend, the essayist and poet Margarete Susman.[155] Susman was known for her cultural interpretation of Zionism, which rejected the idea of a Jewish state.

As far as the Kibbutz idea goes, Landauer was certainly intrigued. Shortly before his death, in March 1919, he corresponded with Nachum Goldman, later co-founder and long-time president of the World Jewish Congress, after Goldman had invited him to a Berlin convention in April

1919 on the question of settlements in Palestine, and a "small preliminary convention in Munich." Goldman had also asked Landauer for advice on a number of economic issues. Landauer shared thoughts on the latter and promised to partake in the Munich meeting, making his participation in the Berlin convention dependent on the outcome.[156] The political developments and Landauer's death, however, did not allow for any meetings or further discussions.

Regardless of all speculation on what Landauer's perspective on the fledgling Kibbutz movement would have been, his ideas proved highly inspirational within Jewish socialist groups of the 1920s and '30s. An impressive number of his texts were translated into Yiddish and Hebrew. The General Federation of Israeli Labor published a tribute to Gustav Landauer in 1939.[157]

That Landauer's influence was indeed tangible in early Kibbutzim is documented in a compelling report by the Austrian writer, psychologist, and long-time communist Manès Sperber:

"Landauer's murder and death were horrific, but for people like me, members of the free Jewish youth movement, Landauer's life had not ended. We felt his presence among us, in particular whenever we discussed a daring plan that, a few years later, would become reality in a far away land on ancient soil. I am talking about the spirited communities established by young pioneers in Palestine. We called such a community Kwuzah, but it later became known as Kibbutz. The Kibbutzim fulfilled the dream of community that was both Landauer's and our own — and they still exist! Today, they are home to third and fourth generations who live in uncompromising individual freedom without private property or hierarchical social structures. They have turned socialism into reality. True, comparatively small examples, but the only ones that have survived many lost or spoilt revolutions. Whenever I visit a Kibbutz, I think of Landauer — and I do not see the tortured face of a murder victim, but Landauer's true countenance, that of a prophet. Landauer was the kind of man whose life and death justifies our being."[158]

Sperber's description is certainly romantic. However, Augustin Souchy, a teenage member of the Socialist Bund, confirms Landauer's legacy among Kibbutzniks. He writes in connection with a visit to Israel in 1951:

"There was a group of about 500 immigrants who had come to Palestine from Germany one year before Hitler took power.

The Jewish National Fund (Keren Kayemet) gave them 500 hectares of land. ... I was surprised to find comrades among them. One of the community's initiators, Chaver Buchaster from Hanover, told me that he and his friends had been inspired by the socialism of Gustav Landauer."[159]

Ruth Link-Salinger claims that Landauer's influence among Jewish radicals even reached to Noam Chomsky through the Zionist student movement Avukah. Chomsky socialized with some former Avukah members during his early university years (officially, the group had already disbanded).[160] While this might be far-fetched, Landauer has certainly left a strong mark in the history of Jewish socialism and anarchism. For example, Paul Avrich tells of a Tel Aviv anarchist group that was named after him in the 1970s.[161]

Scholars have suggested that Landauer's international influence reached as far as Korea.[162] There is not much evidence to support such claims. However, Landauer did leave a mark in South America, mainly due to the translations by Spanish-Argentinean anarchist Diego Abad de Santillán. Santillán had lived in Berlin from 1922 to 1926, frequenting the FAUD circles. He published Spanish editions of "Die Abschaffung des Krieges durch die Selbstbestimmung des Volkes" and *Aufruf zum Sozialismus* in the late 1920s. Between 1929 and 1932, Max Nettlau published a few Spanish articles in Buenos Aires' *La Protesta* and Barcelona's *La Revista Blanca*, most notably "La vida de Gustav Landauer según su corrospondencia" [The Life of Gustav Landauer in Letters][163] in *La Protesta*, July 31, 1929, an issue dedicated to Landauer. Helmut Rüdiger also published an essay on Landauer in *La Revista Blanca* in 1933.

In 1934, Santillán translated the first ever monograph written on Landauer, interestingly enough published in Swedish. The antimilitarist Augustin Souchy had fled to Sweden during World War I and brought out *Landauer: Revolutions Filosof* [Landauer: Philosopher of Revolution] in 1920. Another early foreign language monograph on Landauer appeared in Holland in 1931: *Gustaaf Landauer. Zijn Levensgang en Lewenswerk* [Gustav Landauer: His Life and Work] by Henriette Roland-Holst.

Santillán remained dedicated to keeping Landauer's work alive for decades. In 1947, his translations of Landauer's lectures on Shakespeare appeared, and a Spanish translation of *Die Revolution* was finally published in 1961, again with Santillán's help.

Other translations of Landauer's writings remain rare. In the 1970s, a French translation of *Die Revolution* (1973) and the English edition of *Aufruf zum Sozialismus* (1978) reflected the resurgence of interest in Landauer at the time. The translations were preceded by articles that appeared on Landauer in England's *Anarchy* journal (August 1965), in France's *Recherches libertaires* [Libertarian Studies] (December 1966, a translation of the *Anarchy* piece) and *Le Monde libertaire* [The Libertarian World] (January 1967), and in Sweden's *Arbetaren* [The Worker] (February 23-26, 1968). In the last decade, Giannis Karapapas has published a Greek collection of Landauer essays (2000) and a translation of *Die Revolution* (2001). Charles Daget has edited and translated two essay collections in French (2008 and 2009, respectively). In English, there has been the pamphlet *Anarchism in Germany and Other Essays* (2005), including five Landauer essays, and a reprint of Landauer's correspondence with the Nachum Goldman in James Horrox's *A Living Revolution: Anarchism and the Kibbutz Movement* (2009).

Maybe somewhat ironically – given the lack of translations of his own work – the translations by Gustav Landauer have at times been called his most important contribution to the international anarchist movement.[164] Landauer – often in collaboration with Hedwig Lachmann – translated writers and thinkers such as Guy Aldred, Mikhail Bakunin,[165] Honoré de Balzac, Allan L. Benson, Étienne de La Boétie, Samuel Butler,[166] Voltairine de Cleyre, Margaret Fuller, Peter Kropotkin, Multatuli (Eduard Douwes Dekker), Max Nettlau, Pierre-Joseph Proudhon, Élisée Reclus, John Reed, Jean-Jacques Rousseau, Rabindranath Tagore, Leo N. Tolstoy, Walt Whitman, and Oscar Wilde. In addition, Landauer introduced many more foreign authors to a German-language audience through articles about them or – in the case of German-speakers in exile – commissioned essays. These men and women include Alexander Berkman, Francisco Ferrer, Jean Grave, Emma Goldman, Alexander Herzen, Errico Malatesta, Johann Most, Domela Nieuwenhuis, Robert Reitzel, and Vladimir Solovjov.

Some of Lachmann and Landauer's translations are still reprinted today as the standard German adaptations. Available in any well stocked bookstore are Oscar Wilde's *The Picture of Dorian Gray* (*Das Bildnis des Dorian Gray*) and *The Soul of Man Under Socialism* (*Der Sozialismus und die Seele des Menschen*), Peter Kropotkin's *Mutual Aid: A Factor of Evolution* (*Gegenseitige Hilfe in der Tier- und Menschenwelt*), Étienne de La Boétie's *Discours de la servitude volontaire* (*Von der freiwilligen Knechtschaft*) [English edition: *The Politics of Disobedience: The Discourse of Voluntary Servitude*], the Briefe aus der Französischen Revolution, and the New High German rendition of texts by Meister Eckhart (*Mystische Schriften*).

Following Thomas Esper's ambitious but somewhat dry thesis, *The Anarchism of Gustav Landauer* from 1961, the English-speaking world saw three scholarly works on Landauer appear in the 1970s. These were Charles B. Maurer's *Call to Revolution: The Mystical Anarchism of Gustav Landauer* (1971), Eugene Lunn's *Prophet of Community: The Romantic Socialism of Gustav Landauer* (1974), and Ruth Link-Salinger (Hyman)'s *Gustav Landauer: Philosopher of Utopia* (1977). These volumes have constituted the backbone of every English Landauer study since.

Charles Maurer focuses strongly on arts, on mysticism, and on Landauer's reading of Fritz Mauthner. This makes for a somewhat one-sided reading of Landauer, but the book remains inspiring and informative.

Eugene Lunn's study is the most extensive and provides the best general overview, even if the label of "romantic socialism" seems unfortunate.

Link-Salinger's volume is strong on cultural background, personal analysis, and "Gustav Landauer in Historical Literature" (Chapter 4). The book includes an extensive – if by now outdated – bibliography. Link-Salinger has also edited a couple of collections of Landauer essays and lectures in German.[167]

There are a few shorter texts of interest to the English-speaking reader. Recommended are both C. W. [Colin Ward]'s essay on Gustav Landauer in the London *Anarchy* issue on the Bavarian Council Republic from August 1965 (the issue also contains a translated excerpt of *Die Revolution* entitled "Thoughts on Revolution"), and the introduction to *For Socialism* by Russell Berman and Tim Luke.[168] Paul Avrich dedicates a beautiful, if short, chapter to Gustav Landauer in his 1988 *Anarchist Portraits*.[169] An overview of Landauer's life and work – especially with respect to his influence on the Kibbutz movement – is also provided in the above-mentioned *A Living Revolution: Anarchism in the Kibbutz Movement* by James Horrox. Most recently, Horrox has contributed the essay "Reinventing Resistance: Constructive Activism in Gustav Landauer's Social Philosophy" to the book *New Perspectives on Anarchism* (2009), and an article on Gustav Landauer's Oscar Wilde translations will soon be published in the online journal *Oscholars*.[170]

Out of the Landauer entries in the most widely read histories of anarchism, George Woodcock's *Anarchism: A History of Libertarian Ideas and Movements*, Peter Marshall's *Demanding the Impossible: A History of Anarchism*, and Max Nettlau's *A Short History of Anarchism*, only Nettlau's representation is bereft of factual errors.[171]

1. *Gustav Landauer. Sein Lebensgang in Briefen*, 1: 264.

2. See especially "Volk und Land. Dreißig sozialistische Thesen" [People and Land: Thirty Socialist Theses], first published in *Die Zukunft*, January 12, 1907. "Dreißig sozialistische Thesen" was the original title, Martin Buber added "Volk und Land" later from Landauer's hand-written manuscript; cf. Buber's Preface in Gustav Landauer, *Beginnen* (Köln: Marcan-Block, 1924), III.

3. Russell Berman and Tim Luke, introduction to *For Socialism* by Gustav Landauer (St. Louis: Telos Press, 1978), 8.

4. See the essay "Die Abschaffung des Krieges durch die Selbstbestimmung des Volkes. Fragen an die deutschen Arbeiter," translated in this volume as "The Abolition of War by the Self-Determination of the People: Questions to the German Workers."

5. In translations, this has sometimes been shortened to "minister." However, the distinction between the position of a *Minister* and a *Volksbeauftragter* was important to the council republicans. See Erich Mühsam, *Von Eisner bis Leviné. Die Entstehung der bayerischen Räterepublik* [From Eisner to Leviné: The Emergence of the Bavarian Council Republic] (Berlin: Fanal-Verlag, n.d.; written by Mühsam in prison in 1920), 43-45.

6. Some of these examples also illustrate why it is rarely fitting to equate the German *Volk* with the English "folk." The connotations are rather different, with the closest German equivalent to "folk" being the adjective *volkstümlich*, meaning "from the people" in a "traditional," sometimes "antiquated" and "ritualized" way. In the above examples, "folk kitchen" or "folk theatre" would certainly evoke misleading images.

7. Eugene Lunn, *Prophet of Community: The Romantic Socialism of Gustav Landauer* (Berkeley: University of California Press, 1973), 6.

8. See relevant essays in the bibliography at the end of the book.

9. See also "On the 11th of November" in this volume.

10. Linse, *Gustav Landauer und die Revolutionszeit 1918-1919*, 180.

11. See, for example, Gilles Deleuze, *Nietzsche et la philosophie* [Nietzsche and Philosophy] (Paris: PUF, 1962), and Lewis Call, *Postmodern Anarchism* (Lanham: Lexington Books, 2002); even though Call is often cited as a "post-anarchist" author, he does not use the label himself.

12. Friedrichshagen retains an artistic, if pacified, flair to this day.

13. See Landauer's articles "Die Neue Freie Volksbühne," *Die Schaubühne*, October 19, 1905, and "Die Volksbühne," *Berliner-Börsen-Courier*, September 1915.

14. Landauer gave a talk at the meeting initiating the project on March 31, 1913.

15. *Die Zukunft*, January 5, 1895, published in English as "Anarchism in Germany" in Gustav Landauer, *Anarchism in Germany and Other Essays*, translated by Stephen Bender and Gabriel Kuhn (San Francisco: Barbary Coast Publishing Collective, 2005), reprinted in Robert Graham, ed., *Anarchism: A Documentary History of Libertarian Ideas*, vol. 1 (Montreal: Black Rose Books, 2005).

16. In 1903, *Neues Leben* turned into *Der freie Arbeiter* [The Free Worker], which existed as Germany's most important "proletarian anarchist" journal until 1932. The group behind *Neues Leben* also founded the Föderation revolutionärer Arbeiter [Federation of Revolutionary Workers] in 1900, renamed as Anarchistische Föderation Deutschlands [Anarchist Federation of Germany] in 1903. The organization was largely absorbed by the Freie Arbeiter-Union Deutschlands [Free German Workers' Union] (FAUD) in the 1920s.

17. See "Socialist Hopes" below.

18. Letter dated December 30, 1918, in *Gustav Landauer. Sein Lebensgang in Briefen*, 2: 343-344.

19. Landesarchiv Berlin, Pr. Br. Rep. 30 Berlin C: Polizeipräsidium, Tit. 95, Nr. 16346: Der Schriftsteller Gustav Landauer [The writer Gustav Landauer] 1892-1902.

20. Landauer encountered fierce resistance when trying to present his report, "An den Züricher Kongress" [To the Zurich Congress]. It was later published in *Der Sozialist*, July 29 and August 5, 1893.

21. Heinz-Joachim Heydorn, "Geleitwort" [Foreword] in: Gustav Landauer, *Zwang und Befreiung* [Coercion and Liberation] (Köln: Jakob Hegner, 1968), 14.

22. A part of his prison diary was published as "Aus meinem Gefängnis-Tagebuch" [From My Prison Diary] in *Der sozialistische Akademiker*, various issues from July 1 to September 15, 1895; *Der Sozialist* did not appear during this period.

23. See also "Die Bedeutung des Streiks" [The Meaning of the Strike] in *Der Sozialist*, March 28, 1896. Another interesting strike analysis by Landauer appeared fourteen years later in *Der Sozialist* in connection with a Berlin bakers' strike: "Brot" [Bread], June 1, 1911.

24. *Gustav Landauer. Sein Lebensgang in Briefen*, 1: 4.

25. Landauer published his impressions of the Congress in a series of three articles in *Der Sozialist* entitled "Der Londoner Kongress und die Anarchie" [The London Congress and Anarchy], August 8, 15, and 22, 1896.

26. de Jong, "Gustav Landauer und die internationale anarchistische Bewegung," 218.

27. On June 7, 1896, a bomb was thrown into the crowd at the annual Corpus Christi procession in Barcelona. Around a dozen people died and over thirty were wounded. See also "Ferrer" in this volume.

28. *Gustav Landauer. Sein Lebensgang in Briefen*, 1: 8.

29. First in the article "Der Dichter als Ankläger" [The Poet as Denouncer], *Der Sozialist*, February 5, 1898, then, six months later, in an open letter sent to various newspapers and government offices. Landauer knew about the possibility of imprisonment, but wanted to draw attention to the case. Ziethen was not freed, and died in prison in 1903. See Landauer's pamphlet "Der Fall Ziethen. Ein Appell an die öffentliche Meinung" [The Ziethen Case: An Appeal to Public Opinion] (Berlin: Hugo Metscher, 1898), and the article "In Sachen Ziethen" [Concerning Ziethen], *Sozialistische Monatshefte* 3, 1899.

30. Leuschner, who had long struggled with health problems, died of tuberculosis in 1908. Charlotte moved to live with Landauer and Lachmann.

31. Siegbert Wolf, "...nicht der Staat, sondern die Gesellschaft, die Gesellschaft von Gesellschaften" [...not the State, but Society, a Society of Societies], introduction to the 2003 reprint of *Die Revolution* (Münster: Unrast), 21.

32. Diego Abad de Santillán, "Die tägliche Revolution von unten auf" [The Daily Revolution from Below], in Erich Mühsam et al., *Gustav Landauer – Worte der Würdigung* [Gustav Landauer – Words of Appreciation] (Darmstadt: Die freie Gesellschaft, 1951), 5.

33. "A Few Words on Anarchism," translated in this volume.

34. Mühsam, "Der revolutionäre Mensch Gustav Landauer," 121. Further: "If we began to look for Landauer quotes to justify one particular opinion or another, we would do to him what the political parties have done to Marx and Lenin" (127).

35. Erich Mühsam, "Gustav Landauer. Gedenkblatt zu seinem 50. Geburtstag: 7. April 1920" [Gustav Landauer: Memorial Page on His 50th Birthday], Das Forum, April 7, 1920, here quoted from Knüppel, "Sei tapfer und wachse dich aus," 205.

36. See also "Mexico" in this volume.

37. See various editions of *Kürschners Deutscher Literaturkalender* (KDL); the KDL is an annually updated catalog on German literature, first published in 1879.

38. *Der Sozialist*, March 15, 1911. The terms "anti-politics" and "anti-politician" have been embraced by a number of Landauer scholars. See for example vol. 3 of *Ausgewählte Schriften* by Siegbert Wolf (detailed information in the Bibliography).

39. Ruth Link-Salinger (Hyman), *Gustav Landauer: Philosopher of Utopia* (Indianapolis: Hackett Publishing, 1977), 2.

40. Rudolf Rocker, *Aus den Memoiren eines deutschen Anarchisten* [From the Memoires of a German Anarchist] (Frankfurt am Main: Suhrkamp, 1974), 358.

41. de Jong, "Gustav Landauer und die internationale anarchistische Bewegung," 215.

42. Letter to Max Nettlau, August 10, 1910, in *Gustav Landauer. Sein Lebensgang in Briefen*, 1: 314.

43. Maurer, *Call to Revolution: The Mystical Anarchism of Gustav Landauer* (Detroit: Wayne State University Press, 1971). Thorsten Hinz also uses the term in his study *Mystik und Anarchie. Meister Eckhart und seine Bedeutung im Denken Gustav Landauers* [Mysticism and Anarchy: The Significance of Meister Eckhart in Gustav Landauer's Thought] (Berlin: Karin Kramer, 2000), 12.

44. Landauer published a number of articles on Mauthner around the turn of the century, all in *Die Zukunft*, an eclectic left-leaning journal of arts, philosophy, and politics: "Fritz Mauthner" (Issue 29, 1899), "Mauthners Sprachkritik" [Mauthner's Critique of Language] (Issue 35, 1901), "Mauthners Sprachwissenschaft" [Mauthner's Linguistics] (Issue 37, 1901), "Mauthners Werk" [Mauthner's Works] (Issue 42, 1903). Several years later, "Fritz Mauthners Buddha-Dichtung" [Fritz Mauthner's Buddha Poetry] was published in *Berliner Tageblatt*, December 13, 1912.

45. Hinz, *Mystik und Anarchie*, 14.

46. Included in this volume as "Through Separation to Community."

47. Hinz, *Mystik und Anarchie*, 12.

48. The Socialist Bund also contained a "Freiland" group in Frankfurt am Main.

49. See also Landauer's article "Über Weltanschauungen" [On Worldviews], *Der arme Teufel* 5, 1902, and the letter to Fritz Mauthner from November 28, 1901, in *Gustav Landauer. Sein Lebensgang in Briefen* 1: 100-102.

50. Buber was almost solely responsible for publishing many of Landauer's writings after his death and for keeping his memory alive (see "Landauer's Legacy"). Landauer dedicated a long article to Buber ("Martin Buber") in *Neue Blätter*, Buber Special Issue, 1913.

51. A detailed insight into the relationship is provided by the above-cited book *"Sei tapfer und wachse dich aus." Gustav Landauer im Dialog mit Erich Mühsam – Briefe und Aufsätze*, edited by Christoph Knüppel.

52. English literature on Erich Mühsam is rare. Two books have been published, one of which provides a general overview, *The Eclectic Anarchism of Erich Mühsam* by Lawrence Baron (New York: Revisionist Press, 1976), while the other, *From Bohemia to the Barricades: Erich Mühsam and the Development of a Revolutionary Drama* by David A. Shepherd (New York: Peter Lang Publishing, 1993), is a study of Mühsam the dramatist. Translations of Mühsam texts are almost non-existent, although some excellent renditions have recently been made available on the *erichinenglish.org* website. For more detailed information on the history of Mühsam's reception in the English-speaking world – and the plans to publish an English Mühsam volume with PM Press – see Gabriel Kuhn, "Zur englischsprachigen Rezeption Erich Mühsams und dem Anarchismus in den USA" [On the Reception of Erich Mühsam in the English-Speaking World, and on Anarchism in the USA], in *Wie aktuell ist Erich Mühsam?* [How Relevant Is Erich Mühsam Today?] (Lübeck: Erich-Mühsam-Gesellschaft, 2008).

53. This was also a point of contention during the Bavarian Council Republic; see Mühsam, *Von Eisner bis Leviné*, 57.

54. Michael Matzigkeit, "Gustav Landauer – zu Leben, Werk und Wirkung" [Gustav Landauer – Life, Work, Influence], in: *"…die beste Sensation ist das Ewige…"* […the Best Sensation Is the Eternal…], Düsseldorf: Theatermuseum, 1995, 15. See also Johann Baptist Müller, "Der konservative Anarchist. Zum hundertsten Geburtstag Gustav Landauers" [The Conservative Anarchist: On Gustav Landauer's Hundredth Birthday], *Süddeutsche Zeitung*, April 7, 1970.

55. "Der fünfte Stand" [The Fifth Estate] was published in *Der Sozialist*, July 1, 1910; a related article by Mühsam, "Neue Freunde" [New Friends], had been published on August 1, 1909.

56. See for example "Tarnowska," *Der Sozialist*, April 15, 1910; "Von der Ehe" [On Marriage], *Der Sozialist*, October 10, 1910; the letter to Margarethe Faas-Hardegger, April 1, 1909, in *Gustav Landauer. Sein Lebensgang in Briefen*, 1: 246-250; and the chapter "Gustav Landauer: Kulturphilosoph und libertärer Sozialist" [Gustav Landauer: Cultural Philosopher and Libertarian Socialist] in Birgit Seemann, *Hedwig Landauer-Lachmann. Dichterin, Antimilitaristin, deutsche Jüdin* [Hedwig Landauer-Lachmann: Poet, Antimilitarist, German Jew] (Frankfurt am Main/New York: Campus, 1998).

57. Walter Fähnders und Hansgeorg Schmidt-Bergmann, "'Utopien sind immer nur scheintot.' Hinweise auf Gustav Landauer" ['Utopias Only Appear Dead:' On Gustav Landauer], in *Die Botschaft der Titanic. Ausgewählte Essays* [*The Titanic's Message*: Selected Essays], edited by Walter Fähnders und Hansgeorg Schmidt-Bergmann (Berlin: Kontext, 1994), 296.

58. Ibid., 289.

59. Mühsam, "Gustav Landauer und die bayrische Revolution," 212.

60. Ibid.

61. Mühsam, "Gustav Landauer. Gedenkblatt zu seinem 50. Geburtstag: 7. April 1920," 205.

62. Landauer had already published an article entitled "Fürst Peter Kropotkin" [Prince Peter Kropotkin] in 1900 (*Die neue Zeit. Revue des geistigen und öffentlichen Lebens*, # 325). He published an extensive three-part article entitled "Peter Kropotkin" in *Der Sozialist* in 1912-13 (three issues between Christmas, 1912, and February 15, 1913). Landauer apparently left less of an impression on Kropotkin. Max Nettlau writes in connection with Kropotkin's notorious Germanophobia that certain German-speaking anarchists "could have taught the man a number of things but they never made any impression on him – I am specifically thinking of Landauer" (*Geschichte der Anarchie*, V: 127).

63. Martin Buber, *Briefwechsel aus sieben Jahrzehnten* [Seven Decades of Correspondence] (Heidelberg: Lambert Schneider, 1972), 1: 245.

64. Link-Salinger (Hyman), *Gustav Landauer: Philosopher of Utopia*, 61.

65. Ibid., 64. Landauer already received such critique at the time. See for example his defense in a letter to Fritz Mauthner from October 5, 1907: "Concerning the structure of the text, I dare say that you are absolutely wrong. It is true that structure was not a strong point in my earlier books, but this time I did really well" (*Gustav Landauer. Sein Lebensgang in Briefen*, 1:171).

66. Hinz, *Mystik und Anarchie*, 187-189; Wolf, "...nicht der Staat, sondern die Gesellschaft, die Gesellschaft von Gesellschaften," 21. In the last years of his life, the focus on the Christian communities of the Middle Ages gave way to an increased interest in Judaism and Jewish understandings of community; see, for example, "The Beilis Trial" in this volume.

67. See *Revolution* in this volume.

68. Wolf, "...nicht der Staat, sondern die Gesellschaft, die Gesellschaft von Gesellschaften," 7.

69. Rudolf Rocker, "Das Ende Gustav Landauers" [The End of Gustav Landauer], in Mühsam et al., *Gustav Landauer – Worte der Würdigung*, 39-40.

70. Mühsam, "Der revolutionäre Mensch Gustav Landauer," 124.

71. For German readers, there are two excellent studies that have explored Landauer's understanding of utopia in depth: the above-mentioned *Mystik und Anarchie* by Thorsten Hinz, and Bernhard Braun's Die *Utopie des Geistes. Zur Funktion der Utopie in der politischen Theorie Gustav Landauers* [The Utopia of Spirit: On the Meaning of Utopia in Gustav Landauer's Political Theory] (Idstein: Schulz-Kirchner, 1991).

72. Wolf, "...nicht der Staat, sondern die Gesellschaft, die Gesellschaft von Gesellschaften," 10.

73. See footnote 2.

74. For an explanation of *Bund*, see "Translating Gustav Landauer" in the Editor's Note.

75. See "First Pamphlet of the Socialist Bund: What Does the Socialist Bund Want?" in this volume.

76. *Der Sozialist*, February 15, 1909.

77. Ulrich Linse provides a detailed list of Socialist Bund groups, as well as a general overview of the Bund's organization, in *Organisierter Anarchismus im deutschen Kaiserreich von 1871* [Organized Anarchism in the German Kaiserreich of 1871] (Berlin: Duncker und Humblot, 1969), 289-300. See also Landauer's letter to Fritz Mauthner from June 26, 1908, in *Gustav Landauer. Sein Lebensgang in Briefen*, 1: 198-200.

78. Landauer was banned from entering the Austrian-Hungarian Empire after 1897 due to his political activities; the ban remained in place until the empire dissolved as a consequence of World War I in 1918.

79. Her writings in *Der Sozialist* appeared under the pseudonym Mark Harda.

80. Letter to Margarethe Faas-Hardegger, August 22, 1908, in *Gustav Landauer. Sein Lebensgang in Briefen*, 1: 200.

81. Various letters sent to Faas-Hardegger in 1908-1909, in *Gustav Landauer. Sein Lebensgang in Briefen*, 1: 200-228.

82. Landauer's letter to Faas-Hardegger from April 1, 1909, in *Gustav Landauer. Sein Lebensgang in Briefen*, 1: 246-250.

83. See, for example, Linse, *Organisierter Anarchismus im deutschen Kaiserreich von 1871*, 275.

84. *Gustav Landauer. Sein Lebensgang in Briefen*, 1: 261.

85. Letter dated June 16, 1916, in *Gustav Landauer. Lebensgang in Briefen*, 2: 142.

86. Mühsam, "Gustav Landauer. Gedenkblatt zu seinem 50. Geburtstag: 7. April 1920," 205.

87. Souchy, *Vorsicht Anarchist! Ein Leben für die Freiheit. Politische Erinnerungen* [Beware! Anarchist!: A Life Committed to Freedom: Political Memoires] (Darmstadt und Neuwied: Luchterhand, 1977), 12.

88. *Gustav Landauer. Sein Lebensgang in Briefen*. Buber included five letters written to Hugo Landauer between 1895 and 1897, and one letter to Fritz Mauthner from 1898.

89. Buber mentions in 1929 that Max Kronstein, the husband of Landauer's daughter Charlotte, was planning to edit a collection of "letters, diaries, and

other documents from his youth" (*Gustav Landauer. Sein Lebensgang in Briefen*, 1: VI). Such a collection never appeared.

90. Fähnders und Schmidt-Bergmann, "'Utopien sind immer nur scheintot,'" 286.

91. Gustav Landauer et al., *Briefe nach der Schweiz*, Zürich 1972, 29.

92. See Article Ten of the "Twelve Articles of the Socialist Bund, Second Version," included in this volume.

93. Concerning the entire conflict see Linse, *Organisierter Anarchismus im deutschen Kaiserreich von 1871*, 281-288; concerning the advertisements specifically, see also *Gustav Landauer. Sein Lebensgang in Briefen*, 1: 254 and 259.

94. Gustav Landauer, *Aufruf zum Sozialismus* [Call for Socialism] (Frankfurt am Main: Europäische Verlagsanstalt, 1976), 175-176. Originally published in Berlin: Verlag des Sozialistischen Bundes, 1911.

95. The quote echoes sentiments explained in more detail in "Anarchic Thoughts on Anarchism," included in this volume.

96. Josef Peukert (1855-1910) was a controversial figure within the anarchist movement at the time, accused by some to be a police informer. Vol. 2 of the Siegbert Wolf edited *Ausgewählte Schriften* of Landauer, *Anarchismus*, deals with the debate at length.

97. Gustav Landauer. Sein Lebensgang in Briefen, 1: 259.

98. Max Nettlau, *A Short History of Anarchism* (London: Freedom Press, 1996, based on manuscripts from 1932-1934), 220-221.

99. Landauer reflects on this period and his loneliness in a letter to Constantin Brunner (born Leopold Wertheimer, 1862-1937, Jewish philosopher) from January 2, 1910, in *Gustav Landauer. Sein Lebensgang in Briefen*, 1: 282-285.

100. Ulrich Linse, "Die Anarchisten und die Münchner Novemberrevolution" [The Anarchists and the Munich November Revolution], in Karl Bosl, ed., *Bayern im Umbruch* [Upheaval in Bavaria] (München und Wien: R. Oldenbourg, 1969), 46. See also Linse, *Organisierter Anarchismus im deutschen Kaiserreich von 1871*, 346-376.

101. Rocker, "Das Ende Gustav Landauers," 47-48.

102. The *Aufruf* combined several lectures given by Landauer in previous years; hence the somewhat confusing subtitle *Ein Vortrag* [A Lecture] (dropped in later editions). The essays collected in the chapter "Socialist Hopes" in this volume provide a broad overview of Landauer's understanding of socialism, as well as a number of concrete examples. They constitute both an inclusive, independent summary of Landauer's socialism and a hands-on companion to *For Socialism*.

103. Mühsam, "Der revolutionäre Mensch Gustav Landauer," 124.

104. Santillán, "Die tägliche Revolution von unten auf, 5. Further: "The notion of a daily revolution from below was intrinsically linked to his vision of a free and happy humanity – which was his highest goal" (7).

105. See also Landauer's pamphlet "Die vereinigten Republiken Deutschlands und ihre Verfassung" [The United Republics of Germany and Their Constitution] (Frankfurt am Main: Das Flugblatt, 1918), in which Landauer tries to apply his Socialist Bund vision to the revolutionary situation in Germany.

106. What is probably the most concise articulation of this belief can be found in "Schwache Staatsmänner, schwächeres Volk!", translated in this volume as "Weak Statesmen, Weaker People!".

107. "Was ist zunächst zu tun?" [What Do We Do First?], the second pamphlet published by the Socialist Bund. See below for detailed information on the three pamphlets of the Socialist Bund.

108. *Der Sozialist*, November 1, 1910.

109. Achim von Borries and Ingeborg Weber-Brandies, eds., *Anarchismus. Theorie, Kritik, Utopie* [Anarchism: Theory, Critique, Utopia] (Nettersheim: Graswurzelrevolution, 2007), 381. Originally published in Frankfurt am Main: Joseph Melzer, 1970.

110. Rolf Kauffeldt, "Die Idee eines 'Neuen Bundes' (Gustav Landauer)" [The Idea of a 'New Bund' (Gustav Landauer)], in Manfred Frank, *Gott im Exil. Vorlesungen über die neue Mythologie, II. Teil* [God in Exile: Lectures on the New Mythology, Part Two] (Frankfurt am Main: Suhrkamp, 1988), 148.

111. Mühsam, "Gustav Landauer. Gedenkblatt zu seinem 50. Geburtstag: 7. April 1920," 207.

112. Landauer, *Aufruf zum Sozialismus*, 175. The intriguing ecological implications of Landauer's ideas need yet to be explored.

113. Kauffeldt, "Die Idee eines 'Neuen Bundes' (Gustav Landauer)," 149. The term is based on Landauer's self-description of his ideas, for example in "Ein Brief über die anarchistischen Kommunisten" [A Letter on the Anarchist Communists], *Der Sozialist*, November 1, 1910.

114. Landauer, *Aufruf zum Sozialismus*, 75.

115. One of the very first issues of the "Third" *Sozialist* (April 1, 1909) also included an essay entitled "Der Krieg" [The War].

116. Erich Mühsam, *Tagebücher* 1910-1924 [Diaries 1910-1924], edited by Chris Hirte (München: Deutscher Taschenbuchverlag, 1994), 265-267; Mühsam, "Gustav Landauer und die bayrische Revolution," 212-214; Linse, *Organisierter Anarchismus im deutschen Kaiserreich von 1871*, 361-363. Those who claim Landauer as a pacifist often focus on his articles about Leo Tolstoy: "Lew Nikolajewitsch Tolstoi," *Der Sozialist*, December 15, 1910 (the entire

issue was dedicated to Tolstoy); "Tolstoj," *Blätter des deutschen Theaters*, # 2, 1912; Preface to Leo Tolstoj, *Rede gegen den Krieg* [known in *English as Last Message to Mankind*], Berlin: Der Sozialistische Bund, 1913.

117. Wolf, "'Barcelona ist immer noch besser als Wilmersdorf' – Gustav Landauers Blick in die Welt," 24-25.

118. See also Landauer's analysis of the war in a talk during the Bavarian Revolution on December 18, 1918, later published as "Deutschland und seine Revolution" [Germany and Its Revolution], *Erkenntnis und Befreiung*, January-March 1919.

119. "Der Kanzler des deutschen Volkes" [The Chancellor of the German People], *Der Sozialist*, December 15, 1913.

120. Noteworthy articles from *Der Sozialist* include "Die Sozialdemokratie und der Krieg" [Social Democracy and the War], December 1, 1912; "Vom Krieg" [On War], various issues between November 1, 1912, and April 1, 1913; "Der Kanzler des deutschen Volkes" [The Chancellor of the German People], December 15, 1913; and two pieces directly related to the outbreak of World War I, "Die Erschießung des österreichischen Thronfolgers" [The Murder of the Austrian Successor to the Throne], July 1, 1914, and "Der europäische Krieg" [The European War], August 10, 1914.

121. The history of the Forte-Kreis is well documented in Landauer's letters; see *Gustav Landauer. Sein Lebensgang in Briefen*, 2: 1-16 and 2: 77-92.

122. Joël was banned from the University of Berlin for his political activism.

123. On December 10, Landauer writes in a letter to Martin Buber: "I like Einstein a lot; I hope to meet with him more often..." (Gustav Landauer. Sein Lebensgang in Briefen, 2: 112). No frequent contact developed.

124. Founded in 1914, the Bund Neues Vaterland turned into the Deutsche Liga für Menschenrechte [German League for Human Rights] in 1922. The organization was banned by the Nazis in 1933. After World War II, two organizations claimed its heritage: the revived Deutsche Liga für Menschenrechte, and the more radical Internationale Liga für Menschenrechte. In 2008, the latter awarded its annual Carl von Ossietzky Medal, named after the German pacifist and Nobel Peace Prize Laureate, to the Palestinian Bil'in Popular Committee and the Israeli group Anarchists Against the Wall. Concerning Landauer's influence on radical socialist politics in Palestine/Israel see "Landauer's Legacy" below.

125. The Zentralstelle Völkerrecht existed until 1919.

126. The German Free Corps (*Freikorps*) were raised by the government following the end of World War I in order to bolster its military power. The vast majority of the Free Corps soldiers were monarchist and conservative military war personnel. Effectively, the Free Corps acted as independent right-wing militias.

127. For a general overview of the Bavarian Revolution see Allan Mitchell, *Revolution in Bavaria 1918-1919* (Princeton: Princeton University Press, 1965). Mitchell's report has a strong anti-anarchist bias and ridicules, in the jargon of the German Communist Party, the "First" Bavarian Council Republic as a "pseudo-soviet republic" (*Scheinräterepublik*).

128. *Gustav Landauer. Sein Lebensgang in Briefen*, 2: 296.

129. *Masken* appeared with different subtitles from 1905 to 1933. Landauer published several of his literary essays in the journal.

130. *Gustav Landauer. Sein Lebensgang in Briefen*, 2: 177. See also the letter to Ludwig Berndl from August 16, 1915, translated in this volume.

131. Most revealing regarding Landauer's overall perception of the developments in Germany are the letters from this period published in *Gustav Landauer. Sein Lebensgang in Briefen*. The letter to Margarete Susman in this volume serves as an example. It is planned to include more of these letters in an upcoming PM Press volume on radical currents within the German Revolution of 1918-19.

132. Mühsam had tried in vain to organize a broad anti-war movement after deeply regretting a controversial statement he had published in his journal *Kain* at the outset of the war. He had spoken of "foreign hordes attacking our women and children" (*Kain*, August 3-4, 1914).

133. Printed in *Arbeit und Zukunft*, February 28, 1919, and other journals.

134. Eugen Leviné was the leader of Bavaria's Communist Party who took control of the council republic after the first attack by the ousted government and military units on April 13; executed for high treason on June 5, 1919.

135. In his report, Mühsam concurs with the Communist Party's reasoning at the time, but accuses its leaders of indecision and dishonesty during the decisive days.

136. Erich Mühsam, "Gustav Landauer. Gedenkblatt zu seinem 50. Geburtstag: 7. April 1920," and "Lügen um Landauer" [Lies About Landauer], *Die Weltbühne*, June 24, 1929.

137. Mühsam, *Von Eisner bis Leviné*, 45-46. Due to the delay of the council republic's proclamation by three days and the overall turbulent situation, the document was never published and no complete sketch exists.

138. Mühsam was sentenced to fifteen years imprisonment for high treason. He was freed by a general amnesty in December 1924, the same amnesty that freed Hitler, who had been imprisoned for his 1923 coup attempt. While incarcerated, Mühsam wrote the above-quoted *Von Eisner bis Leviné*, the only detailed eyewitness account of the Bavarian Council Republic from an anarchist perspective. Fourteen years later, Mühsam would be taken into custody again, this time with fatal consequences. In the early morning hours of February 28, 1933, the night of the Reichstag fire, Mühsam was arrested by a Nazi *Sturmabteilung* (SA) unit in his Berlin home. Mühsam, aware of the danger, had train tickets to Prague in his pockets. He was killed in the Concentration Camp Oranienburg on July 9, 1934, and became one of the Nazi death camps' first prominent victims.

139. Landauer hid for two days in the house of a comrade, Alfred Fischer, who would also, like Landauer, be murdered by security forces in Stadelheim Prison after the eventual overthrow of the council republic.

140. For an overview of Landauer's extensive cultural reform program see Linse, *Gustav Landauer und die Revolutionszeit 1918-19*, 233-248.

141. Landauer was uncompromisingly opposed to all hierarchical and authoritarian organizations – this also extended to the Spartacists in Berlin. In a letter to the essayist and poet Margarete Susman, he writes on December 13, 1918: "The Bolshevist Spartacists give much reason for concern: they are pure centralists like Robespierre and his lot; they do not pursue goals, only power; they will create a military regime that will be many times worse than anything the world has seen so far. 'Dictatorship of the proletariat?' I'd rather have Napoleon!" (*Gustav Landauer. Sein Lebensgang in Briefen*, 2: 336). Nonetheless, Landauer gave a eulogy in Munich for Karl Liebknecht and Rosa Luxemburg, the two most prominent Spartacists, after they had been murdered by Free Corps soldiers on January 15, 1919.

142. See "Letters and telegrams to the daughters."

143. Starnberg is a small town southwest of Munich. "Stadelheim" refers to Stadelheim Prison, one of Germany's biggest and most notorious prisons, opened in 1894. Among political dissidents murdered in Stadelheim were also the members of the anti-Nazi resistance group White Rose (*Weiße Rose*) in 1943.

144. Heinrich Freiherr von Gagern (1878-1964), descendant of a military family, received a nominal fine for assaulting Landauer. Another soldier was sentenced to five weeks imprisonment for assault and for stealing Landauer's watch. No one was charged with Landauer's murder.

145. Rocker, "Das Ende Gustav Landauers," 38-39. There are slightly differing reports about the exact circumstances of Landauer's death, but all agree that he was killed by a mob of soldiers. According to a Bavarian government report published in Linse, *Gustav Landauer und die Revolutionszeit 1918-19*, 258-261, Landauer was shot three times.

146. Ret Marut, "Zum Andenken!" [In Memory!], *Der Ziegelbrenner*, March 20, 1920; Ernst Toller, "Brief an Gustav Landauer" [Letter to Gustav Landauer], *Der Freihafen*, 1920-1921, and "Gustav Landauer," *Die Weltbühne*, December 2, 1924.

147. Bernhard Braun, *Die Utopie des Geistes*, 125-126.

148. The German *Jugendbewegung* emerged at the beginning of the 20th century as a movement of youth awareness and independent youth organizing. While its progressive strains included educational anti-authoritarianism, sexual liberation, and environmental awareness, it was predominantly bourgeois and beset by nationalist tendencies that would later feed into the Nazis' *Blut und Boden* [Blood and Soil] ideology.

149. Braun, *Die Utopie des Geistes*, 126.

150. A short article on Landauer, entitled "A Saintly Revolutionary," also appeared in *The Jewish Quarterly*, Summer 1959, written by Alfred Werner. A longer English article on Landauer and Jewish identity, "The Jew as Revolutionary: The Case of Gustav Landauer," written by Paul Breines, appeared in the *Leo Baeck Yearbook*, 1967.

151. This influence – especially strong within the socialist Zionist youth movement Hashomer Hatzair – has recently been traced in a remarkable book by James Horrox, *A Living Revolution: Anarchism in the Kibbutz Movement* (Oakland: AK Press, 2009). Horrox has also made significant contributions to contemporary research on Gustav Landauer (see the bibliography at the end of the book) and is currently investigating the influence of Landauer on contemporary communal experiments in Israel.

152. *Die Arbeit. Organ der Zionistischen Volkssozialistischen Partei*, June 1920.

153. This includes the question of how sympathetic Landauer would have been to increased Jewish migration to Palestine. See, for example, Emil Simonson, "Gustav Landauer als Vorbild der zionistischen Jugend?" [Gustav Landauer as a Role Model for Zionist Youth?], *Jüdische Rundschau*, Berlin, November 2 and 9, 1920.

154. Published in *Selbstwehr*, February 16, 1912.

155. Letter to Margarete Susman, November 4, 1916, in *Gustav Landauer. Lebensgang in Briefen*, 2: 169. Susman's article was published as "Wege des Zionismus" [Ways of Zionism] in *Frankfurter Zeitung*, September 17, 1916.

156. The correspondence between Landauer and Goldman was first published in German in the journal *Akratie*, Fall 1977. It has been made available in English through a pamphlet translated and edited by Avraham Yassour, entitled "On Communal Settlement and Its Industrialization: An Exchange of Letters," published by the University of Haifa without date, presumably in the mid-1980s. Yassour also published reprints of the original German letters and a number of Hebrew pamphlets by and about Landauer around that time. Furthermore, he wrote an English article on Landauer entitled "Gustav Landauer – The Man, the Jew and the Anarchist," which appeared in *Ya'ad*, no. 2, 1989. The correspondence between Landauer and Goldman has recently been reprinted in James Horrox's *A Living Revolution: Anarchism in the Kibbutz Movement*.

157. Link-Salinger, *Gustav Landauer. Philosopher of Utopia*, 102.

158. Manès Sperber, "Der andere Sozialismus. Gustav Landauer oder: Die herrschaftslose Gemeinschaft" [The Other Socialism: Gustav Landauer, or Non-Authoritarian Community], Rundfunkmanuskript [Radio Transcript], in *Nur die Phantasielosen flüchten in die Realität. Anarchistisches Ja(h)rbuch I* [Only Those Without Imagination Escape Into Reality: Anarchist Yea(r)book I] (Berlin: Karin Kramer, 1983), 113-114.

159. Souchy, *Vorsicht Anarchist!*, 190.

160. Introduction to *Signatur: g.l. Gustav Landauer im "Sozialist,"* edited by Link-Salinger (Frankfurt am Main: Suhrkamp, 1986), 39. On Chomsky's relation to Avukah see the chapter "Zellig Harris, Avukah, and Hashomer Hatzair" in *Noam Chomsky: A Life of Dissent* by Robert F. Barsky (Cambridge: MIT Press, 1997).

161. Avrich, *Anarchist Portraits*, 247.

162. Braun, *Die Utopie des Geistes*, 122

163. The essay was based on *Gustav Landauer. Sein Lebensgang in Briefen.*

164. de Jong, "Gustav Landauer und die internationale anarchistische Bewegung," 221; Wolf, "'Barcelona ist immer noch besser als Wilmersdorf' – Gustav Landauers Blick in die Welt," 31.

165. According to Max Nettlau (*Geschichte der Anarchie*, V: 219), Landauer planned an extensive German edition of Bakunin's writings, including his correspondence.

166. Parts of *Erewhon* were published in three subsequent issues of *Der Sozialist* in May/June 1911; although no translator is credited, it is very likely that the translations are Landauer's.

167. For bibliographical references, please see the bibliography at the end of the book.

168. The introduction was reprinted as "On Gustav Landauer" in *The Radical Papers*, edited by Dimitrios I. Roussopoulos (Montreal: Black Rose Books, 1987).

169. Avrich also published an article on Landauer in the December 1974 issue of *The Match!*.

170. For detailed bibliographical references of these texts, please see the Bibliography.

171. Many informative notes on Landauer are included in vol. IV and, particularly, vol. V of Max Nettlau's six-volume *Geschichte der Anarchie*.

CHILDHOOD & YOUTH

TWENTY-FIVE YEARS LATER:
On the Jubilee of Wilhelm II

The essay was originally published as "Vor fünfundzwanzig Jahren. Zum Regierungsjubiläum Wilhelms II." in *Der Sozialist*, June 15, 1913. It is the only Landauer essay that includes details of his youth.

> *Demon: Will the spirit not be inherited?*
>
> *Sleeping King: Of all things that could possibly be inherited, this would be the last.*
>
> **(Bettina von Arnim)**[1]

WHICH DAY OF THE WEEK THE 15th OF JUNE WAS TWENTY-five years ago, I do not remember. The newspapers will certainly address this in all the memorials we will soon be reading. They have better memory because they replace brains with print. I do know, however, that it was not a Sunday like this year. This I know because I was sitting in school. It was in my senior year, shortly before graduation. Between 11 a.m. and noon on said day, all of the town's church bells suddenly began to ring. I instantly knew what this meant and looked expectantly at the teacher; he, however, in his philological fervor, did not (or did not want to) understand what had happened and continued to criticize Sophocles or Plato. This went on until the school's caretaker stormed into the room and ordered us all to the auditorium. There the headmaster told us with the obligatory patriotic ado that Kaiser Frederick III[2] had died.

A few months earlier, I had stood on the auditorium's stage myself, seventeen years old, spewing patriotism. Years earlier, the Grand Duchess Luise[3] had opened a foundation for our school. Senior students whose manuscripts had been approved were granted a patriotic speech every year. Their reward was a silver coin with Fichte's[4] image; the winner got the same coin in gold, and a copy of Fichte's *Reden an die deutsche Nation* – which the Grand Duchess or her advisors had certainly never read or understood.

The whole event was called *Fichte-Akt*,[5] and so, in the name of Fichte, I gave a speech on Friedrich Barbarossa.[6] I tied – in black-red-golden spirit[7] and with passionate references to Heinrich Heine, the teachers' most hated poet[8] – the notions of fatherland, unity of the Reich, and revolution dramatically to the old *Staufenkaiser*.[9] This earned me a harsh public scolding from the headmaster, a pitiful handshake from the mathematics teacher, and, with all sorts of reservations, the silver coin. My mother still has it. I never desired to have Fichte's head, engraved by the Grand Duchess, with me.

Prior to that day, I had a personal encounter with this mother of our country; since this was the only time I ever personally met a crowned head, I want to tell you about it today, on the occasion of her nephew's jubilee.

Our meeting was also at a jubilee. It was the 300th anniversary of our school. Juniors and seniors presented the Sophocles tragedy *Philoctetes* in German. I had only come to this school recently from another, and – not even considering the boredom I felt – there was no reason for me to celebrate. I hardly knew the teachers or the other students and certainly had no particular connection to the place. Nonetheless, I partook in the play as a coryphaeus.[10]

Afterwards, we were presented to the Grand Duchess and her husband; the seniors to him, the juniors – which I was at the time – to her. We know enough today about the way in which monarchs handle their munificent addresses from the *Feldherrnhügel*;[11] I got to experience this first-hand when I was 17. The Grand Duchess, whose Prussian accent I noticed, asked one student a quick question, and then, before he was even able to answer, turned to the next. The student before me was asked something about a professor who had recently died, and then I got the question: "Have you also enjoyed the classes of the professor?" Before I could even open my mouth, the headmaster jumped in and said, "No, this is a very young student."[12] The Grand Duchess looked at me bewildered and said, "Really? And already this tall?" I bowed to hide my grin – even if it was not necessary, as she already spoke to my neighbor.

In the bigger picture, this event, like everything that concerned school, was only an unimportant episode in my development. Even though school, including homework, occupied seven to eight hours of my day as a youth, it meant, with few exceptions, only alternating states of nervous anxiety and relaxation, the ludicrous theft of time, freedom, and dreams, and an obstruction to my own desires, investigations, and experiments. I spent a lot of time as a youth alone, and all that was important to me came from theatre, music, and especially books.

The cheap Reclam volumes[13] of Henrik Ibsen left a huge impression on me and forced my romantic desire to face reality. I had a lot of longing in me for purity, beauty, and fulfillment. I had found nourishment in Richard Wagner, whose operas, performed by Mottl,[14] I enjoyed as often as I could from the age of fifteen. I got tickets on the *Juchhe*, as we called the cheapest stands. But the more effective this magic potion was, the more oblivious I became to the ugliness of reality. And so it was Ibsen who turned my youthful dreams of beauty into a desire for realization; it was Ibsen who forced me, with irresistible power, to no longer ignore reality, to no longer ignore society and its ills, but to be aware and critical and rebellious. It was an individual rebellion at the time, as I did not understand anything about socialism and had no comprehension of national economy. The reason for my opposition to society, as well as the reason for my continued dreams and my outrage, was not class identity or even compassion, but the permanent collision of romantic desire with philistine limitation. This is why I was (without knowing the word at the time) an anarchist before I was a socialist, one of the few who had not taken a detour via social democracy.

Ibsen's influence was soon joined by that of Nietzsche, especially of his *Zarathustra*.[15] Some of the book's contents probably touched me so deeply and strongly because the words made me experience the spiritual struggle that their author had gone through. I had already lived in the minds of philosophers for a long time. I had read Schopenhauer and Spinoza. Now, with Nietzsche, I encountered a thinker in whom thought did not dominate emotion, but in whom thought and emotion were united. Yearning, passion, and fervency were dedicated to an idea like you would dedicate them to a lover. There was poetry, rich and colorful language, compelling verbal imagery, rhythm and dance, devotion and ardor, blissfulness and agony, animality and beauty, courtship and obsession – and it was all about the idea. And yet, as in the case of Ibsen, reality was not disregarded: there was activity in Nietzsche's spiritual quest, there was permanent destruction and creation, collapsing and rebuilding.

I will not say anything here about the fundamental parts of my youth, my heritage, my personality, my experiences at home and among friends. I am only mentioning a few external influences. Yet these alone should explain why my relation to the past twenty-five years of contemporary history is characterized by a strange mixture of detachment and participation. I felt disgust with society way too early to still feel fury or hate towards individuals.

In our times, an artist is defined as someone who has a vision; someone with visions and rhythms that form a separate inner world; someone who can manifest this world on the outside; someone who can create a new, an exemplary, *his own* world through imagination and creative force; someone whose ideas leave his inner being like Pallas Athena left Jupiter's head;[16] someone who then, like an Italian trader of plaster figures, packs the result in a basket and hawks it in "the other world," ordinary reality, where he sells the figures of his dreams and sacred desires to the goblins and caricatures of his artistic mind, all the while advertising, calculating, haggling, arguing, cheating. This is the contemporary artist's mixture of detachment and participation. But mine is another: I want to use reality to create; I want art to be the process of imaginative and communal social transformation, rather than the expression of individual yearning.

Even though it is too early to write my memoirs (I do not lack experience, but I do lack retrospective distance), I have taken the liberty of speaking about myself on the occasion of Wilhelm II's jubilee. If you will, I have given myself a modest torchlight procession.

Wilhelm II does not concern me much, and if I try to relate him to the German people of the last twenty-five years, I can only see him as the guardian of the country's *Simplicissimus* mood,[17] i.e., a spirit of resignation that delights in replacing action with permanent and meaningless complaint; it is the spirit of a fist clenched in the pocket; it is a spirit that has turned the German people into a theatre audience, spectators of the play "German Reich" without any capacity to intervene; it is a spirit that cannot even live up to Grimmelshausen's motto *Es hat mir so wollen behagen, lachend die Wahrheit zu sagen,*[18] because there is nothing pure and productive about today's laughter.

The height of Wilhelm II's twenty-five-year reign was November 1908, when for two days the representatives of all parties held court against him, when the parties unanimously agreed that he had done great damage to Germany,[19] when the majority found words of scorn and ridicule, and when hardly concealed allusions caused great amusement among all present. Finally, the chancellor traveled to Potsdam and the Kaiser made amends.[20]

This was a start; it was but a triviality, but it was something. We would be a little less audience and entourage, and a little more *people*, if we all just remembered on this jubilee that there can only be one monarch: the inner being of each individual. If our situation is to improve, it is this monarch who must claim his rule and point us in the right direction.

---

1. Bettina von Arnim (1785-1859), renowned progressive German writer of the Romantic era. The quote is from her last published work, *Gespräche mit Dämonen* [Conversations with Demons].

2. Frederick III (1831-1888) was Kaiser for ninety-nine days in 1888, the so-called "Year of the Three Emperors." He followed the reign of his father Wilhelm I (1797-1888), Kaiser from 1871 to 1888, and was succeeded by his son Wilhelm II (1859-1941), Kaiser from 1888 to 1918.

3. Princess Luise of Prussia (1838-1923) was Frederick III's younger sister. She became the Grand Duchess of Baden by marrying Frederick I, Grand Duke of Baden, in 1856. Baden, today part of the German state (*Bundesland*) Baden-Württemberg, was a Grand Duchy from 1806 to 1918.

4. Johann Gottlieb Fichte (1762-1814) was a German philosopher and one of the main representatives of German Idealism. His *Reden an die Deutsche Nation* [Speeches to the German Nation] (1808) called for a united German nation state during the time of French occupation. They provided a philosophical foundation for Germany's 19th-century unification.

5. Roughly, the "Fichte Event."

6. Frederick I Barbarossa (1122-1190), King of Germany, King of Italy, King of Burgundy, and Holy Roman Emperor; one of the Middle Ages' most legendary rulers.

7. The colors black, red, and gold — today the color's of Germany's national flag — were first used as a common symbol for the German states during the resistance against French occupation in the early 19th century.

8. Heinrich Heine (1797-1856), German libertarian poet.

9. Reference to the House of Hohenstaufen, a dynasty of German kings in the 12th and 13th centuries; Frederick I Barbarossa was the most prominent.

10. Leader of the chorus in Attic drama.

11. A popular comedy written by Alexander Roda Roda (1872-1945) and Carl Rößler (1864-1948); translates literally as "hill of the field commander."

12. In German, "ein ganz junger Schüler;" in this context *jung(er)* can mean both "new" and "young."

13. The publishing house Reclam was founded in 1828 in Leipzig. Since 1867, Reclam has published the enormously popular *Universal-Bibliothek* [Universal Library] series, providing a wide range of titles, mainly classics, in a standard low-cost format.

14. Felix Josef Mottl (1856-1911), famous Austrian conductor.

15. *Also sprach Zarathustra* [Thus Spoke Zarathustra], published in four parts between 1883 and 1885, is Nietzsche's most widely read work, and considered by many to be the most concise and powerful summary of Nietzschean thought.

16. In Greek mythology, the Goddess of War, Pallas Athena, emerged from the head of her father's, Zeus (Landauer uses the name of Zeus' Roman counterpart, Jupiter), after he had swallowed her mother, Metis.

17. Reference to the picaresque novel *Der abenteuerliche Simplicissimus* (see footnote 95 in *Revolution*).

18. Roughly, "It was so pleasant to laughingly tell the truth."

19. This pertained to chauvinistic comments made by Wilhelm II in an interview published by the British *Daily Telegraph* on October 28, 1908.

20. Potsdam, near Berlin, had been home to the Prussian royals – who were granted emperorship over the newly united Germany in 1871 – for centuries.

EARLY ANARCHISM

ANARCHISM –SOCIALISM

Landauer explains the change of the *Sozialist* subtitle to "Journal for Anarchism-Socialism" (*Organ für Anarchismus-Sozialismus*). The text provides insight into Landauer's early understanding of anarchism, its relation to socialism, and the prospects of a future anarchist society. Originally published as "Anarchismus – Sozialismus" in *Der Sozialist*, September 7, 1895.

JOURNAL FOR ANARCHISM AND SOCIALISM – THIS IS WHAT OUR paper says.

Anarchism is the goal that we pursue: the absence of domination and of the state; the freedom of the individual. Socialism is the means by which we want to reach and secure this freedom: solidarity, sharing, and cooperative labor.

Some people say that we have turned things upside down by making anarchism our goal and socialism our means. They see *an*-archy as something negative, as the absence of institutions, while socialism indicates a positive social order. They think that the positive part should constitute the goal, and the negative the means that can help us to destroy whatever keeps us from attaining the goal. These people fail to understand that anarchy is not just an abstract concept of freedom but that our notions of a free life and of free activity include much that is concrete and positive. There will be work – purposeful and fairly distributed; but it will only be a means to develop and strengthen our rich natural forces, to impact our fellow human beings, culture, and nature, and to enjoy society's riches to the fullest.

Anyone who is not blinded by the dogmas of the political parties will recognize that anarchism and socialism are not opposed but co-dependent. True cooperative labor and true community can only exist where individuals are free, and free individuals can only exist where our needs are met by brotherly solidarity.

It is mandatory to fight the false social democratic claims that anarchism and socialism are as opposed as "fire and water." Those who make such claims usually argue thus: Socialism means "socialization." This means in turn that society – a vague term usually encompassing all human beings who inhabit the earth – will be amalgamated, unified, and centralized. The so-called "interests of humanity" become the highest law, and the specific interests of certain social groups and individuals become secondary. Anarchism, on the other hand, means individualism, i.e., the desire of individuals to assert power without limits; it spells atomization and egoism. As a result, we have incompatible opposites: socialization and individual sacrifice on the one hand; individualization and self-centeredness on the other.

I think that it is possible to illustrate the shortcomings of these assumptions by a simple allegory. Let us imagine a town that experiences both sunshine and rain. If someone suggested that the only way to protect the town against rain is to build a huge roof that covers everything and that will always be there whether it rains or not, then this would be a "socialist" solution according to the social democrats. On the other hand, if someone suggested that, in the case of rain, each individual should grab one of the town's umbrellas and that those who come too late are simply unlucky, then this would be an "anarchist" solution. For us anarchist socialists both solutions appear ridiculous. Neither do we want to force all individuals under a common roof nor do we want to end up in fistfights over umbrellas. When it is useful, we can share a common roof – as long as it can be removed when it is not useful. At the same time, all individuals can have their own umbrellas, as long as they know how to handle them. And with regard to those who want to get wet – well, we will not force them to stay dry.

Leaving allegories aside, what we need is the following: associations of humankind in affairs that concern the interests of humankind; associations of a particular people in affairs that concern the interests of a particular people; associations of particular social groups in affairs that concern particular social groups; associations of two people in affairs that concern the interests of two people; individualization in affairs that concern the interests of the individual.

Instead of both the national state and of the world state that the social democrats dream of, we anarchists want a free order of multiple, intertwined, colorful associations and companies. This order will be based upon the principle that all individuals are closest to their own interests, and that their shirts are closer to them than their jackets. It will rarely be necessary to address all of humankind in order to deal with a specific problem. Hence, there is no need for a global parliament or any other global institution.

There are affairs that concern all of humankind, but in such cases the different groups will find ways to reach common solutions. Let us take the matter of international transport and its intricate train schedules as an example. Here, the representatives of each country find solutions despite the absence of a higher coordinating power. The reason is simple: necessity demands it. It is hence hardly surprising that I find the *Reichskursbuch* the only bureaucratic publication worth reading.[1] I am convinced that this book will receive more honors in the future than the law books of all nations combined!

Other affairs that will need global attention are measurements, scientific and technical terms, and statistics, which are of great importance for economic planning and other purposes. (Although, they are much less important than what the social democrats think, who want to make them the throne on which to build the people's global domination.) Those who are not condemned to ignorance by the conditions that the powerful force upon them will soon make appropriate use of statistics without any global institution. There will probably be a global organization of some kind that compiles and compares different statistical data, but it will not play a very significant role and will never constitute a powerful political force.

Are there common interests within a nation? There are some: language, literature, arts, customs, and rituals all have specific national characteristics. However, in a world without domination, without "annexed territories" and the concept of "national land" (land that has to be defended and enlarged), such interests will not mean what they mean today. The concept of "national labor," for example, will disappear altogether. Labor will be structured in ways that do not follow language or ethnography. For labor conditions in local communities, both geography and geology are very important. But what do our nation states have to do with these realities? (As far as the differences in language go, they pose much less of a challenge than generally imagined.)

Speaking of labor, there are different currents within the anarchist camp. Some anarchists propagate the right to free consumption. They believe that all individuals shall produce according to their abilities and consume according to their needs. They maintain that no one but the individual can know what his or her abilities and needs are. The vision is to have storehouses filled by voluntary labor according to people's needs. The labor will be done because each individual will understand that the satisfaction of everyone's needs demands a collective effort. Statistics and information on labor conditions in specific communities will provide the guidelines for how much to produce and for how much work will be necessary, taking into account both the technology and the overall workforce. The need for laborers will be announced publicly to all those who are eligible. Those who refuse to work – entirely or partly – even though they could, will be socially ostracized.

I think that this is an accurate and unbiased summary of the ideas of the communists. I now want to explain why I consider these notions of labor organization insufficient and unjust.

I do not deem them impossible. I believe that communism and the right to free consumption can exist. However, I do believe that many people will choose not to work. Social ostracization will matter little to them – they can be assured of mutual support and respect among their peers.

This is not the biggest problem though. The biggest problem is that a new moral authority will be created; a moral authority that declares those the "best human beings" who work the hardest, who are ready to do the most difficult and the dirtiest work, and who make sacrifices for the weak, the lazy, and the freeloaders. The constraint of such a morality and the social rewards it promises will be far worse and far more dangerous than the most acceptable constraint we know: egoism. I have reached this opinion after a lot of contemplation. A society based on the constraint of morality will be far more one-dimensional and unjust than a society based on the constraint of self-interest.

Anarchists who share this opinion see a connection between the labor of individuals and their consumption. They want to organize labor on the basis of natural egoism. This means that those who work will primarily work for themselves. In other words, those who join a particular line of work will do so because they expect certain personal advantages from it; those who work more than others will do so because they have more needs to satisfy; those who do the most difficult and the dirtiest work (work that will always have to be done, even if in a less gruesome manner than today) will do so because – contrary to today – this work will be the most valued and highest paid.

The critique of this kind of organization of labor is mainly three-fold: first, one sees it as an injustice against the intellectually or physically weak; second, one is afraid that individual riches will be accumulated and that new forms of exploitation will arise; third, one is concerned that an exclusive class of producers will gain and defend privileges.

I consider all of these concerns unfounded. It is true that there will be a differentiation of labor. However, if people are well educated and their talents well nourished, then everyone will easily find work that suits his or her qualifications. Some will find intellectual labor suitable for them, some manual labor, etc. Those who are unable to work – the disabled, the old – will be provided for in many ways, just like children are provided for. The principle of mutual aid will be central.

It will be impossible for individuals to accumulate riches leading to exploitation, as everyone in an anarchist society will understand that common usage of the land and the means of production is in their individual interest. As a result, those who work the hardest might gain advantages in terms of personal property, but they will not gain any means of exploitation.

Finally, no group would gain anything by becoming exclusive. They would instantly be boycotted. If a certain group were ever to gain an advantage in a certain area of production, new producers would appear and it would not be long before a fair balance was reestablished. When workers come and go freely and when there is truly free competition among equal men, then permanent inequalities are rendered impossible.

It is not inconceivable that the organization of labor, as I have outlined it above, might take two forms simultaneously in different regions or in different fields of labor. Practical experience will soon determine the form that is most feasible. In any case, the goal of both forms is the same: the freedom of the individual on the basis of economic solidarity. There is no reason to argue about the organizational details of the future society. It is much more important to combine our forces to establish the social conditions allowing for the practical experiences that will determine these matters.

Anarchy is no lifeless system of ready-made thoughts. Anarchy *is life*; the life that awaits us after we have freed ourselves from the yoke.

---

1. *Reichskursbuch*: former national German train schedule.

AN ANARCHIST'S RESPONSE TO THE KAISER'S SPEECH

Landauer responds to a speech by Kaiser Wilhelm II threatening the persecution of radical socialists and anarchists. Landauer's defiant comments on the issue of libel must be read in the context of his prison sentence from 1893-1894. Originally published as "Eines Anarchisten Antwort auf die Rede des Kaisers" in *Der Sozialist*, September 14, 1895.

EVERYONE HAS ALREADY READ THE WORDS OF THE KAISER. Nonetheless, these words will be reprinted here, as they ought to be included in *Der Sozialist*. The Kaiser made the following statement to an assembly of military personnel:

> "Our high and noble festivities are disturbed by a voice that does not belong here. This voice has been raised by a gang of individuals who do not deserve to be called Germans; a gang daring to vilify the German people and to insult the holy and honorable late Kaiser. I hope that the entire German people will be strong enough to repel these outrageous attacks! Otherwise, I call on you to lead the fight against this treacherous lot and to free us from such elements."

We have to admit that the Kaiser has not explicitly said who he was talking about. In fact, we kindly ask him to be clearer the next time he speaks of "a gang of individuals who do not deserve to be called Germans." It would simply help to avoid confusion.

The general suspicion is that the Kaiser was talking about the revolutionary socialists; those individuals who neither think that war is wonderful nor that the late Kaiser Wilhelm I was a "great person." If this suspicion is accurate, then the writer of these lines would be a part of this gang – an honor indeed.

The readers most probably know that the monarch stands beyond the law. He enjoys its complete protection, and libel against him is punished severely. Yet, he himself cannot be prosecuted, even if he uses words that would constitute libel if uttered by anyone else, publicly or privately. Even if he addresses us in the most incriminatory ways, we have no legal option for defending ourselves. In general, the derogatory term "gang" alone would be reason enough for prosecution in Germany. Since the Kaiser apparently enjoys using this term without suffering any consequences whatsoever, it would only be fair to allow everyone to use it without legal implications – the writers of *Der Sozialist* included.

In any case, we would much rather form a "gang" than live in isolation. All that I can hope for is that this gang – the "red gang" – will grow bigger and bigger.

The Kaiser says that the people who belong to it do not deserve to be called Germans. Why not? Does a person not belong to a certain people as a simple matter of birth? Are we Chinese or Hottentots instead? Our parents are Germans. What does our political opinion – or our alleged depravity – have to do with our ancestry? Does being German build on any particular merit, something that one has to earn, for example, by being good and exemplary? It seems to me that even robbers and murderers are German if their parents were German. I am convinced that most of the socialists who live in Germany have a German father and a German mother. To me, this means that they are Germans. I would also say that all who have lived in Germany since early childhood are Germans, even if they have a father or a mother from somewhere else. Either one is German or one is not. There is nothing special about being German. However, no one, not even a Kaiser, can take this away from you.

The Kaiser apparently thinks that we do not deserve to be called Germans because we "vilify the German people." However, any German who vilifies the German people vilifies himself. Besides, I have never heard a socialist vilify the rather significant part of the German people who demand a just transformation of society. It might be true that some of our German enemies have been vilified by us. But is this not mutual? Let us think of the oppressed German classes for a moment. Have they not been vilified various times by men like von Stumm and others?[1] They certainly have. Does this mean that von Stumm and his cohorts do not deserve to be called Germans?

The Kaiser furthermore thinks that we do not deserve to be called Germans because we "insult the holy and honorable late Kaiser." I do not think that anyone of us has any interest in insulting a dead person. All that we are concerned with is historical truth, and from our perspective Wilhelm I was no "great man," but – to name only one example – the adoptive father of the emergency laws. (The real father of these laws was Bismarck who was no more venerated in 1849 than he is now in 1895.) Wilhelm I is not untouchable to us. We look at his actions like we look at those of any other person in public office – past or present – and in his case, we find a lot that arouses our anger.

The Kaiser calls on the entire people to "repel these outrageous attacks." Once again, the Kaiser should at least acknowledge that a significant part of the people agrees with us. However, according to him, these people are probably not Germans either. The question that remains then is why the state still makes demands upon us? However, let us not dwell on this; let us ask instead what the Kaiser means by "to repel?" Also in this case, the Kaiser has not been very clear. Maybe he needs to be reminded that the libel against the memory of Wilhelm I can already be repelled legally. His daughter, the Grand Duchess of Baden, has already done so. The words of the Kaiser almost sound like the announcement of a new *Umsturzvorlage*.[2]

Well, we shall not allow ourselves to grow grey hair over this. Times could not get much worse than they were under the emergency laws enacted by the government of the current Kaiser's grandfather, and the workers survived those times. I believe that even *Der Sozialist* – not only the socialists themselves – would survive such a law. If we are not Germans anyway, then we can get rid of as much Germanness as we want. Let us wait and see.

Speaking of new laws: if what the Kaiser said were true, such laws would hardly be necessary. Take, for example, the Kaiser's description of us as a "treacherous lot" (still assuming that his words were directed at us socialists). There are already enough ways to deal with traitors legally. High treason is punishable by death (§80 of the criminal code) or life imprisonment (§81); attempted high treason by no less than five years in prison (§83); and even those who only know about others planning high treason, but do not report them to the authorities, can be imprisoned (§139). Should these laws not suffice against a "treacherous lot?"

The Kaiser does not seem to think so. He instead considers calling on the military to "free" the German Reich "from such elements." Once again, the Kaiser remains very vague when it comes to how he expects the military to do this. There are many people in this country who have been expecting a coup for quite some time. They interpret the Kaiser's words as a sign for the military to seize power if the government will not prove strong enough. I dare not say whether this interpretation is accurate or not, but I would like to ask our Minister of War to check with the Kaiser. The issue concerns the minister directly. If the above interpretation is accurate, then he should feel obliged to resign, since he, as everybody knows, has voiced a very different opinion on the subject in parliament. He declared that the military will not be needed against the socialists; he deemed the use of fire hoses sufficient.

I have arrived at the end of my critical remarks concerning the words of the Kaiser. The critique was longer than the words themselves. The reason is that these words did not make the Kaiser's thoughts and intentions very clear. I hope that we will soon be enlightened. One thing is already very clear, however: we are those who we have always been; and we always will be those who we are!

1. Carl Ferdinand Freiherr von Stumm-Halberg (1836-1901), German industrialist and politician; ennobled by Wilhelm II.

2. A conservative 1894 *Reichstag* (German parliament) motion demanding special laws against government critics; voted down in May 1895.

A FEW WORDS ON ANARCHISM

Landauer summarizes his understanding of anarchism in the liberal Berlin weekly *Die Welt am Montag* [The World on Monday], which ran a series entitled "Die Parteien in Selbstzeichnungen" [The Parties in Their Own Words]. Landauer points to the irony of including an anarchist under such a heading. The article was reprinted as "Ein paar Worte über Anarchismus" in *Der Sozialist*, July 10, 1897. The exact publication date in *Die Welt am Montag* remains unclear.

I HOPE THAT IT IS ACCEPTABLE TO START WITH A CRITIQUE OF THE task I am supposed to perform. I do not intend to be overly pedantic or to split hairs. I want to formulate this critique solely in the name of anarchism. *The Parties in Their Own Words* – an anarchist's opinion does not really fit under this heading. We do not think of ourselves as a party. And even if we did – can a party describe itself in its own words? Reason is needed for such a task, and parties lack reason. First, there exists a logical contradiction: the party is an abstract, authoritarian concept, and not a psychological reality; second, there exists a psychological contradiction: the party naturally lacks reason, self-determination, and physiognomy.

One might say that I am taking the headline too seriously. All that the publishers want is a description of certain political beliefs by someone who holds these beliefs. Well, it appears as if we anarchists always go against the grain, but we have no political beliefs – we have beliefs against politics.

Some might say that this makes us a sect rather than a party; others might add that we are a bunch of lunatics since our beliefs are not even uniform. Such perspectives concern me little. Let the bourgeois and square folks with their common sense think of us as bizarre and outlandish. Those who want to understand us have to understand the ground we stand on.

I agree with the fine American essayist Ralph Waldo Emerson (who knows him in Germany?), who has said that anyone who wants to be a man has to be a dissident.

"Oh," I can see the reader think, "here is an anarchist agenda: to leave the national church!" Yes, we do want to leave the national church, but we want to leave much more: the state and all forced associations; the traditions of private property, of possessive marriage, of familial authority, of privileged labor divisions, of national exclusivity, and of arrogance. All this is essential for the future of human society. Today, we still feel powerless, weak, and alone. However, we need to disengage from everything that we despise, rebel against everything that oppresses and limits us, and take everything that we need and want.

I feel the reader becoming impatient. He has certainly expected to hear about something more exciting given the sensationalist caption. He wants me to talk about bombs, infernal machines, and daggers. Most readers want to read what they think they already know, and that the anarchists throw bombs and demand the same from others appears to be common knowledge.

It is impossible to deny that anarchists have been involved in a number of the last decades' assassinations. However, in principle, anarchism and violence have nothing in common. The anarchist idea is a peaceful idea, opposed to aggressiveness and violence. This does not mean that we are all sheep. But it means that we want to live fully and brightly and as whole and mature personalities. There is something of the Southern intensity, of the temperamental passion of the young peoples in the anarchists. Romance peoples (Italians, Spanish, Southern French) and Russians are much more inclined to be anarchists than Germans, and among the Germans it is the Southerners and those from the Rhine River Valley who have stronger anarchist leanings than the Prussians (if one does not count the big cities where culture has been invigorated).

It is rare that contemplation and reason meet with vibrancy and ardor in an individual. Peaceful light and raging fire seldom mix in a personality. Peacefulness and reason are represented by individuals like the French Élisée Reclus, the Russian Kropotkin, the Austrian Ladislaus Gumplowicz;[1] rebellion and wildness are demonstrated by the French Louise Michel or the Southern German Johann Most (often misunderstood because he is hardly known; a writer of the highest order, a renewed individual, thoroughly original). Only the greatest of people comprise both lucent intellect and fiery passion. One example appears obvious, but who really knows him in Germany apart from us anarchists, a few scholars, and some 48ers?[2] I am speaking of Mikhail Bakunin.

However, back to the assassins: they are not motivated by the ideals of anarchism and they do not pursue anarchist intentions; in fact, intentions have nothing to do with their actions. Neither are they wild *Stürmer*;[3] they are cold, closed haters. The waves caused by their desires break on the dams of a depressing shore: the present. Neither their longing for happiness and freedom nor their most elemental needs can be satisfied. All their emotions are concentrated and compressed. They envision the blessed life of anarchy and the realization of their true inner being, while they cannot even feed themselves and their children. Gradually, many elements of their personality die: reflection, consideration, empathy, even their sense of self-preservation. Their life begins to be consumed by one sentiment only: the lust for revenge. Finally, the moment comes when all that has been hidden rushes to the surface, when all that has been frozen begins to boil and sizzle, when all that has been hardened melts, and when all that has been suppressed explodes. Then, the world reacts with outrage and implements emergency laws to protect itself against the blessed life of anarchy and its secret adherents. This is the same world that never considers measures *against itself*, that never considers oppressing oppression. But, of course, it would not do this. If it did, it would not be the world: *tout le monde* – not only on Mondays, but on all weekdays.

It is easy to condemn the assassins. However, I try to understand them psychologically, and if I were a lawyer, I would defend them against the limitations of bourgeois "justice." My closing words would be: abdicate the authoritarian violence and the protection of privilege and robbery, and there will be no more outlaws and no more rebellious violence! (Those interested in the psychology of anarchist assassins should read the defense speeches by Ravachol, Vaillant, Henry, Acciarito, Etiévan, and many others,[4] and they will find my opinion confirmed. The trial against Koschemann, however, needs not be studied. Koschemann is, in my opinion, completely innocent and the victim of a disgraceful miscarriage of justice.[5])

From what I have said so far, two things follow: first, that anarchism cannot be a mass movement in our times, but only one of individuals, of *pioneers*. These pioneers are able to find far-reaching sympathies and a lot of respect among the oppressed masses. This is becoming more and more obvious, and it is also the case among the social democratic workers in Germany. Many of them – quietly or stridently – have begun to hail the existence of anarchists, even if it still seems impossible or unnecessary for them to be anarchists themselves. Secondly, that we are unwavering optimists despite our principal skepticism. We are not old school individualists. We believe in the good of humanity and in humanity's capabilities. We want an anarchist society; not a society of individual heroes and autocrats, but a society where individuals can live together on the basis of free association and respect; in other (economic) words: socialism.

I have not addressed the German anarchists in particular. I do not think that this matters much. In an article as short as this, it is impossible to say everything. What is most important is that a German anarchist has spoken about anarchism.

The majority of German anarchists are former social democrats who have split from the party during the last seven years. Most of them belonged to factions opposed to the party leadership, in particular to the so-called Young Ones or Independents.[6] Some individuals became anarchists in Germany earlier, inspired by the agitation of Most, Dave, Reve, and Reinsdorf, and by the London journal *Die Autonomie*.[7] However, it has been the publication of *Der Sozialist* – the Berlin weekly that is now in its seventh year and is the most confiscated journal in Germany – that has transformed the anarchist movement from a secret society to a recognized political force. Were it not for the many prejudices harbored against anarchists and for the draconian court sentences,[8] this force would already be much stronger.

1. Élisée Reclus (1830-1905), French geographer and anarchist; Ladislaus Gumplowicz (1869-1942), Polish-Austrian doctor, writer, and political activist, who worked with Landauer in the *Sozialist* collective in the 1890s before distancing himself from anarchism.

2. 48ers: people involved in Europe's revolutionary uprisings in 1848.

3. *Stürmer*: reference to adherents of the progressive literary *Sturm und Drang* movement (often translated as "Storm and Stress").

4. Ravachol, born François Claudius Koeningstein (1859-1892), Auguste Vaillant (1861-1894), Émile Henry (1872-1894), Pietro Umberto Acciarito (1871-1943), Georges Etiévan (deported to the penal colony of Cayenne around 1900) – convicted for assassinations and bomb attacks, and often cited as representatives of the "propaganda by the deed." Landauer incorporated Ravachol's defense speech in his 1893 novel *Der Todesprediger*.

5. The twenty-one-year-old anarchist worker Paul Koschemann was accused of sending a parcel bomb to a Berlin police chief, but always maintained his innocence.

6. Radical offshoot of the German Social Democratic Party in the early 1890s; Landauer was involved with the group – see "1892-1901: Landauer's early anarchism" in the Introduction.

7. Johann Most (1846-1906), Victor Dave (1847-1922), Johann Reve (1844-1896), and August Reinsdorf (1849-85) were prominent German-speaking anarchists; *Die Autonomie* was published as an anarcho-communist German-language journal in London by Josef Peukert and others from 1886 to 1893.

8. There was marked persecution of anarchists and the anarchist press in Germany between 1893 and 1895, and many anarchists – Landauer among them – received extended prison sentences.

ANARCHIC THOUGHTS ON ANARCHISM

Landauer reacts to the assassination of U.S. President William McKinley in September 1901 at the hands of the self-confessed anarchist Leon Czolgosz. Landauer distances himself from the "propaganda by the deed," which he still defended in "A Few Words on Anarchism." In a letter to Fritz Mauthner he announced the essay with the following words: "By the way, I will soon give the anarchists a piece of my mind in an article on the most recent events; I am tired of the glorification of these so-called 'deeds.'"[1]

Landauer had already formulated a critique of the "propaganda by the deed" in *Der Sozialist* on September 17, 1898, in an article entitled "Die Erdolchung der Kaiserin von Österreich" [The Stabbing of the Empress of Austria], a reflection on the assassination of Elisabeth (commonly known as Sisi), the Empress of Austria, by the Italian anarchist Luigi Lucheni. Two years earlier, in the essay "Anarchismus in Deutschland" (*Die Zukunft*, January 5, 1895; translated as "Anarchism in Germany," in *Gustav Landauer, Anarchism in Germany and Other Essays*, by Stephen Bender and Gabriel Kuhn, San Francisco: Barbary Coast Publishing Collective, 2005), Landauer offered an interesting interpretation of the "propaganda by the deed": "It has nothing to do with killing people; rather, it is the renewal of human spirit, of human will, and of the productive energies of large communities. [...] Everything else is passion, despair, or mere misconception."

Throughout "Anarchic Thoughts on Anarchism," Landauer refers to "the anarchists" in the third person, which makes it appear as if he positioned himself outside of the anarchist realm – which he never did. However, the essay is indicative of both a significant change in perspective and of increasing skepticism towards the revolutionary potential of the anarchist movement. It is best read as a companion piece to "Through Separation to Community." The essay was published as "Anarchische Gedanken über Anarchismus" in *Die Zukunft*, October 26, 1901.[2] This translation is a revised version of the rendition published in *Perspectives on Anarchist Theory*, vol. 11, no. 1 (Fall 2007).

I REMEMBER SOMETHING THAT THE ENGLISH ANARCHIST MOWBRAY said at the 1893 International Socialist Congress in Zurich concerning the anarchists' right to participate or not. After stormy debates, a resolution was passed according to which only those who stood for "political" action should be allowed. In this moment, when we anarchists already seemed excluded, Mowbray rekindled the debate by means of a melodramatic joke. He proclaimed that Brutus's deed was an eminent political act, implying that we anarchists also stood for political action and must thus be admitted.

It seems to me that Mowbray's statement is a fitting expression of what has almost become an anarchist dogma, namely to perceive the assassination of people in power as an anarchist act. And, indeed, almost all the people involved in such assassinations in the last decades were motivated by anarchist beliefs. Any unbiased observer would doubtlessly call this odd. For what has the killing of people to do with anarchism, a theory striving for a society without government and authoritarian coercion, a movement against the state and legalized violence? The answer is: nothing at all. However, some anarchists seem to have come to the conclusion that merely educating and talking has not got them very far. The social reconstruction is not to be had because the rulers' force stands in the way. Thus, so they conclude, destruction must be put alongside construction and mere propaganda by the word. They are too weak to tear down all borders, so they turn to propagating the deed – and to make propaganda by the deed. The political parties pursue positive political action – so the anarchists think that they, as individuals, have to engage in a positive anti-politics, a negative politics. These rationales explain their "political action": propaganda by the deed and individual terrorism.

I will not hesitate to say the following in all clarity – knowing that I will not receive much appreciation from either side: the anarchist politics of assassination only stems from the intentions of a small group among them that wants to follow the example of the big political parties. What drives them is vanity – a craving for recognition. What they are trying to say is: "We are also doing politics. We are not idle. We are a force to be reckoned with!"

These anarchists are not anarchic enough for me. They still act like a political party. Their politics are akin to simple-minded reform politics. Assassinations have always belonged to simple men's naive attempts at improvement, and Mowbray's Brutus was just another short-sighted reformist politician. When the American rulers recently hung some innocent anarchists, without any consideration for rights or laws,[3] it was an act that was just as anarchistic as that of any assassin, and perhaps done out of a similar idealism – for only dogmatists can deny that there are fervent and sincere idealists of the state. The majority of anarchists are certainly dogmatists. They will cry out loud that I – who still dare to call my ideals those of anarchy too – declare my truth so openly. Since they are opportunists, they will find that right now it is not the time to say such things. However, I find that right now is the perfect time.

This is another dogma of the anarchists: that every day so many workers, so many soldiers, so many sufferers from tuberculosis are killed by our morbid living conditions, so why all the fuss about just one man? McKinley, they say, counts no more than any of the others.[4] With all due respect, here, too, I will be too anarchic for my anarchist comrades: McKinley's death shook me more – far more – than that of a roofer who fell to his death because of a poorly constructed scaffolding. I readily admit that it might seem old-fashioned, but it contains tragedy for me when an innocent and well-intentioned man, surrounded by the air of power, is shot dead by a fellow human being to whom he extends his hand, and then the eyes of millions turn to his deathbed. Besides, it will only help to idealize this person, who, in fact, might neither have been very intelligent nor very noble. I will gladly add, however, that the assassin also stands closer to my heart than the poor fellow who had put up the scaffolding badly. It means something to be done with life that way.

It is not my intention here to delve into the psychology of the present-day assassins. Perhaps less than being heroes or martyrs they engage in a new kind of suicide. For a man who believes in nothing but this life and who has been bitterly disappointed by it; for a man who is filled with cold hatred against the conditions which have ruined him and which he cannot bear any longer; for such a man, taking one of them down with him while ostentatiously killing himself before the eyes of the world, via a detour through the courts, can be a terribly seductive idea. At least as seductive is a notion that appears in endless variations in the anarchist press: to oppose authoritarian violence with self-determined, "free" violence, the rebellion of the individual.

This is the basic fallacy of the revolutionary anarchists (a fallacy which I long enough shared with them): the notion that one can reach the ideal of non-violence by violent means. At the same time, they object strongly to the "revolutionary dictatorship" that Marx and Engels called for in their *Communist Manifesto* as a short transitional stage after the revolution. But these are self-deceptions. Any kind of violence is dictatorial, unless it is borne voluntarily, accepted by the subjugated masses. But this is not the case in the anarchist assassinations, which are a matter of authoritarian violence. All violence is either despotism or authority.

What the anarchists must realize is that a goal can only be reached if it is already reflected in its means. Non-violence cannot be attained by violence. Anarchy exists wherever one finds true anarchists: people who do not engage in violence. What I am saying is nothing new. It is what Tolstoy has been telling us for a long time. When the King of Italy was killed by Bresci,[5] Tolstoy published a wonderful article that culminated in the words: "One ought not kill them but make them understand that they shall not kill." The article contained such biting attacks against those in power that anarchist papers were happy to print it – including the quoted lines, which, however, were written off as a quirk of personality.

The revolutionary anarchists will object: if we are non-violent, we allow ourselves to be exploited and suppressed and will hence not be free but slaves. When we speak of non-violence, they claim, this does not concern the behavior of individuals but social organization. We want anarchy, the argument continues, but first we must take back that of which we have been robbed and which we are being denied.

However, this is yet another crucial fallacy: that one can – or must – bring anarchism to the world; that anarchy is an affair of all of humanity; that there will indeed be a day of judgment followed by a millennial era. Those who want "to bring freedom to the world" – which will always be *their* idea of freedom – are tyrants, not anarchists. Anarchy will never be a matter of the masses, it will never be established by means of military attack or armed revolt, just as the ideal of federalist socialism will never be reached by waiting until the already accumulated capital and the title of the land will fall into the people's hands. Anarchy is not a matter of the future; it is a matter of the present. It is not a matter of making demands; it is a matter of how one lives. Anarchy is not about the nationalization of the achievements of the past but about a new people arising from humble beginnings in small communities that form in the midst of the old: an inward colonization. Anarchy is not about a struggle between classes – the dispossessed against the possessors – but about free, strong, and sovereign individuals breaking free from mass culture and uniting in new forms. The old opposition between destruction and construction begins to lose its meaning: what is at stake are new forms that have never been.

If the anarchists realized that the core of anarchy lies in the depths of human nature, and if they were able to follow this as a guiding principle, then this would lead them far from the masses, and they would recognize with a shudder what a distance yawns between their convictions and their current actions; then they would recognize that it is all too common and trite for an anarchist to kill a McKinley or to make similarly pointless tragic gestures. Whoever kills, dies. Those who want to create life must also embrace it and be reborn from within.

I would have to apologize here for making "propaganda for anarchism" on neutral ground[6] if I were not convinced that what I call anarchy (without any special attachment to the word) is something that resonates with every man who reflects upon the world and his soul. Every such man will have the urge to give birth to himself, to recreate his being, and — as far as possible — his environment and his world. This extraordinary moment will be experienced by all who, in Nietzsche's words, are able to recreate the original chaos in themselves and to become spectators at the drama of their own desires and deepest secrets. Only once we have achieved this can we decide which one of our many personalities should define who we are. This in turn will define our uniqueness and differentiate us from the traditions and legacies of our ancestors. We will understand what the world should be to us, and what we should be to the world. Those whom I call true anarchists no longer deceive themselves; they have been able to remold themselves through the experience of a deep existential crisis; they can act in the way which their most secret nature demands.

To me, someone without a master, someone who is free, an individual, an anarchist, is one who is his own master, who has unearthed the desire that tells him who he truly wants to be. This desire is his life. The way to heaven is narrow. The way to a newer, higher form of human society passes by the dark, fatal gate of our instincts and the *terra abscondita* — the "hidden land" — of our soul, which is our world. This world can only be constructed from within. We can discover this land, this rich world, if we are able to create a new kind of human being through chaos and anarchy, through unprecedented, intense, deep experience. Each one of us has to do this. Once this process is completed, only then will anarchists and anarchy exist, in the form of scattered individuals, everywhere. And they will find each other. But they will not kill anyone except themselves — in the mystical sense, in order to be reborn after having descended into the depths of their soul. They will be able to say of themselves, in Hofmannsthal's words: "I have rid myself of anything common in me as completely as I have left the soil underneath my feet." Only those who have journeyed through their own selves and waded deep in their own blood can help to create the new world without interfering with the lives of others.

One would misunderstand me deeply if one believed that I preach quietism or resignation, or that I demand the renunciation of action or social engagement. Oh, no! One acts with others; one pursues municipal socialism; one supports farmers', consumers', and tenants' cooperatives; one creates public gardens and libraries; one leaves the cities and works with spade and shovel; one simplifies one's material life for the sake of spiritual luxury; one organizes and educates; one struggles for the creation of new schools and new forms of education. However! None of this will really bring us forward if it is not based on a new spirit won by the conquest of one's inner self. We are all waiting for something great – something new.

All of our art bears witness to the anxiety involved in preparing for its arrival. But what we are waiting for can only come from ourselves, from our own being. It will come once we force the unknown, the unconscious, up into our spirit; it will come once our spirit loses itself in the spiritless psychological realms that await us in the caverns of our souls. This marks our renewal as human beings, and it marks the arrival of the world we anticipate. Mere intervention in the public sphere will never bring this world about. It is not enough for us to reject conditions and institutions; we have to reject ourselves. "Do not kill others, only yourself" – such will be the maxim of those who accept the challenge to create their own chaos in order to discover their most authentic and precious inner being and to become one with the world in a mystical union. What these men will be able to bring to the world will be so extraordinary that it will seem to have come from a world altogether unknown. Whoever brings the lost world in himself to life – to individual life – and whoever feels like a true part of the world and not as a stranger: he will be the one who arrives not knowing where from, and who leaves not knowing where to. To him the world will be what he is to himself. Men such as this will live with each other in solidarity – as men who belong together. This will be anarchy.

It might be a distant goal. However, we have already come to the point where life seems without reason if we do not aim for the unconceivable. Life means nothing to us if it is not an infinite sea promising eternity. Reforms? Politics? Revolution? It is always more of the same. Anarchism? What most anarchists like to present to us as an ideal society is too often merely rational and stuck in our current reality to serve as a guiding light for anything that could or should ever be in the future. Only he who accounts for the unknown gives an adequate account, for the true life, and the human beings that we truly are, remain unnamed and unknown. Hence, not war and murder – but rebirth.

I would be deeply misunderstood if my words were taken as a rejection of free and non-dogmatic socialism, which has in many ways been inspiring, unifying and reinvigorating. Perhaps it is simply not that easy for those of us who have dedicated ourselves to this notion for years to fully acknowledge the futility of our childish faith in radical change outside of ourselves. Maybe it is hard to grasp that socialism is not a new and glorious endeavor that ascends from the ruins of the bourgeoisie, but something that develops within the capitalist world itself, pushing its way into all of its cracks. Such a recognition – as commonplace as it may have become – can still bring a great deal of pain, sometimes too much to allow us to accept the new challenge. Something bright, strong, and practical has entered into modern socialism. This is certainly encouraging. As old dreamers, we were so used to the twilight and the romance of our expectations, as well as to the preparation for a great and sudden change, that we may be forgiven for taking a while to accustom ourselves to our new responsibility.

Luckily, many young people have already taken up the challenge. I am not denying the fact that the masses seeking an escape from social wretchedness have little interest in the higher cultural and mental wretchedness I am talking about here. They do not care what we special ones strive for, and it would be misplaced romanticism if we believed that the changes that the poor and socially subaltern masses need are identical with, or even at all intrinsically linked to, the transformation of the essence of ourselves as human beings. We must learn that there are hundreds of ways – within and outside the state – to help the masses change their plight.

We must break with the habit of seeing each improvement, each innovation, only in relation to our highest and ultimate goal, categorically allowing no other perspective. It is a wonderful thought to combine the material interests and the development of the masses with what I see as our most urgent cultural need – as described above – so that these two struggles can become one; but it is a misguided thought, just as any other rigid and "pure" thought is.

We have long enough misunderstood socialism as a vague, general ideology, a magic wand that opens all doors and solves all problems. We should know by now that everything out in the world as well as within our souls is so jumbled that there will never be only *one* way to happiness. So what I am advocating here has nothing to do with a call on humanity. We have to realize that different cultures exist next to each other and that the dream that all should be the same cannot be sustained – in fact, it is not even a beautiful dream.

I do not ask anything from anyone; I only want to describe the inner condition that might enable some of us to show others by example what communism and anarchy really mean. All I want to make clear is that this freedom can only come to life in ourselves and must be nurtured in ourselves before it can appear as an external actuality. Socialism, too, has gradually become old; it combined many things that are now coming apart. The dogmatism and slogans that formerly proclaimed a new era, the signposts for utopia, are everywhere coming to an end. Everywhere, concepts have turned into reality, becoming unpredictable, shifting, unstable. There is clarity only in the land of appearances and words; where life begins, systems end.

The anarchists have always been far too fond of systems and attached to rigid, narrow concepts. This, in fact, is the final answer to the question as to how anarchists can find value in the killing of fellow human beings. They have become used to dealing with concepts instead of real people. They have separated humanity into two static and hostile classes. When they kill, they do not kill human beings but concepts – that of the exploiter, the oppressor, the representative of the state. This is why those who are often the kindest and most humane in their private lives commit the most inhuman acts in the public sphere.[7] There, they do not feel; they have switched off their senses. They act as exclusively rational beings who – like Robespierre – are the servants of *reason*; a reason that divides and judges. This cold, spiritually empty, and destructive logic is the rationale for the death sentences handed down by the anarchists. But anarchy is neither as easily achievable, nor as morally harsh, nor as clearly defined as these anarchists would have it. Only when anarchy becomes, for us, a dark, deep dream, not a vision attainable through concepts, can our ethics and our actions become one.

1. *Gustav Landauer. Sein Lebensgang in Briefen*, 1: 96.

2. The essay is often falsely referenced as "Anarchistische Gedanken zum Anarchismus" [Anarchist Thoughts on Anarchism].

3. Reference to the Haymarket martyrs – see "The 11th of November" in this volume.

4. U.S. President William McKinley was shot on Sept. 6, 1901, by self-declared anarchist Leon Czolgosz (1873-1901). McKinley died from his wounds eight days later. Czolgosz was executed on October 29.

5. Gaetano Bresci (1869-1901), an Italian-American anarchist, shot dead the Italian king Umberto I (1844-1900) in Monza in July 1900.

6. *Die Zukunft* (1892-1922), where this text first appeared, was a fairly eclectic political and literary journal.

7. See also "The Party" in this volume.

THROUGH SEPARATION TO COMMUNITY

THROUGH SEPARATION
TO COMMUNITY

For bibliographical references, please see "1901-1908: Retreat and Reflection" in the Introduction.

> *Everything that exists now is but the handle of the past and of the future – bottomless, rich, and invisible... I am not happy, as happiness comes from man. I am not unhappy, as unhappiness comes from man too. I am everything, because that is what comes from God.*
>
> *Nothing in the world is lonely, everything is related. The true and the holy are like rays of light that hit everyone whose eyes are open; to see and to be seen is one and the same.*

(Clemens Brentano)[1]

> *We shall be spirit for all things, and all things shall be spirit for us. We shall recognize all things and become one with them in God.*
>
> *This is why I ask God to free me of God. To have no being means to go beyond God and beyond all differences. I was there. I wanted to be there. I recognized the man I created. I am the cause of myself as an eternal being. My birth is eternal. I have always been eternal, I am eternal now, and I will remain eternal. I am also the cause of myself as a temporal being. What belongs to time will die. What comes with time shall vanish with time. My eternal birth includes the birth of all things, and it makes me the cause of myself and of all things. If I did not want to be, I would not be, and neither would there be any things nor God. It is not necessary to understand this.*

(Meister Eckhart)[2]

All my souls slept.
Then the sun rose from its depths.

I am resting: a quiet man in quietness.
A ghosts' horse cart rolls over me,

And a new rich life begins.

The crown that shines around your temples
I have forged a thousand years ago.

The world is full of dark questions.
This is why you have to play the harp.

(Alfred Mombert)[3]

For those of us who see ourselves as part of the vanguard, the distance to the rest of humankind has become enormous. I do not mean the distance between those who one calls educated on the one hand and the masses on the other. This distance is problematic enough, but it is not the crucial one. There are workers who are much closer to the vanguard than educated philistines. One must understand who really belongs to the vanguard. It is not a matter of knowledge or ability, but of perspective and orientation. The social position of the mass individual derives from a heritage that determines his being from the outside as well as from within: he belongs to a certain family and a certain class, he acquires certain knowledge and follows a certain faith, he turns to a certain profession, he is Protestant or Catholic, a German or an English patriot, a shop keeper or a newspaper editor. Authority, custom, morality, time, and class define his existence.

Nowadays, however, there is a young generation that has become skeptical of tradition. We can categorize its members if we want to: then we have socialists and anarchists, atheists and gypsies, nihilists and romantics. Some of them have enthusiastically tried to uplift the masses, to awaken them, to purify them, to arouse anger and indignation in them, to tell them about the coming beauty and splendor, and to organize them in new social and economic unions. Others have chosen different ways: they have turned life into a game and seek the finest and most exquisite for themselves; they have turned into big loners or small hedonists.

I was among those who had gone to the masses. Now I and my comrades have returned. We have lost some along the way – either to a party or to despair. We have brought back others with us – more than them, we could not find. We have come to a realization that took pains to reach: we are too far ahead to be understood. We have developed a sense of clarity that people in their everyday confusion cannot grasp. Our souls cannot tolerate this confusion any longer. The conclusion is that we must cease descending to the masses. Instead, we must precede them. At first, it might seem as if we were walking away from them. But we can only find the community that we need and long for if we – the new generation – separate ourselves from the old communities. If we make this separation a radical one and if we – as separated individuals – allow ourselves to sink to the depths of our being and to reach the inner core of our most hidden nature, then we will find the most ancient and complete community: a community encompassing not only all of humanity but the entire universe. Whoever discovers this community in himself will be eternally blessed and joyful, and a return to the common and arbitrary communities of today will be impossible.

I differentiate between three forms of community: first of all, there is a hereditary power that we can discover deep in the mine pits of our inner self: the inner paleontological treasures of the universe; secondly, there is another hereditary power, one that wants to inhibit, limit, and imprison us from the outside; and thirdly, there are the free momentary associations of individuals based on common interests.

The first of these communities refers to what one usually calls the individual – however, as I want to show, the individual is always a manifestation of the universe. The second refers to the forced communities of bourgeois societies and states. The third refers to the community which is only yet to come: to the one we want to initiate without further delay.

If one wants to find out what we perceive real in the words "individual" and "community," if one really wants to talk about the reality that we keep hidden behind abstract notions and categories, then one must look at the teachings of Berkeley, Kant, or Schopenhauer. Let us admit it: if we make our subjectivity the basis of our reflection, and if we accept the isolation of our individuality, then we give up all other notions of reality; then space and time define all our perception; then all is material, our brain and our senses included (and especially you, dear reader: a ghostly ghost which I, as spirit, have produced); then the past will only be an imagination of our eternally present consciousness – this also means that all evolutionary theory will be rendered impossible.

We might never be able to refute such a notion, nor to prove another. However, the assumption from which this notion stems can never be proven either: my inner feeling that I am an isolated unit can be wrong – and I declare it so, because I do not want to be isolated. Yet, I must be aware of what this declaration means: I leave behind the only thing that seems certain within myself; I now float out into the uncertain world of hypotheses and fantasies. I reject the certainty of my I so that I can bear life. I try to build myself a new world, knowing that I do not really have any ground to build it on; all I have is a need. This need, as a part of life, includes a liberating, joyful strength: I know from now on that I live, that I perceive and act in my own, self-created world. Then, however, in order not to be a godforsaken loner, I accept this world and surrender my I. I do this to feel one with the world in which my I has dissolved. Just like someone who jumps into the water to kill himself, I jump into the world – but instead of death, I find life. The I kills itself so that the World-I can live. And so, even if it may not be the absolute – which really means "isolated" – reality that I create, it is the reality that is relevant to me, born in myself, put in place by myself, and coming to life in myself. We go beyond abstraction, this deadening, emptying, and desolating means of reduction, and instead allow all our forces to combine and pull the universe into the sphere of our own control. Abstraction and conceptual thought have reached their end. They only await their final deadly blow.

Since Kant, conceptual thought has only killed the living world. Now the living world finally rises up and kills the dead concept instead. Yes, even that which is dead must sometimes be killed. The times of the one absolute way to explain the world, and of the both torturous and futile attempts to control it, are over. Instead, we embrace different perspectives of the world that not only exist next to each other but complement each other – we know that they do not show the world "as it is;" yet they do show what the world is for us. This is the way by which we are opening ourselves to what lies beyond our I by using our I. We use our senses to reach out towards what lies beyond them; we attempt to understand the world with the whole richness of our lives, with our passions, and with our deepest contemplation. During our former attempts to touch and grasp the world, we have become tired and complacent; instead of incorporating it into ourselves, we have emptied it and handed it over to the hollow compartments of our general concepts. At the entrance of these unwelcoming quarters – which we keep carefully apart from the more comfortable areas of our lustful opinions and fancy desires – there might be a note of warning: No. 0.

Let us take another way: let us allow the world to pass through ourselves, let us be ready to feel the world, to experience it, to allow ourselves to be grasped and seized by it. Until now everything has been divided into a poor, weak, active I and an unapproachable rigid, lifeless, passive world. Let us instead be the medium of the world, both active and passive. So far, we were content with transforming the world into the spirit of man, or into the spirit of our brain – let us now transform ourselves into the spirit of the world.

This is possible. The old Meister Eckhart,[4] the great heretic and mystic, was right when he said that if we were able to comprehend a little flower and its nature completely, we would comprehend the whole world. He added, however, that we can never reach such absolute comprehension from the outside, i.e., with the help of our senses. "God is always ready, but we are not – God is close to us, but we are far from him; God is inside, but we are outside; God is at home, we are lost."

Meister Eckhart shows us the way – we only have to understand his metaphors of God. He tells of how the ecstatic nun Sister Catherine runs jubilantly towards her master: "Herr, rejoice with me, I have become God!" She has forgotten everything she ever knew and has left herself and everything else. As she comes to her senses again, she first mutters: "What I have found, nobody can put into words." Once words come to her, she says:

> "I am where I was before I became an individual; and all I see is God – and God … You have to know that everything that is put into words or presented in pictures is nothing but a way to lead them to God. Know that nothing is in God but God! Know that no soul can enter God before it does not become God in the way it was before it became an individual … If words suffice for you, this is what you ought to know: God is a word, heaven is a word – those who do not want their souls to move forward, with realization and with love, they should rightfully be called disbelievers … The soul is naked and bereft of all things that can be named … Know that as long as good human beings will live on earth, their souls will continue to exist in eternity. This is why good human beings treasure life."

The way to create a community that encompasses the entire world leads not outward, but inward. We must realize that we do not just perceive the world, but that we *are* the world. The one who can comprehend the flower completely, can completely comprehend the whole world. So let us return completely to ourselves, then we may truly find the universe. Let us make it very clear to us that, as long as we perceive our own inner nature as reality, all matter is indeed a spook, imagined by our eyes, our touch, and our perception of space as the external world (figuratively spoken, because our means of perception are matter too); let us make it entirely clear to us that inner perception only depends on spirit. A spirit that is complex and demanding. If we do not understand this, we will mistake our narrow, ridiculous I for the only thing that is essential. Let us not forget that the acknowledgment of the world is a postulate of our thinking (which serves our life as a scout); this is also true for the acknowledgment of the spiritual world. We must not forget this in order to avoid turning a necessary disposition into a dogma or into so-called science.

There is another thing we must not forget: namely, that the "spiritualization of the world" has nothing to do with a "morality of the world," or a morality which could be derived from a "world principle." The least that our wisdom attains to is an ethical dogma or a so-called scientific justification of morality. Let us make it clear to ourselves – and we now know what it means to make something clear, namely to create a necessary disposition – that past, present and future – as well as the notions of "here" and "there" – are only a unique/unified eternal stream that flows from the infinite to the infinite. There is neither a cause for nor an effect of this world.

Nonetheless, this world is evident to us and therefore true. Assumptions of cause and effect only exist in the realm of isolated bodies, but not in the stormy sea of the soul. It would lead too far to show that one has also, step by step, realized in body mechanics that there are no isolated bodies and no far-reaching effects. The images of flows and waves are also common in the material world (the fact that they are taken from it is self-explanatory). The molecular and ether theory belong here, even if one only understands them as a hypothetical introduction of auxiliary terms or as a kind of justification.

I do not want to deny that the world can be explained materialistically, since there are many possible explanations, an endless number of world views, etc. Spinoza said more accurately, an endless number of divine attributes. But one must understand *everything* materialistically and must refrain from the spiritual completely, because a mixture of the two is not possible. The emergence of the spiritual from the material is unexplainable. Spinoza already knew this. Yet it is only since Locke, Berkeley, and Kant that we understand that matter can, without the smallest remainder, be expressed as spirit alone: either as a reflection of our individual soul – a notion which I reject – or, figuratively spoken, as part-souls of the world-soul: a notion which I embrace. This is the extraordinary advantage a spiritual understanding of the world holds over a materialistic one.

This does not mean that we do not have to study the material; we very much have to in order for our psychological metaphoric language to progress. Our talk of the world-soul would be all but pitiful babble if our senses did not always provide new objective data for our individual soul to interpret. The marriage between us and the world is complicated and difficult; but since the relationship contains various pleasant aspects and since we cannot divorce ourselves anyway, we are best off accepting it. The countenance of complaint and condemnation – which we know as pessimism – is neither enchanting nor uplifting. We say thus: what works, is present; what works, pushes and exercises a certain power; and what exercises a certain power, exists, is that which is alive.

According to this rationale, nothing that is dead could have any effect, or could still be active. Hence, every cause is alive, otherwise it would not be a cause. There are no dead laws of nature. And there is no separation between cause and effect. Cause and effect must exist alongside each other. Our notion of cause-and-effect means a flow from one to the other. And when each pole is enriched by this exchange, and when the exchange becomes eternal, then we probably have what is called a reciprocal effect – because such an effect exists, even if the rigid ones among us do not want to know it. Matter is rigid and stiff; no wonder that materialists are too.

The flow of all that is eternally alive and knows neither isolation nor death is the macrocosm whose discovery makes Goethe's Faust rejoice:

> Am I a God? All grows so clear to me!
> In these pure lineaments I see
> Creative Nature's self before my soul appear.

"Creative Nature" – this is the *natura naturans* of Spinoza, a teacher of Goethe, who takes the term from the medieval mystics and realists. Again and again we do encounter the notion that one can become God; that one can become the world instead of just recognizing it. Perhaps the deepest meaning of Jesus' teachings is reached when Meister Eckhart lets God, who is also the Son of Man, say: "I was human to you, so if you are not Gods to me, then you do me injustice." So let us see how we can become Gods! Let us see how we can find the world in ourselves!

We mentioned the realists of the Middle Ages. They were called realists because they declared the universals, the emptiest abstract notions and generic names, realities. Since they mostly referred to products of both human hands and heads – be it clay, virtue, God, or immortality – they were fair game for their opponents, the nominalists; no matter how hard it was for them to make themselves heard in their complicated times. These concepts, they explained, were not realities, but mere words. Thus the nominalists took on a necessary task: they robbed spooks of their reality and sacredness.

The last great nominalist was Max Stirner, who, with the most radical thoroughness, freed our minds of the spook that abstract notions are. The essence of his teachings can be summarized in the following paraphrased words: "The concept of God has to be destroyed. But it is not God who is the enemy – it is the concept."

Stirner discovered that all actual oppression comes, in the end, from concepts and ideas that are accepted as sacred. With a fearless, strong, and determined hand he took notions such as God, sacredness, morality, state, society, and love apart and demonstrated laughingly their hollowness. According to his marvelous explanation, the abstract notions were but bloated nothingness, and concepts were only words for a group of singularities. However, Stirner then replaced God with the concrete single being, the individual. God was from now on under the ownership of *The Ego and Its Own*.[5] This was Stirner's obsession.

Our task is to prove that the concrete and isolated individual is as much a spook as God. We therefore have to restore the wisdom of the realists that also exists. The objections against them throughout the centuries were important, but now it is time to realize that there are no individuals, only affinities and communities. It is not true that collective names are only sums of singularities or individuals; rather, individuals are only manifestations and points of passage, the electrical sparks of something greater, something all-encompassing. (Whether the generic cut and dried names that we are using are adequate, is another question.)

First, let us remember that there are no more dead causes or dead laws of nature, no transcendent principles, for us anymore. We only know immanent life, only present forces. If therefore the scientists of our days tell us in their rigidness in what ways a newborn individual is determined by heredity, we have to ask: which heredity? Where does it come from? From heaven or from the past? Is the dead, strong, immobile law of heredity the father or godfather of an isolated creature?

Neither abstract heredity exists nor the concrete individual. Heredity as a word hints at the past, while it really means something very alive and present. "The individual" is a rigid and absolute expression for something that is very mobile and relative. Heredity is a very real and very present force which signifies the survival of the ancestors in new forms and shapes. The individual is a spark of the soul stream that we know as humanity, species, or universe. If we see the world only as the outside world, then we do see, touch, hear, taste, and smell individuals. If we turn within ourselves, however, we realize that there are no autonomous individuals. What we are, is what our ancestors are in us. They are active and alive in us, they are with us when we interact with the outside world, and they will be passed on with us to our descendants. What we are part of is an unbreakable chain that comes from the infinite and proceeds to the infinite, even if little segments might tear off and experience complications. Everything we make while we are alive connects us with the universe. And even our dead body is a bridge that is used to continue our journey through the universe. As Clemens Brentano[6] says, "Life is nothing but a piece of eternity that we make our own by dying." The saying *Everything that lives, dies* carries some truth in it, but it is a trivial and meaningless truth. We should say instead: "Everything which lives, lives once and for all."

We have seen that matter and body are inadequate and dated expressions for the complex soul stream that we call the world. Yet, our perspective is so new that we lack proper words for it. Hence, we have to make do with the old expressions under certain reservations. I doubt this will do too much harm, since all our reflections are only metaphorical approaches, which are always pursued under certain reservations. Our world can only be understood if we understand the several parallel, supplementing perspectives by which we have created it.

If we look at this from a material angle, we realize that there can be nothing more certain than that the individual stands in an inextricable connection with the past generations. Sure, the umbilical cord that connects the child with the mother is severed at birth, but the invisible chains that attach our bodies to our ancestors are stronger than this. What is heredity other than an almost eerie yet very familiar and well-known power and domination that the world of the ancestors exercises over our body and spirit? What are power and domination other than presence and community? If we humans have smooth skin instead of woolly hair, a chin that does not protrude, an upright posture, then this is a consequence of heredity, i.e., the domination that is still exercised over us by the first humans who evolved from the state of the apes. Put differently, since these first humans still have an effect on us, they still live in us, and we still experience them in us when we experience ourselves. One finally has to realize that all effect requires presence and that there are no dead, but only living causes.

If we want to get rid of the word "cause" altogether, we could say: "The cause is dead, long live the living effect!" We can also invert Schopenhauer's saying that all reality is effectiveness. We can say instead that effectiveness is reality, that what is real are the connections and the communities, and that all that is real (there is even a Swabian saying that confirms this[7]) is also present and in the moment.

We are the instants of the eternal community of ancestors. It can only help to point out that eternity too follows the rules of time. Even if Schopenhauer calls it "timeless," he means "infinite course of time." I am afraid that if we attempt to create timelessness, i.e., stop the process of time and try to see past, present, and future as a kind of "dead simultaneousness" (the words escape us here), we simply end up with an image of infinite space. Sure, time can be expressed in terms of space, and space in terms of time; time can be swallowed by space and space by time; but to go beyond both notions seems near impossible. To express space through time is maybe one of the most important challenges for the coming generations. All our language is quantitatively spatial and qualitatively facial: the tree, human beings, the mammal – all these categories and many others are built on facial perceptions. It would be good to perceive the world in terms of time instead. Best with the help of hearing. Music can maybe be the simple beginning to this new language.

The great hereditary communities are real; the work of the ancestors is still felt today, hence they must be alive. Of course, our human and animal ancestors – to only speak of those for now – have long become extinct in the outside world; despite searching everywhere, we have only poor remnants. In ourselves, however, these paleontological relics, these dead extinct beings are still alive. It requires only a "second face" to become aware of them. We are what remains of them, and our children will be as much theirs as they will be ours.

The individual bodies which have lived on this earth from its beginnings are not just a sum of isolated individual beings; they form a big and real community, an organism; an organism that changes permanently, that always manifests itself in new individual shapes. As little as our consciousness usually knows about the powerful and real life of our allegedly unconscious desires, reflexes, and physical automatisms, as little do we know about the life of the ancestors in ourselves. And yet their existence is undeniable. If we do not acknowledge this, the meaning of life and the world will remain mysterious to us; they will be all matter, all perception, all spook.

Everything that exists, exists for itself, i.e., is conscious. *Est ergo cogitat* – this is our Cartesian credo.[8] Humanity is no abstract, dead term to us; humanity is real and alive, and the individuals are – together with their consciousness – the individually emerging, changing, and disappearing (another form of changing) shadows that make humanity visible. Humanity, or rather the universe, is the Platonic idea, the *ens realissimum* of the scholastics.[9]

We have to think of the tree which stands in poor soil: it lowers a branch into richer soil and makes the old tree die and pass away, while its own sapling prospers and turns into a new tree. Likewise, we die as human beings and do not die at the same time. In our children, as well as in our deeds, we continue to live in another form and in unity with other human beings. One could say: *Disregard the material and only focus on the spiritual!* However, I would like to respond instantly: *No, no, this cannot be!* The one who only feels the spiritual with his soul while perceiving his body externally has lost all natural perception and has subscribed to some school's dogma. Body and spirit are not separable on the inside, both are expressions of the soul.

Let us look at this artificial separation, let us consider it for a moment: the way that heredity supposedly expresses itself in the individual is only in customs and morals, they say. They speak of "herd morality" and such;[10] but apart from this, the individual is something in and by itself, something special and clearly distinct. The opposite is true: it does not even matter how much customs and traditions of past generations define what we inherit; what matters is that their influence can be felt from the outside, through our social environments and the random communities of authority. However, what really makes an individual is that which is given to him by God's grace and birth; by the hereditary power that we ourselves are.

The individual is the part of ourselves that can only superficially be altered from the outside. The more firmly an individual stands on its own ground, the deeper it retreats into itself, the more it withdraws from the effects of its surroundings, the more it will find itself united with the past, with what it originally is. What man originally is, what his most intimate and hidden is, what his inviolable own is, is the large community of the living in himself, his blood and his kin. Blood is thicker than water; the community, as which the individual finds itself, is more powerful and more noble and more ancient than the weak influences of state and society. Our most individual is our most universal. The more deeply I go into myself, the more I become part of the world. But do I have the means to go this deep, to find what I need? Can what I find be different from a mere perception? Will not the inner perception I can have of myself just be a weak and vague general feeling compared to the clear sensual perceptions I derive from the outside world? Would the community that I advocate be based on nothing but such a weak and vague general feeling that is essentially useless to us?

Well, let us not be too proud of the clarity of our sensual perceptions, and let us not forget that we do not want to *perceive* the community which I advocate, but that we want to *be* and *live* it. The clarity of our sensual perceptions comes from the individualization and separation which we project onto the outside world in order to control it. Likewise, it seems as if the world separates us and turns us into individuals in order to express itself through us. Under such circumstances, it is only in separation and in turning inwards that we can find and feel the world in our body and soul. Since the world has disintegrated into pieces and has become alienated from itself, we have to flee into mystic seclusion in order to become one with it again.

If we want to bring something that we have forgotten into our consciousness, we recall it with the help of the psychological apparatus that we call memory. Our memory, however, is limited to the few and superficial experiences of our individual lives. This means that any understanding of individuality based upon our individual memory is superficial, momentary, and fleeting too. True individuality is deep, ancient, and everlasting. It is the expression of the community's desires in the individual.

Meister Eckhart says that God is not one with the individual, but with humanity. It is humanity that all individuals have in common; it is humanity that gives them value. It is the highest and finest in all individuals' lives. It is what Meister Eckhart calls human nature.

We must not misunderstand this: Eckhart does not speak of arbitrary commonalities enforced by authority. Enforced commonalities are the superficiality of herd mentality. Human nature is not indifferent, superficial, philistine, but eternal heredity, divinity; it is consensus and community, created once all find their deep and genuine core and live according to it. In other words, the true individuality that we find in the deepest depths of our selves *is* community, humanity, divinity.

Once individuals have transformed themselves into communities, then they are ready to form wider communities with like-minded individuals.

These will be new kinds of communities, established by individuals with the courage and the need to separate from the dullness of superficiality.

Individuals who are one with their innermost self and newly born thereof have no "memory" of the ancestors and the community alive in themselves. They *are* this community, they do not perceive anything as external; they *are* this memory, they do not possess it. We are all humans and live human lives. But we are also all animals with animal needs; needs that are older and hence more individual than human needs; the latter always have a touch of superficiality.

Human is our conceptual thinking and our memory; animal – thus both more general and individual – is our observing and witnessing, our feeling, and all forms of subconscious and bodily-spiritual experience. We become most general and divine, "most community," when we are more than animal. The so-called non-organic, the infinite, the universe are part of ourselves as well.

If we follow the teachings of Berkeley and Kant, only the infinite universe, the *natura naturans*, the God of the mystics, can really be called I. I am the cause of myself because I am the world. And I am the world because I am whole. Development comes from an eternal source; the connection is never broken, but our superficial mind cannot remember its origins, cannot recognize the ever-present source in ourselves, and does not allow it to flourish. Nonetheless, we have the most marvelous proof that the human spirit is able to connect to the voice of eternity: music, as Schopenhauer said so well, is the world reduplicated. Music is not necessary, however, to find infinity in ourselves. We must only *become* infinite, we must only become *truly* ourselves and unearth our deepest depths.

There is yet another way to feel the infinite, the most splendid of them all. We are all familiar with it as long as we are not entirely corrupted by the decadence and egotistical superficiality of our distorted and arbitrary communities. I speak of love. Love is such a wonderful and universal feeling, a feeling that spins us round and elevates us to the stars, because it is a cord that connects our childhood with the universe. There lies a deeper meaning in the fact that the name for the experience of community, the feeling that connects us with humanity: love, human love, is the same name that we use for the love between the sexes that connects us with the following generations. Damn the soulless who do not shiver when they hear of love! Damn those for whom sexual satisfaction is nothing but a physical sensation! Love sets the world alight and sends sparks through our being. It is the deepest and most powerful way to understand the most precious that we have.

I have talked about the gap between us, the new human beings, and the masses, and about the necessity to separate ourselves from those united by the state. This might seem to contradict my belief that a love for humanity is part of our most genuine being. Let me explain: on the one hand, it seems clear that all contemporary human beings – the civilized as well as the others – are so closely related to us that it is difficult not to love them as we love anyone who is close to us. On the other hand, the relationship is as difficult as it often is with our closest relatives: they are very close to us in their being and their characteristics, and we do feel the bond of blood and we do love them – but we cannot live with them. Most of our contemporaries have deformed their humanity because of their statist and social lowliness and stupidity; they have also deformed their animalness with their hypocrisy, false morality, cowardice, and unnaturalness. Even during occasional hours of clarity or despair they cannot shed their masks. They have blocked their way to the universe; they have forgotten that they can turn themselves into Gods. We want to be everything though: humans, animals, and Gods! We want to be heroes! So for the love of humanity that has lost its way, for the love of those who will come after us, for the love, finally, of the best in ourselves, we want to leave these people, we want our own company and our own lives!

Away from the state, as far as we can get! Away from goods and commerce! Away from the philistines! Let us – us few who feel like heirs to the millennia, who feel simple and eternal, who are Gods – form a small community in joy and activity. Let us create ourselves as exemplary human beings. Let us express all our desires: the desire for quietism as well as activism; the desire for reflection as well as celebration; the desire for labor as well as relaxation. There is no other way for us!

This intimate belief is born from grief: we want to feel the highest joy of creation because we are desperate. Those who have already experienced it know that the only way to awaken people is by religious genius, i.e., by the exemplary life of those who do everything to rise from the abyss. These individuals know that all these questions are serious existential questions. We who are few, we who are advanced – we need our pride! – cannot, and do not want to, wait any longer! So let us begin! Let us create our communal life, let us form centers of a new kind of being, let us free ourselves from the commonness of our contemporaries!

Our pride must inhibit us from living off their work; there should be no exchange for our finest thoughts – not even for our lowest. Let us engage in physical labor, let us be productive! This way we will be able to present the finest of our spirit to all of humanity. Let us hope that a new generation – to which I address these words based on deep despair – will find itself and unite.

Through separation to community – what this means, is: let us risk everything, so that we can live as complete human beings; let us get away from the superficiality of the authoritarian common communities; let us instead create communities that reflect the world community that we ourselves are! We owe this to ourselves and to the world. This call goes out to all who are able to listen!

---

1. Clemens Brentano (1778-1842), German poet and novelist.

2. Meister Eckhart (born Eckhart von Hochheim, ca. 1260-1328), medieval Christian mystic. Landauer was highly influenced by Meister Eckhart and translated many of his sermons and writings from Middle High German to New High German. Although Landauer's renditions remain respected and published, there exist various competing Eckhart interpretations. This translation follows Landauer's rendition.

3. Alfred Mombert (1872-1942), German poet. The translation reproduces the verses' meaning but no meter.

4. See footnote 2.

5. Common translation for Max Stirner's best known work (also *The Ego and His Own*). The German original is *Der Einzige und sein Eigentum*; literally, "The Only One and His Property."

6. See footnote 1.

7. It could not be established which saying Landauer is referring to here.

8. *Est ergo cogitat*: "It is, therefore it thinks;" Landauer paraphrases Descartes' *cogito ergo sum*: "I think, therefore I am."

9. Meaning literally "the most real being," the phrase has been used by scholastics for God ("the ultimate being").

10. "Herd morality" (*Herdenmoral*), is a term popularized by Friedrich Nietzsche; it is akin to "slave morality" (*Sklavenmoral*) and opposed to "master morality" (*Herrenmoral*).

REVOLUTION

REVOLUTION

For bibliographical references, please see "1901-1908: Retreat and Reflection" in the Introduction.

> *When you see the Way of the Cross, you see demise, because you judge it by those who have walked it in the past; me, I see salvation, because I judge it by those who will walk it in the future.*
> **(Maximus Tyrius)**[1]

SOCIOLOGY IS NO SCIENCE, AND EVEN IF IT WERE, REVOLUTION would elude scientific analysis for different reasons.

This is how exact science evolves: our senses collect impressions which are processed by memory and language and transformed into images of being. Action, effect, and change build on solid, isolated things, which are transferred into notions, abstractions, etc. Science retransforms being (that which has been created to appease our senses and communicative needs) into becoming. Old notions are crushed and – like particles from the sun – disperse under the pressure of reflection and comparison: everything becomes different. Exact science means: the organization and interpretation of sensual perception; a permanent critique of our abstractions and generalizations; a corresponding critique of our understanding of being; and the creation of becoming (a process that aligns our perception with our inner experience).

None of this applies to what I call history (in its widest sense). History has no solid things or substances or elements that notions can be built upon. Even the concrete human bodies that carry history are hardly ever considered in historical study – with the possible exception of those who were tortured or beheaded. In general, our historical data consists of events and actions, of sufferings and relationships.

Science deals with becoming after a long and hard struggle. History deals with becoming from the get-go. Nonetheless, in order to talk about history, we have to form notions akin to those of exact science. They have to be based on processing our perception. As a result, we construct being and we speak of the Middle Ages and of Modernity, of the state and of society, of the German and of the French as if they were facts or entities. However, eventually our analyses always return from these constructions to reality, i.e., the elemental reality of our original and immediate experience: the contact between people, the interaction between individuals, the relations between groups (that support or fight each other), the organization of societies, etc.

Exact science corrects experience: it leads from experience to the abstractions of spirit. The study of history, however, can never lead us to anything but to our original and immediate experience – the more detailed and complex the study becomes, the faster this happens. For the time being, the latest form of historiography, namely social psychology, is the most complex way to dissolve the auxiliary constructions of memory and return to the basics of experience, i.e., to the elemental relationships between human beings.

Since history creates no theories of spirit, it is not a science. History creates something else: forces of praxis. The auxiliary constructions of history – the church, the state, the estates, the classes, the people, etc. – are not only instruments of communication, but the creation of new realities, communities, necessities, and organisms of a higher order. In history, the creative spirit does not generate theoretical insight. This is the reason why the terms "history" and "politics" signify action as much as passive observation (pretending to be neutral, while it is only latent will). There is an apt German word for this process: *Vergegenwärtigung* [to make something present]. History means the *Vergegenwärtigung* of all that has happened. There is an apt word for it in English too: to realize, which means both "to make real" and "to understand," uniting imagination and desire as much as knowledge and creativity. Each investigation into the human past or present creates the future. Once our constructions of history have been dissolved into the elements of individual psychology, they have been destroyed – not only in theory, but also in praxis.

111

We now find ourselves at the heart of what I am aiming at in this text: to study revolution from the perspective of social psychology. Eventually, we will find that social psychology is nothing but revolution itself. Revolution and social psychology are two terms – two shades – for the same thing: to dissolve and to separate general forms and apotheosized images through individualism. The beheading of Charles I, or the Storming of the Bastille, were examples of applied social psychology, while each study and analysis of holy images and supra-individual formations is revolutionary.

There are two strains of history that constitute two strains of historical praxis: on the one hand, the construction of supra-individual entities and higher forms of organization that give life meaning and holiness; on the other hand, the destruction and abolition of these entities when they start to contradict the individuals' freedom and well-being. Rousseau, Voltaire, or Stirner were revolutionaries because they were social psychologists. However, this leads us beyond the objective of our study; for the study's task is not to make revolution, but to write about it.

Let us start at the beginning. I have implied that even if history or sociology were exact sciences, we could not, for different reasons, treat revolution scientifically. I will try to explain this further.

It seems that the best way to prove that something cannot be treated in a certain form is to do this with honesty and sincerity until we cannot carry on any longer. This means that I will attempt to speak of revolution in strictly scientific and deductive terms, asking the reader to scrutinize my every move. It is important to make sure that I am not cheating; especially since I am already announcing that this attempt will be in vain.

I hope that no one expects me to explain why no such thing as inductive science can exist, even if it cannot be denied that most of what is called science today is but a poor mixture of materials and sentiments. So, without further proof, let us state that science is deductive because it is intuitive. Induction and the painstaking collection of data can do nothing but add to the sense of general intuition – they can never replace it. The scientific understanding of revolution hence rests on a general notion that must encompass all of its concrete individual expressions.

The first step in our investigation must be to establish a scientific terminology. All of the terms we commonly employ derive from individual events and therefore lack scientific usefulness. Where can we locate revolution? Revolution concerns communality in all its dimensions. This means not only the state, the estates of the realm, the religious institutions, economic life, intellectual life, schools, arts, or education, but the combination of all of those; a combination that, for a certain period of time, rests in a relative state of authoritative stability. We call this combination – the current state of communality – *topia*.[2]

Topia is responsible for affluence and satiation as well as for hunger, for shelter as well as for homelessness. Topia organizes all matters of communality, wages war, exports and imports, closes and opens borders. Topia implies intelligence and simplemindedness, virtue and vice, happiness and unhappiness, harmony and disharmony. Topia impacts on the sub-areas of communality (those that are not identical with topia itself): the private lives of individuals and families. The borders here are not clearly drawn.

Topia's relative stability gradually changes until a point of labile balance is reached. The changes in topia are caused by *utopia*. In its original sense, utopia does not belong to communality, but to individual life. Utopia means a combination of individual and heterogeneous manifestations of will that unite and organize in a moment of crisis to form a passionate demand for a new social form: a topia without ills and injustices. As a consequence, a utopia is followed by a topia that differs in crucial points from the former topia – but is still only a topia.

This constitutes our **first law**: Each topia is followed by a utopia, which, in turn, is followed by another topia, and so forth. (This law is the result of proper scientific analysis. The empirical induction on which it is based is, as we shall see, only short-lived and without proper definition. The general and necessary character we boldly attribute to it can never derive from experience alone. It derives from the intuition that there exists a common human nature; an intuition that is already reflected in the general terms with which we operate. In this sense it is as certain to us as that one and one make two.)

Corollary: The number of topias and utopias is always the same.

Utopia is a combination of ambitions that will never reach their goals; they will always create but a new topia. Revolution is the period of transition that lies between the old topia and the new topia. Revolution is hence the way from one topia, or from one state of relative social stability, to the next, by way of chaos, rebellion, and individualism (a notion that includes heroism and despicableness; a notion that means the loneliness of the great as much as the loneliness of the atom in the mass).

If we call the topias A, B, C (etc.), and the utopias a, b, c (etc.), then the history of a community goes from A to a to B to b to C to c to D, and so forth. However, using the first letters of the alphabet suggests A as a first topia, while no first topia ever existed. Hence, it seems more appropriate to use letters that lie in the middle of the alphabet: M to m to N to n to O to o to P, and so forth. There exists yet another difficulty of course: do we start with the capital letter or the small? In other words: does the history of humanity begin with society? Or does it begin with a revolutionary idea?

The answer is that while we might argue about whether the alphabet starts with a capital A or a small a, history has no beginning. This is implied in the notion of *Geschehen*.[3] If there is a beginning, there is an end. *Geschehen* has no end, however. Neither is there a historical beginning. Even if we go all the way back to pre-human history, we will find stability and rebellion, community and the individual, the centrifugal and centripetal (or whatever one wants to call this polarity in the creation and re-creation of organic – and not only organic – life). Neither Rousseau's *contrat social* [social contract] can serve as an answer here, nor the silly fight of Antiquity over whether the communality of humans was based on nature (*physis*) or nurture (*nomos*), nor the daft solutions of the Darwinists. If we wanted to find an answer, we have to unearth an origin underneath all the superficial problems entertained by theories of knowledge or philosophies of nature; an origin that would unite both these disciplines, and hence spirit and nature. However, the idea of such an origin appears very unclear and vague. It is hard to reconcile with our scientific ambition. We can proceed, but with less ease and certainty. We proceed on rough ground, knowing that the scientific character of our investigation might soon be shattered. In fact, it might be best to simply forget the ABC and all mathematical masquerades…

As we have seen, each utopia contains two elements: the reaction against the topia from which it arises, and the memory of all utopias that have previously existed. Utopias might appear dead, but whenever a topia rattles their coffins, they are resurrected like Job.

Each topia contains two elements as well – the victorious dimensions of the preceding utopia that had been turned from will to reality, and the remnants of the previous topia. However, these elements alone do not define the new topia. Another element is of crucial importance: the practical demands of the revolutionary period. This, in fact, is so important and general that a second law derives from it.

Second Law: The practical demands of communality during the time of revolutionary uprising and transition entail that the new topia establishes itself in the form of dictatorship, tyranny, provisional government, violence, and similar phenomena.

First Corollary: The new topia arises to save the utopia, but actually causes its demise.

Second Corollary: The practical circumstances that demand a new topia are not reduced to an economy disrupted by revolutionary uprising; they also include – at least very often – interventions by a hostile environment.

We must neither imagine the communities that are established during revolution's journey from topia to topia as isolated nor as original: they are in contact with and affected by other communities on all sides, communities which themselves are in contact with and affected by others, etc. Furthermore, all communities are affected by the natural world: in our times by bad harvests or catastrophes like the Lisbon earthquake;[4] in other times by comets, solar eclipses, or epidemics.

Revolution ignites a general fire among people and transcends borders (which are never stable). Utopia accepts no limits set by nations or states, but demands ideal conditions for all of humanity. In revolutionary times, a heart that remains attached to the past can easily be ridiculed. People trust reason. The world ought to be, as Hegel so audaciously proclaimed, "put on its head;" it ought to "become reason."

In some regions or countries people might be able to retain a stable topia while revolution occurs. Maybe these people have stronger hearts and less reason. Armed confrontations may be the consequence, and revolution might turn into war or long-term economic conflict.

For many reasons, utopia never turns into actual (material) reality, and revolution gets stuck in its transitional role: it marks merely the space between two topias.

I have stated above that each utopia contains the passionate memories of all former utopias. We find the same process in nature, albeit in a more complicated manner. Yeast, for example, makes wine ferment, only to be then taken from wine, and so forth. This means that while each yeast is new, it still contains the reality (or memory – this is one and the same) of all yeast that has ever been.

By the same rationale, utopia always reappears, no matter how often it dissolves and disappears in what it has produced. Revolution is always alive, even during the times of relatively stable topias. It stays alive underground. It is always old and new. While it is underground, it creates a complex unity of memories, emotions, and desires. This unity will then turn into a revolution that is not merely a boundary (or a spate of time) but a principle transcending all eras (topias).

We have already addressed the obstacle that the never-ending past presents for our scientific endeavor. We pushed it aside because we wanted to proceed. The other major obstacle, the never-ending future, we have hardly mentioned. In any case, our investigation has to end here. Our latest definition of revolution declares all our postulates wrong, even though we followed the rules of science strictly. Revolution, in this latest sense, becomes a principle that strides across the centuries.

Our scientific investigation was doomed to fail, because we know nothing of the future; in fact, if we are really honest, we know nothing of the past either. This is important to note, because if we really knew about the past, we could certainly deduce the future by mathematical laws.

Let us exemplify our limited knowledge of the past: let us take one era and try to establish whether it was an era of revolution or not. I suggest the end of Antiquity, the emergence of what I call "rested peoples," and the spread of Christianity.

We have already stated above that a people cannot be treated in isolation. This can hardly be doubted. Of course, we can try to make a new start. We can try to work with a notion of topia that applies to many peoples. However, this will not work because we will not know where to draw the line: we will jump from one people to the next, from there to the animals, the plants, and the earth's metals, then on to the stars and the skies, and we will not stop there either... But let us not think about that. Let us assume for a moment that it was possible to define topia in just such a general way, and let us turn our attention to the simple question (not simple because we are modest, but because the simple contains the complex, and each question contains all other questions) of whether the indicated era constituted a true turning point; whether it was an era of true revolution or not. The problem is that even if we had clarity on this (and were not caught in the darkness in which we are caught), even if we really knew anything about the transition from Antiquity to newer times – which, in fact, was no actual transition, but simply a new beginning of rested peoples, even if it did contain all the elements of Antiquity – then...

But I am digressing. We will return to this. First I must explain what I understand by "rested peoples." Usually one calls them "primitive peoples," or – this being the favorite – "original peoples" (*Urvölker*). Those who want to express some sympathy for them might call them "barbarians;" the others – in particular missionaries – call them "savages." In any case, there seems to be widespread agreement that these people are somehow particularly close to creation. However, this only seems so, because no one really believes it. At least when they are pushed. It is a belief in words only.

A lot of superstition is but convenient convention. People might feel enlightened and modern, but their hearts remain attached to what has been passed down to them; indoctrination goes a long way. Their belief in the "original peoples" is like a card in a game that is passed along without anyone ever looking at it. It even remains unclear what is actually meant by "creation." Creation by an animal? Creation by other people? Creation as a result of a union of allegedly isolated individuals (who do not exist)? Or does the belief in the "original peoples" only imply that they have always lived in some supposed original state? All of this seems to be included in the vagueness in which the belief is expressed.

If I were still using scientific terminology, then this would be a good opportunity to formulate new scientific laws. The first one would be: Using the line of their predecessors as a standard, all people on this earth are the same age. This is as true as the old joke that infertility is not hereditary, and it is as self-explanatory as any triviality and any law ever established. However, it is also perpetually forgotten and overlooked, like everything that is self-explanatory. In any case, the existence of all people reaches back thousands of years, and not only that: since all people already existed before they became human – indeed, before our planet was created – their existence reaches back into eternity; an eternity that can never be imagined *too* eternal.

At this point, many readers might raise the obvious objection that I am confusing social psychology with sociology, and both with history; that I furthermore proceed from there to psychology and epistemology, then to national economy, then to metaphysics, then to biology, then to cosmology – I jump, as they say in German, "from a hundred to a thousand." It is hard to argue against this. However, I am bewildered by how few scientific disciplines ever leave their own confines. One of the virtues of attempting to establish new scientific disciplines along the borderlines of traditional ones – in fact, their true and often their only virtue – is that they break new ground for creativity and abstraction, while tearing down the limitations of traditional faculties. But now back to our treatise...

Just as each human comes from the bottomless depth of time, he also – like all his predecessors – comes from never-ending, boundless, infinite space. What is visible, tangible, and material in a human's life always comes from the outside. It always changes. What constitutes a human beyond metabolism, and what connects him to himself as well as to his predecessors (which is one and the same), is an invisible principle of form, *conscientia et causa sui*,[5] memory; the Archeus[6] that forms itself as well as this microcosm and the eternal unity, the *Weltgeist*.[7]

There is no difference between speaking of predecessors I *have* and predecessors I *am*. I *am* the environment from which I derive. Likewise, there is no difference between speaking of successors I *have* and successors I *am*. I *am* the environment which I become.

There is, however, a difference between you and me, between world and world. To me you are only a fragment, yet at the same time – like me – you are an entire world; and I am only a fragment to you, yet at the same time – like you – I am an entire world.

This is why people of spirit – spirit being love and creating communality – need the family, the herd, the nation (language, customs, arts). These social forms are the bridges of light that connect our different worlds. They also create new forms of community that overcome the rigid forms of community created by hatred, lack of spirit, and meanness. This will be explained in the following paragraphs.

Those who agree with me so far will also agree with the following assertion: each individual's past consists of uncountable peoples and uncountable periods of high, indeed of *highest* culture. The Hottentots, for example, reach back to cultural periods which we know nothing about, but which were certainly – we can safely assume this – many times more advanced than those of the Greeks or Egyptians. There are no limits to imagination – ask the geologists and the chemists. It is true that we hardly know anything about the cultural history of the Hottentots, but this is exactly why we can claim the above with such certainty; any other claim, for example one assuming linear or circular progress, makes no sense whatsoever.

This is what I mean by rested peoples (or tribes). Everything we know suggests that humanity is not progressing as a whole, but that cultures (not the peoples themselves – that is nonsense) sometimes simply vanish. This happens both due to age and the mixture of peoples. The disappearance of a people comes not from extinction, but from mixing with another people. Tribes and peoples interact regularly and without inhibition; between one another, through one another, across one another, etc. In this process they mix. This also means that they are all of the same age, and that the question of whether humanity "derived from a couple" is meaningless. All parts of the world are equally old and have existed forever. All peoples partake in the same honorable and great past, and they all become tired and need periods of rest. They are all sometimes primitive, sometimes original, and sometimes new.

Things are becoming clearer now. We realize that we cannot trace the uneven trajectory of peoples' histories – the change of topias and utopias, of stabilities and revolutions – mechanically. There is no unified humanity and there are no isolated peoples, and the centrifugal as well as the centripetal forces work in very complex ways. The great revolutions that we addressed above (the transition from Antiquity to Modernity and the times of the *Völkerwanderung*[8]) make the revolutions that we actually call by that name look pale in comparison. They remain little more than tiny, ephemeral events.

It is important to note that it was not the rise of Christendom, the demise of Western civilization, or the *Völkerwanderung* itself that marked one of revolution's steps on its stride through the centuries. Christendom is but a small waste product of both the decadence of Antiquity and of Jewish sectarianism, and it would never have had any meaning had it not met rested peoples who were weak enough to be overwhelmed by it. These peoples did not understand cultural heights; Phidias and Sophocles,[9] representatives of a time at its best, meant nothing to them. New times come from decadence and rested deprivation. This is where myth is created – and only when myth unfolds can a new people arise.

How can we trace the footsteps of revolution into the past? The paths that lead us to Rome and Hellas end there. They allow us to find a new beginning, but no revolution. The change from old to new times is not a simple act of progress; it is something entirely different.

The history of humanity goes back several millennia. How can the pitiful episode of the two or three millennia we actually know anything about (and not what is most important) compare to this? What do we really know about revolutions that would allow us to talk about them with cool heads and sober minds? What do we know that would allow us to recognize and analyze them?

We know little about the revolutions of Antiquity. Antiquity is marked by its own trajectory; one that cannot simply be compared with ours. Humanity may be the same in principle, but the forms of communality differ greatly. The people of Antiquity, for example, stood on a horizontal plane that looked towards the Gods. Our lives move on a curve that bends around the globe. But back to our question: what do we really know about revolutions?

The answer is that we only know one true revolution. It does not, however, march through the history of humanity with giant steps. We have seen that there are more significant events in this so-called history of humanity than revolutions, namely the decline of old cultures and the arrival of new ones. These might not occur from eternity to eternity, but at least from ice age to ice age. So when I say that we only know one revolution, I mean a very concrete event in our own history – an event which we are, in fact, still part of. This, in turn, makes it impossible for us to investigate it scientifically since it is impossible to investigate something scientifically that you are a part of, even if only as a silent observing dog. All scientific investigation needs a place outside of what is being analyzed.

The revolution that I am referring to is the so-called Reformation. The stages of this revolution were:

1. the original Reformation with its spiritual and social transformation, its secularization, and its state formation;
2. the Peasants' War;
3. the English Revolution;
4. the Thirty Years War;
5. the American War of Independence.[10]

The significance of the American War of Independence does not so much lie in what happened in America, but in the influence of the war's spirit and ideas on the French Revolution.[11] We will show that the French Revolution stayed alive until 1871; not only in France but all over Europe.

Revolution

The year 1871 marked a clean break, even though I will not claim that it meant the end of an enormous movement whose beginnings extend back to the 16th century. All I am claiming is that we are now witnessing a lull in its development, and that it depends on our nature, our will, and our power whether our time will be a decisive turning point, or a time of idleness and exhaustion. Those who will come after us will know – in a very different way than us.

I do not deny that one can speak of several revolutions that occurred within the last four hundred years, and also of several periods of stability. This should not be surprising given the theory that I have laid out above. One might say that my construction of a single, cohesive, indivisible trajectory of constant ups and downs is arbitrary. I can say little to defend myself, other than pointing out that all historical observation is influenced by our will and our current situation, in short: by *our way*. I would even claim that our historical memory depends much less on the arbitrariness of external influences than on our own interests. If we understand anything about the past, it is only what concerns *our own* past, only what is still relevant for us today; furthermore, we only understand it based on *how we are today*; this is what I mean when I speak of *our way*.

There is only way for us, there is only future. The past itself is future. It is never finished, it always becomes. It changes and modifies as we move ahead.

I am not saying that it is merely the *perceptions* of our past that are changing. This would be too simple. The *past itself* is changing – no matter how paradoxical this might sound. There is no causal chain in which a given cause triggers a given effect that then turns into another given cause, etc. This is not how things work. The notion of causality assumes a chain of given moments, all of which are fixed and stable, except for the most recent one, which is active and causes another moment. But this is not the case. The whole chain is always actively moving forward – not just its last link. All so-called causes change with each new effect.

The past is what we take as the past, and its effects depend on this. In thousands of years, the past will be something very different than what it is today – we journey through time together.

We have to elaborate on this, returning to something I began to outline earlier. There are, in fact, two pasts. They have different forms and belong to different spheres. One past determines our reality, our being, our constitution, our personality, our action. The forces of this past are alive

121

in whatever we do – they reach over and through us. This past manifests itself in everything we are, become, and experience in numerous ways. It indicates a never-ending process within each individual, within each community, and within the relations between all human beings and their environments. Everything that happens, no matter where and when, is the past; *not an effect of the past, but the past itself.*

The other past is something entirely different. It is something we look back at. It consists of the excrements of the other past. This should make clear what I mean. The past that is alive in us leaps towards the future in every moment. It is movement. It is way. The other past is the bits and pieces that have been passed down to us by our ancestors. This is the past we tell our children about. It appears rigid and does not change because it has turned from reality to frozen image. It only changes during revolutions, when history is written anew, when history is altered, when it is dismantled and reconstructed. However, even this past will always remain different for each individual, as each individual has its own perception of the image – a perception determined by the active past within each of us.

All that has been said about revolution so far (and all that will be said about it in the future) speaks of revolution as *way*. To lay out this way is my only intention; I can have no other. It is now possible to repeat our original claim with much more confidence and courage; namely, that to practice social psychology means to make revolution. In other words, we make revolution because revolution makes us. Let us leave strict scientific deduction behind. Not forever of course, but at least until the next ice age.

Let us start all over again. However, what has been said so far about the essence of revolution – with terrible methodology but sound intention – shall not have been in vain. The knowledge we have about revolution – the notion of revolution as it has developed in the revolutionary era (in the era of transformation called Modernity) – suggests a) that we have stepped from one period of relative stability into the next, and b) that the transformations were caused by changes of our ideals. Before the present age of transformation, we experienced an era of strong continuity, a cultural peak that echoed Antiquity. I am speaking of the Middle Ages.

Before we proceed, I have to make one thing clear: in our effort to lay out way, we have to rid ourselves of the stupid classifications of so-called world history and its categories of Antiquity, the Middle Ages, and Modernity. Understanding alone is not enough. One also has to draw the conclusions and cast away moribund names and terms. No decent human being should be allowed to speak of "world history" when all it refers to are pitiful remnants of peoples' activities. Those who speak of Antiquity, the Middle Ages, and Modernity must realize that these are childish categories that mean no more than beginning, middle, and end.

This becomes particularly clear when considering that the last two centuries are usually referred to as the "newest" era, suggesting that we are what "beginners" like Pericles, Sophocles, Julius Caesar, or Dante have worked towards. The Middle Ages then become the "dark stepping stones" between the first cultural peak (Antiquity) and the new glory (Modernity). After us – i.e., after Modernity, hailed as the highest point in humanity's development – history will apparently end. At least the history of man – if any further history were to follow, it would be the history of *super*man.[12]

We must get over the habit of speaking of Antiquity. Even the more acceptable phrase "ancient times" must be abandoned. Parallel to, or even before, the Greco-Roman world, many advanced cultures existed in Asia and Africa – none of which saw itself as a beginning or an end of any kind; each era is a part of eternity. We have to shed our fixation on some linear development according to which all previous periods were nothing more than precursors to our own.

In fact, it would be best if we used no temporal categories at all when speaking of history, since our category of time is all too closely linked to causality. (I am only using the Kantian term here for brevity's sake.[13] It saves me a longer explanation. In general, this could be said better. Kant's categories are but the invention of a philistine. A revision is mandatory.[14]) This means that we are always in danger of confusing predecessors with ancestors, ancestry with backwardness, and a short time span that we happen to know a tiny little bit about with something whole and complete. Instead, we have to look at all people as contemporaries – separated somehow, but not causally or temporally. This is the only way for us to gain an appropriate image of reality. Since humanity is many thousands of years old (this we know for sure; however, I will assume that it is much older until someone provides a convincing reason why it should not be). How can we not regard those who have shared the last few millennia with us as contemporaries? Even if we want to classify eras, the classification must never be strict. We must only speak of different modalities. In this sense, we could distinguish between the following histories:

1. The history of strangers.
2. The history of neighbors.
3. The history of ourselves.

The history of strangers is the history of the Assyrians, Persians, Egyptians, Chinese, Indians, Native Americans, etc. We call this the history of strangers because we do not fully understand the connections between these people and ourselves (or our neighbors – who we will name in a second). For this reason these peoples have also not experienced a renaissance (at least no decisive one) within our own culture even though hints at an Indian renaissance are present and apparent (Friedrich Schlegel[15] had already proclaimed this in the 19th century).

The history of our neighbors is the history of the Jews, Greeks, and Romans. They are neighbors to the European peoples in a wider sense, but neither their ancestors nor their role models. During their demise, the Greco-Romans have passed on both their body and their spirit to the new peoples who were the results of old peoples mixing. The Jews have left a significant legacy of spirit. They did not, however – unlike the Greeks and Romans – become a part of the new peoples themselves. Instead, they slowly, over the centuries, settled near them, and eventually partook in their cultural development, while always keeping a certain autonomy. It may sound paradoxical, but Judaism has also been affected by the Christian Middle Ages, and the Jews of the last centuries are as much characterized by decadence and transition as anyone else, no matter how autonomous their customs remain.

But the fate of the modern Jews whose culture has quietly influenced other peoples is not relevant for our study. We are only concerned with the relationship between the old peoples and our own history. In this history, neither the Greeks and Romans nor the Jews can be called ancestors. Christendom and Europe meant a new beginning: rested peoples might have swallowed and digested elements of Greek, Roman, and Jewish culture, but they also created their own. The demise of the Greco-Roman world, the rise of Christendom among the new peoples (it was among them that Christendom arose!), and the so-called *Völkerwanderung* signify a special era and a new beginning.

We cannot call Greeks, Romans, and Jews role models either, because we go our own way, despite all cultural renaissances. In each renaissance, the revival of old cultural elements has been absorbed by new, healthy forces. What has been crucial within all the so-called renaissances has not been the revived elements of bygone cultures and eras, but the eruption of ingeniousness within the new ones. We do not owe our new cultural forces to Antiquity – much rather these new cultural forces revive elements of Antiquity, making them relevant today. We ought not to be deceived by the philistines who mistake the new for something old.

We have to distinguish very strictly between what the Greeks, Romans, and Jews mean for us – for those who have built new cultures on their ruins and with their gifts – and what they have meant for themselves. We look at solid, mature, and sovereign cultures that do not belong to us, but stand strong and majestic *next* to us. Yet, they are not strangers in the way the cultures named above are. We have absorbed enough of their blood and spirit to perceive men like Plato, Phidias, or Homer, not as relatives, but as soul mates;[16] even if they are figures of a world that is dead to us. This is why we call them neighbors. Our own history relates to theirs in the same way that the history of the German nation relates to that of the French: we face each other as independent strangers – but we do so as neighbors.

A true fusion of our world and that of the Greco-Romans has only occurred once (this also explains all the misunderstandings around renaissances). Namely, at the time when the demise of the Greco-Roman world met with the rested strength and health of the new peoples' awakening. Or, to be more precise: it was the combination of this demise, of the rise of strength and health, and of the intermixing of old peoples that caused the emergence of new peoples and their fledgling cultures.

It seems impossible for us to imagine the emergence of any new cultures – in former or future times – in any different way. The so-called cultural renaissances propagating a return to the glorious times of a Greco-Roman culture that had long been dead were nothing but philistine errors, comparable to the illusion of the German Kaisers that they really upheld Roman culture and the Roman state.[17] The people of those times did not see themselves as part of any "dark" Middle Ages, and they never saw themselves as mediators in any way. They never understood, however, how deep the rift between themselves and the culture of the Romans was.

The German Kaiser was a Roman Kaiser only because he was blessed by the pope. The Greeks and Romans are our neighbors who have gone their own way to the end – for and by themselves. There are times when it is important to look at former cultures that are similar to our own, but a return to these cultures is never possible. Nothing that is dead can ever be resurrected. The European Renaissance meant the rise of the Baroque Age, the awakening of individualism and personalism, and the escape from the confines of the Middle Ages – but it did not mean a revival of the Greco-Roman world that has given us but a dead language (the Latin of the Middle Ages was alive, not classical), a dead (and deadly!) law, and a dead Aristotle (Aristotle had been kept alive during the Middle Ages too[18]).

I do not mean to belittle the wonderful knowledge we might acquire from the Greco-Roman era; yet I argue against all humanist attempts to bring it back. Such attempts will only kill what is alive now.

Let us only think of how a man as wonderful as Theophrastus Paracelsus has argued against the decayed philistinism of the humanists.[19] Paracelsus argued as a man whose nature defied all restriction, making him a true and innovative scholar. Those who know the history of inductive science know that it did not derive from the resuscitation of the Greeks and Romans. The European Renaissance owes a lot more to the purest and deepest Middle Ages than to Antiquity. Much has to be reinterpreted. After all, efforts have been made to turn Dante and Nicolaus Cusanus[20] into Renaissance figures: men who were completely immersed in the Middle Ages.

In general, there exists – especially in Romanic countries – a widespread tendency to view the entire Middle Ages as a predecessor of the Renaissance. This is very unfortunate, even if the era's value as a period of transition cannot be denied.

We will see that the so-called Middle Ages – the only heyday of our own history – marked a synthesis of freedom and constraint. This synthesis defines the peak of every culture. When constraint disappeared, and with it meaning and holiness, freedom took on new forms, became personalized and sometimes riotous and violent. This is renaissance in its original sense: not a return to the Greeks and the Romans, but the demise of a cultural peak and the transition to (as well as the search for) new cultural forms. These new forms of individual freedom and the disengagement from social and spiritual bondage define the way that has become ours; a way that became ever more obvious during the Reformation; a way that I call revolution.

Our own history is the history of the European or Christian peoples; a history that follows the history of the peoples of the Mediterranean. We call this history ours for the simple reason that it is not yet over. We can use the term Christianity for our times as long as we remain aware that today's Christianity has nothing to do with the old Christendom. The one great era of our own history – the era that has led to its cultural peak – was the Christian era; this is what we usually call the Middle Ages. However, this period of Christendom is gone and we have not yet arrived at a new cultural peak. Only once we do will we understand how thorough a break between the Christian era and the still nameless era to follow the Renaissance and the Reformation constituted.

We feel that we are close to the world of the Middle Ages – especially when considering how far we are from the Greco-Roman world. Let us take any Christian painting, any human sculpture or ornament made from stone that adorns a Gothic cathedral, and compare this rather primitive work of art with a classical Greek masterpiece; let us take a walk through the Bavarian National Museum in Munich to revel in the tools and the houses of the Christian era; let us compare medieval mystery dramas with the great works of Greek tragedy, or Hagen and Siegfried with Odysseus and Achilles,[21] or the *Minnesang* of Walther von der Vogelweide or Heinrich von Morungen[22] with the poetry of Archilochus or Horace:[23] everywhere in the Christian world, we will find a soul that resembles ours; everywhere in the classical world, we will find sublime death and strange rigidness.

We must not allow the judgments of rationalism and skepticism to influence our understanding of Christian faith and religion. Rationalism and skepticism say: *this is not...* They lead us away from the Christian era. Christendom said: *this is...* It defined the meaning of communality. It was holy. It was mania.[24]

I believe that, according to what we know about early history and, especially, human nature, we can easily proclaim that all understandings of communality have been based upon mania. It has always been mania that bound humans together, that has motivated individuals to build organizational structures and alliances. Love – making our private and family life possible and secure – is as much mania as the form of vital, life-creating love that once was Christendom. There has been no lack of skeptics who have called the love between the sexes foolish and its consequences bloody, deadly, and treacherous. They were as right as we were when we (also as skeptics) criticized the beliefs of the Middle Ages and set out on our journey to a new mania. However, love is still love, and the peoples of the Christian age too were safe and glorified in their form of love. This is the judgment of history and justice, and, not to forget, of yearning; not a yearning for the same kind of mania (whose return is impossible) but for a new one. Today, however, we reserve the right to defend ourselves against any form of mania with weapons and laughter. We can do this because there is no form that overwhelms us.

The humans of the Christian world were overwhelmed; they were overwhelmed by soul and awe and metaphysical anticipations that concerned the meaning of the world; a meaning that goes beyond earthly life and experience. We can, for example, read Augustine and see how the wisest philosophers turned into children, how the most marvelous speakers began to mutter, how Roman public servants and aristocrats became monks and ascetics. These people were infused. Christianity is a special form of faith, a special form of infusion. It asserts that the world has no reality, but that our life has a goal and meaning; a meaning that goes beyond all earthly life, beyond everything that is worldly, beyond everything that is material.

The particular form of this Platonic doctrine was the symbol of the trinity according to which the spirit (the Holy Spirit), the origin of all things (the Father), and the created human being (the Son of Man) are one and the same. Human beings, however, do not only need symbolism, emotion, and philosophy to be overwhelmed, but also (and especially) event, anecdote, example, epos. This is why the tale of the Son of Man, who was the Son of God and who simultaneously embodied and spiritualized God, cannot be separated from Christianity as a people's religion. Heaven was full of angels, and the earth full of messengers and saints; ascetics and hermits who had already transcended matter, substance, and even desire (just like the Indian sages). This means that – after experiencing complete emptiness – they reached total, unspeakable fulfillment and unity with God. These teachings continued in pure esoteric form – wrapped up and protected by a tale that promised men they could become God: to enter, as saints, the abyss of origin; to go beyond time and space.

This is, in a nutshell, the spiritual content of the dogma and the myth of the Christian people. Such teachings and stories arise in old, declining, tired cultures, characterized by spooks, superstition, and a strange mixture of mystagogy and materialism; a mixture of the spiritual needs of inactive and self-absorbed individuals with the desperation and disorientation of uprooted and expelled social groups. A Plato, an Aristophanes, a Pericles would have turned away with disgust from this jumble and clutter, this amalgamation of downheartedness and ecstasy, of meagerness and snobbery.

However, this rotten product of fermented decadence earns a completely new meaning when it comes in touch with vigorous, rested peoples full of the life and energy that creates, builds, and connects. The effect can be compared to compost reaching the field.

A higher cultural level is attained when multiple social institutions – institutions that are usually exclusive and independent – are filled by a unifying spirit that comes from within them, and yet controls them as an autonomous outside force. In other words, a higher cultural level is attained when multiple forms of organization and supra-individual entities are not united by the threat of violence, but by a spirit that lives in all individuals and that goes beyond earthly and material confines. We have not yet found the right word to name this spirit. The Greeks called it *kalokagathia*.[25] It was represented by Gods and arts.

In our times, this spirit is represented by Christian rites and Christian symbols. Heaven lingers above the fields on which we labor and above the towns in which we work – the eternity of the spirit and men's equality and divinity fly along soulful ways into blue infinity. Romantics like Novalis knew – felt – that blue was the color of Christianity.[26] A color that signifies the darkness of ignorance rather than the light of knowledge, but that still indicates the direction of yearning and the source of light. It is hard to imagine a picture of Mary, the mother of God, without a blue frame.

It is good to be aware of Christianity as a colorful force and to know its color. The further we depart from Christianity, the clearer it becomes that Christianity was not colorless. It was not a gloomy reflection, but magical blue light. We must remember this when reading the great minds of those times: from Dionysius[27] to Meister Eckhart to Nicolaus Cusanus; we must remember it when we encounter a form of ignorance (*Unwissen*) that is actually a form of superior knowledge (*Überwissen*); we must remember it when we encounter a darkness that is actually a light transcending the earth as well as the Gods. The stone towers of the cathedral, rising like trees, reach out to this transcendent reality; a reality that gave people a special form of inwardness, of yearning, of passion, and of sexuality; a reality that gave people faces, postures, tools, and souls; a reality that filled all their institutions and social entities with a common spirit.

Of course, if one entertains the childish idea that the teachings of Christianity were complete, and that they answered everything – an idea found among ignorant humans desperate for meaning and purpose in their lives — then one might detect a gaping contradiction between the earthly, active, cheerful life and creativity of the people and the rigorous Christian teachings. However, this is an abstract notion that builds on poles that never exist with such clarity. There are neither pure beginnings nor abstract constructions. Life is always present in every new beginning, expressing itself in various forms. It is always life that replaces failure and demise.

When Christendom reached peoples in a state of primitive beginning, these were still peoples with traditions, a past, and certain forms of social organization. Among these peoples, Christendom could only beatify and overlay a form of communality that continued with strength and force. In this context, Christendom was only a truth with regard to the people's private and public lives, with regard to their work, their growth, and their expansion — all of which were preconditions and foundations of their existence. If one had told members of a guild or a parish that their positive, creative, and life-affirming unions stood in contrast to the true spirit of Christendom, they would not have understood it. It would have seemed as absurd as asking a physicist today to count the atoms of his body and place them individually on a table. Analyses, dissection, and an antithetical methodology of language and perception can never grasp the realities of life.

I want to repeat at this point: the Christian era represents a cultural level where multiple mutually exclusive social institutions existed side by side, were permeated by a unifying spirit, and constituted a union of many sovereign elements that came together in liberty. We call this principle of the Middle Ages the *principle of ordered multiplicity*[28] in contrast to the *principle of centralism and state power* that always occurs where the common spirit has been lost.

We do not want to contend that there was no state in the Christian era. (Even if a lot could be said for not using the term "state" in connection with institutions that were essentially of a different kind.) However, we can safely say that there was no omnipotent state; no centralized state that overpowered all other forms of community. If there was a state, it was merely an incomplete, rudimentary entity next to other, extremely diverse forms of community. In those times, the state was reduced to a weak mixture of remnants of the Roman state and feeble new statist tendencies; these only became relevant during late Middle Ages' periods of upheaval and revolution.

The Christian era was not represented by the feudal system; nor was it represented by the village or district organization with its commonly owned land and its common economy; nor by the *Reichsversammlung*;[29] nor by the church and monasteries; nor by the guilds, crafts, and brotherhoods with their own judiciary systems; nor by the independent streets, precincts, and parishes of these towns; nor by the unions of towns or the unions of knights; nor by any exclusive and independent forms of social organization. The Christian era was characterized by the totality of these forms – forms that were interrelated and organized without ever creating a social pyramid or totalitarian power.

The social priority of the Middle Ages was not the state but society, or, to be exact: *the society of societies*. What was it that united all these wonderful multiple social forms, allowing them to proceed to higher forms of unity without them becoming uniform? What allowed them to form social institutions without hierarchical domination? It was the spirit that came from the individuals, their characters, and their souls. It was this spirit that filled the social forms, and that returned from there to the individuals with even more strength.

The arts indicate for us whether a certain time marks a cultural peak. During cultural blossoming, the arts are communal and not individual; they are united around a center, but they are not isolated. During such times, they represent the era and its people. During times of dissolution and transition, however, they are products of single, lonely ingenious natures; then they gravitate towards the future and a secret, non-existing people.

The Greek classical arts marked such a cultural peak. So did Christian arts. During the Middle Ages, sculpture and painting were directly linked to architecture (*Baukunst*[30]), representing the longing and the wealth of their time. Compared to these (basically anonymous) "complete" arts, the arts of our times reflect a yearning of special individuals to escape these times. While the Christian art of building represented the building of society and a united and spirited people, our times are represented by the most individual, melancholic, and sorrowful of all the arts, namely music. Music is the symbol of an oppressed people, of communal demise, of greatness being reduced to a few individuals. In a completely different context, architecture has been called frozen music. The truth, however, is that music is thawed, dissolved, melted, individualized architecture (*Baukunst*). Architecture represents a reality. Music represents the yearning for a reality. Music is a refuge for those without a home. The epitome of our times and arts is Münchhausen:[31] a man who substitutes reality for fantasy; a man who is lonely. When Münchhausen creates a factory from bricks of air, he does what music does: music, like architecture, forms glorious buildings and arches – but it does not use bricks; it uses air.

During the Christian era, sculpture and painting were inseparable from architecture, the churches, the town halls, the squares, the streets, the public and private meeting places; they represented society, a multiple people's common spirit. Then painting and sculpture became separated from the buildings and turned into expressions of ingenious individuality. At first, they still decorated the spaces of high society, of princely, courtly, aristocratic, and affluent bourgeois circles. Today, however, the visual arts have become separated from the lives of individuals. Painting and sculpture only refer to themselves. Their products are like poems written to please the poet alone. The arts no longer consider other beneficiaries. They only represent those who produce them, not those for whom they are produced. During times of cultural peaks, the giver and the taker, the artist and the audience, belong together (even if productive ingeniousness remains reserved for a selected few during these times as well). In our times, however, the arts have simply lost their place in society. This is the reason why a new space has been created for them: the museum.

The same goes for poetry. During the Christian era, poetry was present wherever people gathered: in the churches, in the town halls, at indoor meetings, at outdoor assemblies, on the battlefield, during work, in the castles of the knights, and in the palaces of the princes. Today, the place of poetry has become a place of loneliness: the book. And when people experience poetry communally, they gather for this purpose alone, at author's readings and such. While life and poetry used to be one, life is now excluded from the poetic experience and a strange figure takes its place: the poet.

It is slightly different with drama, even though everything said about the other arts, in particular poetry, applies here too: the open stage of the Christian mystery drama connected worldliness with festive and theatrical ritual. However, drama as an art form did not reach its peak during the Middle Ages, but only once the Middle Ages had given way, in England, to a peculiar aristocratic-bourgeois society. Shakespeare owes his greatness, his extraordinary and unique role, to the fact that he stands in both camps at the same time: while he is already an individual and solitary genius, he still represents the people and public life. There is only one other artist who held a comparable position: Johann Sebastian Bach. His music appears to be a crown floating above humanity – but only because the structures on which it was built are gone.

If one wants to understand the connections between the arts and the daily life of the people, one ought to reflect on the following words formulated by a medieval council in Florence: "The community should not concern itself with efforts other than those that derive from its heart – a heart formed by the hearts of all of its members, united in a common will."[32]

It was sentiments like these that brought us the great works of Christian art (we ought to call it Christian art; Gothic art is a meaningless term) and Christian society. This is why even a physical and mechanical description of a cathedral's structure can provide a symbolic picture of Christian society. The Englishman Willis writes in an appendix to Whewell's *History of the Inductive Sciences*:

> "A new decorative construction was matured, not thwarting and controlling, but assisting and harmonizing with the mechanical construction. All the ornamental parts were made to enter into the apparent construction. Every member, almost every moulding, became a sustainer of weight; and by the multiplicity of props assisting each other, and the consequent subdivision of weight, the eye was satisfied of the stability of the structure, notwithstanding the curiously-slender forms of the separate parts."[33]

Willis simply tried to explain the essence of the Christian architectural style. However, since he described it so well, and since the buildings of these high times are a synopsis and a symbol of society, he – unintentionally – described this society as a whole: freedom and constraint; and a multitude of pillars.

There have never been truly isolated individuals. Society is older than the individual. Isolated and atomized individuals are a result of cultural demise, decay, and transition; abandoned people who do not know where they belong. Those born in the Christian era were not just part of vague social alliances or their families. They were part of many groups and unions that overlapped, yet remained independent. If they lived in towns, they were members of the independent communities of their street or alley, of their precinct or neighborhood, and of their town as a whole. The foodstuffs that reached the town from the surrounding area – or from far away, especially salt and grains – were administered by the town's buyers and market regulations, which made speculation and uncontrolled prices impossible. Craftsmen were organized in guilds that bought the resources they needed communally – and often enough sold their products communally too. The guilds even had their own courts that passed judgment on those of its members accused of a crime. The guilds went to war together and entered the town hall together. If someone had to journey by boat, a guild was established for this purpose, as a Hanseatic captain confirmed he when addressed the seamen and passengers on his boat in the following way: "Since our fate is now in the hands of God and the waves, we all have to be equals. And since we are surrounded by storms, high waves, robbers, and other dangers, we have to keep a strict discipline so that we can bring our journey to a good end." A reeve and a lay judge were elected, and at the end of the journey the chairman said: "Everything that has happened on this boat must be forgiven and considered closed; it all happened for justice's sake. This is why we ask you to forget all hostilities in the name of justice, and to and swear by bread and salt that you will harbor no ill feelings. However, if someone feels that he was treated unjustly, he must go to the reeve onshore and ask him for a verdict before sundown."

We only have to read reports like these – chronicles or sermons from the Christian era, or the *Sachsenspiegel*,[34] and other sources of wisdom – to realize that many of our institutions go back to this era. Today, however, these institutions have become cold and dead; their rules and regulations are written on paper, but have no connection to our lives. During the Christian era, they had meaning for human beings and their relationships, and were often created for a specific time and purpose. This was the reason why they attained eternal meaning. Spirit creates laws. But laws do not have the power to create, or replace, spirit.

In the century that Hutten called a pleasure to live in due to the awakening of individual spirits,[35] the spirit of the Christian era began to disappear. Christendom lost its immediate connection to people's lives. It became a school, a *faith*, as a consequence of having turned unbelievable. One got attached to the letters because the spirit was lost. As long as spirit is alive, a tradition needs no letters. It is maintained by the spirit, a force of life shared by all. When it is lost, the ingenious individuals arrive, who walk through the centuries awkwardly, as strangers, with their coats folded over their arms. They are not sociable, self-confident, and multi-talented, but are rather uprooted, torn, one-dimensional, lost, and troubled. Look at Luther: a truly obnoxious man, weak, pathetic, incompetent in all that concerned community and society. The era of individualism arrives in two forms: with the great individuals – and with the atomized and abandoned masses.

I now demand of the readers who have followed me to this point to pause and reflect. I ask you to fill the presented outline of the Christian era and its communality with life and blood. I challenge you to use the terms and thoughts presented to alter your perspectives and change the world that you know and that you have helped create. Turn this world into a world of becoming, of transition, infiniteness, diversity, unpredictability, and inextricableness! The era that I have portrayed was not as arid, naked, and bloodless as it may seem; in fact, there was nothing but life. However, we have to understand this life in the right way. For us – considering everything that has happened since – the lesson of the Christian era is that there was a yearning for holiness that gave society blessing, security, and integrity. Some might want to remind me that there was also feudalism, clericalism, inquisition, and oppression. To those I can only say: I know, but... All history, all understanding is a shortcut, is a condensation. Knowledge does not only come from what we see. It also comes from what we do not see. Life needs forgetting as much as it needs remembering.

We have tried to show that the millennium between the year 500 and the year 1500 was defined by one single tendency, namely ordered multiplicity, fed by a common spirit that united everything. In the same way – and this was the only reason for explaining all of the above – we now want to proclaim that the era from the year 1500 until now (and beyond) is an era without a common spirit. It is an era defined by a lack of spirit. It is hence an era of violence; an era where spirit is present only in certain individuals; an era of individualism, and hence of atomized individuals as well as uprooted and dissolved masses; an era of personalism, and hence individual melancholic and ingenious spirits; an era without truth (like any era without spirit); an era of demise, and hence transition; and an era of human beings without any heart, without integrity, without courage, without tolerance. However, because of all this, it is also an era of experimentation, audacity, boldness, bravery, and rebellion. This is the complexity in which we find ourselves, this is our transition, our disorientation, our search – *our revolution*.

Life in these times is an amalgamation of substitutes for spirit. After all, we need *something* that makes human community possible and that guides it. Where there is no spirit, violence takes over, and the state and the related forms of authority and centralism become consolidated. However, unrecognized expressions of spirit do remain. Spirit never disappears entirely. If it no longer manifests itself among the people, it appears as an abundant and exhausting force in some lonely individuals. The works of beauty and wisdom it produces through them are very different from the works produced during the eras of community.

Our centuries are marked by a desire for freedom and by attempts to attain it. This is what we usually mean when we speak of revolution. The violent surrogates of spirit are enormous. Utopia struggles against a specific form of transition. Wise and courageous individuals, full of spirit and soul, lead a struggle that substitutes one form of transition for another, and so forth, until the period has run its time and a new common spirit takes shape, born from the desires and the distresses of individuals. This new spirit creates new forms of communality and organizes them in new ways. Again, this is our way: to see a common spirit disappear, and to go through a period of violence and rage – a period of distressed masses and a few ingenious individuals – until we reach a new common spirit. It is now the time to document this way, or, in other words, our revolution.

The time frame that I am referring to is rather arbitrary – to make that clear. What could no longer be ignored in the year 1500 was the end of a process that had begun centuries earlier. The mythical force of Christendom had already been lost through scholastic theology[36] and clerical administration. It is hard to understand mythical force in times of logic and reason. We need the guidance of certain forms of female logic or of religious Russians like Dostoyevsky and Tolstoy. We can also call the mythical force faith. Those, for example, who believe within a living Christian culture that Christ is the Son of God feel connected to the deepest foundation of the world (*Weltengrund*) as its children.

The mythical era has – among the Greeks as much as among the Christians; and all other cultures, for that matter – the special merit of believing in symbols rather than letters; or, to be more precise: people do not make such a distinction and perceive and experience symbols physically. It was only church and theological teachings that began to distinguish between symbols and letters and robbed Christendom of its life by focusing on the latter and insisting on literal interpretations of the traditions and dogmas. This is how all true Christians turned into mystics, heretics, and then revolutionaries – while stupidity took hold of the church. All that now matters to the latter is understanding, differentiation, precision, analysis. In short, a rationalist explanation of religion has taken hold. Such stupidity is indeed hard to rival.

The true Christians were soon affected by the Enlightenment and rationalism too. They were forced to claim that everything that they perceived from a Christian – or any religious – perspective was *only* symbolic. As a consequence, they were not only separated from the church and its science, but also from the naïve faith of the people (*Volksglauben*). They became isolated individuals, thinkers, philosophers. This inaugurated an era without a common people and without a common spirit. It also meant that the worldly institutions, the communality of human beings, of society, and of its institutions, were no longer created, maintained, and spirited freely and spontaneously by the community of individuals; instead they became rigid, fell under outside control, or simply dissolved.

The salt loses its flavor. The stupidity of literal interpretation turned deepest meaning (*Sinn*) into mere nonsense (*Unsinn*). Only mysticism understood the symbol of the world. Hereticism rebelled. Nature raged against the "super-spiritual," against the faded, against all that could no longer be understood; at the same time aligning itself with the concrete reality of the external world and its desires. The principle of unification, of life, and of communality disappeared. The minds of the people and the social institutions turned rigid. Science and research awoke. Spirit was no longer free. The inner being lost courage. The lack of spirit began to reign. If we want a symbol for all this, let us name Martin Luther. There is no better symbol for the lack of spirit among people and for times of demise. This sinister man had such enormous power over his time because he represented it so fully. His demonism reflected the dismay, unpredictability, and weakness of his time (although the characteristics of his time were of a different kind than his own).

One hundred years before Luther, there was already a man who rebelled, a man with strong bones, a sober mind, and an iron will; a Christian anarchist way ahead of his time: Peter Chelčický of Bohemia.[37] He had realized that the church and the state were the arch enemies of Christian life, and attempted to save the spirit of Christendom. He described Christian life as an empire of spirit and freedom. Peter Chelčický was conscious of what had only been an unspoken reality before. He campaigned against violence, law, and authority of any kind. He emphasized that the spirit rested inside of each individual and that it promised order for humanity. Proudhon's words about freedom being the mother and not the daughter of order could have been his.[38]

Since the times were already ripe for such wisdom, people listened to this Hussite Tolstoy. However, the times also demanded rational explanations for what had previously simply been taken for granted. To provide such explanations proved impossible. There are prophets with poetic visions who anticipate and create the future; and there are fanatical speakers appealing to our consciousness with clarity and insight. It is the latter who bury the past by understanding and pronouncing the horror of the present. When the common qualities of the individuals who form societies turn into words and battle cries, when inwardness and confidence turn into opposition and demagogy, then an intensity and combativeness is created that might appear youthful and new – yet in reality it only proves that the old is disappearing without hope.

Consciousness kills feeling in the same way that morality kills love and dogma kills holiness. As a result, someone who understands and pronounces the ills of his times further increases them. One of them was Peter Chelčický. Unsurprisingly, the movement he initiated eventually turned into what he originally fought against.

In later times, the same would happen to young revolutionary parties. After a few years – sometimes after a few months – they would resemble what they had set out to abolish. In the case of Chelčický, even his most immediate followers had no real understanding of the connection between external life and inner voice; they did not see the critique – implicit in this connection – of the state and the apparatuses of oppression. They contented themselves in nurturing their pious inner lives and became one sect among many existing alongside the church. Finally, they turned into a confraternity usually known as the Moravian Brethren (*Herrnhuter*). In short, the actions of the fiercest Christian revolutionary led to a pious state of weakness, caressing a tender soul.

We have seen radical attempts in this century to reestablish what has long been called *Urchristentum*.[39] We have also seen national-liberal as well as democratic and revolutionary movements based on Christian beliefs. The passion in the texts of the Hussites, in Friedrich Reiser's *Reformation des Kaisers Sigismund* [The Reformation of Kaiser Sigismund],[40] and in the so-called Peasants' War (for example in Michel Gaismair's *Landesordnung*,[41] or in the appeal of the *oberländischen* peasants[42]) was deeply moving and energizing. At the same time, their practical proposals for social reforms were sensible and politically mature. They stood for a complex blend of spirit and action – most completely represented in Carlstadt and Thomas Müntzer.[43] This blend made for a dedicated struggle; a struggle that motivated the people of entire regions to revive a society in which life was based on the holiness of each individual and the common spirit of a Christian community.

All this, however, came too late. Too many powerful groups had already been established that saw Christian ways of thinking, feeling, and living as indications of ignorance. Humanist circles like those of Mutian, Peter Luder, and Heinrich Bebel[44] turned to playful atheism and polytheism. Renegade monks, jurists, and courtiers became satirical, frivolous, and indifferent, winking at each other, praising Erasmus and soon Rabelais.

This was followed by the authority of natural science and the demonization of nature: external nature had to be controlled to free one's own. There were Columbus and Leonardo,[45] as well as the astrologists with their revolutionizing idea that human will and fate did not depend on divine freedom, but on worldly determination. Then the magicians and chemists came, for example Agrippa[46] and Paracelsus, who freed the spirits from scholastic terminology and the abuse of words, and paved the way from knowledge to powerful dominance. And finally there was Copernicus, of course.[47] *De Revolutionibus Orbium Coelestium* [On the Revolutions of the Heavenly Spheres] brought the *revolutio* [revolution] also to the *orbis humanus* [human spheres]. This was a revolution that threw the individuals perpetually and with centrifugal force out into the void. Some of these individuals soon focused all their energy on themselves and turned into shining stars, while the masses dissolved like particles of dust. Such a revolution lasts centuries before it actually creates something new. In fact, it is not really revolution (*revolutio*) but regeneration (*regeneratio*).

The earth has arisen from its diamond quarters and begun to travel through the ether with enormous power. The heaven of spirit and divinity – the modest human heaven that was formerly nothing but an altar with some candles where humble yearning reigned – has become a never-ending space of worlds and creatures. Man, whose individual worth had formerly depended on being the Son of God and on God's immediate love, does no longer feel like a modest part of the universe; he feels dominant and powerful, a magician and conqueror of heaven and earth; he believes himself to have discovered forces that are keys to wisdom. Power has become the new science. Johann Faust was born a hundred times during this era.[48] Earth was discovered anew. Men boldly traveled around the globe to new shores: Africa, India, the islands and continents of the West. They were carried by new winds in more than just one way.

What would have happened if what lived in the hearts of the greatest individuals – Nicolaus Cusanus, Paracelsus, Agrippa, Giordano Bruno, and Campanella[49] – would have entered the hearts of everyone? What lived in their hearts was no less meaningful than the spiritual life of the late Greek thinkers. What would have happened if it had established itself in small communities? What would have happened if it had been brought and preached in all tongues and with dedication and zeal to the new, rested peoples? What if Bruno's gospel had reached the descendents of Hannibal's peoples in Northern Africa, the children of the Buddha in India, the noble peoples of Mexico and Brazil? What if, as with Christendom's beginning, the old and the new had met and intermingled, spirit with blood, and blood with spirit?

This is only speculation, but it would have caused fundamental change and marked a new era. Instead, we are struggling to refresh and recoup – we are weak and we struggle. We speak of revolutions that are little more than champagne to a patient who is slowly and painfully recovering from a deadly disease.

The newly discovered peoples had met a threefold death: bullets, hunger, and Christendom. The new science, the new philosophy, the new arts, and the new morality, however, have had no real impact on these people. They have only widened the gap between the individual geniuses and the masses; between the educated and the uneducated.

The Renaissance was nothing but the creation of a new aristocracy, a strange aristocracy, we dare even say: an aristocracy of decadence; in other words, an aristocracy not rooted in a people and without a people to lead; an aristocracy without power and soon without status. The only exceptions to this were the times of renewal and connection; in other words, the times of revolution. The renaissance of the peoples was replaced by the so-called reformation of that which had robbed the peoples of their spirit: namely, the church.

What emerged as a clerical Christendom after Reformation and Counter-Reformation was still connected to communality within some circles, especially within sects. Some of them had many members. However, while communality was undivided during the era of true Christendom, the individual was now split in two: while clerical Christendom retained control over private salvation, family relations, and morality, all economic, public and legal affairs – i.e., actual communality – was freed from Christendom, and retained only very thin, uncommitted, and superficial relations with morality. In other words, communality was rendered spiritless.

Something else appeared that one ought not to forget when speaking of the reemergence of classical Antiquity: Roman law. The concurrence of Christendom's reformation and Roman law's reemergence might be the biggest irony in the entire history of humanity. If there was anything in the dying stages of Antiquity that called for spirit and awe, for soul and love; in other words, if there was anything that made the emergence of Christendom possible, then it was the way the conditions of public life and of social relations found expression in the state and in civil law. The new peoples encountering the peoples of Antiquity and Christendom accepted hardly any of these dead customs when the *Corpus Juris Civilis*[50] was assembled, forming the Christian era's Germanic-Romanic code of law instead. This was a consequence of combining the perpetuation of their tribal customs with the arrival of a new spirit.

Today, Christendom has allegedly been saved; in reality, it has died. Its common spirit of unifying love and its body of epic laws and customs have not been replaced by anything that really resembles what existed before Christendom. What we are witnessing are but the ghosts of the era, arising from their graves: Roman Caesarism, Roman trade and usury, late-Roman casualism and literalness, Roman stubbornness, Roman capitalist individualism, Roman slavery – and a corresponding class of men: jurists.

The Roman world never completely disappeared. It has only been suppressed and constricted by the connection of a free Christian spirit and the Germanic spirit of independent federations. Roman constitutional law, Caesarism, and a pagan blessing of the princes all reemerged during the reign of Frederick I Barbarossa,[51] but the common spirit remained strong enough to form alliances and resist these developments and its institutions. Today, however, with spirit disappearing and public life dissembling into all sorts of entities (big and small), Rome seems to have become the only salvation for economy and community – meanwhile, what the new activism, the new world, the new powerful expansion of life would really need are new social forms and vessels.

The irony, of which I spoke, is much more drastic than I have laid out so far. We have to return to Martin Luther: Luther saw and fought the incarnation of the antichrist in Rome in all its forms: scholasticism, clericalism, narrow-mindedness, the transformation of Christendom into a dead system of words. Yet the very same man did everything he could to revive the original antichrist, Rome, the ultimate enemy of everything that true Christendom stands for, the spirit of life. And he succeeded. The Reformers are not only fathers of the principle *cuius regio, eius religio*.[52] These men, and in particular the terrible Martin Luther, have laid the foundation for the acceptance of the absolute power of the princes, and hence for the original forms of the modern state.

Many princes and masters soon understood that the fight against the Roman church would help them increase their power and possessions significantly. The Reformation would never have succeeded had the princes not been able to gain economic profits from secularizing dioceses, monasteries, and pious endowments. Luther and his men supported this as much as they could. After all, the man who always called his teachings *The Gospel* and who called himself (by God's grace of course) Ecclesiastes of Wittenberg,[53] was a witty politician who intended to replace the power he was fighting with his own: the dogma of words and the violence of swords. At the same time of course – conflicted as he was – he did express disgust with the means he employed to make his teachings succeed: "It is obvious that the princes interpret the gospel in their own interest and that they turn into new robbers who prey upon the old."[54]

Let us look at Luther's reaction to the radical revolutionary religious movements of his time. These were headed by the evangelical brothers usually known as the Anabaptists (named after one of their currents).[55] Their teachings derived from the Waldensians and the Bohemian tendencies.[56] During the Peasants' War (rightly referred to as the German Revolution, although Christian Revolution would suit the events even better, especially compared to what we now know as the Christian Reformation), hundreds of thousands of German peasants (and townspeople!) attempted to overcome the ills not only of the church, but of public life in general. They wanted evangelical life to flourish. Both with reason and fanaticism, they meant to restore the spirit as the guiding principle of life. So what did Luther do? He radically separated life from faith and substituted organized violence for spirit. His fight against the people's self-determination of their daily activities (*Werktätigkeit*[57]), which had already led to secularization and the destruction of many institutions of mutual aid now turned into a fight against Christian life altogether whenever it showed ambition to be more than just private.

We know that Luther went through a moment of uncertainty as to whether he should join the masters or the revolutionaries. (He always had moments of uncertainty – then he usually proceeded to push his agenda twice as hard.) First he said – in a particularly awkward and, for a man of his stature, pathetic move – that the reform of the corrupted rulers was not the affair of the people, but of the rulers themselves. Then he suggested – as a token for the rebellion's leaders – that he could not stand in their way as long as they remained worldly revolutionaries and ceased fighting under the Christian flag; in other words, as long as they were fighting as people who "naturally do not want to suffer injustice or ill." However, as soon as these people insisted on fighting in the name of Christ, he, Luther, had to see it as a personal attack against himself and his teachings.

This was the inauguration of pure, abstract, distilled Christendom. In its true sense, Christendom receives its meaning from direct connection with people's lives (*both* private and public), with their work, with their growth and expansion. This is the priority and the basis of everything else. Now, however, a man had arrived who made communality of spirit impossible, and who taught people that their positive, creative, vibrant associations stood in contradiction to the true spirit of Christendom. This man was Martin Luther, the Reformer. It becomes clear why he rejected the meaning of action (*Werkheiligkeit*) and stressed the notion that salvation lies in faith alone. He represents a time when nature, flesh, desire, and worldliness replace inner retreat and sensuality, but still require a blessing. He represents a time when the private relationship between the individual and his conscience is established. And not only that. He also represents a time when public life is no longer filled with and guided by the spirit of freedom and commitment. This marks the beginning of an era dominated by bad conscience. From now on senses, muscles, tendons – everything revealed something that was not Christ. Christ disappeared as an invisible bond between the people. It was impossible for Christ to disappear entirely, though. This is why he was conserved in letters. This allows him to survive his death.

In short, Christendom became bereft of life and turned into an abstraction and a system. Positive alliances became alliances of negation, critique, and rebellion. In both camps, reason replaced spirited reality. Also the will of the revolutionaries had turned from life and truth (as long as they looked towards the past) to reason and understanding. Among the Reformers (including the Catholic ones), reason meant scholastic foolishness. Among the revolutionaries, goodwill meant powerlessness. You cannot create with reason and will alone. I cannot emphasize this enough: *there is no creation without community, spirit, and love.*

It did not take long for Luther to join with the masters and to help implement Caesarism: the untouchable authority installed by God, and the close connection between the throne and the altar. Luther now preached vengeance and violence against anyone who still tried to understand the evangelical freedom of Christians as a principle of life or who dared associate the idea of general priesthood with people's self-determination in worldly affairs. To him, there were no longer people, there was only the mob. Action (*Werkheiligkeit*) was rendered insignificant, both in private and public life. God was reduced to abstraction, to letters, to the church. Holiness, blessing, anointing, everything majestic was handed to the princes and masters. The only relevance that Christendom still had for public life was to help create and control subjects.

To understand how the state expressed itself in the Middle Ages – aside from the smaller and bigger institutions it created – we have to use a word of Goethe: *lässlich*.[58] The state had no stable authority; it was shaky, uncertain, and barely respected. There were many authorities, but there was no holy principle of worldly authority. There were many negotiations and meetings, and many decrees, but no laws in the strict sense of today. The so-called "life of the state" (*Staatsleben*) of the Christian era, the meetings of the estates, the fundraising tours of the Kaiser, even the crusades, contained an element represented so well in Russian literature. Let us only think of the Russian aristocrats described by Tolstoy, for example Pierre and Kutuzov.[59] Logics, causality, and rationalism are not particularly important for people with a creative nature, for people who embrace myth and chaos. While our times follow the mottos of *It has to be done!* and *It is not permitted!*, the motto of those times was *It is happening!* All this changed with Luther. The modern state appeared with its three main characteristics: the absolute power of the prince, absolute law, and nationalism.

Those engaged in the Hussite Wars,[60] the Peasants' War, and similar uprisings were the last to try launching a revolution that would change

life – *all* life, in particular what we today call our economic and social life.
These days, the idea of revolution has practically disappeared. Politics have
been substituted for the Christian spirit – even when people speak of "religious conflicts." The coming era will be characterized by wars between and
within states (this is what is usually referred to as "religious conflict") and
by political revolutions that are in no way abstract and pure, but intrinsically linked to religious confusion, war, and tensions between republicans
and royals.

In Western Europe, political revolution has beset people's minds in
rapid succession: first in the Netherlands, then in Scotland, France, and
England. The origins of revolution are to be found in another country
though; a country that precedes the *Kirchenstreit*[61] and the consolidation
of the princes' power; a country that has inspired all later revolutionary
movements, since all of them begin in spirit before they turn into reality. I
am talking about the country of utopia.

Utopia was first outlined by the Englishman Thomas More in his
book of the same name, published in 1518. It later enthused Protestants
as well as Catholics and found particular reception in France; in general,
the Romanic spirit was more inclined to embrace it. Even though it was
formulated in religious terms at first, it was rapidly secularized.

The notion of utopia was certainly much less powerful than the
Christian spirit. It was built on reason, logic, and tangibility, and was partly
inspired by Antiquity. Yet, it was also more than that. In effect, it constituted a critique, a negation, and a rebellion; it was creative, and – despite its
limitation to the surrogate form of communality, namely the state – it was
spirit as well. We can call this the republican spirit. The men who called on
this spirit as leaders or spokesmen of the following state revolutions can be
called *Monarchomachs*, using the term popularized by Barclay.[62]

Thomas More criticized the conditions of his time with wit and sensitivity. His utopia portrayed a community in which work, science, and the
arts were cultivated peacefully; a community without estates of the realm,
a community administered – for practical reasons – by a prince who, like
all public servants, is elected by the people; a community that tolerates
many different denominations united in a kind of deism that serves as a
state religion and is expressed in the form of public reverence of divinity;
a community, finally, that sees religion as private matter, while morality
serves as a uniting secular principle.

We know that Thomas More was beheaded by Henry VIII. In fact, in the England of Henry VIII we can witness most clearly the defense created against the European state revolutions: the tyranny of an absolute prince condoned by Protestant teachings; and we must indeed speak of tyranny, no matter how overused and trivial the term may appear. There is no other way to describe what the princes became: they became tyrants who disregarded the rights of their subjects and created a conflict between themselves and the will of the people (or the will of those truly representing the people).

The great European state revolutions, led by the Monarchomachs, turned against these princes. They aimed at transforming the state into a social structure where free and prosperous communality could flourish, protected by a constitution and laws. This goal combined two ambitions: first, to reinstall and expand certain social traditions, namely the old institutions of federations, of the estates and of parliaments, of charters and certified contracts; secondly, to employ reason in order to self-confidently reveal and present what is right and natural, while overcoming all that is bad, rotten, pretentious, and unworthy.

The state, supported by Roman law and the teachings of Protestantism, had entered the world as absolutism and the power of the princes. The intention now was to take another step and to turn the state into a general political community; namely, a nation. This was to be done with the help of both the spirit of Antiquity and the new individual love of freedom.

We have already seen that what dies *as spirit* remains as an *opinion*, a *conviction*, or as *faith*. This means that the political revolution still had strong religious connotations. In this respect, there was hardly any difference between Protestants and Catholics. It is not correct to speak of radical Jesuit currents on the one side and Protestant princes on the other. For example, in the country that saw the first great state revolution, France, Catholicism and Protestantism mingled to a degree where they were hardly distinguishable. Protestant Monarchomachs became spiritual leaders of a revolutionary Catholic people's movement.

The man who was the most significant and the most powerful expression of this development was not on the barricades, but was a solitary writer; a man who truly reached beyond all denominations, even beyond Christianity itself. His weapons were the weapons of logic, objectivity, secularism, and individualism. I am talking about Etienne de La Boétie, the more important friend of the more famous Montaigne.[63]

146

It was neither its Caesarian centralism nor its successful kings that allowed France to take the leading role in Europe's political development for a couple of centuries; it was the free and secular French spirit that already had a great predecessor in Rabelais.

In the England of Henry VIII, the connection between Protestantism and the power of the princes found its most extreme and violent form. A common spirit was still alive, however, and the Germanic-Romanic institutions of law, as well as Christian law and its public institutions, resisted Roman law. It was at these intersections that the struggle for the modern state – for the republic (we use this word in its widest sense) – first occurred. It cannot be our task here to study the people's movements and their internal conflicts in detail. We can only provide a sketch of the related history of ideas…

When studying the historical period in question it is necessary to point out the influence of individual people; people who embodied and articulated the new spirit, and who formulated all the relevant questions for the coming centuries. The first example of such a person in England was the bishop John Poynet. The title and the chapters of the volume he published in 1556 summarize the central issue of the struggles that were about to shake Western Europe:

> "A Short Treatise on Political Power, and of the true obedience which subjects owe to kings and other civil governors, with an Exhortation to all true and natural English men: 1. From Where Political Power Grows, for what purpose it was ordained, and the right use and duties of the same: & etc. 2. Whether Kings, Princes, and other Governors have absolute power and authority over their subjects. 3. Whether Kings, and other Governors are subject to God's laws, and the positive laws of their country. 4. In what things, and how far subjects are bound to obey their princes and governors. 5. Whether All The Subject's Goods Be The Kaisers and Kings Own, And That They May Lawfully Take Them As Their Own. 6. Whether It Be Lawful To Depose An Evil Governor, And Kill A Tyrant. 7. What Confidence Is To Be Given To Princes And Potentates."[64]

To raise these questions means to answer them. The historian Grässe[65] wrote a few years before the events of 1848 in reference to Poynet's text: "The worst demagogues of our time do not have more horrendous ideas than the ones laid down in this scripture." This might very well be true. We will see repeatedly that time passes slowly during the age of transition and that revolutions reproduce the same contents over and over again. Grässe could have added that the ideas of the demagogues and revolutionaries of his time had their origins in the conditions of the 16th century – conditions that had not changed much by the middle of the 19th century.

John Poynet himself traces his questions and logical responses back to even earlier times. After all, a love of freedom, and corresponding theories, have always emerged within a people's consciousness when a restrictive and exploitative power tried to establish itself. It was, for example, the German monk Mangold von Lautenbach who suggested during the reign of Kaiser Henry IV[66] chasing away any king who has turned into a tyrant and has hence violated the contract with his people; according to Mangold, he deserved to be treated no different than any "thievish swineherd." In fact, Mangold even suggested following Brutus's example under certain circumstances.

In a similar vein – and at a time when Friedrich Barbarossa and his jurists wanted to revive Roman Caesarism – it was the famous scholastic John of Salisbury[67] who presented a theory of the state in which the prince's role was that of *aequitatis servus* and *publicae utilitatis minister*. John stressed that if the prince diverted from this role, he would abuse the power entrusted in him, turn into a tyrant, and hence become the enemy of the community. As a consequence, it was not only justified to kill him, but a holy duty.

In Italy, when the city-states began to fight for their freedom, it was Marsilius of Padua[68] who presented his idea of a democratic system with a *civis principans* (a "princely president") who was impeachable at any time, since real power lay with the citizens and was administered by expert parliamentarians. Poggio, Aretino, and Machiavelli[69] also proclaimed their support for the republic and turned against the power of the princes. This fight turned from one of isolated rebels to one of revolutionary nations.

Around the same time, the great freedom struggle of the Netherlands against their Spanish king, Philip II, ensued under the leadership of William of Orange. It was successful, and the new spirit – with the help of arms and diplomacy – established the first European state republic governed by the States-General of the Netherlands in 1581.

Meanwhile, the St. Bartholomew's Day Massacre had happened in France under the patronage of Catherine de' Medici,[70] and the French were close to a revolutionary eruption. The French people followed the events in the Netherlands passionately, regardless of whether they were Catholics or Huguenots, clerics, scholars, politicians, or common people. Some went to the Netherlands and took an active part. In fact, two French politicians played a major role in resuscitating Poynet's fight during the revolution in the Netherlands: the famous jurist François Hotman and the great statesman Hubert Languet.[71] They both published highly influential books in the 1570s: Hotman, his work *Franco-Gallia*, and Languet (under the pseudonym Etienne Junius Brutus), *Vindiciae contra Tyrannos* [Revenge Against Tyrants]. Both were Protestants, but that special kind of French Protestant who contributed significantly to the fact that the spirit of the French people was filled with vibrant, sparkling worldliness instead of dead Christendom. These French Protestants were largely responsible for the replacement of an absolute monarch crowned by God's grace with the belief in communal well-being within a constitutional state. For quite a long time, however, these modern Protestants were persecuted in France and had little choice but to serve foreign Protestant princes with their lively spirit, especially in Germany. In other words, the only way they could serve their own country was from the outside.

While the Catholic princes were no longer able to do anything without the modern logical spirit of the Jesuits (who considered the world in all its complexity), the Protestant princes had become dependent on the French Huguenots. Also, Hotman and Languet served many different princes, and what Mornay[72] said about his friend Languet is true for both of them: "He has learned one thing from getting to know the world: to despise it."

Eventually, both Hotman and Languet found themselves involved in the revolution in the Netherlands and published the aforementioned texts, which anticipidated later French publications. In *Franco-Gallia*, Hotman argued that the French kings had always been elected, and that the estates should retain the right to elect them, and, more importantly, impeach them. The much better known Languet directs his words generally *in tyrannos* [against tyrants], focusing on France in particular.

Languet – also a wonderful writer, and, despite his use of Latin, a very modern Frenchman with an elegant tone and a sharp humor – turned into a peculiar and pensive person, but free and self-confident. His extensive travels, which had taken him all the way to Lapland, certainly contributed to this. He tells us of an encounter in Lapland with indigenous people practicing ancient pagan rites (he considered them fire-worshippers) and how this had taught him something he could not have learned anywhere else: an indifference towards all denominations and a natural dignity and nobleness. Languet must have been deeply impressed by the dictates of self-discipline and the commitment to one's ideals within a harsh and unrelenting natural environment. After all, the same qualities character-ized him and the other early revolutionary thinkers we have mentioned: individuals who have lost connection to the people (to a degree that made many of them melancholic), but who were at the same time early protago-nists of all the people now moving towards freedom.

In the case of Languet, his life, his letters, and especially his work *Vindiciae* are all proof of this. Languet knew that it is the spirit that creates and sustains peoples and cultures. Sharing the sentiments of his advanced contemporaries, the spirit that mattered most to him was the spirit of the republic: "Law is spirit; or, if we will, the diversity of united spirits. Spirit, however, is a part of divinity." Arbitrariness, lust for power, recklessness – everything that we would call "anti-social," while he and his time called it "unlawful" – is deemed animalistic: "Those who rather obey the king than the law seem to prefer animal rule over divine rule."

The reader will understand now why I say that the development in the direction of the *res publica*[73] is not simply an expression of reason, but of creative spirit as well. For the early revolutionaries, state and law were God manifested in man. State and law were principles of equality that united the individuals in a higher form of social organization. In their times, this seemed liked the only possible way of uniting people. As we witnessed later (or have we? or will we in the future?), this spirit only proved unifying and divine during acts of aggression, destruction, and revolution. It only developed power in this context. Otherwise, it revealed no positive quali-ties. It was not creative, and neither did it have intrinsic unifying power. As a consequence, once the fighting was over, it turned into what it had originally fought: external violence.

During the time of revolution, those men are the greatest who most decidedly and effectively *negate*. The greatest man is the one whose critique reaches the minds of the people and the subjects. Languet came close. However, he was still filled with remnants of the mild, positive, common spirit of the previous era. He says: "We are all masters. As individuals, we relate to one another as brothers, as cousins, as relatives."

Languet relies even less than others of his era on reason or a golden state of nature. He trusts in the libertarian and federative traditions and institutions of the Middle Ages: *Freibriefe,*[74] contracts, estates, parliaments, and municipalities – and especially the election of the king by the people. He claims, for example, that it had been a common, centuries-old practice for the church in Spain to ostracize a king who had broken his oath to his people. He was denied any legal protections and was left at the people's mercy. These customs, Languet says, were forgotten in his own times: "It appears to be a general rule that *nobody* takes care anymore of what *everybody* should take care of." As a consequence, "the audacity of the kings and the delinquency and indolence of their representatives become so enormous that the kings appear to have forever legitimized their decadence and affectation, because they remain unchallenged ... However, this does not diminish the right of the people! It only increases the injustice of the king..."

Languet anticipated the fate of his country and its royals. Two years after he formulated the above words, the big revolution erupted, leading to the deaths of two kings. It finally failed, however, and absolute power was reestablished with the succession of the Louises who inherited – if we follow Languet's contemplations – the injustice of their predecessors. Two hundred years after Henry III died by the dagger, the same, long buried revolution erupted again, and Louis XVI, administering the legacy of his fathers as a petulant weakling, died at the guillotine.

Meanwhile, the princes had come under increasing pressure both from the men of high spirit and from the people. In Scotland, the great George Buchanan, a famous satirist, poet, and historian,[75] revived the struggle of the Scots against Mary Stuart at the age of seventy-three in his dialogue *De jure Regni apud Scotos* [On the Rights of the Crown Among the Scots] He asks: "What then shall we say of a tyrant, a public enemy, with whom all good men are in eternal warfare? May not any one of all mankind inflict on him all penalty of war?"[76]

It seems obvious that it was not the arrival of the new scholastics – the Jesuits – that caused teachings of individual terrorist struggle. Buchanan was much closer to Protestantism than to Catholicism (even if his free mind cannot really be tied to any particular denomination). He was a friend of Montaigne's, but more prudent and more withdrawn. When he taught in Paris, one of his students was the very young Etienne de La Boétie, who would eventually go far beyond his teacher, not only in energy and powerful poetic expression, but especially in ingenious reflection.

151

Soon it became impossible to hold back the French people any longer. When Henry III – one of the brutal cowards and lewd bigots so common among monarchs – became king (after abandoning the throne of Poland in order not to lose the succession to the throne of France), the country's gallant people were ripe for revolution.

One often interprets the ensuing battle as a struggle between Catholics and Huguenots, and as a fight between a president and a king. This is not really accurate. What was crucial was that a federative and republican revolution fought for ancient rights and freedoms. The spirit that carried the fight against absolute monarchy was a peculiar mix of old libertarian Christian ideals and new principles of reason and lawfulness derived from the spirit of Antiquity and individualism.

The fight was led by the towns, especially Paris with its sixteen precinct representatives elected by the people. The objective was to shake off the king's yoke and declare Paris a free city-state. As the next step, it was planned to summon the estates and to turn France into a free state, following the example of the Netherlands, where quite a few French politicians were active. An enormous number of militant revolutionary pamphlets were published, and the clerics took a leading role in the fight for freedom and people's rights. The priests of Paris released a statement proclaiming that "the assembly of the estates possesses an inalienable sovereignty and the power to unite and to dissolve." Jean Boucher, the priest of St. Binoit, declared that "the prince comes from the people – his power must not rest on hereditary succession or violence, but on free elections." Another priest, Pigenat, contended that the only way in which God would speak was the voice of the people: "*Vox populi, vox Dei.*"

Partly it was the old Christian spirit that was speaking here, now blended with both reason and aggressiveness, and other new forces (sometimes consciously, sometimes not), namely the creative spirit of the democratic idea. In part, the Christian rhetoric was but a matter of habit or strategy. In any case, it stood in stark contrast to the Protestant notion of the "divine right of kings."

Eventually, the priests were joined by the scholars. On December 29, 1587, the Sorbonne declared that "one ought to take away the princes' right to rule when they prove themselves incapable of ruling, just as one takes away the public servants' right to administer when they prove themselves incapable of administering."

In May 1588 came the Day of the Barricades.[77] The people of Paris took to the streets with arms, led by their sixteen precinct representatives and the clergy. The masses advanced successfully to the Louvre, "to fetch Brother Henry to the profession." Henry had fled.

The people proceeded, and for some time it looked as if they were going to follow in the footsteps of the Netherlands. In December, the Bastille – already a stronghold and a symbol of absolutism, provocatively placed in the midst of working people's homes – was stormed. The Arsenal was next, and then the Sorbonne went from the theory of constitutional law to praxis: it renounced the people's duty to serve the king and denied Henry III legal protection. Once again, a monarch was at the people's mercy.

The situation in France echoed that of the treacherous kings of Aragon described by Languet a decade earlier.[78] It was no surprise that King Henry III was killed on August 1, 1589, by Jacques Clément, a young Dominican.

Almost exactly two hundred years later, on August 4, 1789, the Bastille was again taken by the people, this time in the course of the revolution of the Paris Commune. (The Bastille was not only taken to free prisoners – as some still maintain who are busy calculating the numbers of prisoners in the Bastille.) This time the revolution spread across the entire country. The national assembly abolished feudal rights and gave Louis XVI (the heir to Henry III) the title "Restorer of French Freedom." Four years later, Louis was executed too.

Some years before the events of 1848, Richard Treitzschke, the German translator of Languet, called the 1789 revolution a microcosm that "anticipated a slow, but glorious development." I would like to use the word *microcosm* in a different sense: revolution *per se* is a microcosm as it comprises, in an incredibly short amount of time, the spirit of individuals, and demonstrates the achievements possible for the people. It serves as a beacon of hope across all ages.

In revolution, everything happens incredibly quickly, just like in dreams in which people seem to be freed from gravity. Of course, one might experience a similar sentiment when awake: in late hours of reflection, observation, imagination, and creation, we may be convinced that we will achieve all of our goals and that all of the obstacles we face will eventually vanish. Then, however, the day arrives and we can no longer understand our optimism, our courage, our faith. These dark days are long and we will spend many nights remembering them, lying awake downhearted, listless, sad, and depressed. Until another night arrives when we appear to grow wings that will carry us beyond everything that stands in our way; and during those nights, we will remember other nights when the sun rose within ourselves, when everything seemed possible, and when we felt that it was our duty to fight and to achieve our ideals.

This describes the relationship between fast, dream-like revolutions and the tedious periods in-between them. We will go back and forth between these phases until a spirit comes that allows us to realize our nightly dreams every day. Then our spirit will truly come to life. It will no longer be reduced to moments of aggression and destruction that, after some time, always give way to barrenness and anguish.

It is impossible to properly analyze the rise and decline of the French Revolution within the scope of this text.[79] In short, it came to a dispute between the bourgeoisie on the one hand and the people and their representatives on the other. Henry IV cleverly used the opportunity to establish military despotism, while reconciling with the bourgeoisie and the churches. The uprising soon turned into a mere underground surge. The Paris Commune remained antagonistic for some years. There were also many clerics who, for a long time, refused to say a prayer for the king. But broad sections of the French population were wooed by the king's clever diplomacy and impressed by his success in a few wars.

During revolution, people are filled by spirit and differ completely from those without spirit. During revolution, *everyone* is filled with the spirit that is otherwise reserved for exemplary individuals; *everyone* is courageous, wild and fanatic, and caring and loving at the same time. Once the spirit is gone, however, they all want *panem et circenses*, "bread and circuses," again.

The French people of the time wanted victories on the battlefields of both politics and love. Henry IV was able to satisfy them on both accounts. He turned into the "father of his people," as some remarked cynically in the 18th century. When François Ravaillac murdered Henry IV,[80] he did so without a people's movement behind him, but was still connected to the suffocated revolution.

It is common to compare the deed of Ravaillac to the Monarchomach teachings of the Spanish Jesuit Mariana,[81] or the scriptures on constitutional law by the Jesuits Bellarmine and Suárez;[82] scriptures that were hardly more advanced and radical than the bourgeois constitutional theories of Bodin or Grotius.[83] We have seen, however, that we are not dealing with a special Jesuit spirit here, but with a movement that involved the Protestants of Western Europe as much as the Catholics; a movement that drew everyone. Mariana was part of this. His book *De Rege et Regis Institutione* [On the King and Royal Institutions] was published in Toledo in 1598. In the famous sixth chapter of the first volume, Mariana investigates the deed of Clément and declares it great and laudable. He continues to discuss (without any apparent fear) the appropriate measures for dealing with a king who has seized power by violent means and without the people's approval; a king who contradicts the will of the people and "who can be dispossessed and killed by anyone."[84] Mariana concludes that such a king must be judged by the estates. However, if this is not possible, then the following applies: "If someone decides to kill him on his own account, based on the will of the people, it can hardly be called an injustice."[85] Mariana even specifies this: It is brave to attack the tyrant openly – but it is wiser to lure him secretly into a trap. If this works and the conspirators stay alive, they will become heroes. If they fail and consequently die, they will become martyrs who have pleased both God and the people.

As we can see, Mariana's revolutionary theories of war differ only in their dryness from the teachings of the Protestant Monarchomachs. Trying to reduce an enormously broad spiritual movement to the teachings of the Jesuits is nothing but the outcome of denominational quibbling. The "modern men" of the era were not just Romanic Jesuits, but also English sectarians and Dutch and French Protestants. There were also Jesuits who proclaimed Monarchomach ideas, and Jesuit students (assuming it is true that Clément was one) who turned them into practice.

Let us go back sixty years to meet a man who we have already named a couple of times; a man who conceptualized revolution, gave it a psychology and a classical appeal. This ought not to surprise us. In the era of individualism, geniuses precede events. Their work often remains ineffective for an extended period, appearing to be dead. It remains alive, however, waiting for others to apply it practically; men of great and strong spirit, even if they do not necessarily have identical visions and do not share the same fate of solitude.

According to Montaigne, Etienne de La Boétie, who died at the age of thirty-three, wrote his *Discours sur la Servitude Volontaire* [Discourse on Voluntary Servitude] at the age of sixteen.[86] Even if we cannot be certain of the exact age, he was very young and wrote it no later than 1550. A few copies of the text circulated for some time, but it was only shortly after the St. Bartholomew's Day massacre – and long after La Boétie's death – that the text was officially published by some revolutionaries, against strong political objections by Montaigne. The treatise was later republished as an appendix to Montaigne's *Essays*, together with Montaigne's moving memories of the life and death of his young friend.

Etienne de La Boétie always remained within the Catholic Church and seemed to have an intimate but free-spirited Voltairian relationship with God. He embraced what his times (and the entire 18th century) called reason and nature, i.e., an objective perception of things and logic, with independence and courage as associated values. La Boétie was posing the question of his era, if people had only sufficiently understood it: how can an entire people, consisting of countless individuals, allow a single person to torture them, abuse them, and rule over them against their interests and against their will? A person, no less, who is neither Hercules nor Samson, but a pathetic man, often the most cowardly and feminine of the whole nation. If we followed nature, La Boétie proclaims, we would obey our parents, defend reason, and live as nobody's servant.

La Boétie does not want to argue about whether we are born with reason or not. He leaves this question to the "scholars." What is important to him is that nature serves God, guides humanity, is always reasonable, has formed us all according to the same image, and has created us as comrades and brothers. In his view, nature has not created some who are stronger and smarter than others so that they can prey on them like robbers in the woods, but "to allow brotherly love to flourish, and to provide help to those who need it."

So where does the enormous power of the tyrant come from? External coercion cannot be the answer. If two equally strong armies face each other, and one is driven by lust for power, while the other is driven by the will to defend its freedom, then the army of freedom will win. The tyrant's power comes from the voluntary servitude of humanity.

> "How can he [the tyrant] have so many eyes with which to control you if you do not lend him your own? How can he have so many hands to hit you if you do not provide them? How can he ever have power over you if not through you? How can he persecute you if you do not allow him to? What can he do to you if you are not the dealer of the thief who

robs you, and the helper of the murderer who kills you? What
can he do to you if you are not your own traitor?"

Where does such incredible complacence come from? There exists a
natural quest for freedom. If animals knew ranks and honors, then they
would strive for freedom. The answer to our question is this: at some point
– caused by outside attack or internal corruption – human beings lost
their freedom. They were followed by individuals who never knew freedom
and had no idea how sweet it tasted. It became a habit to be complacent in
servitude; and habit is stronger than nature. "The natural may be as good
as it is, but it disappears if it is not nurtured. Nurture will always determine us, whatever form it may take, and regardless of our nature." Just
as fruit trees can be manipulated to bear fruits that are naturally foreign
to them, so can humans be manipulated to accept the loss of freedom.
Humans today do not know any better than to be subservient. They have
always been that way. "They turn themselves into the property of those
who oppress them, because time has made this appear inevitable. In reality,
though, time never rights a wrong but multiplies it endless times." (I repeat
these words here to show that Languet – who uses them too – must have
known La Boétie's book.)

Of course, there are always some who are born with gifts that distinguish them from the masses. When they improve their naturally excep-
tional minds by further study, they acquire knowledge and, most importantly, they experience freedom. Freedom might be completely absent from
their daily lives, but they can imagine it. They feel its spirit. However, they
do not know one another. They have been robbed of the freedom to speak
and act. They remain lonely in their spiritual worlds.

The second reason for servitude is that it both unnerves and softens
people. The tyrants have always done everything in their power to support
buggery, flirtation, playfulness, gluttony, and unmanliness among their people.

The third reason for servitude is that the monarchy has co-opted
religion and has aligned itself with the priests. The crown came to be surrounded by miracles, and the king equipped with holiness and divinity. "The
lies in which the people believe have always been invented by themselves."

The fourth reason for servitude is that a special class of people has
placed itself between the king and the people. The members of this class
try to profit from the king, from the people, and from their peers. Tyranny
creates profits for them that seem to outweigh the pleasures of freedom.

La Boétie's book offers a charming psychological theory of the courtier. He writes that one can pity the king for being surrounded by them. At the same time, one must also pity the courtiers, since they have been abandoned by God and humanity, while being forced to subject themselves to the king and his treatment. The peasants and the craftsmen are oppressed by the king telling them what to do. The courtiers, however,

"have to think what the king wants them to think, and often enough they must anticipate his thoughts in order to please him. It is not enough for them to obey, they have to please him. Serving him destroys them, yet they are expected to share his joy, to abandon their tastes for his, to change their nature and constitution. They have to be attentive to every single one of his words, to the tone of his voice, to his gestures and facial expressions. Their eyes, feet, and hands – everything has to be ready to read the mind of the king and to satisfy his wishes. Is this a happy life? Is this a life at all? Is there any place in the world less bearable than this? And I am not speaking of humans of a higher kind, just of those with healthy senses. Or let's just say of anybody with a human face. What situation is more desperate than not owning a single part of yourself, but being entirely dependent on someone else: for your well-being, for your freedom, for your body, and for your life?"

According to La Boétie, the king suffers too. He can neither give nor receive love. Love and friendship only exist among good people. "Where there is cruelty, dishonesty, injustice, there cannot be friendship." "When businessmen gather, it is not an alliance, it is a conspiracy; they do not support each other, they fear each other; they are not friends, they are accomplices."[87]

La Boétie asks, what can be done against the servitude that has come over humanity? What can be done against this disaster that is a disaster for everybody, for the king, for the courtiers, for the public servants, for the thinkers, and for the people? The Monarchomachs have tried to give plenty of answers, so have the scholars of constitutional law, the politicians, Bodin, Grotius, Althusius,[88] Locke, Hume, and many others. And theirs are not the only answers we have to consider, as the ongoing revolution produces a growing number of theories in many countries. But let us stay with Etienne de La Boétie here: we need nothing, he says, but the desire and the will to be free. We suffer a servitude that is voluntary. It almost seems as if we humans reject the beautiful gift of freedom because it is too easy to attain: "Be determined to no longer be servants and you will be free. I do not encourage you to chase away the tyrant or to throw him off his throne. All you need to do is stop supporting him – you will see how he will consequently, like a huge colossus deprived of its base, tumble and disappear."

Fire can be extinguished by water. But conspiracies to chase away or kill a tyrant can be enormously dangerous when conceived by men who are after fame and glory and hence prone to reproducing tyranny. Such men abuse the holy name of freedom. Modest heroes – like Harmodios, Aristogeiton, Thrasybulus, or Brutus the Elder[89] – who liberated their fatherlands and truly gave them freedom are rare. Brutus and Cassius might have established freedom temporarily by killing Caesar (the most dangerous of all tyrants, because he was not mean and brutal, but deprived people of their rights and freedoms under a cloud of humanity and mildness), but this period died with them.

The point is: tyranny is not a fire that has to be or can be extinguished. It is not an external evil. It is an internal flaw. The fire of tyranny cannot be fought from the outside with water. It is the source that has to be eliminated. The people who feed it must stop doing so. What they sacrifice for it, they must keep for themselves.

> "It is not necessary to fight the tyrant. Neither is it necessary to defend oneself against him. The tyrant will eventually defeat himself. People only need to stop accepting servitude. They do not need to take anything away from the tyrant, they must only stop giving to him. Nor need they change themselves, they need only stop hindering their own development. … When the tyrant does not receive and is no longer obeyed, he ends up naked, without force and without power. He ends up being nothing. He shares the fate of a root that is left without water and nourishment: it turns into a dry, dead piece of wood."

La Boétie's book remains almost entirely unknown in Germany. In France, it was revived by Lamennais.[90] I have summarized its contents here rather extensively for two reasons: one, because I think that when discussing the social psychology and the preconditions of revolution it is best to cite those who first formulated what is essential; two, because this allows us to forego presentations of many later revolutionaries and revolutionary movements, since they have either remained far behind La Boétie or, at best, merely repeated his thoughts; even if some of them are much better known.

The fight against tyrants remained revolution's focus for a long time. Yet the relevance of La Boétie's words does not end here. Even if future revolutionary struggles will focus less on certain individuals and more on the institution of the absolute state, only few of La Boétie's words will need to be altered in order to thoroughly understand this new revolutionary phase. If individual revolutions are recurring microcosms that summarize and precede revolution's general ideals, then La Boétie's essay is the most perfect of all of revolution's microcosms. It represents a spirit that first appears to be solely negative, but soon draws enough power from this negativity to proclaim the positive that has to come even if it cannot be described yet. La Boétie's essay already said what others would later say in various languages: Godwin, Stirner, Proudhon, Bakunin, Tolstoy... The message is: It is *in* you! It is not on the outside. It *is* you.

Humans shall not be united by domination, but as brothers *without domination*: an-archy. Today, however, we still lack the consciousness for such a positive motto, so for now the motto must remain: *without domination*: – .

The negation of rebellious souls is filled with love; a love that is force, in the sense formulated so well by Bakunin: "The joy of destruction is a creative joy." Rebellious souls know that humans are brothers and that they ought to live as such. But they believe that it suffices to overcome external obstacles and external powers. This, however, will make men brothers only while they fight – and maybe overcome – these obstacles and powers. A common spirit can be felt during the revolution – but it does not come to life. Once the revolution is over, it is gone. We can hear people say: yes, but the spirit will remain once the revolution has *truly* been victorious, when the old can never rise again! According to the same logic one might say: if I could hold on to my dreams and mold them by memory and consciousness, then I would be the greatest poet. Both the reality and the idea of revolution define it as a period of health between periods of sickness. If there were no sickness before and after it, it would not be what it is.

A true change of humanity needs a supplement to revolution, something of an entirely different nature. We can add a variation to the motto above: *without domination – with spirit*! It will not suffice, however, to just call upon the spirit. The spirit *has to come over us*. It needs a cover and a form. It does not listen to the mere name "spirit" either. Nobody knows its real name and what it really is. This creates an anxiety that helps us to be committed to transition and progress. Not knowing what to expect means to keep ideas alive. What would ideas mean to us if they were already real?

During the English Revolution, which marked the end of the first wave of the European state revolutions, spirit neither progressed nor deepened. Neither the Independents nor the Rationalists nor the Levellers added anything to the arguments of the Monarchomachs. They followed them like slaves, transforming the originality and fierceness of these early radicals into a kind of new scholasticism. John Milton – uncouth, pedantic, and Rabelaisian, rather than strong and refined – was their most important representative; Algernon Sidney – author of the intelligent but boring *Discourses Concerning Government* – was their last.[91] Their logic was sharp and accurate, but they focused only on the old literary canon, the biblical and Roman examples, as well as on the state; they never took any new developments into account. Hence, the incentive to turn ideas into reality soon faded. We never saw them addressing the conflict in the depths of the human heart. In fact, they never analyzed the true causes for social conflict in any way. Instead, they criticized – as many others had before – the supposed wickedness of men. It is mind-boggling how these republicans could remain blind towards the outside world, towards social and economic conditions, towards all true life and human needs. Milton's praise for the revolutionaries of his time says it all: "No illusions of glory, no extravagant emulation of the ancients inflamed them with a thirst for ideal liberty; it was the rectitude of their lives and the sobriety of their habits that taught them the true and safe road to real liberty."[92] If this is true, we ought not be surprised by where this led them after the execution of Charles I and Cromwell's so-called republic and actual military dictatorship; namely, to constitutional monarchy, the Bill of Rights, economic freedom, the flourishing of British trade and industry – and the most gruesome social conditions imaginable. This was where all of Europe's scholastics and bourgeois scholars of constitutional law had been headed for a long time, and what England's medieval development had prepared: the *clearing of estates*,[93] the eradication of the peasantry, the damage of the soil, and the substitution of agricultural land with pastoral land and hunting grounds. All of this devastated England at least as much as the Thirty Years War[94] devastated Germany.

On the European continent, English developments were followed with extreme anxiety. Charles' execution shocked everyone. However, the people were busy with war, the consolidation of their lands, and the establishment of the nation states. They were exhausted by the enormous loss of blood and the destruction of villages and fields. Furthermore, spirit and community had been almost completely lost, at least in Germany. In France, the gap between the educated (including courtiers) and the uneducated had become enormous. Many sought escape in literature. While some used moving verses to stubbornly ask God for peace, others chastised new fashion trends in uninspired, satirical rhymes. Grimmelshausen wrote his fantastic depiction of German degeneration,[95] and Logau[96] chiseled his malignant epigrams: *"König Karl von Engelland / Ward der Krone quitt erkannt: / Dass er dürfe keiner Krone, / Machten sie ihn Kopfes ohne."*[97]

During these times of ferocious fighting between different states in Europe, and in England between the people and the prince, we meet another figure who preferred to anticipate the future with his eyes rather than with his feet and hands; a man who preferred peace and calm to agitation. He lived in a prison in Naples because his ideas had caused unrest and rebellion. This ought not to surprise us. If a man with a calm spirit decides to interfere in daily affairs, he will inevitably incite people to revolt. In this case, he was a philosopher and a poet. We are talking about the Dominican Tommaso Campanella, who called himself "The Bell." He analyzed his times and presented in barren and dry (almost loveless) words his utopia of the *City of the Sun.*[98]

As a philosopher, he straddled the border between an all-encompassing mystical demonism (in the tradition of the Middle Ages' universalists,[99] in particular Nicolaus Cusanus) and the detailists[100] and psychologists like Gassendi[101] and Locke. In his politics, though, he did not consider the intimate connection between the Christian tradition and the magical forces of the Renaissance. He only saw reason, natural law, and the principle of the state. This caused him to envision some kind of state communism. The relativities, connections, and various associations of former times seemed dead and gone. Individualism only seemed to bring evils. In Campanella's utopian system, the state has taken control of everything: love, family, property, education, religion. Campanella foresees the *absolute* democratic state, the state that knows neither society nor societies; the state that we call social democratic.

Campanella, a terribly lonely man, embraced the world with the love that accommodates and nurtures a thinker's spirit. He found no love, however, in the life around him. He saw only violence resulting from a lack of reason in his time, and violence in the name of reason in the time to come.

Thomas Campanella died and was buried in Paris in the monastery of the Dominicans (who are called Jacobins in France). It is a strange coincidence that the men who were both the children and fathers of the spirit during the great French Revolution – a spirit that he, Campanella, had first articulated – gathered in this very same monastery and took the same name.[102]

The republican spirit played a dominant role in all the revolutions of the 16th and 17th centuries, but religion still mattered. Freedom of conscience was often more important than political freedom. Whenever people fought for domination instead of freedom, the oppression of one or the other religious community was always implied. The final year of the Thirty Years War, however (a war led by states, yet aggravated by religion), coincided with the beginning of the revolutionary times, when the Fronde emerged in France.[103] The day the Peace of Westphalia was signed[104] also brought France a constitution, a Magna Carta of civil rights, and the independence of its parliament.

This revolution was still intrinsically linked to the conflicts between feudal lords and princes. However, for the first time, religious matters were irrelevant. As a consequence, the bourgeoisie, tax policies, and the self-confidence of the townspeople became central political factors – more so even than in England. In its beginnings, the Fronde against the queen regent and against Mazarin[105] was a prelude to (and almost an exercise for) the people's revolution of the 18th century.

At first, the Fronde turned less against the tyrant himself than against the terrible administration of the state and its ministers (as we will see, this is a characteristic of all modern revolutionary movements). It was due to the stupidity and lack of restraint of the queen – the "monarchos-tultitia"[106] – that she, as the wise Cardinal of Retz[107] said, "lifted the cloak that must always cover the truth about the relations between the rights of the people and the rights of the royals if they are to exist side by side."[108] The different contingencies of the Paris parliament soon formed a general parliament and a sort of National Constituent Assembly that took on "the reformation of the state, of the financial administration, and of the wastefulness of the courtiers."[109]

Today, the events in Russia confirm once more how ridiculous and tragic recurring state revolutions are, and how they change individuals in power without changing power's structure. The revolution of 1648 even included a precedent to the famous Tennis Court Oath.[110] In response to the queen's attempt to prohibit further meetings of parliament in the Salle de St. Louis, the parliamentarians responded that "the meetings of the Chambre St. Louis will continue under all circumstances."[111]

On the August 26, 1648, the barricades were up in Paris again. There were around two thousand, manned by one hundred thousand armed Parisians. The barricades had been quickly erected and proved effective. The royals were kept at bay. They remained intimidated for quite some time. The queen, Mazarin, and the entire court fled. A war between Paris and the royals ensued. However, not unlike in England and later in the French Revolution of the 18th century, the soldiers soon took over the leadership of the struggle from the increasingly divided bourgeoisie. Before long, the war was no longer the war of a revolutionary parliament, but of the Prince de Condé.[112] It also made the contradictions between the bourgeoisie and the urban proletariat obvious, and demonstrated how quickly the revolutionary *citoyen* can turn into a peaceful *bourgeois* when the question of property arises and when a tedious armed conflict lasting months or years replaces a passionate, improvised uprising lasting hours.

There was, however, a revival of the revolutionary spirit towards the end of the fighting. A movement emerged that fought both Condé and the royals, that was decidedly federalist and republican, and that aimed at uniting all parliaments, and especially all of the country's towns, in one big alliance. The Cardinal of Retz was one of those involved. He stated: "Given the sentiments in the country right now, the union of the towns can have significant consequences and pose a serious threat to the monarchy. Many want to end royal authority and turn France into a republic."[113] However, there was not enough strength left. This prelude to the modern state revolutions never bore a republic. It ended with Louis XIV seizing power.

It is characteristic of our transitional era that nothing is ever brought to a conclusion, that everything that is spiritually dead rises again physically, and that we have to fight the same fight over and over again. Absolutism has established itself – either in its pure form or, after certain compromises, under a democratic mantle. Even the wars between the different religious denominations and the struggle for the freedom of conscience are not over yet. We are unable to deal with any issue once and for all.

If someone wanted to succinctly summarize what is commonly accepted in philosophy today, or in the sciences, or even in practical life, he would end up with an empty sheet of paper. This would be equally true if he decided to summarize what all can agree is false; in other words, without including any positive agreement. However, such an agreement, and with it unity, exists during revolutionary times. During these times, people are usually bewildered by the chaos and the heterogeneity of the preceding era. Chamfort[114] has left us a marvelous illustration of this with his commentary on the Encyclopedists, Rousseau and Voltaire, written during the earliest phase of the 18th-century French Revolution. He saw it as characteristic that people spoke of events that had happened only a few years before the revolution as something that had happened "back then." In the year of 1791, everything that had happened before the revolution seemed to have happened a long, long time ago. So much had occurred and life had been so rich during the two years of revolution that months seemed like decades and people experienced themselves as part of history. Even simple people were lifted beyond their own limitations. Only such euphoria – only the richness of each minute – can explain why so many seemed indifferent to the terror: they faced death with a laugh, just as they killed with a laugh. Here is what Chamfort had to say about the era before the revolution:

> "France was a peculiar place. ... Antagonism and contradiction were all around. New shining lights battled old misconcep-
> tions. ... Two nations existed within one. This was obvious
> everywhere: in encyclopedias and in absolutions; in the politi-
> cal economy and in Jansenist miracles;[115] in *Emile*[116] and in
> Episcopal mandates; in the royal parliament and in the contrat
> social; in expelled Jesuits, chased-away parliaments, and perse-
> cuted philosophers. The nation had to endure this chaos before
> it was ready for the ideas that would lead to a free constitution."

As we have already seen, each revolution remembers its predecessors and becomes their child at the time of its eruption. However, in the case of the 18th-century French Revolution, the country's 16th-century revolution was completely forgotten. This revolution had to be rediscovered in our times. The reason is that there had been a decisive change within Christianity that did no longer allow the 18th-century French to understand the ways and means of the fight for freedom and a constitution two centuries earlier. If Chamfort returned, he would see that the free constitution that the revolutions of the 16th and 17th centuries aspired to, and that the revolution of the 18th century was able to realize, exists; however, the chaos he described remains as well.

The second wave of state revolutions consists – not considering the prelude of the Fronde – of the American War of Independence, the 18th-century French Revolution, and the revolutions that followed the French example everywhere in the 19th century. Essentially, the ambition of these struggles remained fighting absolutism and the arbitrariness of power, and implementing a constitutional state and a code of law. There were changes, however. The struggles did not – at least not as exclusively as before – focus on the king. They focused less on his brutality and arbitrariness, and more on the incompetence and ignobility of his servants. From the end of the 18th century to the middle of the 19th, the king increasingly found himself on the sidelines. Many no longer considered him particularly relevant, and viewed him with indifference. The *contents* of politics became more important than its form or its representatives. The struggle was no longer a struggle against one person only. Its ambitions could no longer be summarized in one notion. Complexity had replaced simplicity. Revolutions had become specific. The king needed to make horrendous mistakes in order to raise particular attention and ignite a republican movement.

The revolutions of today are but intermediate revolutions; no matter how strong their spirit appears. They are revolutions that no longer focus on the absolute king, but do not yet turn against the new form of totalitarian power: the absolute state. In fact, the revolutions of today support the absolute state, they want to expand and participate in it. The king as the main enemy has been replaced by the estates on which the monarchy rests: the clerics and the aristocracy. It is the estates of the realm that are under attack; in other words, the republican basis of many former revolutions.

The bourgeoisie has become strong through trade and manufacturing. The third estate wants to complete the process of atomization and individualism. There remain remnants of the times of ordered multiplicity and federations in form of privileges and other obstacles to social change. The estates of the realm, however, are as much gone as the guilds; collectively owned and maintained lands (remnants of old commons) are divided; trade alliances are abolished and prohibited. Today's ambitions are not reduced to freedom of conscience and equal participation in the state's affairs. Apart from the rally cry *Freedom and Equality!*, there exists another that is characteristic for this era (meaning almost the same to many as the former): *Freedom and Property!*

The state is expected to secure absolute freedom of trade and business. It is expected to dedicate its laws, the independence of its courts, the guarantee of its subjects' rights, as well as the separation of the legislative and the executive, to this purpose. There shall only be the state and its citizens. No institutions outside of the state shall be tolerated. As far as the freedom of property is concerned, however, even the state must not interfere. Many seem convinced that this is not only the most effective way of guaranteeing the citizens' well-being (no matter whether they are employed or self-employed), but also of increasing the nation's wealth.

A new scientific discipline has been established in connection with both the domestic and international consolidation of the nation state: political (or national) economy. This echoes the emergence of the disciplines of constitutional law and international law as a consequence of the republican movement. At first – already revealed by its name – one thought of political/national economy as little more than an expansion of constitutional law. The state, so one reckoned, ought to administer its economy in the same way that a respectful citizen or merchant administers his personal economy.

The economic movement was in its beginnings the continuation of the republican struggle against the absolutism of the Protestant prince. For the absolute prince there was no difference between national and private property. Everything belonged to him. He could theoretically seize all private possessions and realty if the need arose. He was the country's sole master. It was the republicans and economists who introduced the modern notion of the state.

The first republicans still equated the state with the *états*, i.e., the estates. For the economists the state was equated with the *État*, i.e., a structured administration of an impersonal entity with income and expenses. They soon realized, however, that what was needed was not only a balance of taxes and expenses, but also a balance of trade: a statistics of import and export. Besides state wealth there was also national wealth. This was when the nation, as the union of the people, was rediscovered; a community that was not the state, but not just a sum of individuals and individual achievements either. One discovered that many economic procedures could be described, generalized, and structured: the production and storage of goods; the acquisition of raw materials; the consumption of commodities; the exchange of commodities against money and credit; finally, the various forms of contractual obligations, purchases, and businesses.

Without knowing it – in fact, this is still the case – the second great discovery of the era had been made. The first had been made by La Boétie.

It was probably not he himself but his revolutionary editors who called it *"le contr'un"*: *the one that is not one.*[117] *Le contr'un* is a people consisting of individuals with a sense of individual sovereignty who terminate their obedience to the one and rise above servitude. Along these lines, we might call the discovery outlined above *"le contr'État"*: *the state that is no state.*[118] *Le contr'État* is a community of people outside the state; not as a sum of isolated individual atoms, but as an organic unity, a web of many groups.

We do not know much yet about this supra-individual entity filled by spirit. One day, however, we will understand that socialism is not the invention of something new, but the discovery of something that has existed for a long time. Once the right bricks have been found, the right builders will be found too.

Expanding on this discovery and the new forms of knowledge, we can see two currents developing: one attempts to incorporate all aspects of economic life into the state, including those that have traditionally been independent; the other focuses on the discovery of society (and its own forms of communality) as a third social entity between the individual and the state. A common spirit can only arrive when there is something it can fill and form; something that it can live in and spread out from. (We will address this in more depth below.)

What precedes the common spirit – and the new forms of alliance – is the intuitive, theoretical, creative spirit of science uniting the dispersed elements that have come undone. Political economy is also a science that creates forces of praxis by advancing theory and spirit. At first, political economy tried to establish the so-called laws of individual economy – a senseless and pointless enterprise. Political economy never established useful categories, but led to unifications of reality. The more it chased the laws of capitalism, the more it helped create social economy. It searched for abstractions that are, in the best case, useful names. What it found was instead the reality of unification and spirit. If we consider this in depth, then the old contradiction between nominalists and realists[119] vanishes: the universals are only inadequate *nomina* for what is in fact – not only in human life – an alliance.[120] This is what Plato called an *idea*: a common spirit perceived by individual senses.

This digression was needed. Before we part, let me add this: what I have called a lack of spirit (*Geistlosigkeit*) – a lack that has caused isolated and alienated individuals throughout human history – can also be called sensualism. The senses and sensual perception freed themselves during the Renaissance after a particularly non-sensual spirit had disappeared. However, spirit always inhibits the senses. The Greeks were also a non-sensual people at the peak of their culture. They were mainly concerned with the typical and general.

If a new spirit arrives, a spirit that unites us as a people, then it will be a spirit that will also free the theorists from the ordeal of the indistinct yet inquisitive senses, i.e., from the haunting world of concrete singularities. This spirit will create order and unity in our individual lives, in our communality, and in our thinking.

If I were not writing this text now, in 1907, while we are still in the midst of the events that I have tried to describe; or if I had the power to make things the way I would like them to be; or if I were allowed to use utopian language, then I could say that the two currents outlined above – which had already emerged before the eruption of the state revolutions of the 18th and 19th centuries – will give the revolutions and progressive attempts of the 20th century their character: the first current – that of the "politicians" – will eventually be joined by all political parties with the goal of incorporating economic life into the state, and of solidifying its democratic constitution, not only to protect its citizens from one another, but to also to shield them from poverty, abandonment, and despair. The second current – that of the "socialists" – will come to the conclusion that, after the discovery of society and the free and diverse forces of communality, the state is left with only one task: to prepare its own abolition and to make way for the endless ordered multiplicity of federations, organizations, and societies that aspire to take its place and the place of economic individualism. For the socialists, the state and its economy lack meaning, direction, and spirit.

There will also be a third current, one that stands apart from the others with a smirk and twinkles of joy and hope in its eyes. The adherents of this current believe (rather than openly declare) that the way towards the complete abolition of the state goes precisely through the absolute democratic economic state. Since there has never been an absolute truth, they will probably be wrong too. In fact, all they do is prove the stagnation of our times.

These are the things I could proclaim if I did not have to write this text now. The fact that I am bound to these times, however, forces me to present a utopian image of the revolutions of the 18th and 19th centuries and their ongoing consequences. Our times of stagnation are as distant from those revolutionary movements as from the ones to come. Yet, I have immersed myself completely in them. I cannot say whether I have always been, or whether I am again now. This is of little importance. What matters is that the spirit of regeneration will soon come over us and replace the spirit of revolution; otherwise, we have to evoke the spirit of revolution once more, and maybe more often than that. This is the destiny of revolution in our times: to provide a spiritual pool for humanity. It is in revolution's fire, in its enthusiasm, its brotherhood, its aggressiveness that the image and the feeling of positive unification awakens; a unification that comes through a connecting quality: love as force. Without temporary regeneration we cannot carry on and are condemned to drown.

The obvious weakness of the youngest generation shows even in the fashionable superficiality and political detachment of its greatest talents. Yet it is too early to give up. Let us remember the biggest of all revolutions, the French Revolution of the late 18th century. It has always been the impossible that has created humanity's new realities. In the French Revolution the impossible came over many individuals and over the people as a whole. (This did not show – or only rarely – in the revolution's means and goals, but in its mood and spirit.) In the beginning, it was only about saving France from bankruptcy. Then the same thing happened that had always happened: in the English Revolution, in the Fronde, and especially in the American War of Independence. If the government had not, in rapid succession, made the most incredible mistakes and excelled in foolishness, nothing further might have occurred at all. When the great adventurer Thomas Paine dedicated his pamphlet *Common Sense* to the American people by declaring all government to be corrupt and useless – using the English government as the prime example – it was an Englishman who did so; an Englishman whose spiritual rebellion and progression would not have turned into revolution in America (just as it had not in England) and would not have caused the freest of all republican constitutions, had not the English government (and a broad section of the English people, politicized by the English Revolution) acted so foolishly towards the colonists. What makes the spark catch fire is always the stupidity, brutality, or weakness of those who govern. The people, the thinkers, the poets are a powder keg, loaded with spirit and the power of creative destruction – this proves true every time. It allows us to believe in latent, accumulative force, even when a people is at its absolute lowest.

The case of France is an example of this. When the Comte de Mirabeau[121] dedicated his draft of the Human Rights Charter to the rebellious people of the Netherlands in 1788, the French people were still far from claiming their own human rights – despite all the shining, crackling spirit of the Enlightenment, despite the humor and the freedom of exemplary individuals, and despite the French people's passionate support for the freedom struggle of the Americans. Chamfort – himself a representative of these sentiments – was right when he said that the French Revolution showed that an old and decayed people could suddenly rejuvenate and rise to power and freedom. If this was not the case – so Chamfort argues in the language of the Monarchomachs – then humanity would not only be condemned to eternal servitude but to decline and ruin. After all, we have not forgotten that we are all the same age and that we have all been corrupted more than once.

No revolutionaries had ever been so convinced to do away with all obstacles, to end all ills, to solve all problems, and to create complete happiness as those of late 18th-century France. These revolutionaries felt that it was their duty to implement what Mirabeau had demanded: a government *for the people* and *by the people*. The joy of these revolutionaries was to create peace and happiness for the coming generations thanks to their heroic efforts. This reveals an element of all revolutions, and one that was particularly pronounced in this case: during revolutionary times, people are captured by a spirit of joy.

This spirit even leaks into the grey periods of stagnation. The joyful festivities and street dances that we can still witness in Paris when the city commemorates the Storming of the Bastille is more than just memory – it is an immediate heir to the revolution. We Germans have wonderful words for such joyfulness, even if we have long ceased to be a joyful people (we were during the Middle Ages): *ausgelassen, aufgeräumt, unbändig.*[122] What these words express is a concentration of past events that spread and blossom; events that take control of the outside world and rearrange it; events that have been freed from all chains.

The joy of revolution is not only a reaction against former oppression. It lies in the euphoria that comes with a rich, intense, eventful life. What is essential for this joy is that humans no longer feel lonely, that they experience unity, connectedness, and collective strength. This is why no sensual or spiritual expression of revolution and its conditions is more powerful than Beethoven's Ninth Symphony: after the individual soul goes through deep melancholy, doubt, and fruitless attempts to find happiness and joy in solitude, it reaches for the heavens, rises above itself, and joins all other individual souls in a common ode to joy. Let us not forget its words, borrowed from Schiller's revolutionary poem: "All men become brothers where your gentle wings rest."[123]

Some try to convince us in these flaccid and weak times, bereft of sentiment and ashamed of love and affection that *brotherhood* has become nothing more than a word. Nothing could be further from the truth; we must declare it loudly and without hesitation: *humans are brothers*. This is what all past revolutions have taught us and what we will teach all future revolutions. There are words whose origins are strong enough to withstand all frivolous and narrow-minded adaptations, as well as all forms of ridicule. We owe the word *brotherhood* to the French Revolution. It summarizes its joy: humans felt like brothers – and, let us not forget, like sisters too!

Unfortunately, revolutions decline fast, and not only because of those who La Boétie has warned us about: the ones who seek glory and power. Every revolution inevitably reaches an end even if the utopia that inspires it is always utterly beautiful (albeit more in what it says than in how it says it). Often enough, once a revolution ends, things are not that different than they previously were. The French Revolution reached such an end very soon. The main reason was not that some sought glory and power. Neither was it that the republic was surrounded by enemies, forcing the revolution to turn into war and the republic into a military state (just like England under Henry IV and again under Cromwell). The main reason for the early end of the French Revolution was what I call the Provisional Council.[124] We have already talked about this earlier: since the revolution has no, or hardly any, positive forces that can shape regular life – in other words, since all its power lies in rebellion and negation – it has poor means of communication when it comes to the everyday life of the community. The means that it employs for this purpose are the common and insufficient means of the conditions it aims to leave behind. When, on top of this, a revolution is surrounded – and infiltrated – by enemies, the negative, destructive forces will eventually turn in on themselves. Fanaticism and passion will turn into mistrust – the worst of all sentiments between humans – and soon into bloodthirstiness, or at least indifference, towards the terror of death. Then this terror will become the only means available to those who have seized power – like the members of the Provisional Council. It is a common characteristic of the revolution to be primarily a matter of euphoria, dreams, reverie. This is especially true for the French Revolution, which used the means of political revolution to solve social problems, first and foremost the question of property. Without disregarding all of the other factors involved, this was the main reason why the revolution ceased to be a people's movement very quickly, why the people became increasingly divided, and why the *Emigrantenpolitik*,[125] which created strong external enemies, was successful.

I already mentioned earlier that we will eventually reach a point when state and society – or the surrogate of community and authoritarian power on the one hand, and the true spiritual union on the other – will be separated and when only one of them will prevail. In the meantime, however, they coexist in confusion. Their eventual separation will not be abstract but real – it will be brought on by destruction and creative spirit. For Etienne de La Boétie, retreat and passive resistance against *the one* were still directed against the king – in the future, *the one* will be the state. Then it will also become obvious that it is not a particular form of the state that causes oppression. What causes oppression is self-coercion, self-denial, and the worst of all emotions: mistrust, not only towards others but also towards oneself. All this is engrained in the notion of the state itself; a notion that replaces spirit, inner sovereignty, and life with domination, external control, and death.

In the period of stagnation that we find ourselves in, the confusion of state and society implies the confusion of political and social revolution. Nothing is more difficult for human beings than to realize, and to truly admit in thought and action, that they are not the center of the world but only occupants of a modest spot, somewhere to the left or to the right. This is true for the humans of all eras: they all want to be a peak or a goal or something special – even if they do not make the tiniest effort.

There are many contemporaries who find it hard to admit that our era is only one period of stagnation among many. But it is the truth. The time will come when what the greatest of all socialists, Proudhon, explained in unfading – albeit today forgotten – words will be clearer than it is today: namely, that although social revolution and political revolution are essentially different, social revolution can neither come to life nor stay alive without a series of political revolutions. However, in the end, social revolution means nothing but peaceful construction and organization based on a new spirit and creating a new spirit. Proudhon's *free mutual credit* and *solidary bonds* were economic and sociological terms (this admirably sober destroyer and creator loved such terms) for what we call *common spirit*, and what Proudhon, in his critique of morality (with the abruptness, and probably also baldness, of the initiator) called *justice*.

The great French Revolution – and even more so the European revolutions that followed it – confused the political and the social to the point where the two became undistinguishable. However, there is one issue where the state and society, where politics and socialism, will always touch; where a social decision can only be made by the means of politics: the issue of private land ownership. Private land ownership is not just administered by the state. It has been created by the state. This means that the agrarian struggles of the French Revolution, the struggles against feudalism, were crucial. Yet, already at the time – and even more so during the revolutions of 1848 – there were various attempts to conduct social transformation by common political means, i.e., revolutionary parliamentarianism or violence. This undermined the agrarian struggles. It also led to the proclamation of the *right to work* in the national workshops, and to a commitment of fighting for socialism by violent means (a commitment that was more propaganda than actual attempt). However, as Gottfried Keller has said, freedom's last victory will be bloodless – political revolutions will clear the way, literally and in every other sense.[126] Simultaneously, institutions will be established for a Bund of economic communities; a Bund that will free the spirit imprisoned in the state.

Of course we cannot sit idly until the spirit comes and calls us. The spirit that filled the Christian era found already established *Markgenossenschaften*[127] and many institutions, both diverse and unifying. In other words, it is not the spirit that sends us on our way, it is our way that allows the spirit to rise. We do not walk because we have legs – we have legs because we walk.

Those who have followed me up to this point know where we are headed and what we will build and create. We have dissolved into atoms. We produce goods (alienated commodities) for financial profit rather than for consumption. Money is not a mere convenient means of exchange. Money is a spawning monster. Not to mention the fictitious values that the rich use to rob each other...

Armies of dispossessed people have to serve those who have no interest in creating wealth for them. All they are interested in is creating wealth for themselves. Other armies, mostly composed of the same dispossessed people, have to secure and expand markets for their nations and to keep the peace with weapons in their hands – and pointed against their own chests.

All the enormous economic and technological progress we are witnessing today is integrated into a system of social degeneration. As a consequence, each improvement of the means of production and each improvement of labor conditions worsens the situation of the workers. Our aim is that all those who understand the conditions we live in and who feel incapable of supporting them any longer unite in alliances and work for their own, immediate consumption: in settlements, in cooperatives, and so forth. This will hardly be possible without sacrifice. We will soon have to confront the strongest obstacle imposed by the state: the lack of land. At this point, the revolution – whose trajectory up to this point has been outlined above – will enter a new phase that we can say nothing about. The same goes for social regeneration; we can proclaim it, but we can say nothing about how it will develop. It will depend on the following generations and their judgment. But I plan on speaking about the coming socialism elsewhere.[128]

In countless texts and proclamations from 19th-century revolutionaries – Proudhon, Bakunin, Marx, the Internationalists, all those involved in the various revolutions of 1848, Mazzini[129] and other revolutionaries, the Communards, the Spaniards, etc. – we can see that for many the big revolution was not limited to France, nor was it over at the beginning of the 19th century. In their understanding – and they are right! – there is only one long revolution, with periods of stagnation and sudden re-eruptions. Especially the revolutions of 1848 must be seen as a phase of the revolution delayed by the Napoleonic Wars. There has been a particularly long period of stagnation since the events of 1870-1871. It is the result of a previously unknown permanent state of war that is ironically called peace, and by the rise of nationalism.

The fact that none of the revolutions attempted so far has succeeded in achieving their goals is not sufficient reason to assume that revolution will erupt again. We have already seen that no revolution will ever achieve its goals. Revolution is a means in itself: it serves the revitalization of force and spirit. This does not mean that the revolutions we have seen have not created anything lasting and meaningful. They have. Camille Desmoulins[130] expressed this aptly in a letter to his father written in 1793:

> "The revolution seems to have failed to instill reason in the rulers of the republic. It appears to do little other than replace ambition with ambition, greed with greed. At the same time, it has brought us the freedom of the press, which I consider a great benefit. This we certainly owe to the revolution. The new regime also sees to it that scamps are hanged and imbeciles ridiculed. All in all, the situation is without doubt better than before. In particular because there now exists hope of improving the lives of the people. No such hope existed under despotism, when most were damned to be slaves..."

This summarizes the legacy of the last great revolution. It has certainly become difficult to hang scamps again; but it has also become difficult to guillotine brave and courageous men (even if they might still find themselves in prison). And as far as the freedom of the press goes: it has become much harder to suppress the freedom of opinion in general. Besides, nothing is taken for granted any longer, and nothing is considered holy and unchangeable. Everything is in motion...

I have not talked about the recent developments in Russia in this text.[131] Nobody can say at this point whether this is the beginning of a long revolutionary process or whether the revolution is already on the decline. It is equally unclear whether Russia is merely catching up with the rest of Europe or whether it is actually paving the way for Europe's future.

In the end, we hardly know anything about the path that lies ahead of us – it might lead via Russia, it might lead via India. We only know one thing: it will not lead via the currents and struggles of today – it will lead via the unknown, with sudden turns, and towards buried treasures.

---

1. Maximus Tyrius (2nd century AD), Greek philosopher; also known as Maximus of Tyre.

2. On October 10, 1907, Landauer writes to Fritz Mauthner: "I have created the word 'topia,' as an opposite to 'utopia,' as a kind of joke – but I soon found it rather useful..." (*Gustav Landauer. Sein Lebensgang in Briefen*, 1: 172).

3. The German verb *geschehen* means "to happen," "to occur." In its substantive, mostly philosophical, use, it means "everything that happens."

4. In 1755, Lisbon was almost entirely destroyed by a massive earthquake and subsequent tsunami.

5. Literally, "self-awareness and self-cause."

6. *Archeus* is an alchemical term, popularized by Paracelsus (1493-1541), referring to the principal force of life.

7. Literally, "world spirit" (also translated as "world soul"), the *Weltgeist* is Georg Wilhelm Friedrich Hegel's concept of an all-encompassing absolute spirit as the foundation of all being.

8. *Völkerwanderung* or "Migration Period": widespread and far-reaching migration movements of European peoples from the late 4th to the late 6th century.

9. Phidias (ca. 480-430 BC), Greek sculptor; Sophocles (ca. 496-406 BC), Greek dramatist.

10. 1) The Protestant Reformation is framed by Luther's proclamation of the "Ninety-Five Theses" in 1517, and the Peace of Westphalia in 1648.
2) German peasant uprising of 1624-1625.
3) The rebellion against and temporary abolition of the English monarchy from 1640 to 1660.
4) The Thirty Years War was waged in Europe between Protestants and Catholics from 1618 to 1648 and ended by the Peace of Westphalia.
5) The American War of Independence refers to the American Revolutionary War from 1775 to 1783.

11. When Landauer speaks of the "French Revolution" without further specification, he refers to the French Revolution of 1789. This usage has been adopted in the footnotes.

12. Reference to Friedrich Nietzsche's concept of the *Übermensch* (also translated as "overman"); regarding Nietzsche's influence on Landauer see "1870-1892: Landauer's childhood and youth" in the Introduction, as well as the essay "Twenty-Five Years Ago."

13. Kant taught that human perception was determined by "*a priori* categories" intrinsic in each human being.

14. *Comment by Gustav Landauer:* "I want to bring attention – as I could on many occasions – to the great work of Constantin Brunner, *Die Lehre von den Geistigen und vom Volke* [On Spiritual Men and the People]. The first volume will be published in 1907. I also need to emphasize that many of the sentences in this text could not have been written without Fritz Mauthner's fabulous critique of language." [Constantin Brunner (born Leopold Wertheimer, 1862-1937), German philosopher. The book mentioned by Landauer was published in 1908.]

15. Friedrich (von) Schlegel (1771-1829), German philosopher and literary critic.

16. In German, *lebensähnliche*; literally, "of similar life."

17. The Holy Roman Empire, led by German Kaisers, existed from 843 to 1806. It was mainly a nominal political union.

18. Reference to Aristotelian scholasticism, most famously represented by Thomas Aquinas (1225-1274).

19. Paracelsus (born Philip von Hohenheim, 1493-1541), famous alchemist.

20. Nicolaus Cusanus (1401-1464), pantheist and Catholic heretic.

21. Hagen and Siegfried are characters in the *Nibelungenlied* [The Song of the Nibelungs], a popular German epic poem from the Middle Ages, most famously adapted in Richard Wagner's opera *Der Ring des Nibelungen*. Odysseus and Achilles are prominent figures in Greek mythology and were the title protagonists of Homer's famed epic poems.

22. Walther von der Vogelweide (ca. 1170-1230) and Heinrich von Morungen (ca. 1170-1220) were two of Germany's most celebrated Minnesingers.

23. Archilochus (ca. 680-645 BC), Greek poet; Horace (65-68 BC), Roman poet.

24. The German *Wahn* is difficult to translate. Commonly, both "delusion" and "illusion" are used. In Landauer's usage, the term rather refers to a state of powerful ecstasy, not far from a Nietzschean notion of *will*. Landauer writes in "Volk und Land. Dreißig sozialistische Thesen" [People and Land: Thirty Socialist Theses] (*Die Zukunft*, January 12, 1907): "*Wahn* ... is but a different name for spirit. ... *Wahn* is each banner that people follow; each drum roll that leads people into danger; each *Bund* that unites people and turns a mere collection of individuals into a new form, a new organism. *Wahn* is the human being's most precious, highest quality."

25. Roughly, the ideal of a bodily, moral, and spiritual union.

26. Novalis (born Friedrich Freiherr von Hardenberg, 1772-1801), German Romantic poet. He evoked the symbol of the *Blaue Blume* [Blue Flower] in his posthumously published novel *Heinrich von Ofterdingen*.

27. Pseudo-Dionysius the Areopagite (late 5th to early 6th century).

28. The German original here is *Schichtung*, which usually translates as "stratification." However, in Landauer's usage of the term no notions of hierarchy are implied. Landauer rather refers to the (ordered) coexistence of independent social groups and communities within a social field (society) shared by all. In other words, Landauer's *Schichtung* is horizontal rather than vertical.

29. Political assemblies with varying constitutive power.

30. Literally, "the art of building."

31. Baron Münchhausen (1720-1797), German adventurer famous for bold and incredible tales. There are several literary and artistic adaptations of his life.

32. *Comment by Gustav Landauer:* "I am taking these quotes from Peter Kropotkin's beautiful book *Mutual Aid*, which I have translated. It is full of useful facts on medieval life and society — ideal for those who do not want to go through many lengthy historical monographs."

33. William Whewell, *History of the Inductive Sciences* (London: John W. Parker, 1837), 344-345. Landauer seems to have copied the quote from Kropotkin's *Mutual Aid*, where it is falsely ascribed to the British scholar Robert Willis (1800-1875). William Whewell (1794-1866) was a renowned British polymath.

34. *Sachsenspiegel:* the most important German law book of the Middle Ages.

35. Ulrich von Hutten (1488-1532), German Reformer.

36. Scholasticism: dominant philosophical school in the late Middle Ages, aiming at a reconciliation of Christian faith, Aristotelian philosophy, and the natural sciences.

37. Peter Chelčický (ca. 1390-1460).

38. "Liberty is not the daughter, but the mother of order" — quote from Proudhon's *Solution du problème social* [Solution of the Social Problem] (1848).

39. Literally, "original Christendom;" sometimes referred to in English as the "Apostolic Age."

40. Friedrich Reiser (1401-1458), Waldensian and Hussite; Kaiser Sigismund (1368-1437) was the Holy Roman Emperor during the time of the Hussite Wars. The origins of the *Reformation des Kaisers Sigismund*, a radical anti-clerical treatise, are unclear. Several scholars have questioned Reiser's authorship.

41. Michael Gaismair (1490-1532), Tyrolean peasant leader and social reformer; the *Landesordnung* [literally, "order of the country"] was a draft for an egalitarian and democratic Tyrol.

42. Refers to a 1445 peasant revolt in Switzerland's Bernese Oberland ("Bernese highlands").

43. Andreas Carlstadt (1486-1541), German theologian; Thomas Müntzer (1488-1525), peasant rebel leader.

44. Konrad Mutian (1471-1526), Peter Luder (1415-1472), and Heinrich Bebel (1472-1518) were German humanist scholars.

45. Christopher Columbus (1451-1506), Italian explorer; Leonardo da Vinci (1452-1519), Italian artist and scientist, "universal genius," epitome of the "Renaissance Man."

46. Heinrich Cornelius Agrippa (1486-1535), German alchemist.

47. Nicolaus Copernicus (1473-1543), Polish astronomer.

48. Johann Georg Faust (ca. 1480-1540), German alchemist and astrologer. There are a number of literary adaptations of his life, most famously Goethe's *Faust* (1808).

49. Giordano Bruno (1548-1600), pantheist, burned on the stake as a heretic; Tommaso Campanella (1568-1639), Italian theologian and writer.

50. Comprehensive book of law compiled between 529 and 534 on the orders of Byzantine emperor Justinian I.

51. Frederick I Barbarossa (1122-1190), King of Germany, King of Italy, King of Burgundy, and Holy Roman Emperor; one of the Middle Ages' most legendary rulers.

52. Roughly, "he who rules the region determines the religion." A principle first included in the 1555 Peace of Augsburg, a treaty signed to end violent conflict in Germany between Catholics and Lutheran Reformers. It gave the individual German princes the right to determine the religion of their respective domain. Reconfirmed in the 1648 Peace of Westphalia that ended the Thirty Years War.

53. *Ecclesiastes* in the sense of "preacher." Wittenberg is the Eastern German town where Luther nailed his "Ninety-Five Theses" at the door of the Schlosskirche [Castle Church] in 1517.

54. Latin in the original; translation by Gabriel Kuhn with the help of Manfred Kienpointner.

55. "Anabaptists" is most commonly used as a general term for different radical Reformist groups proclaiming believer's baptism. The German term is *Wiedertäufer*. With "one of their currents they were named after," Landauer most probably means the group around Ulrich Zwingli (1484-1531) in Switzerland.

56. The Waldensians, named after Frenchman Peter Waldo (several spellings, ca. 1140-1218), emerged in the 12th century as an anti-clerical Christian movement preaching voluntary poverty and social justice. Persecuted as heretics over centuries, the movement was all but crushed in the 17th century, and only small communities remain today. The "Bohemian tendencies" refer to the radical Bohemian reformists of the 15th century, mainly Hussites and Taborites.

57. Antiquated German term that in its secular meaning stands for "work," "action." In medieval Christianity it referred to the importance of everyday action – in addition to faith – to please God. The concept of *Werkheiligkeit* [literally, "holiness of action/work"] is related.

58. Antiquated German adjective for "lenient," "forgiving," "soft."

59. The fictional aristocrat Pierre Bezukhov and the historical field marshal Mikhail Kutuzov (1745-1813) are protagonists in Tolstoy's *War and Peace*.

60. Military conflicts in Bohemia from roughly 1420 to 1435 between the political and religious authorities and the radical Reformers led by Jan Hus (ca. 1372-1415).

61. Conflicts between Protestant princes/royals and Catholic commoners in Germany during the first half of the 19th century.

62. Literally meaning "those who fight the monarchs" (from the Greek *makhomai*: "to fight"), *Monarchomarchs* was originally a pejorative term coined by the Scottish royalist William Barclay (1548-1608).

63. Etienne de La Boétie (1530-1563), French jurist, philosopher, and writer. Landauer played a leading role in his rediscovery during the early 20th century; Michel de Montaigne (1533-1592), French philosopher and writer, most famous for his Essays.

64. Quoted from *www.constitution.org/cmt/ponet/polpower.htm*.

65. Johann Georg Theodor Grässe (1814-1885).

66. Eleventh century. Henry IV (1050-1106) was King of Germany and Holy Roman Emperor.

67. John of Salisbury (ca. 1120-1180), English theologian and Bishop of Chartres.

68. Marsilius of Padua (ca. 1275-1342), Italian political scholar.

69. Gian Francesco Poggio Bracciolini (1380-1459), Italian humanist scholar; Pietro Aretino (1492-1556), politically influential and controversial Italian writer and poet; Niccolò Machiavelli (1469-1527), Italian politician and writer, most famous for *Il Principe* [The Prince], written in 1513 and published posthumously in 1532.

70. The St. Bartholomew's Day Massacre refers to a series of Catholic mob attacks and killings predominantly directed at Huguenots. The attacks began on August 24 (the day of commemorating St. Bartholomew, the apostle), 1572, and lasted for several months, killing an estimated 5,000 French Protestants. The massacre was instigated by Catherine de' Medici (1519-1589), the mother of King Charles IX; Catherine was the queen mother of three successive French kings and highly influential during their reigns, which stretched across three decades.

71. François Hotman (1524-1590), Hubert Languet (1518-1581).

72. Philippe de Mornay (1549-1623), Protestant writer and Monarchomach.

73. Literally, Latin for "the public thing/affair." Used as a reference to the organizational structure of society. Widely regarded as the origin of the terms "state" and/or "republic."

74. Literally, "free letter;" a decree issued by a political authority bestowing special rights upon the bearer.

75. George Buchanan (1506-1582), humanist scholar and Monarchomach.

76. English in the original.

77. Popular uprising on May 12.

78. Jacques Clément (1567-1589), radical Catholic, stabbed Henry III (1551-1589) to death during an audience presenting letters; he was immediately killed by Henry's guards.

79. Landauer presented an extensive study of the events in his posthumously published two-volume study *Briefe aus der Französischen Revolution* [Letters from the French Revolution], edited by Martin Buber (Frankfurt am Main: Rütten und Loening, 1919).

80. François Ravaillac (1578-1610), radical Catholic, stabbed King Henry IV (1553-1610) to death in a Paris alley. He was arrested and quartered by four horses two weeks later.

81. Juan de Mariana (1536-1624), Jesuit scholar and Monarchomach.

82. The Italian Robert Bellarmine (1542-1621) and the Spaniard Francisco Suárez (1548-1617) were renowned Jesuit scholars.

83. Jean Bodin (1530-1596), French jurist and political philosopher; Hugo Grotius (1583-1645), Dutch jurist and political theorist.

84. Latin in the original; translation by Gabriel Kuhn with the help of Manfred Kienpointner.

85. Latin in the original; translation by Gabriel Kuhn with the help of Manfred Kienpointner.

86. Landauer's translation of the *Discourse* appeared subsequently in five issues of *Der Sozialist* in 1910-1911.

87. French in the original; translation by Gabriel Kuhn.

88. Johannes Althusius (1563-1638), Calvinist scholar.

89. Harmodios (ca. 530-515 BC) and Aristogeiton (ca. 550-515 BC) were a legendary Athenian pederastic couple who became icons of the Greek democracy movement after assassinating a member of the dictatorial Pisistratid regime; Thrasybulus (ca. 440-388 BC) was a democratic Athenian general; Marcus Junius Brutus the Elder (1st century BC) was a moderate Roman general, father of Marcus Junius Brutus (85-42 BC), the most prominent of Caesar's assassins together with Gaius Cassius Longinus (85-42 BC).

90. Hughes Félicité Robert de Lamennais (1782-1854), French priest, philosopher, and writer.

91. Algernon Sidney (1623-1683), executed for treason against King Charles II.

92. From the *Second Defence of the People of England*; quoted from

www.constitution.org/milton/second_defence.thm.

93. English in the original.

94. See footnote 10.

95. Hans Jakob Christoffel von Grimmelshausen (1621-1676), German writer. Landauer refers to his best known work, the picaresque novel *Der abenteuerliche Simplicissimus* [usually translated as *Simplicius Simplicissimus*; literally, "The Adventurous Simplicissimus"], first published in 1668.

96. Friedrich von Logau (1605-1655), Polish-German poet.

97. Roughly, "King Charles of England wore a crown that was not his to wear, so they took off his head."

98. Tommaso Campanella (1568-1639), wrote the first (Italian) version of *La città del Sole* [The City of the Sun] in 1602.

99. Refers to the *problem of universals*, one of the main theological/philosophical debates of the late Middle Ages. Those who Landauer here calls "universalists" are usually referred to as "realists," believing in the *a priori* existence of general categories/ideas; they are opposed to the "nominalists," who claim that general categories/ideas are *a posteriori* assemblies of similar individual phenomena. Nicolaus Cusanus was not very vocal in this debate, but is named as a prominent "universalist" by Landauer for his radical pantheism, here archaically and awkwardly referred to as "demonism."

100. Uncommon expression for "nominalists."

101. Pierre Gassendi (1592-1655), French scholar.

102. Reference to the Jacobin Club, the most powerful group during the French Revolution; the Jacobins held their meetings in the said monastery — the *couvent des Jacobins* — from which their name derived.

103. Resistance movement against French absolutism from 1649 until 1653; *fronde* means "sling" in French, one of the most common weapons used in the rebellion's beginning. Eventually, the Fronde turned from a people's uprising into an aristocratic movement under the leadership of the Prince de Condé (Louis II de Bourbon, 1621-1686).

104. The Peace of Westphalia ended the Thirty Years War (1618-1648) between Protestants and Catholics in Europe.

105. Jules Cardinal Mazarin (1602-1661), Italian-born prime minister of France from 1642 until his death.

106. Latin wordplay; literally, "the monarchy's stupidity."

107. Jean François Paul de Gondi (1613-1679) was named cardinal in 1652; he was active in the resistance of the Fronde.

108. French in the original; translation by Gabriel Kuhn.

109. French in the original; translation by Gabriel Kuhn.

110. The Tennis Court Oath refers to a meeting of the national assembly during the French Revolution, when, on June 20, the assembly members gathered in a tennis court building after being locked out of their chamber by royalist soldiers. They pledged to continue to meet under all circumstances and to proceed with their plans to write a constitution.

111. French in the original; translation by Gabriel Kuhn.

112. See footnote 103.

113. French in the original; translation by Gabriel Kuhn.

114. Nicolas Chamfort (1741-1794), French poet and writer.

115. Orthodox Catholic movement of the early 17th century, named after Dutch theologian Cornelius Otto Jansen (1585-1638). Successfully suppressed by the church at the beginning of the 18th century.

116. Famous treatise on education by Jean-Jacques Rousseau, first published – amid great controversy – in 1762. Full original title *Émile, ou De l'éducation* [Emile, or On Education].

117. This is Landauer's translation. Literally, "*le contr'un*" translates as "the against-one."

118. Literally, "the against-state."

119. See footnote 99.

120. *Bund* in the original.

121. Honoré Gabriel Riqueti, Comte de Mirabeau (1749-1791), French writer and politician; represented the moderate wing during the French Revolution. In the Introduction to *Briefe aus der Französischen Revolution*, Landauer writes: "The man who I deem the truest representative of the French Revolution's original spirit and its beginnings, and the greatest nature and the strongest mind among all revolutionaries, believed in the rebirth of the French nation and of humankind not in an exaggerated and absolute, but in a realistic and modest, concrete, and balanced manner: Mirabeau was both enthusiastic and skeptical, both revolutionary and political, and if there has ever existed juicy dryness and stubborn humility in this world, then we owe this to him" (XIII).

122. Roughly: *ausgelassen* = jolly; *aufgeräumt* = cheerful; *unbändig* = irrepressible, unruly.

123. *Alle Menschen werden Brüder, wo dein sanfter Odem weilt.*

124. Landauer refers to the reign of the Committee of Public Safety in 1793-1794.

125. Literally, "politics of the emigrants." Landauer refers to French aristocrats who had fled the country and rallied the support of European royals for the French monarchy, a decisive factor for the French Revolutionary Wars that waged in Europe from 1792 to 1802; see also Landauer, *Briefe aus der Französischen Revolution*, 1: 438.

126. Gottfried Keller (1819-1890), Swiss writer. The line *Doch der Freiheit echter, rechter / Letzter Sieg wird trocken sein* is from his poem *Rot* [Red], first published in 1853.

127. *Markgenossenschaft*: rural economic and political cooperative, consisting of a number of homesteads or villages; today basically extinct.

128. Landauer already planned to write *Aufruf zum Sozialismus*, which was published in 1911.

129. Guiseppe Mazzini (1805-1872), democratic Italian nationalist and revolutionary, advocator of a united Italian republic.

130. Camille Desmoulins (1760-1794), journalist and close association of Georges Danton during the French Revolution.

131. Landauer refers to the Russian Revolution of 1905.

SOCIALIST HOPES

WHAT DOES THE SOCIALIST BUND WANT?

This is the first of three pamphlets published by the Socialist Bund to present its goals to a wider audience. "What Does the Socialist Bund Want?" was published as "Was will der Sozialistische Bund?" in October 1908. "Was ist zunächst zu tun?" [What Do We Do First?] and "Die Siedlung" [The Settlement], both of which add little to the ideas presented in other texts in this chapter, were published in January 1909 and in early 1910, respectively. All three pamphlets had print runs of ten thousand and were reprinted in various journals.

THE SOCIALIST BUND WANTS TO UNITE ALL HUMANS WHO ARE serious about realizing socialism.

You have been told that socialism can only replace exploitation, proletarization, and capitalism in a distant and uncertain future. You have been told to wait for things to "develop." We say: *socialism will never come if you do not create it!*

There are those among you who say that the revolution has to come first. But how? And from where? From above? *State socialism?*

Where are the examples, the beginnings, the seeds of true socialist labor, exchange, and community? We do not even have traces or hints; people do not even understand the necessity for these examples. Do they really want to be dependent on lawyers, politicians – "custodians of the people?" Nothing good has ever come from them.

We say that everything must be turned upside down! We refuse to wait for the revolution in order to begin the realization of socialism; *we begin the realization of socialism to bring about the revolution!*

All of the organizations that the working people have so far created for themselves address life *within* capitalism. These organizations can bring about small improvements in the lives of individuals and for certain trades; but they do not lead out of capitalism or towards socialism.

Marxism – an ideology that has played such a large and ominous role in the workers' movement – predicted that proletarization will increase, that economic crises will deepen, that capitalist competition will spin out of control, and that the number of corporations will dwindle. Then, so goes the claim, capitalism will collapse. Has this happened? Does it look like it will happen? What is the *reality*?

What does the state do? It alleviates some of the greatest suffering; it saves capitalism from killing itself using insurance, welfare, and legal interventions; it maintains the system of injustice, of senseless production, and of senseless distribution of goods. *Capitalism proceeds.* This is the result of the state's efforts; and this includes the efforts of the working class and its representatives.

What do the capitalists do? They create trusts and cartels; they pledge mutual assistance and sign contracts; they support one another instead of escalating competition; they help other capitalists to stay alive instead of exterminating them. And crises? The capitalists control crises in the same way they control production. In short, they do everything they can to prove the Marxist prediction false. The workers suffer. Socialism remains distant. *Capitalism proceeds.*

What do the workers do? How do they organize and struggle? What happens in their unions? The unions are organized within capitalism, and they are dependent on the trades and skills that capitalism needs. Through insurances and funds, through the improvement of working and living conditions, the misery of certain trades is sometimes eased, enough for "things to go on." What things? *Capitalism!*

What individuals as producers win, the people as a whole lose; especially the working class as consumers. Who truly pays the wages that the capitalists pay the workers? Those dependent on the capitalists' goods!

Improvements and alleviations are needed as long as we live in capitalism. But they do not lead us out of it; they keep us ever more under its thumb.

What will lead us to socialism? *The general strike!* But it will be a general strike of a special kind, very different to the general strike propagated by the political agitators and embraced by the impressionable masses; by those who applaud in the evening and return to the factories the next morning.

189

The general strike usually propagated suggests that we wait with folded arms until it becomes clear whether it is the workers or the capitalists who have more strength and endurance. We are not afraid to declare the following: given the ways in which capitalists organize these days, it is increasingly likely that *they* will prevail, not the workers. This is true for small strikes, and even more so for big strikes, and it is also true for a *passive* general strike. No one should be afraid to face this truth! Yes, it hurts sometimes to face the truth with open eyes, especially if you have gotten used to dusk and gloom – but it is necessary!

We demand the *active general strike*! This does not mean that we instantly turn to "fighting the state and capital." *We do not begin at the end, but at the beginning*! If nothing has been done for socialism so far, if there are no signs of it yet, then what are we going to fight and die for? For the domination of some leaders, who will tell us what to do, and what to produce, and how to distribute it? Would it not be better if we knew and did all this ourselves? Hence, we say: the action of the working people is … *work*! In the active general strike, the workers will starve the capitalists, because *they will work for themselves and their own needs*!

You capitalists will still have money, documents, and machines of course. Eat them! Exchange them! Sell them! Do whatever you want. If it does not help you, however … *then work*! Work like us. You will no longer get our labor. We need it ourselves. And we have freed it from your restraints. We now use it for the creation of socialism.

The day when this happens will mark the only true beginning of socialism. I hear some say, "Oh my, this is a long way off! *The socialist beginning is only occurring now?* We thought we were close to the end!" How can you be close to the end if you have not taken a single step yet? However, once you start your journey, you will soon see your goal clearly! The very first step is to accept the truth. It tastes bitter, just like certain roots; but once it grows, it will bear sweet fruit.

These are our first words to you, and soon you shall hear more. We will tell you in detail how to leave capitalism, how to stop serving it, and how to begin and expand socialism until capitalism – due to inner understanding or external force – will have to capitulate.

THE SOCIALIST WAY

Landauer explains his understanding of socialism through a critique of the common "individualism" vs. "communism" divide. First published as "Vom Weg des Sozialismus" in *Der Sozialist*, July 1, 1909.

W E HAVE BEEN ASKED MANY TIMES WHETHER WE "STAND on the ground" of communism or individualism. My answer will surprise many, as it not only demonstrates the inappropriateness of the terms, but of the entire question. Hopefully, it will cause people to reconsider what they are asking. The answer is: we stand on the ground neither of communism nor of individualism, but on that of capitalism. In other, and less captious, words, we are dealing with a question rife with assumptions that must be examined. These assumptions are that socialists must propose – or may even limit themselves to proposing – a complete theory, and then try to convince humanity, or a particular class of humanity, of its authority; by preaching or by other means. However, the "ground we stand on" can only be the ground of reality, the ground of conveyed and well-established institutions, injustices, and ills – no matter how much we may wish that we were standing elsewhere.

The ground we stand on is a ground we want to leave. We desire different forms of human relations. A complete theory, a utopia, a "reasonable" idea of what we want, a "proper" understanding of what is right and what is wrong are not necessarily needed. The first step in the struggle of the oppressed and suffering classes, as well as in the awakening of the rebellious individual's spirit, is always insurgency, outrage, a wild and raging sensation. If this is strong enough, realizations and actions are directly connected to it: both actions of destruction and actions of creation. This sensation is not opposed to knowledge and contemplation. However, it is no science, and it does not provide clear, extensive declarations of what we want.

The combination of innocent emotions, active forces, and instinctive knowledge of the people have already brought many great things to this world. Science and scholarly analyses have often lagged behind and only formulated theories that corresponded to what had already been created by the unified, undivided spirit. During such times, conscience is strong and effective. Conscience is the knowledge of feeling; a knowledge connected to imagination, energy, and force. What we usually call knowledge – reflection, division, categorization, dissolution, and reassembly – only reigns when conscience is weak. This is what defines our times. Our times are times of low energy and a lack of confidence, of waiting rather than experimenting and creating, of sluggishness rather than motion. The longer these times remain, the more abstruse the science and theory of society and its laws will become. As a result of our inability to head towards the dark, the unknown, and the impossible, we have philistinism instead of reality, speculation instead of life, abstraction instead of fulfillment.

In times like these, we must no longer reflect upon the reality that surrounds us and the ideas that fill our minds. We must find the people who are willing to leave this ugly, oppressive, and corrupting reality behind and proceed to a new one. We have to ask who *the creators* are. We have to ask not about people's theories and ideals, but about their strength to no longer *partake*.

No one has asked these questions yet. Everyone has always appealed to the "community," the "whole;" either in the form of the "state," the "people," or a significant, but overrated, section of them, namely the "proletariat." Everyone has appealed to mass politics – as if the masses consisted of noble and glorious individuals who only need to be told the truth before instantly turning towards it. We, however, are the first who proclaim: *Through separation to community*!

Who are the people who have the strength to no longer partake, you ask? Who are the people ready to create new forms of community? It is *the few*! There is no other answer. The ever increasing dominance of capitalism – something that Marxists have tried to sell us as a blessing – and the degeneration and spiritual decline of the people have gone too far. This is why we are forced to call upon the few who have the strength to precede. They need to do so for themselves, for their self-esteem, and not least for the people. We need them as role models and shining examples for the whole world. They must realize decency, justice, and beauty.

This is our new theory of movements: masses have always started moving only because certain individuals began moving within themselves; this gave birth to external movements that pulled others along.

I can already hear people accusing us of individualism. In fact, we do not object to this honorable attribute. We only ask for clarity. No longer must people lump together two very different things under one and the same name. We will explain this in more detail soon. First we must answer the individualists whose irritation and outrage we can also hear: we have turned to "the masses" or "the people," they say. Never! We have never called upon anyone but the individuals, the egoists, the *Eigenen*![1]

The individualists, the individualist anarchists, have always called upon the pride, the self-respect, and the sovereignty of the individual. Their usual advice for the oppressed has been: if you had as much egoism as your masters, you would not have any masters. As a simple calculation this is not entirely wrong: egoism keeps egoism at bay. The individualists have always taught that the proper egoist will respect the rights of others because he respects himself; furthermore, he will be smart enough not to attack others in order to avoid being attacked, etc. There has, from its beginnings with Mister (and Master) Stirner, always been a certain coldness of reason in these teachings. Everything remains abstract, and there is nothing more alien to these individualists than the realms of life where warmth, passion, fervor, depth, and darkness reign; where the soul unfolds its powers. However, only those who feel comfortable in these realms can understand the impact that cold abstractions can have on people at certain times. The realms we are talking about are the realms of history.

I do not think that the individualists have ever shown any understanding of why things today are the way they are; they have never shown any understanding of the relationship of the individual, the masses, and social circumstances. They always appear to believe that what exists today will continue to exist for a very long time, and that nothing can be done but to proclaim the pure doctrine over and over again. The individualists seem to be patiently waiting for several periods of transition, lasting centuries or even millennia, before monopolism disappears, before social democracy wins – and then disappears, before there will finally be a mass of egoists. They are proclaimers, "waiters;" they are inactive, they *do not do* anything. If you need an illustration of the stubborn and melancholic solitude of the individualists, the paralyzed and paralyzing isolation of those who do not separate from the masses to create new forms of community with like-minded folks, then look at Benjamin Tucker and his journal *Liberty*.[2]

The individualists often connect their ahistorical abstractions with the both wonderful and powerful economic theory of Proudhon, a theory that builds on the principle of free and just exchange of equivalent products between people united in towns, associations, and cooperatives. It seems to me as if there are two things that individualists do not understand: first, that this economic theory belongs to very specific historical circumstances; second, that it is in no way necessarily linked to the rest of their doctrine, namely the self-centeredness and the sovereignty of the *Eigenen*.

In their clear, cold, and sober language, the individualists often tell us that human beings are either respectful or disrespectful egoists. However, if there are egoists who are respectful by nature, then why worry about economic theory to begin with? Will they not naturally be decent? How could there be any danger that the wrong economic circumstances would corrupt them? Maybe we can get the individualists to agree that the theory of corrupting social circumstances – particularly popular among minds contaminated by Marxism – is vastly exaggerated. Those who are, for example, corrupted as parliamentarians are probably people who are already prone to corruption. (For the record: we do not rely on such arguments against parliamentarianism; we have better ones.) However, the consequences that we think need to be drawn puzzle quite a few egoists. We say that *no one is better suited to maintain a communist economy than true individualists. In fact, a communist economy can only be maintained by true individualists.*

Eventually, the individualists will have to agree. The most glorious of all economic theories, Proudhon's notions of free exchange and a popular bank, can only be implemented under specific historical circumstances. These existed in the past and they will exist again in the future. They need an entire people to be involved, or at least a great number of producers from all trades. This was the case during Proudhon's time, when France was petty peasant and petty bourgeois. The revolution of 1848 also allowed for the introduction of credit without interest and joint guarantee. Since then, however, Proudhon's recipe has never been applicable. People trusted Marx: they trusted historical determinism and allowed capitalism to develop into a monster.

Are there any individuals today who refuse to passively watch the trajectory of capitalism? Individuals who have understood that capitalism, the state, and even the workers themselves have provided the capitalist system with enough means to prove wrong the prophecy that capitalism will inevitably crumble? If such individuals exist, then their task is self-explanatory. They must find their inner self, they must gather, they must assess their forces. They must also direct calls for liberty, self-determination, and glory towards the souls of the servants. But they will only do so because they know that some individuals like them are hidden underneath the masses and need to be found, as they belong to the few that we rely upon. In any case, there are more of them than anyone today might think.

If the few adhere to any particular theory, they will be ineffective. They will also be ineffective if they despise the masses and retreat into their own minds and into aestheticism. We demand that they act, that they secede, and that they unite. No theory will tell them what kind of relationships or what economic systems will be possible. They will learn from the historical moment, from their numbers, their values, their determination. If possible, they will found cooperatives and popular banks, as well as their own markets. They will form an economic alliance, because they are few, but also because they will want to experiment with mutual aid and respect, knowing that economy is a collective matter, just as spirituality is an individual matter.

Historical socialism – in other words, *socialism as beginning, as way, as action* – takes abstract entities for what they are, namely images that inspire. There is no place in historical socialism for hollow ideas that only serve as melancholic mind games for isolated and inactive individuals. Historical socialism overcomes the opposition of communism and individualism; it elevates both and merges them into a higher union. It paves the way of the pioneers who turn bawdiness into self-discipline.[3] It paves the way for those who are first in creating a new people. It paves the way to the beginning of peoples uniting in freedom.

---

1. *Der Eigene* was a term used by Max Stirner for a sovereign individual; literally, "someone who owns himself." Stirner writes in *Der Einzige und sein Eigentum* (commonly translated as *The Ego and Its Own* or *The Ego and His Own*): "*Der Eigene* is he who is born free, the original free man; *der Freie* [literally, "the free man"], on the other hand, only longs for freedom, he is a dreamer and a longer."

2. See also "Tucker's Revelation" in this volume.

3. *Aus der Unzucht zur Selbstzucht*; the German wordplay cannot be reproduced.

THE SETTLEMENT

This is the most concise summary of Landauer's belief in autonomous rural communities as the most promising way to socialism. Not to be confused with the third pamphlet of the Socialist Bund. In the Bund pamphlet, Landauer adds more thoughts on the questions of land and economic organization, while this essay has a stronger manifesto appeal. It was first published as "Die Siedlung" in *Der Sozialist*, July 15, 1909.

PEOPLE WHO ARE UNHAPPY WITH THEIR LIVES HAVE LEFT TOWNS to found settlements in the country for a very long time. This has happened in North America, Brazil, Australia, England, Switzerland, and elsewhere. It is not true that these attempts have always failed. Quite a few of these settlements exist to this day. Some live according to communist principles. Others produce goods for the capitalist market, for example handicrafts, and unite in sales cooperatives.

There is one aspect, however, that separates us from these people. Most of them were content to create a space for themselves, a community that pleases their souls. Some of them were successful. They gathered enough private means to leave the misery and ugliness of capitalist existence and to create their own happiness; a happiness that suits their desires and their hearts – but cares little about others. We want to care about others; and we want them to care about us. In the midst of our country, in the midst of our people, we want to plant a pole and tell everyone who can hear us: *Look, here is a signpost – follow it!*

Psychologically speaking, one could of course say that we do what we do for ourselves as well. Yes, it is for us, it is for our satisfaction. However, we will not be satisfied if we are isolated! We want to be with our people! "Our people" – this often means people who move against those who surround them; people who move away from those who remain helpless in their misery, who do not know what to do, and who often enough do not want to do anything. *Our people* are the *new people*; they are the people and the culture that our spirit envisions. This also means that while, in a certain sense, we secede and precede for our own sake, we mainly do so for the sake of the *way*, for the sake of an ineradicable and deeply rooted desire, for the sake of what we have made the center of our being. We do not primarily separate for our *comfort* – we do it for *us*; in other words, for the revolution.

This word – "revolution" – truly helps to mark the line between us and the loners – those who do not aim at the whole and who do not understand that our movement must have a historical impact, that it must create a new spirit and new conditions; otherwise, it cannot be our movement. However, when we speak of revolution, we must also draw a line between ourselves and those who call themselves "revolutionaries," even if they are dormant or only half-awake and never do more than imagine and talk.

It can be of no great concern to us whether ten or fifty or one hundred and fifty men found a settlement, or how many new settlements will emerge in a given period of time. Our movement has centuries behind it, and now heads forward into future centuries. Some years here or there matter little. We are proud and secure enough to demand a new age; an age where people live in a beautiful and joyful world.

We want to directly link the production of consumer goods to the needs of the people. We want to create the basic form of a new, real, socialist, free, and stateless society, in other words, a *community*. However, we could use the help of everyone who desires socialism, even if they are not able to separate from the current social conditions as thoroughly as we are. They can find ways to support us even if they – at least for now – stay in their parties, unions, and cooperatives. They can help us create the example that we want to create. This will be a challenge and it will demand sacrifices.

We address in particular those who are our closest friends without knowing it: the peasants. We have to make them understand that we are not as peculiar as some of those people who call themselves socialists; we have to make it clear that we would never want to take away their land! What for? It is for them, and they already have it. If anything, they have too little of it. It seems that even the peasant associations have now forgotten something that has been repeatedly recalled since the Peasants' War, most recently in 1848, namely that the peasants used to have much more land to work.

Peasants, your enemies are not the workers in the industrial centers! Your enemies have always been the aristocrats and the big landowners! Now we want to join you and struggle for land together – we want to unite with you! You must have land, and we want it too! Once everyone – townspeople included – joins the struggle for land, and once the rally cry *Land and Freedom!* becomes the motto of the German people, there will be a cultural movement for a better life that is much stronger than anything the industrial workers have ever been able to create. It will be impossible for the rulers to withstand such a movement. They will be forced to implement far-reaching governmental measures to regulate the redistribution of land, as happened in France on August 4, 1789, when the king earned the title "Restorer of French Freedom"...[1] All this belongs to history, however. Let us stay with our own cultural beginnings...

The peasants will desire culture once we awaken their true being. Their intellect, their creativity, their liveliness, and their joy have all suffered tremendously under the reign of feudalism, aristocracy, the state, public servants, and especially the clergy. Today, peasants live between the extremes of dull, monotonous silence, and raw, uncontrolled wildness. This is why hardly anyone sees the depths of the soul, the profound understanding of the world resting inside these peasants; the beauty, passion, and determination that lies within their minds. Only those who can read people really well are able to detect the continuing greatness and refinery of the peasants of this country. All that is required is an awakening.

A difficult, yet rich and glorious task has been handed to us. No one so far has tried to bring love and spirit to the peasants. The spirit we speak of is a spirit of *realness*; a spirit that transforms, plows, and harvests both social conditions and humanity.

The peasants need people who support them; people who settle with them, who help them to work their fields, who join them in artisanry and industrial work during the winter months, who share practical skills with them, who loosen their stiffness, who rouse them from their fairy-tale sleep, and who show them how to stride and dance – and it will be a different kind of dance than the one practiced in the village inns today!

As far as tradition is concerned, it cannot be forgone completely if we want to create a beautiful settlement. We cannot create a beautiful settlement from ideas and theories alone. It is best to join an already existing village, where we can revive the old, almost forgotten communal institutions in a new kind of union.

The socialist village, with workshops and village factories, with meadows and fields and gardens, with cattle and flocks and chickens – you big city proletarians, get used to the idea, as alien and strange as it may at first seem! This is the only remaining way to begin the realization of socialism. Socialism is the return to natural labor; it is a natural, multi-faceted connection of all activities; it is the union of intellectual and manual labor, of artisanry and agriculture, of education and work, of play and work. Think about how your children grow up today! Think about the horror of child labor in capitalism! Think about how alienated today's schools are and how they produce empty hearts and barren minds! Think about how self-explanatory the union of work, recreation, and education – including the most advanced sciences – will be in rural settlements!

It is not only the urban proletariat that must get used to this idea before it will eventually turn into will and desire. There are also the artists, the scholars, the stay-at-homes, everyone who is doing pure intellectual labor. They are all separated from reality, from realization, from nature, from the use of all of their organs and muscles. However, they have not adopted the division of labor voluntarily; a division that leads to some people only working physically and losing their spirit, with others turning the highest that life has to offer – life's luxury, life's religion: knowledge, reflection, feeling – into a commodity, a daily job, a business. The latter are all "journalists," in other words: intellectual peons. It is much the same concerning those who remain outside the "brain market" – most of them are still alienated from reality and occupy nothing but their intellect, day and night.

There are many people today who see no alternative to the lives they live. This must change! Once the change has come, it will no longer be necessary to make your leisure hours as long as possible and haggle over every single one of them. Labor – and leisure – will become part of life's natural flow. Everyday life will be transformed. Your personalities will grow; like boulders, like mountains – high and strong! A new life will come. You will have hours to yourself, and you will share the hours that belong to everyone with the community. This community has to be created – for yourselves and for others. It does not mean that anyone will deprive you of your solitude, but that solitude will regain its rightful role: religion, ceasing to be what it has become today: a commodity.

You will find what has been said strange and confusing. Do not forget, however, that we have only begun to turn to you and to everyone else! Those who are part of us will hear what we have to say, and will descend into this new element, into the future life; they will fill our ideas with their own experiences, their own desires and observations; they will think *beyond*; and they will finally recognize the natural as what it is, no matter how fantastic it might look at first; they will join us in our way; they will help us lay the ground for a new communal life – a ground from which beautiful and rich new individuals shall arise.

We have drawn a first sketch of the settlement that we must create, and of what we have to do. This sketch reveals the necessity of setting many things in motion in order to turn what is now in our spirits and hearts into reality. We are facing innumerable challenges. There is plenty of unfarmed, barren land. We have to start from nothing. No one has even attempted *to begin* yet; *to realize* socialism. This Herculean task evokes a feeling that I will describe with the following words: everything around us appears fallow, derelict, inactive; at the same time, we can sense how something in us is emerging, an insatiable desire: we want to transform, we want to realize, we want to be ten times the number that we are, we want to make each day last twice as long, we want a hundred arms to help everywhere. After all, we can hear the calls from across the land: *Seize, push, act! Make it a pleasure to live!*

---

1. At a meeting of the National Constituent Assembly abolishing feudalism.

SOCIALIST BEGINNING

This is one of Landauer's most popular pieces. He provides concrete examples of how to implement socialism within the confines of the capitalist state. First published as "Sozialistisches Beginnen" in *Der Sozialist*, September 1, 1909.

MEANS AND ENDS ARE NOT TO BE DISTINGUISHED IF ONE pursues a real life, i.e., the realization of thought. It is an old mistake to impose an invented ideal, a blinding fantasy. It is an old mistake to name a goal, and then ask with resignation, "What can we do to achieve it?" No worthwhile goals can ever lie ahead of us in some distant future. Our goals must lie behind us and push us forward. They have to drive and motivate us. We have to free ourselves from the apparitional and schematic notion that there can ever be complete socialism and that all that needs to be done is to remove the fine line between the social conditions of today and the social conditions we wish for. "America is here – or nowhere!"

Socialism is not an end that requires means. Socialism is action that carries its ends within itself. The social conditions of today are the legacy within which we operate. Too often do we accept this legacy as a dark, dull, and inescapable destiny. Socialists are the ones who do not see things this way; they are the ones who question. Socialists are those who want to organize their common affairs reasonably and purposefully on the basis of a humane, good, honorable, and respectful conviction. True socialism is clear, simple, and self-explanatory – at least for those who do not mistake "traditional" for "right."

Socialists do not share the prejudices of traditional schools, sects, and parties. They do not believe that one class of people is destined to make better socialists than another. (At least as long as there is no evidence of one class of people having more reason, decency, and energy than another.) Socialists will also abstain from wincing every time money or capital is mentioned – contrary to the half-wits and dogmatists. Money and capital can be harmless and useful things. Money can be nothing but a signifier of credit, i.e., of mutual trust and solidarity. Even metallic currency, despite its traces of exploitation and violence, can be part of reasonable and decent interaction. In any case, money is indispensable for the time being. Socialists are so secure in their good will and righteous nature that they are of good conscience and a light heart.

It is certainly true that we are few, and it is likely to remain this way for quite some time. However, we must not despair and become gloomy. What we need are cheerful voices; voices that remind us that the few will turn into many!

People have already acquired means for the first socialist settlement – they have appealed for support, sold stamps,[1] saved pennies, etc. We welcome this and nothing can be said against it. However, there are means that seem more valuable to me than asking for the support of sympathizers. Means that are *more* than means, means that are *immediate expressions of socialism*. All they require is going beyond talking about the Socialist Bund to *become* the Socialist Bund. What is required is that those of us who are committed, determined, and cheerful move to the center of all those who want to leave the emptiness, confusion, and misery of random capitalist commodity production in order to reach reason and unity.

Sometimes we are disheartened. This is normal for beginners. The same is true for sometimes being dark, pensive, vague, and secretive. The ignorance and the poorly digested doctrines of the masses organized in political parties often rises up before us like the Chinese Wall. It is little wonder that we can get angry. However, we must not forget that the masses have been turned into what they are over hundreds of years. The individuals who are different show themselves because we approach all individuals as if they were different – this is how we find those who truly are, making it possible for them to join us. This is an apt and well-tested strategy: if you want to awaken reason and energy from dormancy you have to assume that they are not dormant. You cannot awaken someone if you do not approach them as if they were not sleeping.

I can be more concrete when talking about means as immediate expressions of socialism. Let us, for example, talk about the amalgamation of consumption. It is something that we have already talked about before, but without ever going into much detail. We have often remained too general by pointing out that as consumers we are not part of capitalist production, which also allows us to come together and unite as human beings. However, we must not leave it at the level of such general declarations. We must instead aim straight at reality and make changes. So let us provide some examples of what is possible...

Not too long ago, we have heard that the central branch of the German Book Printers Union alone has almost seven million Deutschmarks in savings. The money has been invested in state and local bonds, and similar things. These millions come from membership fees and predominantly serve the purpose of guaranteeing support in cases of unemployment, sickness, invalidity, and travel in search of work. The Book Printers Union is just one example of many. Numerous millions of Deutschmarks are owned by German unions.

Any individual with a socialist spirit within these unions would ask: Why do so many of us travel? Why are so many of us unemployed – and not because of the economy, but voluntarily? Why do some rejoice when they are laid off? Why do we become sick voluntarily; or at least stay officially sick longer than what we actually are? (No honest person will deny that this is often the case.) Such an individual would also ask: What do we need the most when we suffer from weariness and sickness, when we are convalescent patients? The answer is: change and recovery! In terms of change, we need change in our working environments; we need labor that frees us from the monotony of capitalist commodity production. In terms of recovery, we need sanatoria, homes for the sick, and access to nature. In short, *we need socialism to recover from capitalism*. For any thinking person this is self-evident.

What our unions have to do is to build true and effective institutions of support and solidarity. They have to create *realities*, immediate aspects of socialism. If the unions want to help those of their members who suffer from the monotony of labor, who feel that they lead alienated lives, or who have other physical and mental problems, then they have to create settlements. They have the means to create them all over Germany! Maybe the idea has been lacking up to this point. This is no longer the case! The next step is to form the right organization to implement it. We must also propagate the idea, and we must not be deterred by the conciliatory and defensive objection that "the workers will not want to do this." This is just too simple. When have people ever immediately understood what serves their interests best? We will defend and realize our idea, and we will not back down!

I will give you another example. Every summer members of all classes go on vacation. This is yet another expression of the need for recovery. Some travel near, some far, but there are millions of people every year who leave their familiar surroundings in order to recuperate from the work that they have grown tired of. In cities like Berlin, Frankfurt, Nuremburg, or Munich – to name but a few – the guesthouses are overcrowded. People have to pay exorbitant sums for accommodation, especially in the abovementioned travel hubs. What if the vacationers and travelers were organized? What if they committed themselves to only staying and eating in guesthouses that they themselves – i.e., the organization that they have founded – have built? It would be easy to secure credit through a mortgage and we could very quickly end one of the most despicable forms of exploitation. Those who travel will then always live at home, in houses that have been built for them out of solidarity. On a small scale, the traveling salesmen have already shown what is possible if travelers' unite their interests. However, they were content with pressuring the guesthouse owners for discounts. It is characteristic to be content with halfway and insufficient solutions if you are only looking for personal benefit. This will not be the case among those who aim at a true transformation of our economic foundations. These people will demand a new spirit. They will go far and will lead many initiatives of the kind outlined here.

These were only two random examples from an enormous range of cooperative possibilities. Nowhere is the cooperative idea stronger than in our Bund. Our Bund is destined to found and stimulate these wonderful, inspiring associations that will unite millions of people to eradicate intermediary trade and to establish consumer unions and alliances. We know that the working class and the petty bourgeoisie already have some consumer alliances. However, they do not understand the real potential of consumer organizations. They do not know that these organizations are destined to create a new society, a society where people will have land to work. Without land, people are still in transition. We, the Socialist Bund, are destined to transform unions and cooperatives and to give them what they need: holistic thinking, in other words: *life*.

Let us not waste any time! Let us get to work! The work that needs to be done requires deep intellectual understanding as well as hard manual labor. We have no other choice. If the circle of those who want to join a settlement remains small, not much can be done. But we are optimistic. We feel strong. We are ready to take the loose reins out of the hands of those "socialists" who have lost both vision and direction.

We have only been able here to give a couple of examples of the many activities needed to implement our idea. We will say more in the future; we will go into the details, the possibilities, and the demands. However, we will not talk about means and ends. We will not even talk about "tactics." All these old formalities have no meaning for us. We follow the principle of action that carries its ends in itself, and we urge everyone to do the same. Everyone is capable of doing this, and everyone has a two-fold interest in it: it will be personally beneficial, and it will contribute to a united and cheerful life – the kind of life that is missing today. It is our joyous task to create it!

1. A group within the Socialist Bund sold so-called *Siedlungsmarken* (literally, "settlement stamps") that could also be used as postal stamps to collect money for planned settlement projects.

THE PARTY

Landauer reports on the 1909 party convention of the German Social Democratic Party in Leipzig. The essay was published in two parts as "Die Partei" in the October 1 and 15, 1909, issues of *Der Sozialist*. It is a thorough critique of party politics and includes a description of the German Social Democratic Party's "revisionist" and "radical" wings. In this translation, some paragraphs on contemporaneous issues of domestic politics have been omitted. The subheadings have been added for clarity.

The Politician – Public and Private

AS USUAL, THE DELEGATES WHO GATHERED IN LEIPZIG THIS year to parade Germany's Social Democratic Party did so to quarrel behind closed doors, deceiving the public with a charade of power and unity. [...] This, however, was largely unsuccessful. No matter how hard these professional politicians tried to convey calmness and self-control, they once again appeared as an assembly of neurasthenics and hysterics – agitated, self-indulgent, and with an apparently inherent need to display violent temper. In the company of such men, it is almost impossible to resolve misunderstandings, to clarify facts, to leave the mania of political individualism behind, or to bridge antagonisms through mutual respect. Party conventions are gatherings whose most important people do not belong in the public eye but in a sanatorium.

I do not intend to insult the often talented, devoted, hardworking people who wear themselves out for the party in tedious political legwork. However, what kind of times are we living in when it requires a zeppelin or some similar showpiece to capture the interest of the people?[1] When people fall prey to habitual loudmouths? When this demagogy and menagerie leads the loudmouths to self-importantly compete once a year? When it appears as if this competition serves the purpose of lustful relief? It is the shameful passivity and indifference of our people that causes the sensual barbarism of their representatives. It is the people's sleep that brings about the insomnia of their representatives, and it is the people's silence that leads to the shouting of their representatives.

Our representatives no longer see themselves as a part of the people. They no longer feel accountable to them. Every year, they become more shameless in manipulating the people. This year, they used the crying injustices of the tax policies of the Reich and its states. What they refuse to understand is that if any of their boohooing ever really inspired people, there would be nothing to decry. Our political professionals must realize that the only thing their yearly *Janitscharenmusik*[2] ever arouses is their own anxiety.

What distinguishes the true and genuine politician, i.e., a leader of spirit, is quietness and inner balance. Such a man is the same person, no matter whether he retreats or engages in public affairs. There is no contradiction between his private and his public life.

The demagogue, i.e., the dangerous and immoral party leader, could once upon a time be characterized as a hypocrite flaunting righteousness in public, but leading a corrupt private life. The epitome of this was Tartuffe.[3] Today, the party demagogue can no longer be described in such a manner. Calling him a hypocrite is too simple. The situation has turned around: today, the party leader is a respectable, virtuous, upright, and honest man in his private life, while deploying the most ignoble, detestable, hideous, and shameful weapons in what is referred to as his public "fight."

If one is able to look beyond martial and war-like images, one realizes that there are more important, more sincere, and nobler things in this world than "fighting." Those party leaders who only fight are, in the best case, people who have given up or given in; in the worst – and usual – case, they are sad traitors to the people. The reason is that those who only know how to fight do not know how to build, to organize, and to guard. What they usually fight for are their own interests. Hence, their fight is directed against everyone else – individuals as well as groups. However, they cover this individualistic fight in the clothes of the most sacrosanct fight of all: that between the classes, the "class struggle." In the name of this struggle, they can act as ruthlessly and unconscientiously as they want – even when they are very considerate and conscientious in their private lives.

No one ever demonstrated this more clearly to me than Wilhelm Liebknecht.[4] I met with him regularly over the course of the final years of his life. The unforgettable M. von Egidy,[5] unknown by all who have never met him personally, brought us together. He did so in response to Liebknecht's wish to discuss our common advocacy for the barber Ziethen. Ziethen had been sentenced to death for a murder he did not commit. His sentence was commuted to imprisonment, and he died incarcerated.

In the 1860s, in his fight against Bakunin and the anarchists, Liebknecht had already made it obvious that he was ready to use any means necessary against his political foes. He did not hesitate to grossly distort their beliefs either. As a result, I had abused him verbally.[6] When we met, I intended to be polite yet reserved. As someone who had been deeply offended by him, I wanted to limit our interaction to the discussion of the issue at hand. Liebknecht, however, approached me with a disarming friendliness. This was an eye-opening experience; not only concerning him but concerning humankind. Liebknecht dealt so habitually with offenses (both actively and passively) that I got the – probably correct – impression that he had completely forgotten my verbal abuse, although not even two years had passed. Subsequently, we developed rather friendly relations, and I realized how frighteningly lonely the centerpiece of a great party can be. Liebknecht was the most famous of all social democrats, and in the public eye, the party's authority. Yet, even as the chief editor of *Vorwärts*,[7] he exuded almost no influence during his final years, neither on the journal nor on the party.

I do not regret the friendly relations that we established. Liebknecht had a lot of natural righteousness, rooted in his character. In his private life, he was virtuous and respectable. He showed both gentleness and excitement. In short, he was a "good man" – some might also say a petty bourgeois. An anecdote from his earlier years illustrates this. I went on an excursion with Ledebour,[8] and the two young Liebknechts,[9] who were both students at the time. Ledebour was like a private mentor to them. One of the two – I do not recall whether it was the antimilitarist and high traitor of today or his brother,[10] and I'm afraid history will have to live without ever knowing – lost his pocket knife. On the way home, he repeated over and over again: "Oh, what will father say!? Oh, what will father say!?"

This is what he was like. The same man who would later, in his public role, strangle every alleged enemy of the party, whether he came from inside the organization's ranks or was considered an outside threat. I related the harmless personal incident concerning the pocket knife to demonstrate this contradiction and to clarify that no person is depraved per se. What makes them depraved is a certain role that they occupy within society, within the state, or within the party. When they wash off the ink from their editorial offices and print shops, and when they take off their work clothes, hats, and canes, they cast off a mask and become entirely different beings. Real beings.

"Radicals" vs. "Revisionists"

How is it possible that a party can exist for decades with such contradictions? The answer is that German social democrats have been wondering for decades about what to think of parliamentary politics. They have a party that wants to make laws – and that does not want to make laws; a party that wants to participate in state-building – and that does not want to participate in state-building; a party that wants to improve the state gradually – and that wants to leave the state behind (at least the current one); a party that wants to compete with other parties for seats in parliament – and that wants to prepare for violent revolution. The vagueness of their practical and legislative demands (the ones that follow the Marxist part of their program) parallels the vagueness of their understanding of the relation between principles and tactics.

I once witnessed chickens being hypnotized by a chalk line on the ground. They were no longer able to move. Social democrats resemble these chickens. They stare at the chalk line with horrified, glassy eyes. In this case, the line is nothing other than the divide between the capitalist state and the socialist state. Social democrats stare at it hypnotically; they criticize, demonstrate, and talk revolution. Once they come out of hypnosis, however, their principles frighten them and they frantically turn to tactics – after all, there are millions of voters to "entertain."

The party's so-called "radicals" cling to their statist, centralist, and authoritarian socialism. They are afraid that the party loses sight of its goals if it focuses too much on lawmaking within the confines of the current state. They are afraid that this would make for a democratic workers' reform party. Some claim that this has already happened and that there is no turning back. Bebel,[11] for example, wrote in 1898 on behalf of the party's executive committee: "In the entire history of humanity there has not been a single example of a great social movement that took generations to reach its goals. Either it reached these goals quickly, or the entire movement disappeared with no goals attained." Men like Bebel believe that it is impossible to demand revolution while wearing oneself out in the slow, tedious processes of legislation.

The response of the party's "revisionists" is that it is time to rise above radical sloganeering. They demand that their party be recognized as a democratic and parliamentarian workers' party. They call upon the radicals to stop complaining. They want unity.

The radicals reject this unity. This makes them dislikeable. They want the party to follow their ideas because to them socialism and the party are one. This is the contradiction that they are caught in: they are nothing if they do not have mass support, but they can only gather mass support through electoral and parliamentarian politics. When their opinion has no influence on the implementation of a law, they are – "in the name of the masses" – against it, even if it would mean an improvement. When their opinion can influence the implementation of a law, they – "in the name of the masses" – support it. They try to gain and maintain power by appealing to destructive, belligerent proletarian instincts that question all peaceful politics.

The revisionists, on the other hand, demand political education and civility. They know that – given the power distribution of political parties in Germany and the country's electoral system – the radicals might be able to gather many votes, but will never become an influential force in parliament. The revisionists are more realistic, like their friends in France and Austria. They know how to go beyond the nimbus of revolution and towards real political power.

To call the radicals "radical" and to compare their "revolutionary" politics to the "reformist" politics of the revisionists is a distortion. It is impossible for anyone to say whether or not there will be a political revolution in Germany in the foreseeable future. If a revolution should occur, it will only concern the abolition of the feudal remnants and the further implementation of democratic, possibly even republican, institutions. Something that can be proclaimed very confidently, however, is that the revolutionary speeches by the proletariat's radical representatives prevent a revolution rather than generating one.

The politics of the revisionists are much more likely to provoke clashes between Junkerdom[12] and modern democracy than those of the radicals. However, a far-reaching democratization and republicanization of the bourgeoisie remains a precondition. There is no country in which the proletariat alone will ever affect political transformation. The revisionists, first and foremost Bernstein,[13] understand this. They are far-sighted. They aim to create a democratic bourgeoisie, as they know that a democratic bourgeoisie could not possibly resist far-reaching social reforms.

If we concede that the revisionists have the clearest idea of how to reach an additional political revolution – all revolutions are but additions to the bourgeois revolution of 1789 – then we must also admit that socialism cannot be attained merely through struggles over political power. If there is no socialism in everyday life, then all attempts to reorganize our economic conditions will repeat the experience of 1848, and our desires will remain unfulfilled.[14]

Social reforms or power politics will not give us socialism. However, certain reforms can be the beginning of significant political transformation; for example, in the field of ownership structures, especially concerning land. Certain reforms can be the beginning of something new.

There is deception, misapprehension, and ignorance in both of the party's factions. Neither side sees things as they are. Neither side understands that it alone cannot create socialism among the people. Neither side understands that socialism has to be constructed from an inner desire and requires the awakening of a new spirit.

Right now, the Social Democratic Party is not only stumbling in "ideological" darkness, but is also beset by personal rivalries. We see not only competing convictions, but also ambitious individuals struggling for power. As both sides know that the decisive moment of their internal struggle has not yet arrived, they engage in well-concealed skirmishes over posts in bureaus, offices, and local as well as regional assemblies. A particular characteristic of this war within the party is that while the officers and corporals fight bitterly – usually with muted anger, which becomes open anger during party conventions – the rank-and-file shows hardly any interest.

This is not an open contest. It is restricted and often malicious. There is no popular involvement. It is a contest between clever theorists and well-trained practitioners. Their personalities are weak; they lack liveliness, force, and persuasion.

Social democratic voters often do not even know which strain of the party they are supporting, and they hardly ever care. At the same time, neither radicals nor revisionists have any interest in people thinking for themselves, or in guiding them from dangerous angry instincts to quiet and earnest reflection. After all, this might cause people to think beyond the party!

---

1. In August 1908, the fourth prototype based on Ferdinand von Zeppelin's rigid airship model was destroyed during a test flight for the German military. A highly successful fundraising effort among the German people secured the continuation of the Zeppelin program.

2. March music played by Ottoman military bands related to the Janissaries (*Janitscharen*), elite infantry units; reputedly the oldest variety of military march music. *Janitscharenmusik* is a common German term for indicating a great spectacle.

3. Main character in a Molière (1622-1673) play of the same name, first performed in 1664.

4. Wilhelm Liebknecht (1826-1900), one of Germany's most influential 19th-century social democrats, and the father of Theodor and Karl Liebknecht. See also Landauer's article "Der Fall Liebknecht" [The Liebknecht Case], *Der Sozialist*, August 29, 1895.

5. Moritz von Egidy (1847-1898), long-time military officer, later pacifist and Christian reformer. Landauer reflected on Egidy's ideas in "Christentum und Anarchismus" [Christendom and Anarchism], *Der Sozialist*, October 19, 1895, and published "Im Kampf um die Weltanschauung: Stimmungen zu M. von Egidy's Tod" [The Struggle About Ideology: Reactions to M. von Egidy's Death], *Der Sozialist*, January 14, 1899.

6. See "Der Fall Liebknecht" [The Liebknecht Case], *Der Sozialist*, August 29, 1896.

7. *Vorwärts* [Forward], daily paper of the German Social Democratic Party from 1891 to 1933.

8. Georg Ledebour (1850-1947), prominent German socialist.

9. Theodor Liebknecht (1870-1948) and Karl Liebknecht (1871-1919), sons of Wilhelm Liebknecht, both prominent socialist politicians; Karl was murdered by security forces after the defeat of the Spartacist Uprising in Berlin in 1919.

10. Karl Liebknecht was sentenced to eighteen months in prison for a 1907 antimilitarist treatise, "Militarismus und Antimilitarismus" [Militarism and Antimilitarism].

11. August Bebel (1840-1913), highly influential German social democrat; accused Landauer of being a "police informer" at the 1893 congress of the Second International in Zurich.

12. *Junker*: antiquated term for aristocrats and big landowners in Prussia and Mecklenburg.

13. Eduard Bernstein (1850-1932), one of the most prominent revisionists within the SPD in the late 1890s.

14. Reference to the defeat of the bourgeois revolution in Germany in 1848.

WEAK STATESMEN, WEAKER PEOPLE!

This short piece contains one of Landauer's most quoted lines, namely his definition of the state as "a social relationship; a certain way of people relating to one another." First published as "Schwache Staatsmänner, schwächeres Volk!" in *Der Sozialist*, June 15, 1910.

A PALE, NERVOUS, SICK, AND WEAK MAN SITS AT HIS WRITING desk. He scribbles notes on a sheet of paper. He is composing a symphony. He works diligently, using of all the trade secrets that he has learned. When the symphony is performed, a hundred and fifty men play in the orchestra; in the third movement, there are ten timpani, fifteen anvils, and an organ; in the final movement, an eight part chorus of five hundred people is added as well as an extra orchestra of fifes and drums. The audience is mesmerized by the enormous force and the imposing vigour.

Our statesmen and politicians – and increasingly our entire ruling class – remind us of this composer who possesses no actual power, but allows the masses to appear powerful. Our statesmen and politicians also hide their actual weakness and helplessness behind a giant orchestra willing to obey their commands. In this case the orchestra are the people in arms, the military.

The angry voices of the political parties, the complaints of the citizens and the workers, the clenched fists in the pockets of the people – none of this has to be taken seriously by the government. These actions lack any real force because they are not supported by the elements that are naturally the most radical in each people: the young men from twenty to twenty-five. These men are lined up in the regiments under the command of our inept government. They follow every order without question. It is they who help camouflage the government's true weaknesses, allowing them to remain undetected – both within our country as much as outside of it.

We socialists know how socialism, i.e., *the immediate communication of true interests*, has been fighting against the rule of the privileged and their fictitious politics for over one hundred years. We want to continue and strengthen this powerful historical tendency, which will lead to freedom and fairness. We want to do this by awakening the spirit and by creating different social realities. We are not concerned with state politics.

If the powers of un-spirit and violent politics at least retained enough force to create great personalities, i.e., strong politicians with vision and energy, then we might have respect for these men even if they were in the enemy's camp. We might even concede that the old powers will continue to hold onto power for some time. However, it is becoming increasingly obvious that the state is not based on men of strong spirit and natural power. It is increasingly based on the ignorance and passiveness of the people. This goes even for the unhappiest among them, for the proletarian masses. The masses do not yet understand that they must flee the state and replace it, that they must build an alternative. This is not only true in Germany; it is also the case in other countries.

On the one side, we have the power of the state and the powerlessness of the masses, which are divided into helpless individuals – on the other side, we have socialist organization, a society of societies, an alliance of alliances, in other words: a people. The struggle between the two sides must become real. The power of the states, the principle of government and those who represent the old order will become weaker and weaker. The entire system would vanish without a trace if the people began *to constitute themselves as a people apart from the state*. However, the people have not yet grasped this. They have not yet understood that the state will fulfill a certain function and remain an inevitable necessity as long as its alternative, the socialist reality, does not exist.

A table can be overturned and a window can be smashed. However, those who believe that the state is also a thing or a fetish that can be overturned or smashed are sophists and believers in the Word. The state is a social relationship; a certain way of people relating to one another. It can be destroyed by creating new social relationships; i.e., by people relating to one another differently.

The absolute monarch said: I am the state. We, who we have imprisoned ourselves in the absolute state, must realize the truth: *we* are the state! And we will be the state as long as we are nothing different; as long as we have not yet created the institutions necessary for a true community and a true society of human beings.

THE TWELVE ARTICLES OF THE SOCIALIST BUND, SECOND VERSION

The Twelve Articles functioned as a program of the Socialist Bund and represent the most succinct summary of Landauer's understanding of socialism. The first version was written as "Die zwölf Artikel des Sozialistischen Bundes" in June 1908 and was subsequently published in various anarchist journals. It is available in English as an appendix to *For Socialism*. The significantly altered second version was published in *Der Sozialist*, January 1, 1912. The "Twelve Articles" are a reference to the "Twelve Articles" of the German peasants during the 1524-1525 rebellion.

1. Socialism is the creation of a new society.

2. Socialist society is a Bund of economically independent communities that exchange their goods fairly. The individuals of these communities are free in their personal matters, and voluntarily united in all that concerns the common good.

3. The Socialist Bund is destined to eventually replace the state and capitalism. It can only become a reality when active socialists organize their daily lives communally and exit the capitalist economy as far as their circumstances allow.

4. Socialist settlements will be prepared by communal consumption and by replacing the monetary economy with mutual credit. This will allow working people in independent communities to produce and exchange the products of their labor without the mediation of parasitic profiteers.

5. In the Socialist Bund, today's capital will be replaced by two social factors: a) institutions based on a connecting spirit and guaranteeing the satisfaction of the working people's needs (both with respect to production and consumption); these institutions and the spirit of mutuality will replace the usury and the emptiness of the monetary

economy; b) land: land is a necessary requirement for any economy, capitalist or socialist; it belongs to nature in much the same way that the institutions belong to spirit.

6. The requirements for the true and all-encompassing creation of socialism among the peoples are expropriation and redistribution of land among independent communities; this must be based on principles of justice, on the true needs of the people, and on the understanding that there cannot be permanent land ownership.

7. To make the necessary transformation of land rights possible, the working people have to realize as great a degree of socialism as their numbers and their energy allow. They have to provide examples of socialist reality. This has to happen on the basis of a common spirit (the capital of us socialists) and its institutions.

8. As long as examples of socialism cannot be realized and lived, the hope for a transformation of social relations and property rights remains futile.

9. Socialism has nothing to do with state politics, demagogy, or the working class fighting for power. Neither is it reduced to the transformation of material conditions. It is first and foremost a movement of spirit.

10. Anarchy is just another – due to its negativity and frequent misinterpretation, less useful – name for socialism. True socialism is the opposite of both the state and the capitalist economy. Socialism can only emerge from the spirit of freedom and of voluntary union; it can only arise within the individuals and their communities.

11. The further socialism extends and the more it expresses the true nature of human beings, the faster men will turn away from the spiritless institutions that have led to oppression, stupidity, and pauperization. An all-encompassing social contract will replace authoritarian violence, and the Bund of free communities and associations – what we call *society* – will replace the state.

12. The creation of the Socialist Bund demands the proletarians' departure from the industrial towns and their resettlement in the country, where agriculture, industry, and artisanry will form a union, and the distinction between intellectual and physical labor will be abandoned. Labor will be joyful and there will be a sense of belonging; this will allow us as individuals to form both communities and a people.

ON WAR & NATIONALISM

A FREE WORKERS' COUNCIL

This essay, based on a talk delivered by Landauer in Berlin in September 1911, marks his transition from optimistic socialist activity to desperate defense against the war. Landauer begins the essay by clarifying misconceptions regarding the Socialist Bund, in particular its relation to the working class. He then turns to the apparent threat of military conflict and propagates an "active general strike" as the most effective means of prevention.

"A Free Workers' Council" is one of the most crucial and telling texts in Landauer's political biography. The written version was first published as "Vom freien Arbeitertag" in *Der Sozialist*, October 1, 1911. *Arbeitertag* is a variation on *Reichstag*, the German parliament, and *Landtag*, a provincial assembly. Since the representative body that Landauer envisioned was clearly not parliamentarian, "council" appears to be a more apt translation. He expanded the essay's theme in *Der Sozialist* a few weeks later (November 15, 1911), in the almost identically titled article "Freier Arbeitertag."

SOME PEOPLE HAVE CLAIMED THAT ALL THE SOCIALIST BUND wants to do for the creation of socialism is to establish workers' colonies and settlements. This is far from the truth. Those who believe this have misunderstood us completely. Similarly, the recent actions of the Socialist Bund group "Arbeit" [Work] in Berlin[1] – actions that have now been joined by other groups – must not be perceived as a turn towards the proletarian perspective, the perspective of class struggle. It is ludicrous to assume that we have abandoned our goals and ways. We have not changed at all. You, however, dear listeners, will now get the opportunity to change your opinions by getting to know us better. We have always said that we cannot explain and illustrate what we stand for all at once. Hence, it is not surprising if you are still confused about what we want and about who we are. However, all will be revealed.

The governments of the European states seem to enjoy teasing the people with war: first Germany, then France, England, Spain, and now Italy and Turkey.[2] This is one reality we are facing.

Another is that German social democracy and trade unionism are in a pathetic and miserable state. Their representatives certainly talk a lot – and do nothing. As a result, we believe it impossible to initiate socialism among the German workers by propaganda and education alone. How can such means have any effect when there is not even a *sense* of what true socialism means? How can they have any effect when the workers' souls and minds, their patience and their courage, have been battered for sixty years?

Furthermore, we do not believe that socialism merely belongs to the so-called working class. Appealing to the people alone will not help us. Appealing is the trade of professional con artists and comedians. What we have to do – and this goes for everyone of us, the members from all classes – is to show others and ourselves what socialism means *in action*. We must realize as much of socialism as possible *right here and right now*.

As far as active social and cultural development is concerned, we cannot expect more from the working class than from other classes; however, things look very different in terms of anger and rejection, of emotion and strength, which are mandatory for effective resistance. That which calls itself the "socialist movement," or "workers' movement," today has been formed by many different currents and sects. There exists unity concerning the most important principles – the only ones who disregard them are the leaders, the public servants, the bureaucrats. This is why the entire movement is in danger of disappearing or of merely keeping its clenched fist in its pocket. This is where our task begins. We have to identify, clearly and without any reservation, what is at stake; we have to motivate those who are led by others – almost by their noses, it appears – to return to themselves, to rekindle their self-awareness and self-determination. This is the reason why we must say the following.

True socialist workers have no patriotic interests. Of course, they love the landscapes they live in, and they love their language and their customs. However, they know that the quarrels between governments are not over landscapes, languages, or customs. They are over money.

True socialist workers do not want war. They would even reject any revolution that committed systematic mass murder the way the state does in times of war. They oppose war not only because they cannot identify with its purpose, but because they detest it.

There is something that any true socialist worker feels, in his hands and in his twitching muscles, while he is laboring: when production stops, no government can go to war.

It is the duty of all socialists to turn this feeling into knowledge and will.

In the case of war – in fact, even in the case of bellicose governmental threats, the workers have to prepare an all-encompassing labor stoppage. The governments need to know what they must anticipate. Plenty of decisions have to be made before it is too late: the form of the strike, the trades it must focus on, the exact time and manner of its declaration.

One of the strike's benefits will be that the socialist workers will realize that, on the basis of their shared principles, they can form, despite all differences of opinion, an actual union, a Bund. This will trigger a lot more future action based on a common spirit.

We need to understand the following – something that is already felt by many: as much as governments and the politically, socially, and economically privileged are the enemies of the working class, the biggest obstacle to the workers' actual development and effectiveness is the bureaucracy that they themselves have created in forms of parties and trade unions. The actions of the workers can only be effective when they abandon the system of permanent representation, the ruinous system of parliamentarism that they have copied from the state. Instead, they must unite in groups and alliances that are based on particular trades and on local communities. Permanent debate within these groups is of utmost importance.

At times, representation might be necessary for practical purposes, but representatives must only be appointed for specific tasks and must never lose touch with those who have delegated them. We know that this is not the case in the Social Democratic Party nor in the centralized trade unions. These institutions know no real democracy; parliamentarian demagogy and governmental bureaucracy reign. German workers do not know of self-determination, of the life of a united people, of freedom and of unity (*Verbündung*[3]). If they want to take their destiny into their own hands, they have to take the first step: they have to come together in a Bund and *take action*!

The Socialist Bund has formed for this purpose. But it is not a means to an end. Workers uniting in self-determined action is already a decisive part of the creation of a true society, a true people, i.e., true *socialism*.

We call on the German workers to prepare a general free workers' conference.[4] This will send a clear sign that they are ready to turn their will into action and take control of public affairs. A committee to prepare such a conference is already forming. It will soon make concrete proposals to the German workers. These proposals should then be discussed wherever workers gather, on construction sites, in factories and workshops, etc. Eventually, groups shall be formed that represent certain trades – but directly, not within party or trade union structures.

The conference, the beginning of a free workers' council, does not have to be an assembly in one place. Parallel meetings in various towns and regions would demonstrate and strengthen the workers' unity just as well.

We have no illusions about this venture. It is an enormous challenge. On the one hand, we do understand what we have to do, what we should do, and what can do; on the other, no one can foresee the outcome: it might be something gigantic, it might be something modest, development might be fast or slow. However, if each and every one of us does his part, we can certainly prove wrong those who preach inactiveness because they have "no faith in the masses" (while all they truly lack is faith in themselves). Diffidence and hesitation have never led to anything.

The task of all those who support our idea is to propagate this socialist beginning among the workers wherever they can: in factories, workshops, and so forth. Whoever has suggestions to make, general or specific, please speak up! This is not about theory, scholarship, science, or philosophy. We strive for something simple, for the given, the natural, the self-evident. It will be realized by the people. We call on them to determine their own destiny, to speak up, and to act in their own name!

---

1. The group "Arbeit" had signed a call for a German workers' council, authored by Landauer in September 1911.

2. Reference to the Italo-Turkish War of 1911-1912 over the domination of present-day Libya.

3. Literally, "to come together in a Bund."

4. Such a conference was never realized, and no free workers' council was established.

THE ABOLITION OF WAR BY THE SELF-DETERMINATION OF THE PEOPLE: QUESTIONS TO THE GERMAN WORKERS

This anti-war pamphlet was released by Landauer in December 1911 under the title "Die Abschaffung des Krieges durch die Selbstbestimmung des Volkes. Fragen an die deutschen Arbeiter." One hundred thousand copies were printed, and almost immediately confiscated by the police. Landauer escaped the ensuing court cases, since the publication did not carry his name. The text was eventually reprinted in *Der Sozialist* on October 1, 1912. It echoes a lot of the sentiments expressed in "A Free Workers' Council," but renders them more concrete by a didactic question-and-answer format. This translation is an abbreviated version.

What is War?

WAR IS A VENTURE CARRIED OUT BY ONE STATE AGAINST another state. Every venture can be divided into its purpose and in its means. Are you asking about the purpose or the means?

You are right: one thing at a time. What is the purpose of war?

The purpose of war is to plunder, to conquer, to extend the power of certain states, to diminish the power of other states, and to secure markets for industry and trade.

Do the workers have an interest in this?

No. Plundering is for exploiters who do not want to work. As far as conquering goes, no worker of one state can wish for the worker of another to experience the form of oppression that he is experiencing. The quarrels of states over power and over their subjects have nothing to do with workers – workers are the subjects in question. And with respect to securing markets for industry and trade, this is the very reason for the boundless misery of the people, especially the poor, and for the insecurity of our economies; economies built on production that only serves the money bags of the traders, the factory owners, and the bankers, instead of the needs of the people. This is true for each country, each province, and each town. Trading belongs to war; working belongs to peace.

So what are the means of war?

Now we can leave the purpose behind and start talking about what war actually is. Let us not even consider the despicable side effects of war; effects that are not arbitrary, but as old as war itself: the cruel instincts, the raw perversion that shows in the slaughtering of children, women, and the old. Let us suppress our emotions, force ourselves to be calm and define war technically: war is a situation in which several hundreds of thousands of men attempt to kill one another by the most sophisticated technical means after decades of preparation.

Do the workers of a country ever want war?

The workers can never want war; even if their conscience allowed them to murder, their reason would not allow them to kill themselves.

Do the workers have any means to prevent war?

[...] If the workers stopped working at the right time, in the right way, and with the right intentions, then war would not be possible.

But when is the right time?

Each war begins with a declaration of war. Then mobilization for war follows. A declaration of war is an announcement exchanged between hostile governments. Mobilization is an order of the government to all of its subjects drafted for military service. However, before there can be a declaration of war and mobilization, public opinion has to be won (at least in our time). A warlike mood must be engendered in the public. The government also needs to make (more or less) clear demands; demands that the public must be aware of. In most cases, it will be very obvious that a government is preparing for war before it actually declares war. As soon as it is known that one or more governments want war, the governments can be brought to reason and forced to find peaceful solutions by a strike, the workers' ultimate means.

So there is no point in calling a general strike once the war has already started? It has to be called before?

Exactly. The arguments that have recently been brought forward against such a general strike have little meaning, because they all refer to the "missed moment." It is true of course that the moment has been missed once war has caused an international economic crisis, increased unemployment, dejection, hunger, sickness, misery, and despair. No strength to act and no option for interfering will remain at that point. However, contrary to what these smart arguments say – arguments that are presented by very scared men – the solution will neither come from the atrocities committed by our rulers and privileged classes nor from the passivity of the workers. It is preposterous to call this combination of atrocity and passivity "progress."

Can you be certain that the workers would endure such a strike; that they would win it; that they would achieve their objective?

Certain? No, I definitely cannot be certain! It signifies the decay of our times that people always want external certainties. In reality, this only increases the external uncertainty of their situation, and the unstableness of their mind and their conviction. When it comes to our ultimate means for preventing atrocity, we can neither rely on God nor on Marx to provide us with any certainty. We need certainty in ourselves. This is the certainty that has always led the way to victory; it is called *courage*. We need to have the will to be victorious, and we have to try.

But even during the worst of times and in the face of the worst possible dangers, no sober person will do what seems futile. So let me ask you: is it probable – or even possible – that the workers will endure, that they will win, and that they will reach their goal?

Endure? For how long? *Win?* What are they going to win? *Goal?* What goal do you mean? This is no ordinary strike. It has no goal. It can win nothing that strikes usually try to win. This strike is about right preparation and right organization. It has no purpose but itself; or, if you will, its only purpose is to bring work to an end – *their* kind of work. When there is no more transport of people and goods, when the factories lie idle, when neither electricity nor coals are being delivered, when towns are without light and water, it will not remain that way for very long. People will start organizing themselves. State governments no longer know what self-determination of the people means. If the above scenario occurs, they will be reminded. This is the strike's meaning: to make an impression in one country and to cause other countries to follow suit.

Do you think that the best possible outcome of the strike would be the government promising to stop provoking war, so that the workers can return to their workplaces in peace?

Do I know that? Do we always have to know everything in advance? Maybe that will happen; maybe it will not. Furthermore...

Wait, before you continue: Will the enemy not attack us when it sees that the people do not want war and that the government has been weakened?

The enemy? We workers are friends, and we will use our friendship across borders in unprecedented ways if only one courageous people stands up for its rights. If we have international agreements, and if they are kept, fine. But what is much more important is to set an example. If we do the right thing, and if our actions inspire others to act, then no government will be able to unleash mass murder. There is no doubt about this.

You speak of international agreements, yet these do not seem very important to you. Why not?

Because I cannot stand pomposity. It is easy for a few party bureaucrats to exchange meaningless phrases. But these are hardly more significant than the chatter at international peace congresses or in the peace declarations that the governments have agreed upon in The Hague.[1] First the workers of a nation, of a people, have to come to agreements after solid, direct, profound, and multilateral discussions. Then, they have to respect these agreements. Even if history provides no example, it is evident that if the working masses of a single people demonstrate – not only through words, resolutions, and articles, but also through collective action at their workplaces – convincingly and truthfully that they respect their lives, that they are ready to take the necessary steps to prevent the outbreak of looting and murder, and that their will is unbreakable, then this – an animation of dead words – will spark a fire among all peoples. [...]

Could it not be the case that even if the general strike were to begin today, we would still have war tomorrow? And then what? What will be left to do?

225

The spirit behind this question is the spirit of disaster. The minds of the workers – and nowhere is this truer than in Germany – are twisted and wrecked. They are not sober people, and it is difficult to rely on their ideas; they put all their hopes in spontaneity, in the unknown, in miracles. They have no understanding of how to realize ideas step by step and stone by stone, and this is why all they do is feverishly dream of a sudden transformation in which night turns to day and mud to gold, while in reality, they carry on with the monotony of their pitiful lives that seem to move like mire in a clogged runlet. Their entire idea of socialism is a fairy-tale: here comes – one, two, three, you can't even seen it – the cudgel in the sack or the big *Kladderadatsch*,[2] and then, with the twinkling of an eye, the wishing table and the miracle land of a future state where mules will drop gold from all openings for the benefit of their masters. Always fast, always sudden, always fantastic – such are their dreams. However, the real implementation of a different society looks very different. It is not enough to talk and dream. Yet, we must not despair. Rome was not built in a day either. [...]

The workers must take the first necessary steps, they must prepare themselves. For once, they must not think of what others can do for them. They must think of what they themselves can do. They must think what they really think. They must be what they really are.

What do you mean? "They must think what they really think and be what they really are?" Is not everyone what he really is and does not everyone think what he really thinks?

If everyone was what he truly is and if everyone thought the thoughts that truly live inside of them, then there would be no need to oppose war and the world would be a very different place. There would be socialism within us and around us. No, people dare not to think their own thoughts. There is a lot of hidden awareness and secret knowledge inside of them, but they do not allow it to surface. No worker truly wants war. They also all know – even if they are not aware of it – that only a general strike can prevent war, and that a strike has to be called to prevent a call for war. However, are we close to this awareness? No. Have we seen even the tiniest effort to prepare the emergency strike that is needed? No. It seems as if the people's true knowledge has fallen into a deep well, from which it is almost impossible to retrieve. [...]

So do you think that it is our duty to help people realize what they truly are, to awake them from their sleep and their apparent death, and to bring to light what they truly think? Why have individuals and peoples lost their true being, and why have their true thoughts disappeared into this well?

There are many reasons – but the main one is the passivity and compliance that has reigned for centuries. This is why it will take a long time for people to develop peaceful co-existence and a spirit of mutual aid, even if the way there is very simple and self-evident. People today only think of what is closest to them, of what affects them directly and immediately. They think slowly and egotistically and are narrow-minded.

In this sense, the threat of war actually brings hope. War concerns people's lives directly – as well as the lives of their sons and fathers – and it wields the scepter of unspeakable horror. This presents us with an opportunity to make a change; we have to do whatever we can to make use of this opportunity. People think slowly because their parents thought slowly. Schools never taught them a different kind of thinking either. Schools do not teach people to think. As a result, people are happy to give up early and let others do their thinking for them. The main reason for their misery is the system of representation!

So you think that the workers let themselves be governed and directed and will not govern and direct themselves? However, if governments were abolished, the workers would not declare war on one another!

Well, governments and states will not be abolished any time soon. We will not be able to motivate the masses to abolish them today and to create a new order. Besides, we have a government in Germany that claims to be a government of and for the workers. And indeed, this government – and our entire system of representation – has been ratified by the workers. If the workers want to make decisions about peace and war, they have to free themselves from this government and this system. The workers' party, its bureaus, and its central committees are nothing but institutions that the workers surrender their thinking, their acting, and their freedom to. Has there been any progress at all?

For example: the government taxes foodstuffs or declares war. What do the people do? They protest. They still believe – despite of centuries of evidence proving otherwise – that things might get better if other people or other parties ruled. Things never get better, however. They only get worse. The reason is that people have lost the ability to intervene and no longer know what self-determination means. This applies also to the union governments that the workers have recently added to the state governments. Union representatives might, for example, come to a wage agreement with the capitalists; a wage agreement that determines the well-being and the misery of tens of thousands of people. The union representatives have the right to do so because their helpers, the workers, have given it to them – renouncing their rights in the process. And then what happens? They shout again and protest and deny responsibility. If they are really angry, they will vote for different candidates the next time; candidates who inevitably will follow in the footsteps of their predecessors. How can this happen? It can happen because the workers are not alive and are not used to doing things for themselves. Where the masses do not really *live*, decadence is inevitable. All decadence in the upper levels of society comes from its lower levels. Government stinks. How could it be different? Rotten people are on top because rotten people are at the bottom.

What exactly must the workers do now?

They must not hesitate to test the truth of what has been said here: namely, that workers as a great, connected mass think uniformly about war and about the possibility of preventing it. They must realize that it can neither hurt nor do injustice to anyone if they, just for once, tried to uncover their true thoughts and turn them into reality. They must realize that this is not a question that depends on theories, on scholarliness, on programs, or on so-called science. They must realize that they are the working people and that they must rely on simple things that are close to them and that live within the heart of every true worker. They must realize that the quarrels between social democrats and anarchists, between Marxists and revisionists, do not really concern them. They must realize that something else is at stake, something more important (something most important!), something that leaves us no time to quarrel and no reason to wait and to be passive. They have to realize that it is they themselves who need to become active and take care of things!

It seems that in order for the workers to do this and to come to binding agreements they have to gather. How will they do that?

I believe that the workers have to organize the biggest convention that we have ever seen. Until now there has always been a mediator between

the workers and their goal: a party, a union, a parliament. There has always
been a priest who forced himself between the believers and their God.
However, this can never serve the interests of the people (people who are
alive) but only those of an organization, of the church, of idols. It is time to
leave this distortion behind. What we need to focus on are the assemblies
of workers in the workshops, in the factories, on the construction sites.
That is where the workers must talk and realize their unity, where they
must carefully discuss their plans and all related questions, where they
must send messengers on their way between groups, branches, towns –
until there is enough communication and clarity to summon councils in all
provinces on one and the same day. [...]

**Do you know what this reminds me of? Do you know that there
exists an example of this in history?**

Yes, I know, even though we did not think of it originally. During the
Great Revolution in France, the districts and sections of Paris and of other
towns were organized in this manner; the people gathered regularly and
controlled and advised their delegates directly. This secured their self-determination and allowed them not only to provide a precious example for
the future, but also to create a vibrant, cheerful public life in the present.

[...] Whether the workers today will do the same thing, whether
they will free themselves, whether they will speak and act for themselves,
whether they will determine their own destiny – this can only be answered
by the workers themselves.

---

1. Peace conferences in The Hague, Netherlands, in 1899 and 1907, led to
the first legal regulations for international warfare and the definitions of war
crimes, known as the Hague Conventions.

2. Antiquated Berlinian vernacular for "a loud boom."

REVOLUTION, NATION, AND WAR

An often-overlooked Landauer essay exposing the state as the perpetrator of war and the obstacle to people's revolutions. First published as "Revolution, Nation und Krieg" in *Der Sozialist*, February 15, 1912.[1]

OMRADES, WHEN YOU OPPOSE WAR, THERE IS ONE THING THAT you must never forget: you are right in what you do; you are right in feeling anger and disgust; you are right in opposing not only all aggressive expansionist politics but also all standing armies during so-called peaceful times; armies that turn as much against internal enemies and their own people as against external enemies and foreign people. Look at a globe to comprehend the space that the earth's peoples occupy; look at history to comprehend how our own times rest on the becoming of other times.

During the greatest of their revolutions,[2] the French people united and formed a new, self-conscious nation. It was not enough for the "patriots" who achieved this to fight against their country's monarchy and feudal aristocracy; they soon had to defend their freedom and their revolution against the powers of the coalition: Prussia, Austria, Spain, Sardinia and Piedmont, etc.

There were also elements of aggression and expansionism within the revolution; indeed, under Napoleon the newly born French nation soon attacked Spain, Germany, and other countries, stirring the spirit of revolutionary nationalism. In the beginning, however, the violence and military organization of the revolutionary French nation was used to defend it against the foreign royal armies that had been solicited by the king and the aristocrats. What would have become of the French Revolution and the French nation had it not been for the inspired action and the organizational genius of Danton and of the Committee of Public Safety, especially Carnot?[3] What would have occurred without the young generals of the revolution who arose from the midst of the people, and without the belligerent revolutionary fire of the masses that found such striking expression in the Marseillaise? At that time, no antimilitarist could have been a revolutionary or a patriot. The revolutionary nationalists had to act in self-defense.

Let us take a look at the world today. What is the danger for the revolution in Mexico, in Persia, or in the enormous land of China? What gets in the way of the Turkish movement? It is mainly the threat of external enemies.

The revolution in Mexico is in full force. We know that Madero has only been able to oust Díaz[4] because he had promised land to the proletarians and the Indians. All of the numerous revolutionary leaders emerging today – Reyes, Gomez, Zapata, Salgado, and all the others[5] – only find followers because they instigate agrarian reforms. We must not believe, however, that the people can always be betrayed. While the revolutionary leaders use them to solidify their power, the people use the leaders' power for their own interests. The people also make use of the revolutionary disorder. Indians and serfs, for example, settle the land they want to occupy – which is usually the land that used to be theirs. All this might be achieved, and the revolutionaries might win and prompt significant changes to establish a new social order – if it was not for the United States of North America, which are only concerned with their own political agenda and the interests of their billionaires. At the right moment, they will intervene and send their troops. What happens then? Hopefully, an enormous revolutionary nationalist fervor will unite all of the Mexican people and there will be what we have to call war.

The situation in Persia is evident: the Russians and the English shamelessly follow agendas of power, while the Persians want to establish fairness and freedom.

The consequences of the Turkish Revolution – a revolution that succeeded mainly thanks to the country's military – were inevitable given the situation in Europe: the Turks are forced to build up their army due to the hostility of their foreign enemies.

The situation in China is evident too: the young Chinese republic is surrounded by enemies who are not only waiting for its collapse, but who are trying to provoke it by all kinds of dirty tricks. Their intention is to rob, plunder, and exploit. The threat is imminent. No one will be helped by abstract announcements that demand an end to all domination, including that of the Chinese republic. Neither will anyone be helped by declarations that oppression at the hands of the Chinese or the Manchu is as bad as oppression at the hands of foreigners. There are always levels of oppression, and they always matter for the oppressed. Perpetually reiterating that one thing is "just like the other" is akin to playing dodgeball with words. It has nothing to do with reality and it lacks empathy. There is no "just like the other." The domination of English, Russians, French, or Germans over China is something entirely different from a Chinese republic created by revolution. The foreign powers do not even treat the Chinese like human beings – they treat them like things.

The danger that comes from the outside has great significance for China's development. The Chinese have a natural tendency for federalism, not least because of their diverse tribes. Who could be happier about a federative republic than we socialists and anarchists? However, if China remains China and is not torn apart by foreign bloodhounds, then centralism – both of the government and of the military – will most probably win. This is a harsh realization. But things go the way they have to go, and the defense of the Chinese Revolution will require the militarization of the country's numerous peaceful tribes. Whether the consequence of this will be expansionist aggression under a Chinese Napoleon or a new Timur,[6] we – or our children – will find out in the future.

We have to realize and admit that the war between states – or, in general, state politics – do not only produce conflicts that concern the states. State politics also produce revolutions, and these revolutions might in turn produce wars as a need of defense against foreign aggression.

It is of course right to rally behind slogans such as: "We have to get rid of the state!" or "We have to create a different social order!" However, this does not change the fact that states *do exist* and that we have to deal with them. Neither does it change the fact – and let me emphasize this, as it is very important, but all too often overlooked – that it is not only states that go to war, but also young nations united and created by revolution; nations that are forced to defend themselves against the aggressor states.

What can we do in Germany, France, Austria-Hungary, Italy, Russia, England, or America? What can we do while we are active in these countries trying to create new forms of socialism from below? We have to do whatever it takes to prevent belligerent, aggressive, and exploitative activities of our governments directed against the rising (*becoming*) revolutionarily peoples. We have to do this both for our humanity and for humankind. No people can guarantee freedom and a just order when there is no solidarity among all peoples in the struggle against war and the state. As long as this struggle is not won, war will remain a reality – not only between the states, but also as a means of defense of revolutionary nations.

What has been laid out here should prove enlightening for those who think it through. They will come to an essential realization; a realization for which there are plenty more examples than the ones provided here. Yes, the emergence and action of an individual, a group, a people, or the masses can be sudden, immense, fierce, and powerful. However, the outcome will be but a tiny step forward. During all our work – no matter where it takes us and how long it lasts – it is mandatory for us to remember this.

This is bitter medicine, I know. However, there is also consolation. Dear friends, whatever you do, it is not so much the external result that counts, it is what you can give to yourself! You follow your own nature and you have to do whatever leaves you at peace with what is inside of you. Who will be most effective in the struggle for external social transformation? It will be those whose actions are righteous and courageous and who are able to look at themselves with pride, satisfaction, and strength. Whoever is whole and reliable in the present will be whole and reliable in the future. The generations to come will be grateful if we do not live for them *but for our own souls.* This is the greatest gift we can give them.

1. A related Landauer essay is "Zum Problem der Nation. Brief an Herrn Professor Matthieu in Zürich" [On the Problem of the Nation: A Letter to Professor Matthieu in Zurich] (*Der Aufbruch*, August/September, 1915); Jean Matthieu (1874-1952) was a socialist priest and teacher.

2. The French Revolution of 1789.

3. Georges Danton (1759-1794), moderate leader of the French Revolution, guillotined under Robespierre and the "Reign of Terror." The Committee of Public Safety was the de facto French government in 1793-94. Danton was its first president. Lazare Carnot (1753-1823) was mainly responsible for building up the French Revolutionary Army.

4. Porfirio Díaz (1830-1915) was Mexican President from 1876 to 1880 and from 1884 to 1911. Francisco Madero (1873-1913), an upper-class democrat, ousted Díaz in a coup in 1911, a major event in the Mexican Revolution. Madero soon lost control over the revolution's development and was killed in 1913.

5. Bernardo Reyes (1850-1913), Emilio Vazquez Gomez (1888-1913), Emiliano Zapata (1879-1919), Jesús Salgado (1873-1919); Reyes, a former army general under Díaz, was involved in killing Madero in 1913.

6. Timur (1336-1405), Central Asian conqueror who established the Timurid dynasty encompassing virtually all of Central Asia from 1363 to 1506.

PEACE TREATY
& PEACE ADMINISTRATION:
A LETTER TO WOODROW WILSON

This is possibly one of Landauer's most curious pieces. A letter sent to
Woodrow Wilson in December 1916 (Landauer writes "Christmas 1916").
Landauer had great hopes in Wilson's peace initiatives – in Max Nettlau's
words, the result of a "ridiculous overestimation"[1] – and decided to share
his own vision of an international body of national representatives as a
precaution against military conflict. The letter had to be smuggled out of
Germany, and it is not known whether Wilson ever received it or whether
it had any influence on his leading role in the post-war foundation of the
League of Nations (transformed into today's United Nations at the end of
World War II). In fact, the English version of the letter has never been
found. The German version was first published as "Friedensvertrag und
Friedenseinrichtung. Ein Brief an Woodrow Wilson" in *Rechenschaft*, a col-
lection of Landauer texts published in 1919.[2]

A PEACE TREATY MARKS THE TRANSITION FROM THE VIOLENT
activities we know as "war" to people living together in
what we know as "peace;" it belongs to the former as
much as to the latter.

This is why a peace treaty can never provide a complete
guarantee of peace. It always includes elements of the violent
imposition, extortion, and misery of war that one accepts with
disgruntlement and ill future intentions. A peace treaty only
provides peace as an infected legacy of war.

In 1648, the Peace of Westphalia[3] attempted to create a true
balance between the European powers. Diplomats of the warring states used to employ international law. The attempt was
repeated during the Vienna Congress.[4] International law was
supplemented by constitutionalism and even by notions of brotherhood and Christian love envisioned as principles of public life.

These attempts were not entirely ineffective. But the results were far from satisfactory. They did not result in any significant changes.

There is no doubt that it will be similar this time. All sides will soon strongly feel the necessity to end the war. Everyone will be happy when this end comes. Even the bonds will no longer work as an excuse to prolong the war;[5] especially not for those who profess dedication to the idea of permanent peace. At the same time, once the war has ended, there will be so many different interests to consider that only a frail makeshift roof will be able to cover the house of humanity. There appears to be no possibility that a peace treaty can implement reliable measures against the recurrence of a war as terrible and insane as the one we are now witnessing.

However, one thing does seem possible: the peace treaty can demand *commitments to strengthening peace and to preventing war.* Such a clause would, in fact, also accelerate the process of signing the treaty: if there is a common commitment to working for peace, then any changes of European borders will be easier for everyone to accept, because there will be a joint guarantee, signed by all states, of the freedom and self-determination of all peoples.

The European War developed and erupted in 1914 because since 1870-1871 Europe had accepted the rule of armed peace, costly armaments, and year-long detention of almost the entire male population in a stratified institution with the purpose of professional technological destruction. This created a system of both standing and reserve armies of millions in ways unknown before.

Unlike other nations, Germany reached its unity not through internal liberation and renewal, but through war against a neighboring people.[6] This led the nation's leaders – whether correctly or not is irrelevant – to believe that the position of the German Reich in the concert of the world powers will always depend on its capacity to threaten others with violence. The other states allowed themselves to be intimidated year after year, decade after decade. As a consequence, they followed the German example and wasted inestimable material means and the creative forces of spirit and soul on contributing to a system of violent intimidation.

The attempts to end this system made at the conferences in The Hague were much too modest.[7] It was not even the true leaders and statesmen who gathered there, but political academics who were allowed a side stage to make some decisions of minor significance or without binding power. The constitutional assembly that had originally been planned was never realized. Its purpose would have been to replace violence with a declaration of international laws as a necessary supplement to the declaration of human rights.

Everyone who has studied the history of these conferences recognizes the major responsibility of the German Reich for their failure. However, once again none of the other states challenged the Germans openly. Instead, they met and decided on their measures behind closed doors. The result was that – instead of a profound unified effort to bring about change in Europe – we witnessed the emergence of two ever more hostile military blocks.

There was no real policy of peace during those decades. Every "peace talk" between powers not aligned with Germany made Germany a target – or at least that is how it was perceived by the Germans. There has never been an attempt – or at least it did not succeed – to revive the spirit of 1871 and to rectify the mistakes that were made at the time; this also includes, perhaps especially, the mistakes made by the neutral powers.

What is needed this time is an amendment to the peace treaty that demands immediate preparations for an international state congress with binding decision-making powers. This congress must include all warring states and all neutral powers. It must be able to decide on matters that are not directly related to the (provisional) peace treaty; matters that have always been declared to be simply "internal matters." This has proved fatal. *There are two matters that affect all peoples equally:*

1. armaments; and

2. the implementation of constitutional law within individual states; meaning that the participation of all people in the politics and governance of an individual state must be institutionally guaranteed.

Re 1) No matter what has been declared for more than forty years, armaments and violent intimidation are not simply internal affairs. The arming of one state concerns all others. Silence as a consequence of intimidation is a precondition for war. The idea of preserving peace with armaments is shameful, dangerous, and draining even for the strongest among us. In fact, the idea contradicts peace. Armaments are but the first stage of war. War's full eruption will follow inevitably.

In the future, such a situation has to be avoided by all means. This cannot happen if the task is left to individual governments or to bilateral talks they might occasionally engage in. What is needed instead is an institution of public law whose decisions are binding and enforceable. If preparations and talks commence immediately after the troops have returned home, if the talks are open, and if 2) falls under the jurisdiction of this institution as well, then we can expect that its decisions will be put into effect in each country by the moral power of its people.

Re 2) The existence of politically privileged and underprivileged classes within a state is also not a simple matter of internal affairs. It is important for all states that an individual state's foreign policies are based on the will and the responsibility of the entire people. The last war proved the international danger posed by secret governments, shadow governments, irresponsible military cabinets, and the uncontrolled political influence of professional armies. People have paid a heavy price for state relations oscillating between two extremes: fear and non-interference during times of peace; and the unleashing of incomprehensible violence during times of war – a violence knowing no borders, no scruples, and no limitations. This is why a new institution has to be established, a community of states interested in true peace; a community that, in the interests of everyone, must no longer tolerate state constitutions that grant political privileges to certain classes, dynasties, or individuals.

During the times we called peace, the relations between the states were defined by cautiousness, contemplation, prudence, and deception. Then war came and suddenly there were passionate outbursts, brutal rants, and credulous defamations. In both cases, untruth prevailed.

The true peace we aim to create now must be built on truth, openness, and mutuality; this is why we need a new international institution.

There are many qualities that reemerge during times of war in a ghost-like fashion: courage, chivalry, heroism, endurance, camaraderie, loyalty, sacrifice. We need them all, but we need them in alive, quiet, gentle, and discrete forms; in forms that are not only determined by a reminiscent past, but by a prophetic future; in forms that will allow peoples to unite and work together in order to initiate true peace.

These short contemplations I present to Mr. Woodrow Wilson, the President of the United States of America, with the request to consider them. I also urge him to keep in mind that they come from a German who strongly believes that the German people will eventually atone for the harm that they have caused humanity, and that they will live up to the promises and creations of the great representatives of their spirit; they do, however, need the trust and the support of others, just like all tribes and peoples on their way to creating humanity.

I allow Mr. Wilson to make use of this text in any way he deems appropriate.

Hermsdorf near Berlin, Christmas 1916
Gustav Landauer

1. Nettlau, Geschichte der Anarchie, V: 263.

2. For bibliographical references, please see the bibliography at the end of the book.

3. See footnote 104 in *Revolution*.

4. The 1814-1815 Congress of Vienna attempted to redefine the European order after the Napoleonic Wars.

5. The German government financed the war mainly through war bonds. This tied the war effort closely to economic concerns that were regularly used as justifications for continued military engagement.

6. The German nation state was a result of Germany's victory in the Franco-Prussian War of 1870-1871.

7. See footnote 1 in "The Abolition of War by the Self-Determination of the People."

ON AMERICA

THE 11TH OF NOVEMBER

Article on the eight-year commemoration of the Haymarket martyrs' hang-ings. Published as "Zum elften November" in *Der Sozialist*, November 9, 1895. Landauer published three more articles on the Haymarket events in *Der Sozialist*: "An die Lebenden. Zum 11. November" [To the Living: On the 11th of November], November 11-13, 1897, "Die Bedeutung des 11. Novembers im Jahre 1898" [The Meaning of the 11th of November in the Year 1898], November 12, 1898, and "Zum 25. Gedenktag des Justizmords von Chicago" [On the 25th Anniversary of the Judicial Murder of Chicago], November 11, 1912.

MANY BATTLES WILL BE COMMEMORATED THIS YEAR. A battle that we want to commemorate is the the one that peaked on the 11th of November, 1887, in Chicago. It was a battle waged against proletarians who struggled for freedom.[1]

A significant segment of German freedom fighters are under the impression that there have never been more reactionary times than ours, in which people are persecuted for libel against the crown. It is true, these are bad times, and if our enemies had it their way, many of us would have already been hanged, beheaded, or burned alive.

However, we have to understand that our enemies' rage – which, so far, has remained without significant consequence – is nothing compared to what happened in America eight years ago. Imagine that, after the murder of the factory owner Schwartz in Mühlhausen,[2] the spokespeople for the German proletariat would have been arrested, accused of conspiracy to murder, tried, found guilty, and then killed in the name of the law; imagine that one of the men hosed down by police during the battle in Friedrichshain[3] had thrown a bomb, leading to all of the spokes-people of Berlin's proletariat being killed after an appalling traves-ty of justice; these scenarios give you an impression of the scandal of Chicago that led to the killings of the 11th of November.

The killings were not committed in a monarchy, nor under a military or aristocratic regime. They were committed in the American republic, which takes pride in having the freest political institutions. A land of equal rights and people's militias. It is of deep symbolic significance that the killings occurred in this country that is the most advanced in the eyes of the bourgeoisie and politicians. This can only clarify what the country's political institutions, and participation in them, are really worth. These things are not what hold us in chains; we are held in chains by an economic system that forces us to serve a class of masters. The less restricted the system of exploitation is, the more brutal this class becomes.

It is not only the outrageous callousness with which five men were killed that makes us commemorate the 11th of November as a day of special significance; it is also – and particularly – the idealism and greatness that these five heroes demonstrated. And heroes they truly were – no one must speak of victims! We must recall their wonderful individual traits again and again...

Louis Lingg has to be named first. When, after his conviction, he was encouraged to petition the governor for mercy, he responded with the marvelous words: "In our situation, the instinct of self-preservation is the biggest crime!" Robert Reitzel,[4] who quoted the words in his commemoration speech at Waldheim Cemetery, explained that not everyone can climb to such sunny heights, before continuing: "However, we can demand that everyone understand and honor this man's true courage, which made him put ideals and the struggle for their realization above ordinary life. His ideals were those that have been pursued and taught by every great man and that are ridiculed by every scoundrel: love, truth, and rights for all!"

Let us name Spies next. He had, for a short time, considered to petition for mercy, but upon hearing that some of his comrades refused to do so, he wrote the following lines in a letter to the governor:

> "During our trial the desire of the prosecutor to slaughter me,
> and to let my co-defendants off with milder punishment was
> quite apparent and manifest. It seemed to me then, and a great
> many of others, that the persecutors would be satisfied with
> one life – namely mine. Take this, then! Take my life! I offer it
> to you so that you may satisfy the fury of a semi-barbaric mob,
> and save that of my comrades. I know that every one of my
> comrades is as willing to die, and perhaps more so than I am.
> It is not for their sake that I make this offer, but in the name

of humanity and progress, in the interest of a peaceable – if possible – development of the social forces that are destined to lift our race upon a higher and better plane of civilization. In the name of the traditions of our country I beg you to prevent a seven-fold murder upon men whose only crime is that they are idealists, that they long for a better future for all. If legal murder there must be, let one, let mine, suffice."[5]

It might be the most disturbing detail of this dreadful tragedy that the two men who did petition for mercy were granted clemency, while Spies was executed with three of his comrades "upon his wish." As we know, Louis Lingg did not climb upon the gallows. He killed himself in his cell on the 10th by blasting a bullet in his mouth. During his agonizing last hours, the inhuman prison personnel argued about whether he ought to be hanged the next day or not!

Of Parsons we think in grief. A contemplative, heartfelt man who combined the love for his friends and his wife with a love for humanity.[6] Only a few hours before his death he remembered in melancholic resignation the warm, blooming life he was to leave behind, and sang a Scottish folk song:

Maxwelton's braes are bonnie / Where early fa's the dew /
'Twas there that Annie Laurie / Gi'ed me her promise true /
Gi'ed me her promise true / Which ne'er forgot will be / And for
bonnie Annie Laurie / I'd lay me down and dee.

Engel was the oldest of the group, he was killed in his fifty-first year. The day before his murder he recited for his comrades Heine's "Silesian Weavers" in a moving manner.[7] It says in a report that has reached me: "The wardens came to Engel's cell, but he did neither see nor hear them. With a proud face, and as if he had escaped the confines of prison, he declaimed the stirring verses. There was solemn silence when the old man had finished. He looked around as if waking from a dream, before resting his head on his hand."

Then there was Fischer who intoned the prophetic words of the Marseillaise on the afternoon of the 10th:[8]

Von uns wird einst die Nachwelt zeugen,
Schon blickt auf uns die Gegenwart.
Frisch auf, beginnen wir den Reigen,
Ist auch der Boden rauh und hart.[9]

We must also name the three men who escaped the gallows: Fielden, Schwab, and Neebe. It was Neebe who had said to the court:

"I will ask you to do it – that is, to hang me, too; for I think it is more honorable to die suddenly than to be killed by inches. I have a family and children; and if they know their father is dead, they will bury him. They can go to the grave, and kneel down by the side of it; but they can't go to the penitentiary and see their father, who was convicted for a crime that he hasn't had anything to do with. That is all I have got to say. Your honor, I am sorry I am not to be hung with the rest of the men."[10]

Another person must be mentioned. It is the Governor Altgeld of Illinois. This just and courageous man gave freedom to Fielden, Schwab, and Neebe in 1893. He had proven in a comprehensive report that the executed were innocent and had been killed unlawfully. This is why he has the honor to be named here in connection with them. He deserves this in particular because the furious American master and exploiter class would have killed him too had it only had the option.

Two months ago the *Sedantag*[11] was celebrated with much pomp by all good Germans. None of these people were good Germans during the farce of Chicago which they watched in silence and without sympathy. This despite the fact that five among the eight men who were killed or imprisoned were Germans. A fact that might almost justify patriotism. However, these men were not good Germans either. They had left their fatherland to find a hero's death on foreign soil; a death that makes them immortal.

Let us pledge today: we want to be Germans like they were! Their ideals, documented in word and text, are ours too: anarchy, free labor, and a free life. If it will ever be our fate to fall into the same hands as they, we can only wish to depart as they did!

---

1. After the Chicago police had killed six workers on strike for an eight-hour workday on May 3, 1886, a workers' rally was held on Chicago's Haymarket Square the next evening. At the end of a relatively uneventful gathering, police officers moved in to disperse the crowd. A pipe bomb was thrown, killing one of the officers. The police opened fire, which was returned by armed workers. The shootout left eight police and an unknown number of workers dead; approximately sixty police officers and an estimated two hundred workers were wounded. The person who threw the bomb was never identified. Of the eight radical labor organizers who were arrested and put on trial for conspiracy to murder, the majority were of German descent. All but one were sentenced to death. Oscar Neebe (1850-1916) was sentenced to fifteen years in prison.

Samuel Fielden (1847-1922) and Michael Schwab (1853-1898) appealed to the governor and had their sentences commuted to life imprisonment. Louis Lingg (1864-1887) committed suicide the night before the execution. Albert R. Parsons (1848-1887), August Spies (1855-1887), Adolph Fischer (1858-1887), and Georg Engel (1836-1887) were hanged on November 11, 1887.

2. Heinrich Schwartz was killed in 1895; Mühlhausen is a small town in Southern Germany.

3. Landauer refers to three-day battles in the Berlin suburb of Friedrichshain between unemployed workers and police from February 24 to 26, 1892.

4. Robert Reitzel (1849-1898), German-American anarchist and long-time editor of the Detroit journal *Der arme Teufel* [The Poor Devil] (1884-1900); see "In Memory of Robert Reitzel" in this volume.

5. August Spies, letter to Richard Oglesby, Governor of Illinois, November 6, 1887; quoted from *www.spartacus.schoonet.com.uk/USAspies.htm*.

6. Albert Parsons grew up in Alabama. He married Lucy González (1853-1942) in Texas in 1871. The couple moved to Chicago where they got involved in radical labor politics. Lucy Parsons remained a dedicated labor activist until her death in 1942.

7. Heinrich Heine (1797-1856), libertarian German poet; the "Silesian Weavers" (Die schlesischen Weber), published as "Die armen Weber" [The Poor Weavers] in 1844 in Karl Marx's journal *Vorwärts!* [Forward!], is one of his most popular poems, also known as the "Weberlied" [Song of the Weavers].

8. Landauer refers here to the "German Workers' Marseillaise," written by German poet and labor activist Jacob Audorf (1834-1898) in 1864 and sung to the original Marseillaise tune.

9. Roughly: *We will make the future, the present is already watching us. Let us begin our dance, even if the ground is rough and hard!*

10. Oscar Neebe, speech at the trial of the Haymarket Martyrs, October 1886; quoted from *www.chicagohistory.org/hadc/books/b01/B01S003.htm*.

11. The *Sedantag* [Day of Sedan] commemorated the Prussian victory over Napoleon III in the Battle of Sedan on September 1, 1870.

IN MEMORY OF
ROBERT REITZEL

The essay commemorates Robert Reitzel, founder and long-time editor of the German-language anarchist journal *Der arme Teufel* [The Poor Devil], published in Detroit from 1884 to 1900, and revived from 1902 to 1904 by Erich Mühsam and others in Berlin. The essay was published as "Zu Robert Reitzels Gedächtnis" in *Der Sozialist*, May 7, 1898, a special issue dedicated to Reitzel.

ROBERT REITZEL IS DEAD. HIS PHYSICAL REMAINS HAVE BEEN cremated. He wished for his friends to commemorate him with joy, song, and wine. However, I have rarely had a feeling of such irretrievable loss. Robert Reitzel demonstrated complete love of life; he knew how both the smallest and the greatest things can enrich our existence; he was always ready to fight for what he believed in; he was a rebel, a revolutionary, an artist of language and of life. Robert Reitzel was unique, and he will not return.

We had gotten so used to his illness that his death came unexpectedly. Especially since his life did not seem finished. Nothing about Robert Reitzel ever seemed finished. He was always in a state of becoming and of recreating himself. He grew permanently before our eyes, until the bitterness of destruction took us by surprise. We are deeply saddened by how much life death has taken from us this time. Robert Reitzel was like a soap bubble that continued to grow bigger, more beautiful, more colorful, and more mesmerizing – until it was suddenly gone.

In Germany, Robert Reitzel is only known among a few, mainly the readers of *Der Sozialist*. But as long as he lived he had great influence among German-Americans. Those who read his texts and his journal *Der Arme Teufel* could not remain indifferent.[1] The clerics' talk about how the dead have no enemies is certainly not true for him. Many still hate Robert Reitzel. Many more, however, love him.

Reitzel was particularly hated among priests of all sorts: the priests of the church (he had fought both Catholics – with love – and Protestants – with contempt); the priests of the state; the priests of the political parties; the priests of morality; even the "free-thinking" priests. Besides, Reitzel was hated by professional writers, the writers of America's compliant press, the writers paid by capital.

Robert Reitzel educated German-Americans about classical German literature: Goethe, Heine, Scheffel, Gottfried Keller, Storm, Vischer.[2] He also educated them about the literature of our German youth. He introduced many names to America: Henckell, Mackay,[3] in his last years particularly Nietzsche. Germans he educated about American literature: Emerson, Henry David Thoreau, Walt Whitman.

Der Arme Teufel enabled the gathering of diverse elements: old fraternity members, young fraternity members (the old Heidelberg student never liked the *Blasen*[4]), the Catholic priest Hansjakob, the blasphemer Panizza, the free-thinker Ruedebusch, the democrat Conrad, the communist Most, the individualist Tucker, scholars, merchants, workers.[5] It was Reitzel's great, gripping personality that attracted them all.

How can we describe this personality? Reitzel was no man of programs, of parties, of dogmas. He liked to call himself an anarchist whenever it was a dangerous thing to do – like in the year 1897 after the murder of Cánovas.[6] What attracted him to revolutionary socialism was not future models and doctrines, but the rebellious spirit of both the individual and the masses. His greatest virtue might have been that he was able to interest people, who had initially only admired his sophistication, his prose, and his free-thinking approach to religion, in his rebellious character, his nihilism, and his anarchist spirit. He was often told that his true domains were peace, beauty, contentment, and joy. Every time he responded emphatically that in our times war, hate, anger, and violence are still needed.

At the same time, Reitzel taught the proletarians that they have to wrap their swords in roses. He made it clear to them that it is not only the stomach that suffers hunger and thirst, but the spirit and the soul too.

Without end, Reitzel sang us the song of songs of pleasure and celebrated the soul by wine and love! How this man could love, and how he could tell us about love! To Anna and Röslein, to Grete and Liese, and to many others. When he thought about his past and his home, he laughed and cried, he rejoiced and dreamt.

The few examples of his writing that we have collected for this commemorative issue will prove his wonderful use of language. They will demonstrate what a complete man he was. The remainder of the issue will consist of nothing but articles and poems by him.

In recent years, whenever someone who Reitzel loved had died, he liked to pronounce the following words – words I would now like to pronounce as well:

> *Ho! stand to your glasses ready!*
> *Tis all we have left to prize.*
> *A cup to the dead already.*
> *Hurrah for the next that dies.*[7]

---

1. The journal *Der arme Teufel* [The Poor Devil] was published in Detroit from 1884 to 1900 and briefly revived in Berlin from 1902 to 1904 by Erich Mühsam and others.

2. Heinrich Heine (1797-1856), Joseph Victor von Scheffel (1826-1886), Gottfried Keller (1819-1890), Theodor Storm (1817-1888), Friedrich Theodor Vischer (1807-1887); German-language poets and writers.

3. Karl Friedrich Henckell (1864-1929), German writer; John Henry Mackay (1864-1933), Scottish-born German writer and anarchist.

4. A loose, fraternity-like student group.

5. Heinrich Hansjakob (1837-1916), politically engaged Catholic priest and writer; Oskar Panizza (1853-1921), German psychiatrist and poet; Emil F. Ruedebusch (ca. 1870-1920), German-American libertarian writer; Michael Georg Conrad (1846-1927), German writer and liberal politician.

6. Antonio Cánovas de Castillo (1828-1897) was an influential Spanish monarchist shot dead by the Italian anarchist Michele Angiolillo (1871-1897); Angiolillo was executed for the killing.

7. English in the original.

TUCKER'S REVELATION

Landauer criticizes Benjamin Tucker's preface to the sixth edition of *State Socialism and Anarchism: How Far They Agree and Wherein They Differ*, published in London in 1911 (first edition 1886). The text was published as "Tuckers Eröffnung" in *Der Sozialist*, May 15, 1911.[1]

TWENTY-FIVE YEARS AGO, THE AMERICAN BENJAMIN R. Tucker wrote a short essay entitled "State Socialism and Anarchism: How Far They Agree and Wherein They Differ." Tucker had avidly studied the theoretical skeletons of two great socialists, the American Josiah Warren and the Frenchman Pierre-Joseph Proudhon. He combined the two and created a new, fleshless and bloodless, skeleton that he called the only true anarchism – while, in fact, it is more aptly called "anatomism."

Tucker claims the following: economic conditions will be perfect when free, total, unrestricted competition reigns. Today, this competition is restricted by monopolies that are protected by the state. Four such monopolies are central. First, the *money monopoly*, capital's interest. (If the banks and the institutions of circulation were forced to compete, then they would receive financial rewards for administrative duties, but no extra tributes.) Second, the *land monopoly*. (Protected by the state, huge land and mining areas are the property of individuals who do not take after these areas personally. This protection by the state must go. Land must only be possessed for personal use.) Third and fourth, *tariffs* and *patents*. At the right moment, the people will – by appropriate means, mainly organized tax refusal – undermine the power of the state. In turn, the protection of the monopolies will vanish, free competition will hold sway, and the era of anarchist socialism will begin.

In its abstract form – bereft of all psychology and historical differentiation – this theory has always been weak and childish.

However, it still included the great discoveries of Proudhon in certain ways, and those who knew how to equip the skeleton with flesh and the corpse with life could benefit from it; even if Proudhon's thoughts were anatomized, dogmatized, and systematized to a degree that leaves them barely recognizable.

What has always been dangerous, however, is Tucker's use of abstract terms without reflecting upon reality critically and linguistically. This is especially dangerous for half-educated dilettantes who take the "state" and "capital" as much for realities as they did the land. It seems that Tucker's individualism never noticed that for the independent and courageous individual, the "state" is only reality insofar as one wants to live in peace and undisturbed comfort. Yet there have always been individualists of another kind, i.e., anarchists, who have shown what the state truly is, namely a spook. They have shown that the state is no reality that exists independently from the people. There is no "state" on the one hand, and people who live in it on the other. The "state" much rather belongs to what people do and understand. People do not live in the state. The state lives in the people.

The individualist Tucker is insofar a state socialist as he is totally dependent on the state, the masses, and the majority. As long as the "state" is not abandoned, not even the tiniest bit of Tucker's free competition of capital can be realized. Tucker knows nothing about the possibilities of free and direct exchange of producers who have unified their consumption by means of mutual credit, checks, and clearinghouses. Tucker knows nothing of the things that Owen, Proudhon, Busch, and Mülberger knew.[2] He knows nothing about how the paradigms are created that allow the masses to free themselves of the state and capital when humans begin to organize the exchange of their products beyond privileged capital – capital and the state do not exist as external realities, but as internal deficits. Tucker knows nothing about the destructive and productive forces of the individual. He knows nothing about creativity and is hence the opposite of an individualist. He is a philistine who is not connected to life but battles spooks. He takes the "state" and "capital," both of which exist as relations between people, for the exact same kind of reality as a piece of land or nature.

We do not want to enter the controversial debate around land ownership and personal possession and use here. Bernard Shaw has criticized Tucker successfully in this respect.[3] It ought to be mentioned, however, that Tucker is a completely ahistorical person with no comprehension of communities and communal ownership. In the way he articulated it, the abolition of land monopoly – land being after all a natural reality that one has or does not have – only means that after the end of state protection, the parts of the land that are not actually used by their owners are confiscated and redistributed.

Tucker's great love for passivity shows here. People have to "abolish the state." But how? It is fascinating that Tucker manages to never say a single word about this. He simply sweeps over it.

Tucker's theory is like hard bread that has to be dipped into reality to make it digestible. If we do this, however, its consequences cannot be overlooked. An end to land monopoly means the beginning of a new form of land ownership. For example, the servants who have helped a master to use his land might now take possession of the land themselves. Since the protection by the state is gone, they will somehow take from the monopolist what he does not need. *Somehow*. As soon as one tries to fill one gap in Tucker's theory, another one appears.

Tucker wrote this essay twenty-five years ago. He celebrates the anniversary in curious ways. If he were a drummer and this essay was his finest drum, we could say that he now beats it so hard (probably being happy that it held up for twenty-five years) that its gaps become increasingly obvious. Let us consider the postscript to the essay's sixth edition,[4] which was recently published in London – it is short but telling:

> "[Twenty-five] years ago, when the foregoing essay was written, the denial of competition had not yet effected the enormous concentration of wealth that now so gravely threatens social order. It was not yet too late to stem the current of accumulation by a reversal of the policy of monopoly. The Anarchistic remedy was still applicable.

> Today the way is not so clear. The four monopolies, unhindered, have made possible the modern development of the trust, and the trust is now a monster which I fear, even the freest banking, could it be instituted, would be unable to destroy. As long as the Standard Oil group controlled only fifty millions of dollars, the institution of free competition would have crippled it hopelessly; it needed the money monopoly for its sustenance and its growth. Now that it controls, directly and indirectly, perhaps ten thousand millions, it sees in the money monopoly a convenience, to be sure, but no longer a necessity. It can do without it. Were all restrictions upon banking to be removed, concentrated capital could meet suc-

cessfully the new situation by setting aside annually for sacrifice a sum that would remove every competitor from the field.

If this be true, then monopoly, which can be controlled permanently only for economic forces, has passed for the moment beyond their reach, and must be grappled with for a time solely by forces political or revolutionary. Until measures of forcible confiscation, through the State or in defiance of it, shall have abolished the concentrations that monopoly has created, the economic solution proposed by Anarchism and outlined in the forgoing pages – *and there is no other solution* – will remain a thing to be taught to the rising generation, that conditions may be favorable to its application after the great leveling. But education is a slow process, and may not come too quickly. Anarchists who endeavor to hasten it by joining in the propaganda of State Socialism or revolution make a sad mistake indeed. They help to so force the march of events that the people will not have time to find out, by the study of their experience, that their troubles have been due to the rejection of competition. If this lesson shall not be learned in a season, the past will be repeated in the future, in which case we shall have to turn for consolation to the doctrine of Nietzsche that this is bound to happen anyhow, or to the reflection of Renan[5] that, from the point of view of Sirius,[6] all these matters are of little moment."

Tucker has always chosen the imprecise word over the precise, the vague over the clear. If we nonetheless try to understand what he is saying, the gist would be that there is only one thing to do: spread the right doctrine, i.e., anarchism according to Benjamin R. Tucker. How is this anarchism spelled out? We need the great revolution and the redistribution of property. However, since it will take some time for this to happen – and Tucker does not seem upset – there is little use for us individualists to propagate and realize the revolution. It is enough to educate by word and text. The actual work can be done by those who we despise: state socialists, communists, and professional revolutionaries. They can also take care of the confiscations of property. Due to our influence, the blessing of free competition will then simply follow. The rest does not concern us. It is also untimely to redistribute property and work for the revolution now. The time is not yet ripe, and humans are not yet ready for the millennium. History might repeat itself. We individualists, however, wash our hands in innocence.

A lot can be conceded to Tucker. Our overall situation has become more difficult. The working masses will never care much about the thousands of millions of the Standard Oil Group and the billions of other trusts, corporations, and capitalists. The only things they care about are the land and its products. They can do without the gold and the silver, and without the paper and the ink that the books are kept with. However, land ownership has become ever more concentrated. As we have seen, Tucker once called the confiscation of illegally owned land the anarchists' second main task after the abolition of the state. He explained this hazily and left it to others to think further and expand the confiscations to products that are owned as extensions of the land and as a consequence of illegal monopolies; for example houses, factories, machines, and accumulated goods. Now he pulls back and gives up the only part of his doctrine that ever had an active element. (No matter that it was left to those who the Tuckerite anarchists want to have nothing to do with, other than to instruct them on what to do after the revolution.)

The real difficulty does not even lie in the concentration of the only true wealth: land and land products, but in the fact that the workers lack what is true "capital": mutualism, forms of work, and modes of exchange that are independent of the capitalist global market, and first indications of socialism which can lead to its expansion and to a redistribution of property. Such state socialists and true believers as Tucker and Marx bear a major part of the responsibility for this. They get people used to waiting and hoping, and they teach them to desperately stare into the future. They have told people again and again: there is nothing to be done now; a certain development must come to an end first.

Tucker and Marx belong together. Both are fanatical believers in the state. It is true, one wants to extend the state, while the other wants to abolish it. However, they both see the state as a fact, when in reality it is only a condition of the soul. One waits until the state develops into socialism, and engages in politics that are supposed to speed up the process. The other also waits for the state to develop into socialism, but thinks that the state will disappear during this process. This difference is less important than the commonality: both delay socialism and have no idea what to do now.

Tucker thinks that, due to their enormous reserve funds, trusts can throw goods on the market so cheaply that they can eliminate all competition. What, however, is Tucker's scenario? His text describes a situation where a people, or various peoples, have "abolished the state" by means of organized passive resistance ("tax refusal, etc." – he is too clever to elaborate on the "etc."). It never occurs to him that the general strike is an essential part of his famous passive resistance, and that the trusts can hardly throw goods on the market, no matter the price, when there are no hands to produce them.

However, let us not talk about Tucker's vision of a future that we will never see. Let us talk about the socialism that is real and that is in its beginnings. If socialists communalize their consumption and begin to work for themselves, if they, in ever increasing numbers, establish settlements, workshops, and factories, if they create popular banks and other means of circulation – will the capitalists not kill them as soon as these new creations become a threat? Here we reach the weakest part of Tucker's theory: he knows of no other motives than those of economic advantage. Without egoism of a higher kind – known as sacrifice, passion, fire, love, and community – not even the faintest idea of socialism will ever arise and nothing will ever challenge economic monopolies.

Tucker and his followers probably know this. They know that there will never be a true socialist beginning without individuals who dedicate themselves to ideals, to heroism, and even to temporary communism. Tucker and his followers are unable to do this. This is why they preach passivity and caution. They do not act but calculate. This is the final explanation for all the gaps in their theories. With his latest words, Tucker has made them even bigger.

The lifelessness, rigidness, shrewdness, and coldness of Tucker's philistine doctrine cannot be emphasized enough. Tucker says: "I proclaim an absolute ideal and I stand by it. For this ideal to become reality, revolution is a necessary precondition and will bring with it the redistribution of property. To bring about the revolution, however, is not my duty. In fact, I am concerned that it will come before the time is ripe for it. So all I do is proclaim the absolute ideal. Should history repeat itself: in other words, should it come to another heroic effort by the people to redistribute wealth in a way that I, Tucker, do not agree with, what will I do? Nothing. I just stay in my armchair, or retreat to the star Sirius, and continue to proclaim."

Is not Tucker himself a repetition of history? Is he not Ahasver, the eternal Jew? Just like Ahasver constantly wandered, Tucker constantly sits in his armchair, writing his treatises and mumbling something about "repetitions of history." The Peasants' War returns, and Florian Geyer once more heads for the fields, the theorist Carlstadt courageous on his side[7] – Tucker in his armchair mumbles: "Repetition of history." He travels

253

with his armchair to England to meet the royals and, in the same way Milton fought the king during the English Revolution, opens the bag he has slung over his shoulder, hands them a brochure – and mumbles just like the poet of the paradise lost and regained: "Repetition of history." The eternal Tucker travels to North America to watch the War of Independence unfold, and then heads to France to witness the Great Revolution and subsequently the events of 1830, 1848, 1871, and so on – having the scriptures announcing the millennium and the armchair always with him, he once again mumbles: "Repetition of history."

For active natures, there is no repetition of history; everything is unique, original, essential, and alive. Nor is there ever complete fulfillment of ideals; the fulfillment of ideals needs permanent struggle and (re)creation. Passive, dogmatic, philistine, and dead natures, on the other hand, are convinced of the opposite. What they reject is always the same, and their ideals are always the same too. All that needs to be done in order to fulfill them is to spit them out over and over again.

Now we know what this newest revelation of Tucker is. It is not the final word of his doctrine. It is not his legacy. It is not the revelation of his testament. It is the revelation of his bankruptcy.

---

1. For a Landauer critique of John Henry Mackay, Germany's most prominent individualist anarchist, see "Ein Leumundszeugnis für Herrn John Henry Mackay" [An Assessment of Mister John Henry Mackay], *Der Sozialist*, October 10, 1898.

2. Ernst Busch (1849-1902) and Arthur Mülberger (1847-1907) were German followers of Pierre-Joseph Proudhon.

3. In the pamphlet "The Impossibilities of Anarchism," published by London's Fabian Society in 1893.

4. The edition quoted by Landauer was not accessible to me. I here quote the slightly revised version of the 1911 postscript, published in the 1926 edition of *State Socialism and Anarchism* by Vanguard Press in New York.

5. Ernest Renan (1823-1892), French writer and historian.

6. Sirius is the brightest star in the night sky.

7. Florian Geyer (ca. 1490-1525), a leading figure during the German Peasants' War of 1524-1525; Andreas Carlstadt (also: Karlstadt, born Bodenstein, ca. 1482-1541) was a German theologian and reformer.

McNAMARA

In this article on the bombing of the *Los Angeles Times* offices on October 1, 1910, which killed twenty-one people, Landauer mainly targets the hypocrisy of the defense campaigns for the brothers James and John McNamara, both radical labor activists, who, after months of denial, eventually admitted to the deed. The *Los Angeles Times* had been targeted for its strong anti-union positions. James, who had planted the bombs, was sentenced to life, John to fifteen years in prison. Published as "MacNamara" [sic] in *Der Sozialist*, March 1, 1912.

I
N LOS ANGELES, NEAR THE MEXICAN BORDER, THERE HAS BEEN an enormous explosion in an office building in which both the daily *Los Angeles Times* and a big steel plant had their offices. Twenty-three people died.[1] Immediately after the incident, two explanations were offered, both drawing on experts' reports: some people claimed that it was a terrorist attack; others maintained that it was a gas explosion.

In particular, the workers' papers insisted that the unfortunate victims were not only victims of an accident, but of criminal capitalist negligence. They called the accusation of capitalists and state persecutors that members of socialist workers' organizations had planted a bomb infamous. This did not deter the state prosecutor from arresting numerous leaders of the local labor movement, among them the McNamara brothers. In turn, a protest movement was initiated by syndicalists and anarchists that soon encompassed all strains of the American labor movement and expanded across the entire country. The movement was dedicated to fighting what it saw as a disdainful attempt to exploit a terrible accident for the demonization of socialism and the destruction of the lives of innocent socialist activists.

Many parallels were drawn to the judicial murders in Chicago.[2] The same had happened there. A bomb was thrown, the leaders of the labor movement were arrested, and, in a scandalous trial, declared responsible for the deed of an unknown person because of their speeches and writings. Some of them were executed, others imprisoned. Years later, the state's highest public servant, Governor Altgeld of Illinois, conducted an extensive inquiry into the matter, declared all of the accused innocent, and immediately freed those who were still alive.

In Los Angeles, the situation seemed even worse: a mere accident was to be used to put innocent socialists on trial and to accuse them of a terrible deed that had not even occurred. The outrage among the workers grew with every passing week. Then, suddenly, the two main suspects confessed, declaring that they were responsible for the explosion.

It is understandable that the social democratic and union leaders were ashamed. They had thought that they were fighting for innocent men. Those who embrace the principle of vengeance are probably most likely to understand their reaction: in their anger, rage, and indignation, they now furiously demanded the most severe punishment for the guilty.

The workers were in a difficult situation. People should never be turned into means – social democrats must abide by this as well. During the protest campaign, Victor Berger[3] and other social democratic leaders were used and hailed – even though they never acted out of any other motive than a "bourgeois" sense of morality incited by an unjust persecution. Their calls for vengeance were only a logical conclusion. Throughout the entire case, they did nothing other than follow their nature. Now, however, they were assailed by radical workers.

There are circles within the workers' movement that stubbornly deny that socialism requires human nature of a different kind; one that does not embrace violence. In these circles the fight for socialism is seen as a war following war's laws. This is why it might very well be that the initiators of the protest movement were in fact hypocrites and liars. I am saying this for truth's sake. The commitment to truth is an essential part of the human being required by socialism. Did these protesters not know, or at least feel, that this had been a deliberate attack? Was not their main intention to do everything they could to save the comrades who were in danger? Did this not mean that they denied the deed, and rallied against the persecution of allegedly innocent men only for tactical reasons?

This cannot be determined, and I do not want to examine all the dirt behind the scenes. What do I mean by "dirt?" A fight that is led by Jesuit means. A lot of idealism can be part of such a fight, but not the purity of truth. Capitalist exploitation and statist oppression are able to beset the souls of those who maintain them, because these souls have no real desire for purity and truth. Neither do so-called socialists and revolutionaries who believe that they are engaged in a war between the oppressed and the oppressors; a war in which all means are justified. In most cases, these people are on the side of the oppressed because they have not had the opportunity to be on the side of the rich. Their nature is no different. In fact, their lack of responsibility might even be greater. They often mistake the restlessness and libidousness of gypsies for freedom and rebellion.

True socialism is something entirely different from the fight of a social group against another. Being unable to enter the ranks of the rich – as a result of both external and internal circumstances – does not make you a socialist. Being a servant to a master or to your own reflexes and instincts does not make you a socialist. Socialism is not a war between people. Socialism is first and foremost a struggle of man against himself; secondly, it is a war against war.

There is a remarkable aspect to the Californian act of war. Usually, there is no need to guess whether something was a terrorist act or not. It might be understandable – considering the logic of war, revenge, and propaganda – if the individual perpetrators deny having committed the act in order to save their lives; both for their own sake and for that of further action. However, the intentions behind the act will still be communicated to the public. What kind of sense does it make to blow up a building and kill people, and then speak of it as an accident?

We can assume that the consequences of the deed, the property destruction as well as the death of innocent people, were not deplorable to the perpetrators. Sane people would not have conceived such an act to begin with. What, however, is left of their deed when no one even knows that it was deliberate? It might make some kind of sense for a group of individuals to kill a Russian tsar by poisoning him over time without ever telling anyone. Despite history teaching us differently, they might believe that the death of a particular leader might help the people. However, such logic does not apply to the terrible act of Los Angeles.

After the McNamara brothers had changed their minds and confessed, heated arguments ensued within the workers' movement. All across the globe, people now debated the act's possible justification. Of course – and I say this with great sadness, as it ought not be self-explanatory – there are various strains of communist anarchists and revolutionary syndicalists who defend the action. On the opposite side, one finds mainly Marxists and other parliamentary socialists. Their arguments, however, for example the ones that Kautsky directed against the American syndicalist and social democrat Haywood,[4] are pitiful, as they only concern tactics. "Individual activism" is decried because it hurts the official labor movement. In Kautsky's words: "Everything that makes the organization of the proletarian masses more difficult, or that keeps the masses from organizing altogether, has to be rejected!" Kautsky stands on the same ground as the embracers of vengeance: Jesuitism. In this case the Jesuitism of the party.

Within all this calculating bleakness one longs for a word from the heart. However, no such word can be found; let alone a word that leaves behind the paradigm of war and heads for the true foundation of socialism.

In the pages of this journal, socialism has recently been described in the following manner: "It does not strike back when it is attacked. Instead, it tries to understand the reasons behind the attack and seeks to avoid further aggression by changing the conditions that give rise to it. Socialism is not about responding to ills in a reactionary manner. It is about ending ills by transforming the reality that feeds them."[5]

Haywood and other apologists of the deed committed by the McNamara brothers argue that socialism fights property and that property must hence be destroyed. This, so the argument continues, frightens the capitalists and eventually renders capitalism impossible. Such foolish and superficial pronouncements pass as particularly radical.

I could not care less whether one calls me a radical or not. I can easily do without labels. Neither superficial garishness nor garish superficiality are indications of radicalness. The same goes for smashing fanfares. "Radical" is not, as it is often claimed, the opposite of "moderate," but of "superficial."

Superficial are all those who tamper with symptoms rather than turning their attention to the roots. Even wild agitation and excessive hate can be very superficial. On the other hand, quietness, contemplation, and caution can be very radical. I see Tolstoy as an eminently radical figure, much more so than many who have risked their lives under the influence of superficial theories that they combined with their natural instincts. I do have a lot of respect for these people though. They might not have thought radically, but the connection that they made between their feelings and their lives, between their desires and their deeds, was genuine and radical. What I find difficult is to muster respect for those who build their radicalness on the deeds of others, who turn superficiality into theory, and who reduce essential human questions to mere tactical questions.

There are those who believe that within our economic war, the capitalists and oppressors are on one side, while the chosen ones – like themselves – are on the other. This is not a radical but a superficial belief, no matter how wildly the believers behave. The idea that they only have to win the war to introduce socialism only confirms this.

The people who maintain capitalism and who are at the same time damaged and oppressed by it are on both sides of the divide. Capitalism makes all of us ill. No matter what our material conditions, we are miserable. True socialists want to escape capitalism and war. Those who coerce because of coercion, oppress because of oppression, and act violently because of violence are not socialists. Neither are those who want to replace one government with another. People who respond to blows with blows are unhappy. They are only courageous and heroic because they have been victims for a long time. The ones who turn such libidousness into theory and tactics are superficial tinkerers. They become party leaders instead of socialists.

"Property is theft." What does this famous phrase mean? It relates the possession of one's own property (something that has traditionally been held in high regard) to the theft of someone else's property (something that has traditionally been held in low regard). Now let us consider the fact that those who steal live off others. What does this mean for those who do not live off their labor, but off the interest of their property? They also live off the labor of others. Hence, the owner is a thief. This is the lesson of the phrase. Does it justify theft? No! What confusion! Everyone knows what a thief is. What needs to be understood is what an owner is.

People like Haywood claim that we cannot have socialism now and that it will come later. They add that property is theft and that war is murder. Hence, those who are destined to die must respond with theft and murder to be like the rich and powerful.

Here we have it: "to be like them." If it were only true. Those who say these things realize and admit that the ills of our society lie in robbery and war, while the rich and powerful do not. This is why there should only be one thing for the former to do: begin with the creation of a better life and the renewal of society. Who else is to do this? And how else could it be done? And when will it ever begin?

As long as "socialists" continue to dance their dance and add murder to murder, robbery to robbery, and revenge to revenge, as long as the action of "revolutionaries" is reaction, and as long as neither engages in transforming the individual and society and in creating something new, then everything will only become worse and these so-called socialists and revolutionaries will remain accomplices of the status quo – and they will be particularly guilty, because they knew, but failed to transform their knowledge into action.

Such is the true propaganda by the deed: to actively turn the truth in our minds into social reality.

1. On October 1, 1910.

2. Reference to the Haymarket martyrs – see "On the 11th of November" in this volume.

3. Victor Berger (1860-1929), socialist journalist and co-founder of the Socialist Party of America in 1901.

4. Karl Kautsky (1854-1938), Czech-German social democratic theorist; Bill Haywood (1869-1928), union activist, best known for his prominent role in the Industrial Workers of the World (IWW).

5. From Landauer's article "Organisierte Reaktionen" [Organized Reactions], published in *Der Sozialist*, February 1, 1912.

FROM MEXICO

In 1911, Landauer published two articles on the Mexican Revolution in *Der Sozialist*: "Zur Revolution in Mexiko" [On the Mexican Revolution], on May 1, 1911, and "Aus Mexico" [From Mexico], on September 15, 1911. "Aus Mexico" provides the more comprehensive analysis. Both articles express Landauer's sympathies for the Magón brothers and the Mexican Liberal Party, as well as Landauer's critique of U.S. imperialism.

T HE REVOLUTION IN MEXICO IS NOT YET OVER. HOWEVER, ITS development certainly does not serve the interests of the North American railway kings and land thieves. It also goes beyond a mere quarrel about words or about presidential or ministerial posts. No battles have been waged yet and no towns occupied. The recent change in leadership, however, will not please the country's inhabitants. They have been violently and fraudulently robbed of their lands and sold into bondage on plantations and in factories. They will not accept that the leader of their masters shall now be called Madero instead of Díaz.[1]

They know that Madero is one of the country's richest land-owners and is interested in nothing but power and land acquisition. In the countries we live in, we do not properly understand what it means to be a rich landowner in Mexico. One needs to travel for weeks to cover Madero's estate. Besides, Madero is an agent of the North Americans who want to control and exploit Mexico. This, however, is the reason why there was a lot of international press coverage on the revolution (never truthful of course). Those in power were interested in the revolution as long as it was indeed Madero's revolution, i.e., as long as the capitalists were able to exploit the rebellion of the poor and downtrodden. Now that the rebellion is turning against the oppressors and land thieves, the coverage has ended. There are no reports about the tearing down of fences, the destruction of ownership records, the occupations of lands, the strikes on plantations, and the walkouts in factories.

The party that still supports the rebellion is the Mexican Liberal Party.[2] It has adapted the slogan *Land and Freedom*. Its leaders, the two Magóns and others,[3] have been imprisoned by the United States authorities for "violation of neutrality." Their courageous and outspoken journal *Regeneración*, published in Los Angeles, California,[4] has been prohibited in Mexico by Madero. Nonetheless, it is distributed and read. It will also soon include an English section that will enlighten those in North America who are willing to be enlightened.

Such enlightenment is more than necessary. The position of the radicals and social democrats in the United States is scandalous. They feel, with good reason, that the struggle in Mexico is a struggle for true freedom and realization. For party socialists of all countries, however, true freedom and realization has always spelt Beelzebub and anarchism. The Mexican Liberals have become anarchists by getting in touch with reality. They do not object to the label, as long as it is interpreted correctly. For the United States social democrats of course this is reason enough to deny these socialist revolutionaries support. And not only that: it is reason enough to abuse them.

It should not surprise us that the land reformers and single taxers, the heirs of Henry George, do not care the least about this heroic and desperate struggle of workers against parasites, of the poor who toil the land against the capitalists who steal it. The saying *There are no roses without thorns* cannot be turned on its head: there are plenty of thorny bushes that never carry roses. In other words: those who expect the land reformers to have an interest in a true struggle about land – a struggle that affects millions of people – are wrong. I doubt that the German land reformers have even heard about the Mexican land thieves and the shameless methods that they are using. Accordingly, the German land reformers have probably not heard about the enormous struggle against them either.[5]

It had to be expected that the United States social democrats would use this opportunity to wrap their cowardliness and petty jealousy in Marxist colors. Thus, they find an appropriate reason to leave the Mexicans to their fate. "They have not yet gone through the capitalist stage." True. They are for the most part peasants, and for the most part they have not been chased from their lands because their properties were needed, but because there was a demand for serfs. In Marxist reasoning, this means that these developments mark "original accumulation" and belong to a precapitalist era. This also goes for the cruelties committed by Díaz, Madero, the North American billionaires, the land thieves, and the railway shareholders. It goes for everything that these capitalists have done against men, women, and children.

The Mexican serfs are still beginners in misery. This is not intended to belittle their misery. Not even a German party secretary could claim that the misery of a German industrial worker is greater than that of a Mexican peasant chased from his land. What being a beginner in misery means is that one still has the force and spirit to rebel!

When capitalism has blossomed, when the time is ripe for transformation, there will no longer be revolutionaries and beginners. The Marxists' *Verelendungstheorie*[6] is correct; but it must also be understood correctly. The more capitalism blossoms, the weaker the heart and the mind of the proletariat become.

You brave Mexicans, your revolution is still at its beginning. Our workers have already taken a few steps. You are still a long way from scientific social democracy. In other words: you have not been robbed of your mind long enough yet to be social democrats. This is the truth. Only those who have lost their minds can adhere to the bizarre botanical studies of scientific cowards who are waiting for capitalism to blossom because they are unable to find and eradicate its roots.

1. See footnote 4 in "Revolution, Nation, and War."

2. The Mexican Liberal Party (*Partido Liberal Mexicano*) existed from 1906 to 1913 and was strongly influenced by anarchist ideas. For some months during the Mexican Revolution it controlled Baja California.

3. Ricardo Flores Magón (1873-1922) and Jesús Flores Magón (1871-1930).

4. *Regeneración* [Renewal] was published from 1900 to 1918.

5. German land reformers were mainly organized in the Bund deutscher Bodenreformer [Association of German Land Reformers], led by Adolf Damaschke (1865-1935).

6. Marxist theory about the necessary pauperization (*Verelendung*) of the working class in capitalism.

MEXICO

On August 10, 1914, Landauer published this update on the Mexican Revolution in *Der Sozialist*. He continues to sympathize with the Mexican Liberal Party and stresses the importance of the land question. His analysis of the "anarchist" Liberal Party's role helps clarify his understanding of anarchism and provides a very tangible example for his reflections in *Die Revolution*.

THERE IS NO DOUBT THAT THE REVOLUTION IN MEXICO — AS it has been explained in this journal before[1] – persists for so long only because it is based in a social revolution and is not reduced to a political one. This is the only reason why no political careerists have so far been able to establish authority with the help of the monopolist classes. A social revolution does not accept "peace and order" before it reaches its conclusion. In order to find followers, political careerists have to strengthen the country's "disorder" – then it is easy for them, even if their personalities are not particularly compelling and their connections to the privileged classes not particularly strong.

It seems that there are numerous claims that this revolution is about political power, and that guerilla war and expropriation are its main means. However, the true meaning of the revolution is economic transformation, is the fight against property and monopoly. This alone makes it so durable.

Sometimes we may get the impression that the so-called Mexican Liberal Party of the Magón brothers,[2] in reality an anarchist organization, only exists in Southern California, that it has exaggerated the social significance of the revolution, that it has romanticized its ambitions, and that it has described for fact what is but wishful thinking. However, we now know for certain that Zapata and his followers have written the motto *Land and Freedom* on their banners, and that they act accordingly; the same goes for the peasants and the land laborers (mostly Indians and half-castes, so-called peons[3]) who have united with them.

The Zapatistas, about ten thousand armed men, operate in the north of the country. Their activities have recently been described by the predictably outraged correspondent of the *Frankfurter Zeitung*.[4] They demand the partitioning of all big estates and have begun to execute this in the states they occupy. According to *Regeneración*, the journal of the Mexican Liberal Party,[5] these are Morelos, Southern Puebla, Michoacán, Guerrero, Veracruz, Northern Tamaulipas, Durango, Sonora, Sinaloa, Jalisco, Chihuahua, Oaxaca, Yucatán, and Quintana Roo.

The *Frankfurter Zeitung* describes the Zapatistas' actions thus: they burn all archives and try to destroy any memory of the old regime. The article adds that the program of these northern rebels is full of "socialist phrases." However, the Zapatistas' politics seem hardly limited to "phrases." As the correspondent confirms, the Zapatistas have confiscated all of the private property of the rich, and their provisional government now administers mines, breweries, and factories. Since our country's bourgeois press is enraged, it is probably true when *Regeneración* writes that "the bourgeois press in Mexico has to admit that the workers have themselves taken possession of the land; that they have not waited for some patronizing government to do it for them..."

If this is true, we need not be surprised about the impression shared by an American writer, John Kenneth Turner,[6] in the June issue of the respected journal *The New Review*[7] under the headline "Why I Am For Zapata": "Unlettered as they are, the mass of Mexicans who are fighting with guns know better what they want than any equal number of 'superior' Americans going to the ballet-box know what they want – and they know better how to get it."[8]

In the face of this reality, we need not be surprised if both the U.S. President and the American land monopolists slowly come to realize that Mexican land belongs to the Mexican people, i.e., the people who actually work it. The importance of the issue will not surprise those who remember the ruthless exploitation and slavery-like conditions under which workers on the country's Mexican and American-owned *latifundios*[9] were kept (see the articles in *Der Sozialist* from 1911). It was hence only logical that President Huerta[10] tried to save his rule a few weeks before he was forced to resign due to pressure from all sides by proposing a far-reaching agrarian reform. The mouthpiece of the Californian exploiters, the *Los Angeles Times*, denounced Huerta's proposition as "the greatest plan of confiscation ever proposed by a government."[11]

We can see clearly now that the Mexican Revolution not only builds on the land question, but that the revolutionaries also actively reclaim land, and that they have had respectable success, not least in the way their actions have been embraced by the public, as well as by certain politicians. We can also see clearly now that the Mexican Liberal Party does not only produce forceful revolutionary manifestos, full of wonderful Spanish expressiveness and emotion, but that it also constitutes a real social force. The party might call itself "liberal," but it declares its anarchist leanings openly. Such an organization being the strongest faction within this great revolution must not be underestimated. Characteristically, this "Liberal Party" now turns to the International Anarchist Congress[12] with a precise and proud declaration that demands the recognition of the Mexican Revolution as "not just a war of capitalists, politicians, and bandits," but as a venture where the repossession of land by the working people is seen as "the first step to secure bread and economic freedom." The Mexican Liberal Party further demands that the actions of the Mexican revolutionaries are acknowledged as exemplary for all peoples.

These are two different things, however. The first has to be accepted without reservation: once the revolution – we must not forget: for political reasons[13] – had broken out, the Mexican peons acted in ways that suited their thinly populated country where land is still plenty: they took what they needed from the monopolists and the land trusts. As far as the question of providing a model is concerned, however, there is no denying that the conditions in our countries[14] are significantly different, and that we, as anarchists in these countries, still have many things to do before we can emulate the example of the Mexican peasants. This means that it will take us a long time to get what they are close to getting now. However, it also means that we will not encounter the same problems that they are close to encountering now.

Let us be clear: whatever land the Mexican people have already conquered, and whatever land they will conquer in the near future (although they will have to be quick!), will most probably remain theirs.[15] This is an enormous success that all of humanity will benefit from and that deserves to be celebrated. At the same time, we will see how this success will soon be compromised; namely, by its bureaucratic administration at the hands of the new political entity that will inevitably emerge from the revolution, whether it will be called the North American Union or the Mexican Republic.

As certain as social and economic realization marks the height of this revolution, new forms of political power will mark its end – and hence a return to its beginnings. True anarchy will not be established, nor will true society, true freedom, or true justice. On the basis of the significant improvements that will remain, there will be new violence, new monopolies, new exploitation – and there will be new struggles. History has not spared a single people. What we must wish for is that in Mexico, and anywhere else, the intermediate times, the times of peace, will be used for the preparation and creation of socialism.

We have used the term "anarchist" in connection with the revolutionary Mexican Liberal Party. This is far from typical for us. Anarchism and party politics are contradictions. In this case, however, we are truly dealing with an anarchist *party* – which explains both its current success and its inevitable future defeat.

There are three major kinds of anarchist activity. All deserve the name. First, because it has been used by their practitioners; and second, because they all share the rejection of the state and the desire for freedom and voluntary union as the basis of their beliefs. *One kind* of anarchist activity is individual struggle in times when the masses content themselves with speeches. This kind, marked by the so-called propaganda by the deed and by insurrection, belongs to history. *A second kind* is the radical interference in political revolutions that have gathered mass support. *The third kind* is the preparation and the creation of the spiritual and economic foundations of a stateless society of societies.

The Mexican anarchists became active in a revolution whose eruption they had hardly influenced. This means that they can only engage in the second kind of anarchist activity; for the third, the fundamental one, it is too late. This means that their anarchy can never do more than help to reclaim land for the dispossessed by violent means. The Mexican Liberals will not be able to prevent the institutionalization of new authoritarian violence once the revolution ebbs away, nor will they be able to stop this authoritarian violence from serving the privileged classes and curtailing the working people.

A social revolution cannot be made. The Mexican Liberals have not made one either. They were only able to serve as tools for political revolutionaries – and to use these politicians as their own tools for socialist expropriation. Revolutions as decisive interruptions of history will probably play a part in the great social transformation that will bestow new forms of society and spirit upon us; but the social transformation as a whole can never be reduced to such interruptions.

It cannot be our task to emulate a great revolutionary episode in a thinly populated and barely industrialized country. Our only task can be the third kind of anarchist activity named above. In our situation, this must be the absolute priority. Once again, the objective *is the preparation and creation of spiritual and economic foundations for a stateless society of societies*.

We do believe in *true* an-archy. We believe that capitalist exploitation will one day be brought to an end, just like feudalism was brought to an end. Then no new form of economic privilege will arise, but communities and alliances – *a humanity* – that will create institutions of fair exchange. We believe – in fact, we can clearly see! – that hate and violence, and all their terrible consequences, will turn into a mad and evil dream as soon as the foundations, forms, and the smooth functioning of a society without exploitation have been secured.

This is why we have to take a different approach than Mexico's anarchist-revolutionary "party": we have to allow the spirit – a spirit that has always known the right thing to do – to materialize; we have to create humanity; we have to prevent every great historical interruption and its success from being compromised by law and arbitrariness.

We salute the brave revolutionaries of Mexico! And we invite them to go beyond the thrilling and tempestuous revolutionary work against society's rottenness and decay and to join us in the even more important, yet slow and gradual work of freeing and creating spirit, thereby allowing humanity's peoples to establish economic cooperatives, communities, and alliances.

1. See "From Mexico," including the introductory comments.

2. See footnotes 2 and 3 in "From Mexico."

3. Originally impoverished migrant laborers; derived from the Spanish *peón*, someone who walks as opposed to riding a horse.

4. The liberal *Frankfurter Zeitung* appeared from 1856 to 1943.

5. See footnote 4 in "From Mexico."

6. John Kenneth Turner (1879-1948), U.S.-American journalist and writer with socialist leanings; active supporter of the Mexican Revolution.

7. *The New Review: A Weekly Review of International Socialism* was published in New York from April 1913 to June 1916.

8. John Kenneth Turner, "Why I am for Zapata," *The New Review*, vol. II, June 1914, 325.

9. Quasi-feudal land estates, generally known as *haciendas* in Spanish-speaking Latin America.

10. Victoriano Huerta (1850-1916) was a military officer who assumed the Mexican presidency from February 1913 to June 1914.

11. Re-translated from Landauer's text. I have not been able to access the original.

12. The planned 1914 International Anarchist Congress was not held due to the outbreak of World War I.

13. Landauer refers to the coup of 1911 as the beginning of the Mexican Revolution (see also footnote 4 in "Revolution, Nation, and War").

14. Landauer presumably means the European countries.

15. For the turbulent history of 20th-century land struggles in Mexico see Gustavo Esteva, *The Struggle for Rural Mexico* (South Hadley: Bergin and Garvey, 1983).

OPINION & JOURNALISM PIECES

THE PETROLEUM WORLD MONOPOLY

This is an early essay by Landauer on the control of international petroleum production and trade, and on the possibilities of resistance. Published as "Das Petroleum-Weltmonopol" in *Der Sozialist*, September 9, 1895.

TODAY, THE PROFITS OF THE WORLD'S OIL WELLS ARE BASICALLY united; namely within an enormous ring of exploiters whose heads are the American Rockefeller, the Russian Robel, and the International Rothschild.

We must assume that this monopoly ring prays to nothing but boundless profit, yet if they prayed to God, they could use the words of the great rogue Franz Moor:[1] "Hear me pray, God in Heaven (it is the first time, and it shall never happen again): I have never dealt with little things, my Lord!"

It is indeed no little thing to control without restriction a commodity that uncountable millions of people are dependent on. Neither is it a little thing to earn millions by doing so. The enormous recent increase in oil prices is the work of this clan of crooks, and if Rockefeller felt like it, he could double, or quadruple, this colossal price again in another few weeks. The consumers are entirely at the mercy of the exploiters.

Many propositions have been made for changing this, but they are all useless. Admirers of the state have presented a state monopoly on petroleum as an answer. Such a monopoly could not bring relief, however, because the state owns no oil wells and has to buy from the ring too. Nothing can stop the ring to take as much money from the state as it does from private buyers.

Some might believe that a state monopoly could destroy the ring due to the great demand that unified mass consumption would generate. This means that the individual owners of the oil wells, the so-called producers, would be better off delivering directly to the state rather than to the ring. This, however, is not true. The so-called producers, i.e., the relatively petty exploiters, always fare best when they align themselves with the big exploiters. In fact, in this case, they do not have any other choice. Firstly, the ring can sell petroleum below its value anytime it wants and drive smaller competitors out of business. Secondly, it can offer the highest prices to the owners of the wells – all it has to do is to demand even higher prices from the buyers who are dependent on them.

The so-called producers are by no means connected to the ring by bonds of love. But they are forced to obey it, because otherwise they would be crushed. A state monopoly cannot change this situation in any way. Especially since the powerful within the state have no interest in touching their own freedom of exploitation. The landowners would oppose such a move as well, as the owners of the oil wells are also landowners, and crows do not pick crows' eyes.

In Egidy's *Versöhnung*,[2] Dr. Mülberger makes a suggestion that would essentially lead to the same conclusion as the aspirations of the state monopolists.[3] Mülberger claims that the establishment of municipal oil reserves would solve the problem. He calls for the foundation of petroleum consumers' unions controlled by the municipality, hoping that a unification of consumption will allow the consumers to establish direct contact with the producers, i.e., the petty exploiters.

It has been explained above why such hope is futile, no matter how unified the demand for petroleum is. Neither the state nor the municipality – the latter even less so – can bust the interest groups of capital. Even if the petroleum consumers of the entire world united, they would not be able to get one drop of petroleum from a source other than the ring. As long as the ring stays united, the global consumers' union can do whatever it wants to do – if it wants petroleum at all, it will be forced to pay the prices demanded by the union of exploiters in the end. If the entire raw product is in the hands of the alliance of exploiters, consumers' unions remain entirely powerless, no matter how big they are. I have already explained this in the pamphlet "Ein Weg zur Befreiung," published in May.[4]

There are only two options for the consumers: one is a palliative; the other is a radical measure that, unfortunately, has only little chance of being realized.

The palliative would consist of limiting petroleum consumption. Especially in the crowded environment of big cities, tenants' unions could pressure landlords into installing gas pipes and gaslights, or even electric lighting. If this was widely implemented, it would make a difference. The difference would be small, but at least lighting would no longer be dependent on petroleum and the ring controlling it. However, no one knows what would happen next. Consumers and tenants' unions usually elicit a strong unified response on the part of the exploiters.

This is no argument against consumers' unions. They are extremely important, if only to make the frontlines clear. We have to assume, however, that a success of tenants' unions in reducing dependency on petroleum would only be partial and temporary. While it might make petroleum cheaper, it would probably make gas more expensive.

The radical measure would be the interference of the *true* petroleum producers: the masses of workers at the wells. A worldwide general strike of petroleum workers, supported by the consumers of every nation, has a chance to destroy the ring and to lower the prices of petroleum. Its success would also improve the living conditions of the workers.

Unfortunately, hopes of getting the two most important communities of petroleum workers united are dim: the American workers seem less than enlightened, and the Russian workers languish under despotic rule. Furthermore, the workers would have to go on strike and attempt to break the arrogance and the reign of the exploiters, not primarily in their own interests, but in the interests of the consumers. Finally, there exists another difficulty: even if – with enormous sacrifices – such a strike could be organized, the wells would still remain the private property of the capitalists who could then form another ring, which would then make another strike necessary, and so forth. This would continue until the oppressed – the workers and the consumers alike – arrived at the realization that a gradual fight against the concentration of capital is useless and meaningless.

Once capital is concentrated, it is not enough to purse your lips, you actually have to whistle. In other words, society has to be lifted to a new level; a level at which neither the land nor the means of production are privately owned, and at which no one is exploited or excluded from society's riches.

1. Protagonist in Friedrich Schiller's play *The Robbers* (*Die Räuber*).

2. Journal edited by Moritz von Egidy (1847-1898), a pacifist and Christian reformer, formerly a military officer, from 1894 to 1898. See also footnote 5 in "The Party."

3. Arthur Mülberger (1847-1907), doctor, writer, and advocate of Pierre-Joseph Proudhon's economic theories; Landauer references Mühlberger's essay "Die Petroleum-Frage" [The Petroleum Question] in *Versöhnung*, Year 2, # 35, 1895.

4. "Ein Weg zur Befreiung der Arbeiterklasse" [A Way to Liberate the Working Class] was published in May 1895 in Berlin.

DO NOT LEARN ESPERANTO!

This is Landauer's contribution to the Esperanto debate that had engulfed European socialists after the first Esperanto workers' groups had been established in Sweden (1903) and Germany (1905). Esperanto had been conceived as a means to foster international peace by the Polish school teacher L.L. Zamenhof (1859-1917), who published his outline for an easy-to-learn international language in 1887 under the pseudonym Doktoro Esperanto (*esperanto* meaning "hopeful" in the language itself). Landauer vehemently argues against the unifying virtue of Esperanto, castigating it as an "artificial language" that undermines what he sees as the basis for humanity united in socialism: the cultural regeneration and self-determination of the peoples.

The essay appeared as "Lernt nicht Esperanto!" in the November 1907 issue of *Die Freie Generation* [The Free Generation], a journal edited by the Austrian anarchist Pierre Ramus.[1] Landauer's text is a response to Ramus' pro-Esperanto remarks in the article "Aus dem Tagebuch eines Propagandisten" [From the Diary of a Propagandist], published in the *Freie Generation* October issue of the same year. Ramus added a response to Landauer's article, characteristically entitled "Lernt Esperanto!" [Learn Esperanto!].

Landauer remained opposed to the idea of creating "artificial" languages for easing international communication throughout his life. In a letter from April 1917, he congratulates Martin Buber for opposing a Dutch initiative demanding the establishment of an International Academy to develop a common global language.[2]

I N THE LATEST ISSUE OF *DIE FREIE GENERATION*, PIERRE RAMUS, the journal's editor, has urged his readers to learn the so-called language of Esperanto. Had he recommended reading Goethe's *Faust* once a year, I doubt that he would have had much success. However, I am sure that many readers are already sitting over Esperanto language guides because of Ramus' short remark. Human beings, radicals in particular, have the tendency to embrace everything – often fanatically – as long as it appears out of the ordinary. The challenge of the ordinary derives from reason and appeals to reason. However, reason is one of the two main enemies of spirit – the other is stupidity. The two often merge in spiritless intelligence. Esperanto is a perfect example.

Anarchists need to understand that the basis of both individual life and human co-existence is something that cannot be invented. It is something that has to grow. Society as a voluntary union of humanity, for example, has grown. Nowadays, this union has been *overgrown* by a dreadful artificial product, the state. The people's languages and dialects have also grown. It is sad that different languages are often cited as excuses for hostilities between nation states. It would be even sadder, however, if humans really believed that the diversity of languages was the reason for disunity. Ineradicable, real difference does not only exist between peoples, it exists between all human beings. Each human being talks, thinks, and feels differently than others. In fact, humans can understand and talk to one another because they are different. If they were all the same, they would hate one another. Total equality is not only impossible; it would also be dreadful.

The diversity of languages is nothing to be lamented. Even less so it is something that we can abolish. What we need to abolish are the conditions that keep humans from learning foreign languages. Are anarchists not always opposed to palliatives and gradual improvements within the state and capitalist society? Esperanto is nothing but that – and it is a particularly ugly, useless, and dangerous palliative.

Only the most trivial, petty, and unimportant things can be expressed by an artificial product: only what is old and has been endlessly regurgitated – nothing new, fermenting, creative, ingenious. Language is alive. It has not only grown – it grows continuously. It contains a never-ending past, just as it contains a never-ending future.

Artificial creations do not allow humans to think further and to craft new things. They can only translate what has already been said many times. They can never capture what is most important in a language: the fine shades, the nuances, the unspeakable. In the grown languages, a lot of what is said lives between the words as an unutterable element. In Esperanto we can only blabber.

Even for practical purposes – for example as a language for conferences – Esperanto is useless and dangerous. When the French speak Esperanto, they still think in French, and their original thoughts will only be a distant memory when expressed in this alleged "common language." At the same time, the German or English will interpret what they hear in German and English. People might believe that they understand each other, while there will only be misunderstanding. It is much better for people not to understand each other at all than to misunderstand one another without noticing.

Misunderstandings during discussions in Esperanto can only be avoided when the discussions are reduced to banalities and platitudes. There would be neither subtlety nor refinement; nothing would be from the heart. For anarchism this would be disastrous, as there is nothing more important for anarchism than to delve into the depths of our mind and our spirit and to explore our inner being, our personality, our character, and our human nature. No artificial language can ever do this.

I remember the Zurich anarchist conference of 1893[3] and our Italian comrade Molinari.[4] His speech was fiery and wild; he gestured with his arms and hands, and captured our attention with wide, passionate eyes. I did not understand a word of what he was saying and could only compare his incredible presentation to a roaring waterfall. Then Molinari was translated into German by the late comrade Körner.[5] Körner spoke in a soft, impassionate manner. This allowed me to understand everything: the thunderous appearance of the Italian as well as the calm and modest words of the translator. Had Molinari spoken in Esperanto, I would have missed an important part of this experience; an important part of life.

The German, French, English, and Italian understood one another incredibly well at the conference. They embraced one another with open and curious eyes. No stammering could get in the way of understanding. Shall we give up such moments of deep unity for Esperanto? Never!

For those who have the time to learn languages, I have a different proposal. Learn your own! Germans shall learn German; Englishmen shall learn English, and so on. Do not understand this as an expression of arrogance. Me too, I am still learning German every day; not its grammar, but the language of its great poets and thinkers. If, after you engage in this with love, you still have extra time, learn a foreign language. Not least because it will help you to understand German better; you will discover its intricacies and complexities. If you do learn a foreign language, deal with the grammar as briefly as possible! Start reading as soon as you can! Do not only translate. This is very harmful. Translating can be added later. What is important is to first learn how to read the foreign language, i.e., how to think and feel it.

Do Not Learn Esperanto!

Here is my advice: practice thinking and feeling as it needs to be practiced! Practice the intricacies and complexities of grown languages – especially your own! Never give up the study of your own language! And do not learn Esperanto!

PS: I recommend reading what Fritz Mauthner has written about Esperanto in his recent essay *Die Sprache*.[6]

1. Pierre Ramus (born Rudolf Grossmann, 1888-1942), Austrian anarchist; published *Die Freie Generation* from 1906 to 1908, and *Jahrbuch der Freien Generation* [Yearbook of the Free Generation] from 1910 to 1914.

2. *Gustav Landauer. Sein Lebensgang in Briefen*, 2: 178.

3. Landauer refers to the independent anarchist meeting held after the anarchists had been excluded from the congress of the Second International.

4. Luigi Molinari (1866-1918), Italian anarchist lawyer and educator.

5. Wilhelm Körner (1869-1896), German anarchist; an obituary was published in *Der Sozialist*, January 1, 1896.

6. Mauthner had dedicated his text *Die Sprache* [The Language] to Landauer. It was published in Frankfurt in 1906, as no. 9 of the *Die Gesellschaft* [Society] series, published by Martin Buber. Landauer's *Die Revolution* appeared in the same series one year later as no. 13.

MAY 1

This essay is one of the most thought-provoking in a long line of Landauer commentaries on May 1. They began with enthusiastic support: in 1893, Landauer attended the May 1 celebrations in London as an international delegate and vehemently demanded the date's declaration as a national holiday. In 1894, he hailed May Day in a stirring prison diary entry.[1]

In the essay translated here, published fifteen years later as "Der erste Mai" in *Der Sozialist* (May 1, 1909), Landauer expresses deep frustration with the ritualization of May Day celebrations and the ritualization of political action and protest in general. In an article entitled "Der Arbeitstag" [Work Day], published in *Der Sozialist*, May 1, 1912, Landauer specifically focuses on the social democratic instrumentalization of May Day and its ever increasing reformist character.

An article published about May 1 in 1900 – "Der erste Mai," *Die Welt am Montag*, April 30, 1900 – remains untraceable.

AFTER THE NORDIC PEOPLES WERE VIOLENTLY FORCED UNDER the yoke of Christendom, they had to celebrate their sacred natural festivals in secrecy. Groups of heathens were forced to sneak to mountain tops under the cover of darkness in order to observe the festival of spring on May 1: the festival of nature's resurrection from the ice.

In earlier times, they had celebrated the day jubilantly and openly. Under their Christian masters, all those who gathered for godless natural rites and devotions to joy were gruesomely tortured and murdered. Some heathens succeeded in turning the Christian fear and horror of demonic natural forces against their masters. They made terrible noise once they reached the mountains and made Christians believe that a wild army of witches, devils, and evil ghosts had gathered there. This made them flee instantly, and the pious children of nature were able to greet the arrival of spring with crackling mountain fires. This marked the first Walpurgis Night and led to the belief among Christians that on the eve of May 1, the witches, devils, and evil ghosts rode to the Brocken[2] and to other wild, lonely peaks.

In one of his most beautiful poems, Goethe portrays, with gracious and profound rationalism, how May 1 once was, in old and happy heathen days, a festival of spring, and how it then disappeared under Christendom and was replaced by the night of the Witches' Sabbath.

What we have been witnessing for about the last twenty years as a new form of May Day celebration has nothing heathen, nothing happy, and hardly anything natural about it. It is a colorless, artificial, and institutionalized event that gives no one joy. Nonetheless, people cling to it fanatically. On occasion, they try to connect it to the old festive day in order to give it the air of tradition. This does not really work, however.

The decision of the Paris International Socialist Congress of 1889 to demonstrate every year on the same day for the demands of the workers – in particular for the eight-hour workday – is characteristic of a movement that lacks initiative, spontaneity, and vibrancy. It indicates a movement that has replaced these virtues with discipline and structure.

No effective demonstration has ever been arranged ahead of time – especially not by some delegates at a congress. Effective demonstrations need a trigger, a spark, a particular concern that connects with hope. It must be assumed that it was not the purpose of the congress' tactical decision to prevent such demonstrations. However, it was certainly the result. The "intensity" and "energy" we witness at May Day demonstrations today are nothing but theatre.

Even more pointless and dangerous was the idea of combining the annually pre-assigned demonstration with an annually pre-assigned general strike. What distinguishes revolution – and this is the only true sense a general strike can have – from war is that war is a state institution. As such, it can be prepared, trained, and, to a certain degree, anticipated by wargames. Revolution, on the other hand, is a sudden interruption of ordinary life; a time of disorder that no one can prepare for and that no one can arrange (in particular not annually). Those who demand orderly disorder once a year for the duration of one day are either deceived or deceivers. Wargames are for armies. For the proletariat, there is only the gamble of revolution.

Those who organize today's May Day celebrations are deceiving everybody and are supported by the deceived. Those who are the loudest in demanding a stoppage of labor are also those who ask their masters and employers to grant them a holiday. Every year, communities of workers have to come up with new ways to compensate for the fines of those who have been taken to court. It is fascinating how stubbornly sacrifices are made for an event that has no other purpose (and cannot have any other) than to try to demonstrate power that does not exist. Every year means are employed that have tragic consequences for many individuals; yet its overall effect on society is little more than comical. And still this is knowingly repeated year after year. It is a sad comedy.

What is characteristic of non-productive movements is that they first decide on something that is wrong and worthless, and then, when inevitably nothing comes of what they have decided on, they search for scapegoats. Parliamentarians of the opposition criticize everything as long as their vote does not count. Yet they are more than eager to compromise as soon as their vote might allow them to partake in power. The same is true for many of those who cling orthodoxly to May 1 as a once-and-for-all implemented holiday, because they cannot even create their own meaningless rituals.

True socialists have nothing to do with such pretense and disguise of weakness. We have no maneuvers and no spring parades; we do not regulate our actions according to the calendar. "Passion is no herring which one pickles."[3]

May 1 as an institution is typical and fitting for the revolutionary party. Once upon a time, there was an old chicken that had lost its strength. It had become dry and infertile and could no longer lay eggs. However, it still ran around and cackled incessantly: "Egg, egg! Egg, egg!" This earned the chicken much esteem, making it known as *the big egg chicken* among those who did not really care about the brave chickens that really laid eggs. The same is true for those – whatever they may call themselves – who concentrate on verbal revolutionism only because they lack the creativity and force for real action. As long as the revolution was alive in Western Europe, i.e., as long as people had clear goals and took clear action, there were no revolutionary parties. These only appeared once the revolution was over and the era of pretense began. These parties maintained that the revolution was still alive and would re-emerge in full force any day. They did so to secure power. Revolutionary parties are dependent on stable governments. Their goals are vague and abstract. None of their members knows how to attain them; and no one dares to either.

Some say that they the party needs to achieve democratic power
before there can be socialism. Others say that there needs to be a revolution before there can be socialism. In fact, there is very little difference
between the two perspectives. The adherents of the first demand democratic government. They will, however, be very happy with undemocratic
government if it is their own. The adherents of the second view demand
– knowingly or unknowingly – undemocratic government. However, since
their politics are bereft of positive ideas, as well as of creativity and force,
but are instead characterized by bloody dilettantism, their government will
inevitably give way again to democratic government.

Look at Turkey. Have the Young Turks called themselves a "revolutionary party" for the last half century? Have they preached decade after
decade that we cannot attain anything without seizing political power? No.
They had real goals, and they organized accordingly. They did not desire
revolution. They desired a constitution and autonomy. They finally reached
these goals in a revolutionary manner because they were determined to
reach them and worked hard for it.

Were there a truly revolutionary party in Germany, it would be a republican party. It would not be ineffective from the outset. Neither would
it be so ridiculous as to announce everywhere – in meetings and declarations – that it wants revolution. Instead it would begin where every effective movement begins: in assessing the realities and possibilities provided
by the current constitution. It would not jump ahead and prattle arrogantly about the final stages of social development, but it would announce its
goal, a republic, and then pursue it with quiet determination.

The French got a constitution in 1791 because they desired it. They
got a republic in 1792 because they were tired of their unfaithful and
treacherous king. They abolished the tithe because they no longer wanted
to pay it. During all those years, no one ever said, whispered or shouted:
We want revolution! or *We want revolutionary power so we can transform
society!* Had they done this, they would have gotten no constitution, no
republic, no revolution, and no freedom. Not for the peasantry, nor the
townspeople, nor the bourgeoisie. All they would have gotten were their
heads kicked in.

I am speaking in parables here. I am trying to teach. What is crucial
is not to propagate temporary measures, but to prepare the realities that
one desires. The socialism we want is no socialism of political institutions

but of communal organization. We know as well as our enemies (or even more so) what must disappear if we want to attain our goal. However, we also know that it will not simply disappear as a result of agitated condemnation. This is the belief of the downhearted. It signifies lack of creation wrapped in the pompous cloak of radicalism. What really counts is to actively build something new.

If you want socialism, i.e., if you want to live in beauty and happiness and in communities of justice and solidarity, then create it! Look for the cracks in capitalism and find ways to escape the economic war. Figure out how to no longer produce for capitalism's commodity market, but to satisfy your own needs. This is a collective process: the more that individuals are able to unite their needs, their creativity, and their lives, the more effective they will be.

We are still few, and we are seen by others as a strange and foolish lot. However, we know what our task and our goal are, and we have found our way. This means that we can afford the worst heresy of all, the one that no one forgives: *we want to be happy!* This May Day shall see for the first time something that will shock the bureaucrats of revolution: happy socialists!

The objective conditions of our lives are no better than those of fellow proletarians or of others who are oppressed. However, we have put up with the desperation and ineffectiveness of complaint and condemnation long enough. The time has come to replace this with hope, confidence, and creative desire.

All misery comes from social conditions. We know what these conditions are today. As long as people accept the role that the demise of the spirit allots them, they will live and suffer under these conditions. As soon as they are filled by the spirit of community and creation, they will be whole humans again and masters of their own destiny.

The first year of our Bund is coming to its end. We have found ourselves and our creative force. We feel like we have come to life again. We feel desire running through our veins. We move from the fumes of the cities to the land. We feel one with nature whose children we are. We wander around and see things in ways in which we have never seen them before. We understand that this is *our* land. The peasants we meet have stern and distant looks. We greet them with a new love because we have come to them as helpers. We will work the land with them. They need us as much as we need them. The delicious gift we have to offer is a spirit that will bring them happiness after centuries of emptiness and boredom.

May 1

Humanity today is sunken, but it shall rise again once it has found its vital energies and creative forces. A time will follow in which humans, devoted both to themselves and to their surroundings, will once again climb mountains together to celebrate the renewal of life with fire and light. Inside of us, this time has already arrived. All we need to do now is to keep it alive and spread it. Let us thus celebrate the coming May Day as a festival of spring, in other words: a festival of renewal!

1. Gustav Landauer, Landauer Papers at the IISH, Amsterdam.

2. Highest mountain peak in Northern Germany; traditionally described as the center of Walpurgis Night activities.

3. *"Begeisterung ist keine Heringsware, die man einpökelt auf viele Jahre"* is a line from the Goethe poem "Frisches Ei, gutes Ei" [Fresh Egg, Good Egg] (1815). (Landauer writes *"…lange Jahre."*)

FERRER

Landauer writes about the arrest and ultimate execution of Spanish anarchist educator Francisco Ferrer. Ferrer had been indicted as an instigator of the Barcelona rebellions during the so-called Tragic Week in July/August 1909, in which anarchists, socialists, and republicans clashed with government forces over the deployment of reserve troops for the Second Rif War.[1] The essay was published as "Ferrer" in *Der Sozialist*, October 15, 1909. Two weeks later (November 1), Landauer published a follow-up piece, "Die Ferrerbewegung" [The Ferrer Movement], as well as "Protestversammlungen und Demonstrationen" [Protest Meetings and Demonstrations], a report about German protests against Ferrer's execution (*Der Sozialist*, November 1, 1909). Max Nettlau and Gustav Landauer continued the discussion in the November 15 issue under the heading "Die Fortführung von Ferrers Werk" [The Continuation of Ferrer's Work].

On October 13, 1910, one year after Ferrer's murder, Landauer spoke at a commemoration event in Berlin. Groups of the Socialist Bund held similar events in other German towns. The *Sozialist* issue released on the same day was dedicated to Ferrer's memory. On October 20, 1914, Landauer published another memorial piece for Ferrer, "Zum Gedächtnis" [In Memory], in *Der Sozialist*.

Landauer's interest in matters of education had always made him follow Ferrer's work closely. He also published in Ferrer's journal *La Huelga General*: "Nuevos Corrientes en Germania" [New Currents in Germany], appeared on January 25, 1903. The contact had been arranged by the Cuban-born anarchist Tárrida del Mármol, who Landauer met while living in England in 1901-1902.

Already in the late 1890s, when Spanish anarchists suffered severe state persecution,[2] Landauer was active in international solidarity campaigns. He published the articles "Die Anarchistenhetze in Spanien" [The Persecution of Anarchists in Spain], *Sozialistische Monatshefte*, I, 1897, and "Spanien," *Der Sozialist*, August 15, 1910.

In the United States, Ferrer's theory had an important impact on the Free School Movement;[3] Landauer himself wrote "Call for a Free School" ("Aufruf zur freien Schule"), a text that was widely distributed by the Socialist Bund and published in *Der Sozialist*, January 15, 1910.

THERE ARE TWO COUNTRIES IN EUROPE WHOSE INTERNAL AFFAIRS THE rest of the continent always feels compelled to comment on. This is usually done with outrage. The two countries are Russia in the east and Spain in the west. In the pages of this journal, we have already referenced the collection of abominable facts that Peter Kropotkin put together under the title *The Terror in Russia*.[4] This book, full of atrocities and horror, summarizes the protest of Europe against the barbarism of the Russian counterrevolution. It is available in various German editions.

As far as Spain is concerned, we saw the last big wave of protests against the country twelve years ago. It went through all of Europe. Anarchists – or those who were accused of being anarchists, even if they were simple republicans – were imprisoned and tortured in the most gruesome manner after a bomb had been thrown by an individual.[5] The Spanish author Tárrida del Mármol[6] has documented how one of them, Thomas Ascheri,[7] eventually succumbed to the ordeal, admitted to the bombing, and named various fellow prisoners as co-conspirators. Eight men were executed, forty sentenced to twenty years in prison, twenty-seven to eight years in prison. It is known who truly threw the bomb and who built it.[8] These people had no connections to those who were tortured and never went to court. There was also widespread protest in Germany at the time.[9] Not only anarchists, but also M. von Egidy, Friedrich Spielhagen, Judge Krecke, August Bebel, and especially the editors of the *Frankfurter Zeitung* were determined to disclose the truth.[10] Nonetheless, we unfortunately have reason to believe that the torturers are still active in Spain, especially in the fortress Montjuïch near Barcelona.[11]

Again and again Barcelona! All of Spain's industry, commerce, activity, spirit, and freedom are concentrated in the province of Catalonia, particularly in the city of Barcelona, near the French border. This will remain the case as long as not everyone leaves for South America, as so many have already done. The true, vibrant Spain is no longer in Europe, it is in Argentina. A young Argentinean writer, i.e., a Spaniard who is no longer a Spaniard, Manuel Ugarte[12], describes the kingdom of Spain as follows:

> "Spain has always been a reactionary power. It was only of significance in Europe when intolerance and tyranny ruled. Fanaticism and oppression were not the country's only characteristics during its heyday, yet it is evident that the more Europe escaped darkness, the less power and influence Spain had. To this day it preserves the stubborn haughtiness

of the Hidalgos,[13] despite the arrival of the democratic era;
it preserves its contempt for material progress and scientific
achievement; it preserves its disdain for modern life under the
illusion that its long faded crest is still shining brightly..."

Hardly anywhere do wealth, luxury, and presumption exist side-by-side with poverty, scarcity, and depression as they do in Barcelona. You will find narrow-minded priests and brutal soldiers next to enlightened and scientific men and women of high spirit.

A few months ago, a people's rebellion broke out in Barcelona in connection with the African War.[14] As Catalonians know where the main enemies and tormenters of their country reside, their rage was mainly directed against the monasteries. After some days, those in power were able to control the situation. They also knew where to find their main enemy: he now stands between life and death, sharing the fate of all those who have already been massacred, executed, and thrown in jail. His name is Ferrer. It seems that a court martial has sentenced him to death in a mockery of justice they called a trial. The decision of the highest council of war is still pending.

Who is Ferrer? According to trustworthy reports, he had personal relations to Spanish revolutionaries who played a role in the rebellion, but he himself did not take part and knew nothing of its imminent eruption. He had not been politically active for years. Instead, he had focused on re-introducing culture and humanity to an unhappy people – the most important task that Spain faces today. Ferrer had founded a school movement: the establishment of private secular schools for the people's children. It allows each child to learn about nature and spirit. Ferrer employed knowledge to fight the superstition, stupidity, and ignorance in which the monks – the accomplices of the powerful and rich – keep the people. He challenged death with life, stagnancy with movement, and narrow-mindedness with openness. These are the reasons why Ferrer is now the prisoner of the inquisitors and those who rule by the sword. These are also the reasons why all of Europe follows the struggle of a single righteous man who is the head of the Spanish people; a head that those in power aim to sever from its torso.

No one must believe that our Socialist Bund is reduced to only one method or way. We do not close our eyes to the diversity of our times. We want reality; we want *realization*. We embrace everything that leads to it. If we wanted to summarize our beliefs in one sentence, we could use the words of Goethe: *Act, don't speak!* This must be our motto. (Although no one must overlook the power of a word that comes from, and goes to, the spirit and the heart.) This is why we say today: indeed, we want to *act* for Ferrer rather than to *speak* for him! If we had the means, many of us would already be on their way to Spain. They would go there to free Ferrer – using both means of violence and of intellect.

Unfortunately, we do not have these means. Maybe others do and know the right way. Maybe they can act before it is too late. We will do the little we can: join the protests of Europe and encourage others to do the same. Not enough has happened in German-speaking lands so far. Ferrer is still alive. He might still be alive when these words reach the readers. If this is the case, then we encourage all to do whatever they can to bring his fate to the attention of the German peoples, and to carry their protests to the representatives of the Spanish state in Germany, Austria, and Switzerland. Ferrer is a noble and strong ambassador of life. He must not lose his own.

      * It is too late to protest. Francisco Ferrer was murdered on the morning of October 13, 1909. Soldiers shot him dead. They loved their life more than the light. Damn the Spanish people as long as their miserable lives are worth more to them than to breathe freely – even if it is only for a moment! There was only one ray of hope: the officer who had, by coincidence, served as Ferrer's defender found fiery words of truth and pointed out the scandalous character of this charade. This man, by the name of Galcerán, saved Spain's honor – and was instantly thrown into the dungeons.[15] The judges showed vengeance, the king no clemency. This has been the case in Spain for decades. Who will be next?

1. The Second Rif War was fought in Morocco in 1909 over Spain's colonial possessions.

2. See page 24.

3. See Paul Avrich, *The Modern School Movement: Anarchism and Education in the United States* (Princeton: Princeton University Press, 1980).

4. An excerpt of Kropotkin's book was published in *Der Sozialist*, August 1, 1909.

5. On June 7, 1896, a bomb was thrown into the crowd at the annual Corpus Christi procession in Barcelona. Around a dozen people died and over thirty were wounded.

6. Tárrida del Mármol (1861-1915), Cuban-born Catalan anarchist and friend of Gustav Landauer. ·

7. Thomas Ascheri (ca. 1870-1897), born in Marseille, moved in anarchist circles, but was a suspected police spy; executed on May 4, 1897.

8. This assumption of Landauer's was not true.

9. Landauer was among the speakers at a protest in Berlin on March 3, 1897.

10. Moritz von Egidy (1847-1898), military officer turned pacifist and Christian reformer; Friedrich Spielhagen (1829-1911), German writer; Hermann Krecke (1852-1904), court magistrate and active in the establishment of cooperatives; August Bebel (1840-1913), prominent German social democrat; *Frankfurter Zeitung* (1856-1943), bourgeois-liberal daily journal.

11. The fortress, built on a hill of the same name in the 17th century, was a notorious prison, torture chamber, and execution site under authoritarian Spanish regimes until the end of the Franco dictatorship.

12. Manuel Ugarte (1878-1951), Argentinean socialist writer.

13. Spanish nobles.

14. Landauer refers to the Second Rif War (see footnote 1). The protests were mainly directed against the deployment of reserve troops.

15. Francisco Galcerán Ferrer (1874-1954). The claim that he was persecuted for his defense of Francisco Ferrer is disputed in the book *The Life, Trial, and Death of Franciso Ferrer* by William Archer (London: Chapman and Hall, 1911).

JAPAN

Landauer reports about the execution of the anarchist circle around Shūsui Kōtoku in Japan on January 24, 1911. The article was published as "Japan" in *Der Sozialist*, February 1, 1911. It is a follow-up piece to "Ein Tendenzprozess in Japan" [A Biased Trial in Japan], published in *Der Sozialist*, December 15, 1910. Landauer also petitioned the Japanese ambassador in Berlin with regard to the case in a letter dated January 6, 1911.[1]

T
WELVE ANARCHIST SOCIALISTS, ONE OF THEM A WOMAN, HAVE been executed in Japan.[2] Twelve more had been sentenced to death, but had their sentences commuted to life-long forced labor. Two more have been sentenced to many years of imprisonment.

We do not know what those who were sentenced did or what they had planned to do. Neither do we know whether they were guilty according to Japanese law or not. We do not even know if their trial was fair and within the confines of the law. It is impossible to claim – as some do – that the entire case was the making of the police.

One day the truth will be revealed, even though the correspondents of the great European and American journals have done terrible work so far. There is strong suspicion that the so-called "public announcement" of the sentence was nothing but a staged spectacle for the West. It is said that no one was at the announcement except members of the Japanese government and foreign diplomats. Allegedly, the Japanese people never knew anything about it. If this is true, then it would be a breach of the Japanese constitution.

Whatever the exact circumstances, it does not seem that there has been any opposition to these horrible events among the Japanese. In the United States, in England, in France, Holland, Belgium, Germany, Switzerland, Austria, and Italy protests were organized by people who demanded the truth.[3] No Japanese person seems to have joined these protests, neither in Japan nor abroad.

Regardless of whether those who were sentenced were guilty according to Japanese law or not, the entire case means that militarism and the politics of expansion have received their first major blow in Japan. The events reveal that Japan faces internal crisis and conflict, and that an internal war has erupted. This explains the open anger of the Japanese government and the fearful secrecy surrounding the events. The advantage that Japan had over other oppressive states has been shaken – no matter whether this was indeed a terrorist conspiracy or whether the sentenced were, in the eyes of those in power, simply guilty of revolutionary socialist propaganda and treason. Japan's said advantage was still evident during the Russian-Japanese War: a whole people seemed united in bellicose sentiment and in the lust for conquest and expansion.

Everywhere in the old Europe and America, even in England, patriotism has been shaken by the new socialist ideal. Many people have realized that the "nation" and its expansionist ambitions are but a mask for the desire of the privileged who aim to expand their wealth and power. Everywhere we can see patriotic ideals being replaced by calls for internal renewal and economic as well as political transformation. So far, the different socialist and revolutionary movements might have been unable to find promising ways of realization. However, antimilitaristic and anti-patriotic sentiments are ever increasing – even among those who are called for military service: army, reserve, militiamen – and obstruct the politics of aggression. The governments know this.

So far, this has not been the case in Japan. More so than those of any other country, the politics of Japan have been characterized by intimidation, expansion, and conquest. Those in power will certainly believe that they have successfully prevented all opposition by suffocating its first breath. However, they have made the same mistake that those in power have always made, no matter where. There is nothing more certain to awake the spirit of rebellion and the desire for renewal than the blood of martyrs.

We are told that Dr. Kōtoku and his friends[4] reacted to the death sentences with cheers. Reliable reports are lacking, but we can imagine vividly with how much happiness the twelve went to the gallows. Right now, the Japanese people are still quiet and motionless. However, the blood that has been spilled will, drop by drop, enter the veins of men, women, and children, and bring their own blood to a fiery boil.

Kōtoku had begun to translate Marx, Bakunin, Kropotkin, and Tolstoy. This work was crowned by the death of him and his comrades. They have translated socialism into Japanese. Among future historians, their execution will count as the true birth of socialist awareness in the country.

Violence, and violence against violence... It is always the same. Japan does what all other countries have done. We will see developments echoing those of Europe and Russia. A people usually do not learn enough from another people to avoid making the same mistakes in its own development. Everything will be repeated and copied. Japan has taken significant shortcuts in copying Europe's and America's capitalist and militaristic civilization. The phrase "*affenartige Geschwindigkeit*"[5] seems to apply perfectly. No one can tell what this means concerning Japan's socialist development. Will the country overtake ours soon? Maybe the people of Japan will understand before we do that both the expansionist violence of the state and the violent resistance against it only indicate the absence of true power. Physical violence directed against the state will, in the end, never create anything but another state. Violence, conducted by individuals or masses, is always an unmistakable sign of powerlessness. There is only one true, one real power: the power of the spirit – as demonstrated by Jesus.

I only have power if I am able to affect other people because of what I am. I have power if I can help other people find their own being; if I can help them develop their own unassailable power. There are those who see the state as an incarnate entity that can be – and has to be – overthrown, and capital as an external reality that can be taken away and confiscated. Such beliefs cover up helplessness in thought and action by means of superficial sham-powers.

What we really need is an entirely new understanding of social transformation. People have to realize that the state that they are fighting lives within themselves, and that their complacency and passiveness are its guardians. People have to realize that capital is not something to be seized, but a mechanism that ties their hunger to labor. People today often turn to state mediators for protection from the scrounging economic mediators. These people have not yet understood that they have to free the power that lies within themselves and that both parasites – the economic as well as the political – need to be left behind.

Things will develop the way they have to. Wrong ways are ways too. Maybe the right destinations can only be reached by wrong ways. Maybe clarity can only be reached by fermentation. Maybe safety can only be reached by passion. Maybe we can only reach the great, quiet, creative, inner force that unites us by wasting our energies in external conflicts. Maybe this is the only way to bring an end to brutality, whether it comes from above or from below.

Let us find what we, what each one of us, can do to live up to the moment. And let us, in all this horror, in all this confusion, in all this dreariness, not lose the joy that we need to grow and to stand tall.

> *Some fountains may still sprinkle*
>
> *And the grass may still glow red*
>
> *But freedom's true and proper victory —*
>
> *It will be dry*

(Gottfried Keller, "Rote Lehre")[6]

---

1. It is not certain whether the letter was ever sent. A draft was found among Landauer's papers after his death. Published in *Gustav Landauer. Sein Lebensgang in Briefen*, 1: 335-336.

2. On January 24, 1911.

3. In London, a great rally was held on December 8, 1910. In 1911, London's Freedom Press published the pamphlet "The Japanese Martyrs. Kōtoku's Life and Work."

4. Shūsui Kōtoku (1871-1911), journalist and anarchist, was considered the "ringleader" of the executed anarchists.

5. Literally, "ape-like speed;" German turn of phrase for "lightning speed."

6. Gottfried Keller (1819-1890), Swiss writer. *Rote Lehre* literally means "Red Teachings."

THE BEILIS TRIAL

Landauer began to address Judaism in depth only during the last years of his life. His comments in *Die Revolution*, for example, still reflect the conscious detachment of a secular radical. Even in his early mystical interest he reaches out to Christian rather than to Jewish teachings. In June 1909, however, the following note can be found among his letters: "I am not in the least inclined to forget the joy of my Jewishness even for a day."[1]

In 1913, Landauer publishes two of his most important essays on Judaism, "Sind das Ketzergedanken?" [Are These Heretic Thoughts?] and "Der Beilis-Prozeß" [The Beilis Trial]. The former is included in a book entitled *Vom Judentum* [On Judaism], edited by the Bar Kokhba League of Jewish Students in Prague. According to Hanna Delf, Landauer calls himself therein "a conscious Jew for the first time."[2]

"The Beilis Trial" addresses the 1913 court case against the Jewish builder, Mendel Beilis, in Kiev. Beilis was accused of ritually murdering a Christian child to bake matzo with the child's blood. He was eventually acquitted, but Landauer was appalled by the anti-Semitism that had made such outrageous allegations possible. He entitled the November 5, 1913, issue of *Der Sozialist* "Kiew" and dedicated it to Beilis. Next to "The Beilis Trial" (entitled "Kiew" in the *Sozialist* issue, renamed in later printings), the issue included articles commissioned by Landauer from non-Jewish friends. Landauer wrote in the editorial: "Socialism means action among human beings; action that must become reality within these human beings as much as in the outside world. When independent peoples propose to create a united humanity, these propositions are worthless when even a single people remains excluded and experiences injustice."

Landauer further reflects on Judaism in his 1913 essay on Martin Buber ("Martin Buber," *Neue Blätter*, Buber Special Issue), and in "Ostjuden und Deutsches Reich" (*Der Jude*, October 1916), a reflection on the relations between the Jews of Eastern Europe ("Ostjuden") and the German nation state. Noteworthy is also "Zur Poesie der Juden" [On Jewish Poetry] (*Freistatt*, August 22, 1913). Concerning Landauer's relations to Zionism and his influence on the Kibbutz movement please see "Landauer's Legacy" in the Introduction.

PEOPLE EMBARK ON LONG JOURNEYS TO DISCOVER THE PEOPLES OF ASIA, of Africa, and of the Pacific Isles. They describe the manners and customs of the so-called savages and barbarians that they find carefully and meticulously. However, I know of no more heartless barbarism than the one executed by scholars and publicists all over Europe against the Jews – a people who live right among them.

Six or seven million Jews live in Poland and Russia. Their forefathers emigrated there from Germany during the Middle Ages. Our linguists record every Alemmanic, Bavarian, and West Low German local dialect – yet they ignore a language that has retained the beauty of Middle High German at least to the same degree as Swiss German has.[3] They do this because common prejudice against the Jews is stronger in their philistine hearts than scientific curiosity. They detest nothing more than the Yiddish language.

There are dictionaries and scientific treaties on the language of gypsies, of outlaws, or of criminals. None of them have been written by gypsies, vagabonds, or criminals; nor were any written by their friends or on their behalf. They have all been written by scholars. However, if the Jews had not begun to explore their language and their folk songs themselves, this history would be an area even whiter than the white areas on the maps of Africa. This is just one example for something that applies very generally: nothing is known about the real life, about the manners and customs of the Jews. The reason is that no one wants to know anything about it.

Are any other people treated similarly? The Jews live in the midst of other peoples. Their lives are open, nothing is hidden. Yet all that is supposedly known about these lives rests on mere rumors. Let us say that a missionary described the following scenario: somewhere in the interior of Africa there live a people numbering one hundred thousand men and women. Among them live a smaller group of people numbering about five thousand men and women. Every now and again, the small community slaughters a child of the big community in order to drink its blood at the altar of their idols. Would we believe this?[4]

Everyone who wants can learn about the religious life of the Jews. All that is needed is to approach their communities with basic respect and kindness. Behind a number of superficial customs revolving around renunciation and penance, the following will soon appear as the core of the Jewish religion: the complete absence of Antiquity's representative priesthood; the sanctification of man; and the connection with the heavens and the unspeakable – a connection that fills the whole community as well as the individual who lives guarded by his family.

I will intentionally not speak of the indelible traits of a Jewish national spirit that remain in myself and others like me – those who have separated themselves from traditional Jewish life. Instead, I will speak of the manners, the customs, and the ways of the communities where the confession is still alive.

Let us picture a small German village where the lives of the people revolve around plows, hoes, and manure. In the middle of all the neat small white-painted brick houses, on the village's highest point, stands a wide Romanic church built from centuries-old blazing sandstone. In its interior, there are high vaults, pillars, and paintings. The air is filled with incense. When I enter such a church, I do not just think of superstition and error. I also think of greatness and the longing for eternity; I think of the exuberance that must have filled this village once. But then I hear the litanies of the priests and I see the apathy of the old women and men who gather in the church and I know that this exuberance is gone.

Among the Jews who live in true, unspoiled communities there is no distinction between priests and laypeople. Every pious Jew, no matter how dirty his worldly affairs, begins the day by turning to God. And every now and again throughout the day, he will take fifteen minutes to do the same. In their *shul*[5] – a word that Jews prefer to the foreign word "synagogue" – it is the community as a whole that celebrates holiness. It is hard to find the same repentant longing for purity elsewhere.

I speak of true Jewish communities here; not the ones modernized and trivialized by today's Christian priesthood and its Sunday celebrations; not the ones that have desecrated the work day. I speak of those Jewish communities that are – repeatedly and everywhere – accused of adding the blood of slaughtered Christian children to their Easter bread.[6] What lies behind these accusations – as currently in Russia and as in Western Europe before – has been summed up by one of the attorneys during the last ritual murder case in Germany in 1892 in the town of Cleves: "This case is not unresolved because the accused is a Jew – the accused is a Jew because the case is unresolved."

What allows this to happen? It is the fact that a mixture of superstition, shyness, fear, and contempt keeps a society's majority from getting to know

the Jewish people, as well as the fact that those in power encourage this ignorance and use it for distraction; we only have to look at the despicable way
in which the corrupt, bureaucratic tsarist Russian state does this right now.

When I try to appeal to the German spirit to revolt against this bestial-
ity, I usually lose heart and have to lower my pen. What we are witnessing
in Russia right now also remains possible in Germany. Even the finest German minds do not recognize Jewish life and do not acknowledge it in the
same way that they acknowledge other spiritual and national communities.

Haggling defines Jewishness as little as drinking beer defines Germanness. Jewishness is not cowardice, just as Germanness is not rowdiness.
Jewishness is not intellectual coldness and calculation, just as Frenchness is
not rhetoric and phrase. Neither is Jewishness excrescence and deteriora-
tion of Jewishness.

Jews are as bellicose as any other people, but their bellicose spirit has
turned inwards. This is not only a result of their dispersion and dissolution among foreign peoples. "I did not come to bring peace but to bring
the sword." These are not just the words of Jesus the Jew and Muhammad
the Arab; these are first and foremost the words of Moses who stands as
the biggest of all war heroes in the midst of the Jewish people. Through
him the war to unite with God, the war against sin, the war for purity
and sanctification has entered the heart of the Jewish people, of the Jewish community, and of each individual Jew. It is a war that is led by no
representative, no pioneer, no savior, no saint, and no priest. It is a war
of renouncement, of cleansing one's soul, of going inwards, of praying, of
uniting the community in repentance.

Many customs that have once been meaningful have turned meaningless, but there is neither superstition nor fetishism. And since there is no
fetishism, there can be no cannibalism either, and it becomes impossible
for the soul's holy war to turn into a bloody war against people of a different faith. It has indeed long been impossible for soul-searching Jews to go
to war against others, or to cause wounds to anyone but to themselves.

Jews always kept their spiritual, their national uniqueness, even if
individual Jews who decided to join humanity have hid their Jewishness or
have tried to overcome it. The movement that goes through Jewry today,
mostly under the name of Zionism, should have, no matter the developments around it, the following aims: to help Jews shape their particular
being – that they, like any other nation, have developed over millennia –

purely, creatively, and under the guidance of spiritual and strong natures; to defend their freedom, their self-determination, their unity of soul, and their embrace of holiness both from the mess of ignorance and from mechanical habit; to fill the Jewish community with vision and life; to allow Jews to give themselves to humanity – humanity that cannot forgo Jewry or any other stage or shade of humankind. Humanity does not mean sameness; humanity means alliance of the plenty.

It is not only Jews who have to find themselves if they want to join humanity. The same goes for all nations on this planet. However, none of these nations can truly find itself and join humanity if it does not seek to understand the Jews, their inner being, and their reality. After all, there are twelve million Jews dispersed across the planet who constitute an indivisible entity. Half of them live in big communities among other nations.

There are of course some who already know that Jews have no cannibalistic customs; who know that Mendel Beilis, like so many before him, is persecuted and tortured as an innocent man. These people must not keep quiet. They must speak out. Privately and publicly. Wherever they may be.

1. Letter to Constantin Brunner (born Leopold Wertheimer, 1862-1937, Jewish philosopher), in *Gustav Landauer. Sein Lebensgang in Briefen*, 1: 262.

2. Hanna Delf, "'Wie steht es mit dem *Sozialist?*' Sozialismus, Deutschtum, Judentum im Briefwechsel Gustav Landauers und Fritz Mauthners" ['How Are Things with *Der Sozialist?*' Socialism, Germanness, and Jewishness in the Correspondence of Gustav Landauer and Fritz Mauthner], in Ludger Heid and Arnold Paucker, eds., *Juden und deutsche Arbeiterbewegung bis 1933. Soziale Utopien und religiös-kulturelle Traditionen* [Jews and the German Workers' Movement until 1933: Social Utopias and Religious and Cultural Traditions] (Tübingen: J.C.B. Mohr (Paul Siebeck), 1992), 127.

3. Modern Swiss German remains much closer to the German of the Middle Ages than other German dialects.

4. Landauer refers to blood libel, i.e., the accusation of slaughtering human beings – often children – for ritual consumption of their blood. Although diverse social groups have been accused of blood libel, the accusations have most commonly been raised against Jews, already in Antiquity.

5. Landauer uses *Schule*, the German word for "school."

6. Landauer uses the Christian term *Osterbrot* instead of matzo here.

LETTERS

TO PAUL ELTZBACHER
Hoppegarten near Berlin, April 2, 1900

Landauer comments on Paul Eltzbacher's *Der Anarchismus. Eine ideenge-schichtliche Darstellung seiner klassischen Strömungen* [Anarchism: A History of Ideas of its Classical Currents], first published in 1900 and remaining one of the most widely read studies of anarchism's main strains to this day.[1] Landauer sees Eltzbacher's scientific classifications as directly opposed to anarchy's inherent diversity, fluctuation, and openness.

D EAR MR. ELTZBACHER,

A lot could be said in response to your questions. They are extremely perceptive. I am planning to include an analysis of your book in an upcoming article of mine.[2] This might allow me to deal with your questions in depth. For now, a few words must suffice.

I deem "anarchism" the best term to describe my understanding of life. It is not true that I have abandoned the belief in a future anarchist society. I have only questioned the belief that such a society can be established anytime soon by the men and women of today. However, I believe that some people – those with understanding and good will – are able to do so now.

I believe in the possibility of small anarchist settlements that might, eventually, be left in peace by non-anarchists. Your critique is based on the unspoken assumption that anarchism has to involve all of humanity, or at least all of the so-called civilized people. I do not consider this a necessary implication of the anarchist idea – not even according to your strict definitions.

Some of your definitions I consider too strict in fact, particularly in the last part of your book. I see more commonality among the different schools of anarchism. You, like all men of science, overestimate the *word* and fail to see what is essential, namely the unspeakable, the mood, that which is not easily measured, identified, and categorized. I do not care much for scientific classification. After everything has been diligently divided, it will inevitably mingle and blend again anyway.

However, the manner in which you have presented the subject will be useful for those who are unfamiliar with it. Your work is enlightening and virtuous. We anarchists – and everyone eager to learn – have every reason to be grateful to you. I must congratulate you in particular on your unbiased definitions of the law, of the state, and of property. These definitions reveal the intellectual and spiritual freedom of a wise man.

Warm greetings,

sincerely,

yours,

Gustav Landauer

---

1. First translated into English in 1907 and published by Benjamin Tucker; latest English reprint with Aslan Press (2008).

2. Without naming him, the last paragraphs of "Anarchic Thoughts on Anarchism" include an implicit critique of Eltzbacher's approach.

TO JULIUS BAB
Hermsdorf (Mark), September 15, 1904

Landauer met Julius Bab, a dramatist, in the Neue Gemeinschaft. In 1904, Bab published the book *Die Berliner Boheme* [Berlin's Bohemia]. Landauer's letter is a response to Bab's comparisons between the bohemian and the anarchist. Landauer used the opportunity to clarify his understanding of anarchism at a time when he was not publishing political texts.

Landauer and Bab remained lifelong friends,[1] and Bab gave a eulogy for Landauer at the Volksbühne Berlin on May 25, 1919.[2] In 1933, Bab was a co-founder of the Kulturbund Deutscher Juden [Cultural Union of German Jews], a legal Jewish organization trying to protect the rights of Jewish artists in Nazi Germany. Quickly instrumentalized by the Nazis, the Kulturbund Deutscher Juden existed until 1941. Bab had emigrated to the United States two years earlier. He died in New York in 1955.

D EAR MR. BAB,

Thank you for your note! It is everyone's right to use and evaluate my work – or anyone else's.

However, I find your definitions unsettling. If you really want to call "bohemia" a complete negation of social life, then you should at least mention in a footnote that in previous times a bohemian was also called a recluse or a hermit – a special form of which was the stylite. And this is just one example.

I am of the opinion that such general terms as "bohemia," "anarchism," and "nihilism" defy formal definition. They are terms that have developed historically and can only be understood historically. For example, "anarchism" is a collective name for *transformative ambitions* (the fact that many of its adherents – though not all of them – share a certain rebellious attitude is a secondary characteristic); "bohemia," on the other hand, is a collective name for a certain personal *lifestyle*, i.e., for a particular way of negotiating poverty, (often weakly developed) spiritual and artistic productivity, and (usually strongly developed) sensitivity and such.

(Sometimes, but not often, the attempt is made to elevate this curious mixture of voluntary misery, essential weakness, and secondary strength to a *principle*, and hence a transformative ambition.)

In short, if you compare the anarchist to the bohemian, you compare two very different things. It is like writing a thesis entitled "The Wandering Students and the Anabaptists: A Comparative Study."

If I had to characterize the bohemian with one phrase, I would say that he is a man who makes a *vice* of necessity. The anarchist, however – just like any other socialist – wants to abolish material misery. He wants to see a world of freedom, personal development, collective action, and so forth. What comparison do you see between the two? It is true that, due to his rejection of bourgeois society, the anarchist is often condemned to live the life of a bohemian. However, his aim still contradicts bohemia: the anarchist aims at an *order*. *Ambition* is the *tertium comparationis* of anarchism and everything that can be likened to it; *lifestyle* is the *tertium comparationis* of bohemia and everything that can be likened to this concept.

If you want to go even deeper (and I have a tendency to do so, but do not find many who are willing to join me), you could only call those people anarchists who possess the aforementioned ambition naturally; people who have worked so hard on their own transformation that, once they find enough like-minded spirits, they are instantly able to establish an anarchist society – despite the difficulties and sacrifices involved in detaching oneself completely from the bourgeoisie (which happens by means of a common organization of labor).

With such a definition, even the last, secondary, link between anarchy and bohemia is severed. No bohemian is ever mature enough for anarchy. If he is an "anarchist on the side," then only as an idealist whose lifestyle does not live up to his principles due to an inept rejection of productive labor (a main characteristic of the bohemian).

And so forth. – I am also sending you the books I have promised to send. Thank you very much. Greetings!

Yours,
Gustav Landauer

1. There is an interesting exchange concerning Landauer's *Aufruf zum Sozialismus* in *Der Sozialist*: the November 11, 1912, issue includes a critique of the book by Bab, published as "Ein Brief an den Verfasser des *Aufrufs zum Soz-*

ialismus" [A Letter to the Author of the *Aufruf zum Sozialismus*]; Landauer's response entitled "Antwort auf einen kritischen Brief" [Response to a Critical Letter] appeared in the following issue, December 1.

2. Without naming him, the last paragraphs of "Anarchic Thoughts on Anarchism" include an implicit critique of Eltzbacher's approach.

TO ERICH MÜHSAM
Hermsdorf (Mark), May 3, 1907

Landauer comments on some of Mühsam's writings. The letter is an indication of the tutor role that Landauer often assumed in their relationship.

DEAR MÜHSAM,

I was delighted to hear from you after such a long time. I sent you birthday wishes too. You needed them! [...]

I have read your work in *Die Fackel* and a short article in *Der Freie Arbeiter* today.[1] I was not impressed. The style lacks refinement and clarity. The contents lack rigor and strength. I wish we could sit down together and go through it all sentence by sentence. You would have to concede – like you have had to previously – that I am right when I speak of playful and unabashed superficiality. Nonetheless, you would do it all over again the next time...

Your prose is as bad as W's.[2] He also feels that he needs to comment on each and every thing without a second of hesitation. Your prose feels cold, yet you have so much inner warmth, and such a fine heart! Some of the things you write are truly shameful. To give you but one example, you write that "anarchism means nothing but the rejection of all forms of domination, or, in positive terms, the unrestricted autonomy of each individual." I really have to reference myself here: for years I have been trying to work against the usage of such empty terms. I have been trying to fill the words we use with soulful, historical, true content. "Individuals?" "Autonomy?" Do these things even exist?! Do you really think that we can get anywhere by endlessly regurgitating such dry and hollow phrases? I assume this is called "agitation."

Our attempts to strengthen humanity's spirit will go nowhere if – despite the claim to say and do "glorious," "deep," and "wonderful" things – everyone just dives back into the same old water; which is exactly what you do in your article.

Nothing can be said against writing and distributing a so-called declaration of principles, or against the federalist organization that you propose. It is also true that the anarchists' fear of their own principles is pitiful. However, none of these well-intentioned ideas will help us if they remain formal and have no real content. Just wait, one day you will see! [...]

I greet you warmly and hope that you are doing well.

Yours truly,

Gustav Landauer

1. "Zur Naturgeschichte des Wählers" [On the Natural History of the Voting Citizen], *Die Fackel*, April 12, 1907; "Prinzipienerklärung" [Declaration of Principles], *Der freie Arbeiter*, May 4, 1907.

2. Albert Weidner (1871-1946), co-editor of *Der Sozialist* from 1895 to 1899.

TO MAX NETTLAU
Hermsdorf near Berlin, June 7, 1911

Landauer carried on a regular correspondence with the famed anarchist historian Max Nettlau after they first met in the 1890s. In this letter, written in a response to Nettlau declining the offer to take an active role in the publication of *Der Sozialist*,[1] Landauer summarizes his socialist ideas and announces the publication of *Aufruf zum Sozialismus*.

D EAR NETTLAU,

I found your comments very convincing and I do understand your reasons. However, you are right in the assumption that I have considered these points before. Maybe you could try to look at things from my perspective and analyze them with my terms. You will understand these terms better once you have read my *Aufruf zum Sozialismus*. It is indispensable to distinguish material realities like the land and its products from complexities like the state and capital. Without such a distinction, neither real understanding nor real action are possible. The state (and the same goes for capital) is a relationship between human beings; it is a form of (active and passive) doing and enduring that has been passed down from generation to generation. Etienne de La Boétie has explained this once and for all.

I refuse to divide people into those who are the masters of the state and those who are the state's servants. Human relationships depend on human behavior. The possibility of anarchy depends on the belief that people can *always* change their behavior. In order to change ourselves and our social conditions, we must use the limited freedom that we have. It is up to no one but ourselves to do so and to create as much freedom and unity as possible. Who can deny that we have made very little use of the possibilities we have?

We are like small children who have plenty of things to play with but stubbornly refuse to use them because all we want are the dolls of our older siblings. The more attentively we play with the bricks, the more insignificant the doll will become. Eventually, it will turn into the lifeless ghost of passivity and lethargy that has haunted our ancestors and that now haunts us. (Of course we know that these ghosts cling to living people. These people are like corals or snails that hide in a house carried by themselves.)

The above also implies my response to your comment on Tucker. You say that Tucker has the right to reject a revolution that does not pursue his goals. Of course. I see no problem with this. Whether to join revolutions or not is a difficult question that everyone has to answer for himself – even though no certain answer can be given before the revolution actually breaks out.

I only object to the passiveness of those who cannot find a task to pursue *right now* at any given moment. As long as the anarchists – no matter what school they adhere to – put an eternity between themselves and what they want to create, they will never create anything. I will evoke the motto of *Hic Rhodus, hic salta*[2] as long as we have a chance to do something, no matter how limited.

Those who speak incessantly of all the obstacles we are facing and of what we must do to overcome them, only do so because they have nothing better to do. I want to act. This also means that I refuse to reduce the relations between people to trading matches, rocks, or fields. I am not afraid of people fighting people. Neither am I afraid of advocating such a fight. But I believe that it only becomes necessary once we have used all the possibilities that our enemy's leave to us without getting in our way.

My book will show how we own "capital," but lack land and its products. The fight against our human enemies can only begin once we use our capital and demand land. The same is true for the realm of the state. We are caught in spider webs – if we were not, then our cooperatives, settlements, and federations would do the most incredible things. We lack heartiness and clarity. If we did what we could do, our so-called enemies would be very troubled.

But who is "we?" And how many are we? We could be many more – more than most of us can imagine – if we were only able to speak the right language, the language of naivety instead of philistinism. This – and not only this – implies self-criticism. Me too, I am only starting to free myself from the spider webs. I have to learn to speak very differently. However, once we have learned to speak the right language, we will be so many that it will be possible to use the language that truly counts: the language of example and beginning.

Warm greetings!

Yours,

Gustav Landauer

---

1. Landauer had sent a letter proposing the collaboration on May 19, 1911. The correspondence is archived among the Max Nettlau Papers at the International Institute for Social History (IISH) in Amsterdam.

2. Literally, "Here is Rhodes, now jump!" The saying's meaning can be compared to "walking the walk after talking the talk;" based on a Greek tale about an athlete boasting about his long jump achievements in Rhodes until his companions challenge him to prove his excellence right there and then.

TO BERNHARD KAMPFFMEYER
Hermsdorf i.d. Mark, July 5, 1912

The letter, addressed to Bernhard Kampffmeyer, a friend of Landauer's since the days of the Friedrichshagener Dichterkreis, concerns the seventieth birthday of Peter Kropotkin. Landauer intends to establish a fund to provide for Kropotkin financially. He also discusses the idea of proposing Kropotkin for the Nobel Peace Prize.[1]

DEAR KAMPFFMEYER,

As you know, Kropotkin will turn seventy this year. Nettlau confirms that he has problems financially. In a letter I received from Kropotkin himself some days ago, he mentions that his strength is declining and that his work suffers from it. His general health, however, is better than it was a few years ago. The doctor even allows him to permanently live in England now – however, not in London. This is why he has moved to Brighton.[2]

I think that the best thing that could happen for his seventieth birthday would be a collection among sympathetic people to alleviate his financial problems.[3] There would be several advantages: Kropotkin would not have to worry about his daily bread; many people would find relief in knowing this; and Kropotkin would be able to bless us with more insights and marvelous work.

I believe – and so does Adolf Otto[4] – that rich people could be found to provide the funds. I would like to keep all of this a private affair, however; the collection of funds as well as their deliverance.

My favorite option would be to give him a certain sum unconditionally, at the same time making it clear to him that the money had been gathered for his personal sustenance and not for general political activities. If he wants to benefit humanity, the best he can do is to look after himself. Ideally, he would receive a life-long pension, subsidized by a number of people.

In England, Otto named Mr. Rowntree.[5] In Germany, I think Franz Oppenheimer should oversee the search for benefactors.[6] He is a great admirer of Kropotkin and has met him personally. I think we can also get useful advice from Nettlau whose current address I have and which I am allowed to use for such purposes. In France, I do not know anyone.

I also mentioned the idea six weeks ago to Domela Nieuwenhuis.[7] He contacted me concerning a special international gift for Kropotkin (a marble cast);[8] I have not received an answer yet.

Nettlau also had the brilliant idea that P. K. should receive the Nobel Peace Prize for *Mutual Aid*. This sounds more like a propagandistic fantasy than a realistic possibility, but it is not entirely unfeasible. After all, it is difficult to find someone year by year who has really done something for peace. In any case, I think this is of secondary concern to us.[9]

I hope that you will support my idea and that it will come to fruition! It would also be a reason to finally meet again. I would be delighted!

Warmest greetings from house to house, yours,
Gustav Landauer

---

1. Four years later, Landauer would be among the international anarchists outraged by Kropotkin's contribution to the "Manifesto of the Sixteen" (1916), which supported the Allies' war against Germany.

2. Kropotkin lived in Brighton until 1917, when he returned to Russia.

3. Money was indeed collected for Kropotkin's birthday. According to Martin Buber (*Gustav Landauer. Sein Lebensgang in Briefen*, 1: 410), he received between 300 and 400 Pounds.

4. Landauer's brother-in-law, active in the Socialist Bund.

5. Joseph Rowntree (1836-1925), Quaker philanthropist.

6. Franz Oppenheimer (1864-1943), sociologist and political economist with socialist sympathies. Oppenheimer was an adherent of Theodor Hertzka's *Freiland* idea (see Introduction).

7. Ferdinand Domela Nieuwenhuis (1846-1919), prominent Dutch socialist.

8. It does not seem that Kropotkin ever received such a gift.

9. Nettlau's idea remained an idea.

TO LUDWIG BERNDL
Hermsdorf i.d. Mark, August 16, 1915

In this emotive letter, Landauer expresses his grief in the midst of World War I. Ludwig Berndl was an editor, writer, and translator friend of Landauer.

D EAR FRIEND BERNDL,

    We are, all in all, doing fine; my wife has returned from her journey. We have lost close ones in these times of trial, there is no denying this. What provides hope, however, is that we will be understood by many more after this experience is over. [...]

We cannot escape this war, and we should not. It is true that I cannot understand how people can show such contempt for humankind – they seem to forget that they are human beings themselves. However, wishing for an idyllic escape is no answer, even if this means anguish and suffering. Our hope must be the purity in ourselves. If we are pure, and if we know that people would treat each other differently if they were like us, then we have the comforting certainty that what is alive in ourselves can be alive in others as well. No one lacks the ability, the disposition, the potential. All humans are equal.

If we see nothing but guilt – guilt of action as well as of acceptance – around us, then this reminds us that an enormous task lies ahead of us. So let us all experience this horror, let our hearts be filled with sorrow, and let us come to the brink of complete hopelessness. However, let us not despair. Let us rather defeat despair through action! This is the way of the warrior, and we all have to be warriors. Only heroism can save humanity. However, we must understand heroism correctly. It has nothing to do with the madness of the state.

It is said that the current wars are – "in reality" – fought for economic reasons. This might be true as far as their results are concerned; it is not true as far as their motivations go.

If we want to change people's behavior, we have to change people's motivations. And these can be changed. What lies at the core of the eruption and the execution of wars is the power and the honor of states. We have to make clear that it is not the peoples that are enemies, but the states.

The "state" is a twisted and antiquated form of (internal as well as external) organization for the sake of the economy, peaceful exchange, and public safety. The following has always been true, is true right now, and will always be true: people live together in communities; people exchange goods and services over long distances; people are differentiated by language, custom, desire, and need; people believe that everyone looks out for his individual interest; however, some people stand up, make a change, and point the direction for the spirit and the courage of others. This is the reality that will always remain.

The slaughtering that is happening now has nothing to do with this. It is utterly meaningless, an unreality, nothingness. Our task is to undo this unreality. The results of this war will help us with this task – regardless of the exact shape they take. The entire war will help us.

It is this conviction – and my ongoing belief in the power of action, something I call *hope* – that saves me. I might only see what I see in order not to despair. However, I am not willing to debate with anyone who sees despair as an option.

With love from house to house,

yours,

Gustav Landauer

TO HUGO LANDAUER
Hermsdorf near Berlin, February 9, 1917

Hugo Landauer, his cousin, always remained Landauer's most important contact within the family. This letter expresses Landauer's continued abhorrence of the war, his outsider position even within the German left, and the hopes he put in Woodrow Wilson.

D EAR HUGO!
[...] Not only do I understand Wilson perfectly, but I predicted everything: his call for permanent peace, as well as the German Submarine War[1] and its inevitable consequences.

Wilson's position is entirely logical. It would be entirely illogical if the wise and exemplary views expressed in his speech to the Senate did not lead him to treat Germany as the enemy of humanity: a state that threatens to kill peaceful Americans if they maintain relations with states that they have no quarrels with. This must be obvious for everyone who is not blind! "Germany" whimpers of course: "We have no merchant ships that can conduct the trade war without bloodshed, capturing other merchant ships, and confiscating contraband. This is why we have to use submarines and why blood has to be shed." How do we expect a state that is not even involved in the war to react to such ludicrous explanations? Why should America care whether Germany wins or whether a legitimate blockade backed by international law forces it to ask for peace?

Germany is condemned to lose. What we are witnessing is its last attempt to win and to defy international law. As everyone with a clear mind knows, this attempt is doomed to fail. The tragedy is that so many people, most of all we Germans, will still have to suffer enormously for nothing at all. It will still take some time before those who are responsible for the war will admit what even they already know.

If there has ever been a reason for a responsible state leader to cut diplomatic ties, Wilson would have it now. However, he will – and now especially – maintain that a "Peace without Victory" has to be reached. He has explained very well what he means by that.[2] The German government and military rebuffed the idea.

You are deeply wrong concerning the first two responses to Wilson's original call for freedom. He proposed to announce the conditions for peace publicly. This is also what the Entente has done – albeit in a clumsy and agitated manner. The concessions demanded of Russia were also very harsh. However, the difficult military situation makes such demands necessary. Everyone understands this. The Germans, however, arrogantly rejected them. Their message remained: "Let us all get together and make peace!" What idiocy! What embarrassment to approach the world with the air of a victor: "We want peace." Who does not want peace?! They could have said this the very second that the war started. States go to war to make peace – a peace that will be favorable to them. In order to have serious negotiations one has to state one's aims. One has to say what was desired from the beginning – or what is desired now. One has to declare what has been learned and what one regrets. Otherwise, one only appears foolish and pathetic.

The war had no meaning when it started, and even if the Germans – as they imagined – had won before the end of 1914, it still would not have had one. Now, however, it does have a meaning, and this explains the necessary double role of a reasonable, free, and dignified man of peace like Wilson: what we have now is a war against war; a war that is meant to be the last war of them all.

History has made the German Reich the representative of war. This is – without exception – our fault, our dishonor, and our punishment. Should the other states just accept that we condone the cast of belligerent militarist men that form our government? Should they accept that the spirit of our people reflects the most idiotic and limited type of man: the high school professor? Those of us who knew better from the beginning – those of us who are relatively innocent – can only hope that we will survive this flood of sin; together with a pitiful and dumb people. There lies a sinister logic in 1917...

Warmest greetings!

Yours,

Gustav

PS: My hands are freezing. It is impossible to heat this room. Hence, the particularly bad writing. It is fortunate, however, that I do not have to write with my feet – they are freezing even more.

1. Landauer refers to German submarines attacking Allied merchant shipping in the Atlantic.

2. Wilson gave a speech under this title in front of the U.S. Senate on January 22, 1917. It was an attempt to motivate all parties to engage in negotiations. The attempt failed. The United States declared war against Germany on April 6.

TO MARTIN BUBER
Krumbach (Swabia), November 15, 1918

In this letter to one of his closest spiritual companions, Landauer reports on the revolutionary situation in Munich and about his personal involvement.

D EAR BUBER,

   I have recovered enough to return to Munich to-night. It is best for me to be there, even if it is not ideal. You should come too; there is enough work to do. I will write to you once I have found a suitable task. In the meantime, let me make it clear that I am strongly opposed to summoning the national assembly soon![1] If this happens, it is only in the interest of the rotten parties. They are shameless enough to pretend that the national assembly has already regained legitimacy. This is not the case. There has to be a new spirit first, born by new conditions. Such conditions can only be instigated by revolutionary interventions. We need an entirely new press. I would not condemn any act of violence that helps destroy the old. I am thinking of an advertising monopoly for the state and the municipality; right now this means the workers' and soldiers' councils.

   I am in total opposition to the pompousness of "intellectual councils!" There shall be no more divisions between manual and intellectual workers – and hence nothing that resembles the idea of Hiller's *Herrenhaus!*[2]

   I wish I could go to Berlin as a representative of Bavaria. I would like to see you in the same role in Vienna. For now, how-ever, this is only my personal idea. Tell me what you think!

   What the train schedules will look like on the December 1 no one knows. I do count on you coming to Düsseldorf though.[3]

Ask the director – Mr. Keller – to telegraph you concerning the possibilities on the 29th.

Warm greetings to you all [...].

Yours,

Landauer

1. After Germany was declared a republic in Berlin on November 9, 1919, moderate, parliamentarian sections demanded the convocation of a national assembly; more radical sections demanded a council republic based on direct democracy.

2. Kurt Hiller (1885-1972), libertarian German essayist, propagated a kind of Nietzschen *Geistesaristokratie* [literally, "aristocracy of the spirit"] in a 1918 essay entitled "Ein deutsches Herrenhaus" [A German Manor House].

3. Landauer, although having just rejected the call as dramatic adviser to the Düsseldorf Theatre in order to support the Bavarian Revolution in Munich, visited Düsseldorf regularly in his role as temporary editor of the Theatre's journal *Masken*.

TO MARGARETE SUSMAN
Krumbach (Swabia), January 13, 1919

Margarete Susman was a left-leaning German essayist and poet. Landauer responds to her pamphlet "Die Revolution und die Frau" [The Revolution and Women], published in Frankfurt am Main in December 1918. The letter includes a concise assessment of the revolutionary developments in Germany.[1]

D EAR FRIEND,

Your beautiful pamphlet has passed a hard test: I read it right after I received the first results of Bavaria's parliamentary elections.[2] The results confirm everything that I expected. However, this provides no joy, as it means that we are back in times when those in solitude remain right – and lonely.

The revolution should have never trusted the business of voting and parliamentarism. It should have used the new social structures to remodel and educate the masses. I fear that we will now have to deal with the old party politics again, i.e., with the counterrevolution. This will last a long time – until things will become so miserable that people will finally no longer accept it.

Kurt Eisner has a pure spirit and pure goals. However, due to a mixture of prudence, calculation, naiveté, and optimism, he has left his true way and chosen to engage in deceitful political games. He was horrified by the revolutionary energy. He has lost his bearings between Spartacus and compromise. He has postponed his own way, which he never recognized as clearly as I did. He has been a social democrat for too long. The entire German Revolution is bound to fail because its dependency on the social democrats.

The Spartacists will not be able to win.[3] Neither should they. As frightening as it may be: we need a power vacuum. Misery has to rise in Germany for the creative spirit to emerge. My only conciliation is that the struggle will continue. It is a struggle for meaning – even if it now expresses itself in meaningless ways.

There is one part of your pamphlet where you miss the point. What you say on page six and seven needs additions.[4] The revolution has to bring people happiness – in every respect. It has to provide people with a reality, a here and now, a salvation. For a few hours, maybe for a few days, our revolution was great and real, because it meant liberation, physical joy, and redemption to our soldiers. Then, it did not know how to proceed and was not able to provide people with anything real – something to do, something that could have changed their plight. This caused a pause in its development – a pause that we are still in.

Help can only come from a new economy. Only an emergency social-ism can provide what we require. It will arise from a combination of free action and desperate need. Some of this I have already said in the preface to the new edition of *Aufruf zum Sozialismus* – you should receive a copy soon. A lot remains to be said, however. [...]

With love to you both,

Gustav Landauer

[...]

1. Susman published two essays in Landauer's honor after his death (both enti-tled "Gustav Landauer"), in *Masken*, 1918-1919, and in *Das Tribunal*, June 1919.

2. The January 12, 1919, elections were the first elections after Bavaria had been declared a republic in November 1918. Eisner's USPD, which had carried the revolution in November, was heavily defeated both by the SPD and the conservative Bayerische Volkspartei [Bavarian People's Party].

3. Refers to the 1919 January Uprising in Berlin, led by the *Spartakusbund* [Sparta-cist League]. The very day that Landauer wrote this letter, right-wing militias from all over Germany entered Berlin to crush the uprising. The two most prominent Spartacists, Karl Liebknecht and Rosa Luxemburg, were murdered two days later, on January 15. Landauer gave a eulogy for them in Munich on February 6.

4. Susman calls "atonement" the "essential meaning of revolution," and writes that revolution is "about the future, not the presence" (Margarete Susman, "Die Revolution und die Frau," Frankfurt am Main: Das Flugblatt, 1918, 6-7).

TO FRITZ MAUTHNER
Postcard with Landauer's photograph[1]
Munich, April 7, 1919

Landauer informs his long-time friend and mentor about the proclamation of the Bavarian Council Republic and about his personal role.

THANK YOU, DEAR FRIEND. THE BAVARIAN COUNCIL REPUBLIC has honored me by making my birthday a national holiday.[2] I am now the "people's delegate" for propaganda, education, science, arts, and a few other things. If I'll have a few weeks, I hope I can achieve something; however, it is very likely that it will only be a few days, and then all this will have been but a dream.

I wish both of you all the very best,
Your Gustav Landauer

---

1. One in a series of postcards from the council republic's proclamation.

2. The proclamation of the Bavarian Council Republic – declared a national holiday – coincided with Landauer's birthday.

TO HIS DAUGHTERS

These letters and telegrams to his daughters, dated April 14 to 16, 1919, were Landauer's last messages to his family.

Monday, April 14, 1919, 11 a.m.

MY BELOVED CHILDREN,

I am still free and secure, as I wrote yesterday. Apparently, there was fighting in Munich, but the council republic prevailed. Some of my friends were or are still imprisoned. But do not worry about me! I am looked after well in every respect and I will be cautious!

My greatest concern is that false rumors will reach and worry you. I do not know how long it takes for my messages to arrive, but I do hope that you have received the telegrams that I have sent.

My second concern is that agitated bourgeois and peasants might harass you. I hope not. If it does happen, however, be wise and prudent. If you decide to leave Krumbach for some time, go to the Bernsteins[1] who will assist you. Do not forget to take the little bit of money that is in the house, as well as your and your mother's jewelry.

I have found someone who can probably help us move. In the meantime, write immediately to Aunt Else[2] and give her the exact address of Mr. Schuberts![3] Write her regularly!

I hope to hear from you soon!

Now I kiss you, dear Landauer and Eisner children.

Your father.

PS: Greet Helma![4]

In imitated children's writing
Munich, April 14, 1919

Father is well.

Telegram, Munich

April 15, 1919, 11 a.m. 46 N.

I am okay. Send news quickly! Pack your belongings. I want you here. Helma too. Willy will fetch you.[5] Notice of departure necessary.

Dad

Fragment, never sent

Munich, April 16, 1919

MY BELOVED CHILDREN,

I am writing a letter again. Yesterday I telegraphed. I wonder whether you received the message. In any case, I have not received the response I had asked for. I wanted you to come to Gr.-Hadern; however, there is no way to reach Munich right now anyway. If you are harassed even in the least, start traveling to Uncle Hugo – all of you. It will be his pleasure to be your host. As far as I am concerned, I am all right staying here, although I am starting to feel rather useless.

---

1. Distant relatives.

2. Else Eisner, Kurt Eisner's widow, who Landauer's daughters were staying with.

3. The identity of Mr. Schuberts is not clear. Probably, he was the owner of the house that Landauer had rented in Düsseldorf before heeding Eisner's call to Munich.

4. Helma Rosenthal looked after Landauer's children.

5. Wilhelm Klebsch, Kurt Eisner's medical orderly, did make it to Krumbach. However, by the time the children attempted to travel to Munich, all roads and railway lines had been shut by the military. The children traveled to the Lake Constance (Bodensee) residence of Landauer's cousin Hugo instead.

BIBLIOGRAPHY

IN GERMAN

Books and pamphlets by Landauer published in his lifetime

"An den Züricher Kongress. Bericht über die deutsche Arbeiter-bewegung" [To the Zurich Congress: Report on the German Workers' Movement]. Berlin: Der Sozialist, 1893. Landauer's report to the 1893 congress of the Second International in Zurich – due to the anarchists' exclusion he never got to present it.

Der Todesprediger [The Preacher of Death]. Dresden: Heinrich Minden, 1893. Landauer's early novel.

"Ein Weg zur Befreiung der Arbeiterklasse" [A Way to Liberate the Working Class]. Berlin: Adolf Marreck, 1895. Landauer propagates the idea of a consumers' cooperative as an important part of establishing autonomous structures for workers.

"Von Zürich bis London. Bericht über die deutsche Arbeiter-bewegung an den Londoner Kongress" [From Zurich to London: Report on the German Workers' Movement to the London Congress]. Pankow bei Berlin: self-published, 1896. Translated into English and published as "Social Democracy in Germany" – see below.

"Der Fall Ziethen. Ein Appell an die öffentliche Meinung" [The Ziethen Case: An Appeal to Public Opinion]. Berlin: Hugo Metscher, 1898. A pamphlet to defend the barber and inn keeper Albert Ziethen; see "1892-1901: Landau-er's early anarchism" in the Introduction.

Macht und Mächte. Novellen [Power and Powers: Novellas]. Berlin: Egon
  Fleischel, 1903. The two main pieces, *Arnold Himmelheber* and *Leb-
  endig Tot* [Alive Dead] were written in prison in 1894.

Skepsis und Mystik. Versuche im Anschluss an Mauthners Sprachkritik
  [Skepticism and Mysticism: Essays Inspired by Mauthner's Critique
  of Language]. Berlin: Egon Fleischel, 1903.

Die Revolution. Frankfurt am Main: Rütten und Loening, 1907.

"Die Abschaffung des Krieges durch die Selbstbestimmung des Volkes.
  Fragen an die deutschen Arbeiter." Berlin: Verlag des Sozialistischen
  Bundes, 1911. In this volume as "The Abolition of War by the Self-
  Determination of the People: Questions to the German Workers."

Aufruf zum Sozialismus. Berlin: Verlag des Sozialistischen Bundes, 1911.
  See *For Socialism* below.

"Ein Weg deutschen Geistes" [A Way of German Spirit]. München: Forum-
  Verlag, 1916. Essay about Johann Wolfgang von Goethe, Adalbert
  Stifter, and Georg Kaiser – Stifter was a popular 19th-century Austri-
  an novelist, Kaiser a German dramatist and Landauer contemporary.

"Die vereinigten Republiken Deutschlands und ihre Verfassung" [The
  United Republics of Germany and Their Constitution]. Frankfurt
  am Main: Das Flugblatt, 1918. Landauer describes his vision for a
  radically socialist and federalist Germany.

"Wie Hedwig Lachmann starb" [How Hedwig Lachmann Died]. Krumbach: self-published, 1918. Landauer intended this only to be
  distributed among his closest friends.

Rechenschaft [Account]. Berlin: Paul Cassirer, 1919. Collection of texts
  written between 1910 and 1916, most of them previously published. Compiled by Landauer.

Books by Landauer published posthumously

Shakespeare. Dargestellt in Vorträgen [Shakespeare. Presented in Lectures].
  Edited by Martin Buber. Two volumes. Frankfurt am Main: Rütten
  und Loening, 1920. Collection of Landauer's extensive lectures on
  Shakespeare's plays.

Der werdende Mensch. Aufsätze über Leben und Schrifttum [The Becoming Human: Essays on Life and Literature]. Edited by Martin Buber. Potsdam: Kiepenheuer, 1921. Collection of essays from 1903 to 1918. Buber included the note, "Edited according to the testamentary instructions of the author."

Beginnen. Aufsätze über Sozialismus [Beginning: Essays on Socialism]. Edited by Martin Buber. Köln: Marcan-Block, 1924. Essays from 1907 to 1912. Same Buber note as in *Der werdende Mensch* (see above).

Gustav Landauer. Sein Lebensgang in Briefen [Gustav Landauer: His Life in Letters]. Edited by Martin Buber and Ina Britschgi-Schimmer. Two volumes. Frankfurt am Main: Rütten und Loening, 1929. Collection of Landauer letters. No responses are provided, but the letters are annotated.

Zwang und Befreiung. Eine Auswahl aus seinem Werk [Coercion and Liberation: Selected Works]. Edited by Heinz-Joachim Heydorn. Köln: Jakob Hegner, 1968. Combines essays from *Rechenschaft* and *Der werdende Mensch*, with an extensive introduction by Heydorn.

Entstaatlichung. Für eine herrschaftslose Gesellschaft [De-Statization: For a Society Without Domination]. Edited by Heinz-Jürgen Valeske. Afterword by Stefan Blankertz. Westbevern: Büchse der Pandora, 1976. Essays from 1909-1910, mainly related to Landauer's understanding of socialism.

Erkenntnis und Befreiung. Ausgewählte Reden und Aufsätze [Knowledge and Liberation: Selected Lectures and Essays]. Edited by Ruth Link-Salinger (Hyman). Frankfurt am Main: Suhrkamp, 1976. Nine political lectures and essays from 1895 to 1918.

Signatur: g.l. Gustav Landauer im "Sozialist" (1892-1899) [Signature g.l.: Gustav Landauer in *Der Sozialist* (1892-1899)]. Edited by Ruth Link-Salinger (Hyman). Frankfurt am Main: Suhrkamp, 1986. Landauer's essays from the "First" and "Second" *Sozialist*, 1892 to 1899. Extensive introduction by Link-Salinger.

Briefe nach der Schweiz [Letters to Switzerland]. With Erich Mühsam, Max Hoelz, Peter Kropotkin. Zürich: Limmat, 1972. Intriguing little book centered around Swiss syndicalist Margarethe Faas-Hardegger, who Landauer fell in love with and who collaborated with various known anarchists. She was an important force in reviving *Der Sozialist* in 1909. The book includes correspondence between Faas-Hardegger, the named authors, and other socialist activists.

Auch die Vergangenheit ist Zukunft. Essays zum Anarchismus [The Past is Future Too: Essays on Anarchism]. Edited by Siegbert Wolf. Frankfurt am Main: Luchterhand, 1989. Wide-ranging essay collection, extensive introduction, bibliographical notes, and timetable by the editor.

Die Botschaft der Titanic. Ausgewählte Essays [The Titanic's Message: Selected Essays]. Edited by Walter Fähnders and Hansgeorg Schmidt-Bergmann. Berlin: Kontext, 1994. Wide-ranging selection of essays, extensive afterword by the editors.

Gustav Landauer – Fritz Mauthner. Briefwechsel 1890-1919 [Gustav Landauer – Fritz Mauthner: Correspondence 1890-1919]. Edited by Hanna Delf. München: C.H. Beck, 1994.

Zeit und Geist. Kulturkritische Schriften 1890-1919 [Time and Spirit: Writings on Culture 1890-1919]. Edited by Rolf Kauffeldt and Michael Matzigkeit. München: Boer, 1997. Wide-ranging essay collection focusing on Landauer's writings on culture, literature, and the arts. Extensive appendix.

Dichter, Ketzer, Außenseiter. Essays und Reden zu Literatur, Philosophie, Judentum [Poet, Heretic, Outsider: Essays and Lectures on Literature, Philosophy, Judaism]. Edited by Hanna Delf. Berlin: Akademie Verlag, 1997. This was planned as vol. 3 of an eight-volume Landauer Collected Works edition. It includes Landauer's writings and lectures during World War I. No further volume of the planned edition has been published.

Arnold Himmelheber. Eine Novelle. Edited by Philippe Despoix. Berlin: Philo, 2000. Individual publication of the 1894 novella *Arnold Himmelheber*, originally published in *Macht und Mächte*. Like *Der Todesprediger* strongly influenced by Friedrich Nietzsche. Commentary by the editor.

"Sei tapfer und wachse dich aus." Gustav Landauer im Dialog mit Erich Mühsam. Briefe und Aufsätze ["Be Brave, Grow, and Mature": Gustav Landauer and Erich Mühsam: Letters and Essays]. Edited by Christoph Knüppel. Lübeck: Erich-Mühsam-Gesellschaft, 2004. Traces the relationship between the two seminal German anarchists.

Notable essays by Landauer on anarchism and socialism not included in the Reader

"Wie nennen wir uns?" [What Do We Call Ourselves?]. *Der Sozialist*, April 1, 1893.

Zur Frage: Wie nennen wir uns? [On the Question: What Do We Call Ourselves?]. *Der Sozialist*, April 8 and 15, 1893.

"Manchesterfreiheit – Staatshilfe – Anarchie. Politische Unfreiheit – politische Mitarbeit – Negation des Staates" [Manchester Liberalism – Help of the State – Anarchy: Lack of Political Liberty – Political Participation – Negation of the State]. *Der Sozialist*, June 24, 1893.

"Etwas über Moral" [On Morality]. *Der Sozialist*, August 5, 1893.

"Arbeiter aller Länder, vereinigt Euch!" [Workers of the World, Unite!]. *Der Sozialist*, September 28, 1895.

"Zur Entwicklungsgeschichte des Individuums" [On the History of the Individual]. Various *Sozialist* issues from November 2, 1895, to February 8, 1896.

"Die Krise in der revolutionären Bewegung" [The Crisis in the Revolutionary Movement]. *Der Sozialist*, June 4 and 18, 1898.

Preface to *Michael Bakunin* by Max Nettlau, Berlin: Paul Pawlowitsch, 1901.

"Proudhon und Bakunin. Eine Charakteristik" [Proudhon and Bakunin: A Representation]. *Der Sozialist*, January 15, 1909.

"Zur Geschichte des Wortes 'Anarchie'" [On the History of the Word "Anarchy"]. *Der Sozialist*, May 15, 1909.

"Organisationsfragen" [Questions of Organization]. *Der Sozialist*, July 1, 1909.

"Marxism and Socialism" [Marxism and Socialism]. Various *Sozialist* issues from December 15, 1909, to April 15, 1910.

"Zum 40. Gedenktag der Pariser Kommune" [On the 40th Commemoration Day of the Paris Commune]. *Der Sozialist*, March 15, 1911.

"Vierzig Jahre nachher" [Forty Years Later]. *Der Sozialist*, April 15, 1911.

"Die Arbeit der Kommune" [The Work of the Commune]. *Der Sozialist*, April 15, 1911.

"Gott und der Sozialismus" [God and Socialism]. *Der Sozialist*, June 15, July 1, and July 15, 1911.

"Individualismus" [Individualism]. *Der Sozialist*, July 15, 1911.

"Alexander Herzen (Aus Anlaß seines 100. Geburtstages)" [Alexander Herzen (For His 100th Birthday)]. *Hannoverscher Kurier*, March 22, 1912.

"Arbeitselig" [Laborious]. *Der Sozialist*, May 1, 1913.

"Zu Michael Bakunins hundertstem Geburtstag" [For Mikhail Bakunin's 100th Birthday]. *Der Sozialist*, May 20, 1914.

"Michael Bakunin. Daten seines Lebens" [Mikhail Bakunin: Facts of His Life]. *Der Sozialist*, July 1, 1914.

"Stelle Dich, Sozialist!" [Show Yourself, Socialist!]. *Der Aufbruch*, July, 1915.

"Vom Sozialismus und der Siedlung. Thesen zur Wirklichkeit und Ver-wirklich-ung" [On Socialism and Settlement: Theses on Reality and Realization]. *Der Aufbruch*, October, 1915. An extended version of this essay, compiled by Buber from Landauer's hand-written notes, is included in *Beginnen*.

Notable essays by Landauer on arts, literature, and culture not included in the Reader

"Über epische und dramatische Dichtung" [On Epic and Dramatic Poetry]. *Deutschland*, January 4 and 11, 1890.

"Das neue soziale Drama" [The New Social Drama]. *Deutschland*, April 12, 1890.

"Die Zukunft und die Kunst" [The Future and the Arts]. *Die neue Zeit. Wochenschrift der deutschen Sozialdemokratie*, January 13, 1892.

"Gerhart Hauptmann." *Die neue Zeit*, January 29, 1892.

"Dostojewski." *Das Neue Jahrhundert II*, April to September Issue, 1899.

"Die blaue Blume" [The Blue Flower]. *Die Nation*, # 28, 1900.

"Streit um Whitman" [The Whitman Dispute]. *Das literarische Echo*, 1907.

"Der Dichter und sein Volk" [The Poet and His People]. *Der Demokrat*, # 33, 1910.

"Strindberg." *Blätter des deutschen Theaters*, 1912.

"Dem größten Schweizer" [To the Greatest Swiss]. *Der Sozialist*, July 1, 1912. On Jean-Jacques Rousseau.

"Strindberg." *Neue Jugend*, 1916.

"Friedrich Hölderlin in seinen Gedichten. Ein Vortrag" [Friedrich Hölderlin in His Poems: A Lecture]. *Die weißen Blätter*, April-June, 1916.

"Die Zukunft der deutschen Bühne. Eine Umfrage" [The Future of German Theatre: A Survey]. *Die Zukunft der deutschen Bühne*, 1917.

"Eine Ansprache an die Dichter" [An Address to the Poets]. *Die Erhebung. Jahrbuch für neue Dichtung und Werte*, 1919. Lecture given on October 18, 1918.

"Goethes Politik" [Goethe's Politics]. *Masken*, January 14, 1919.

Selected translations by Landauer

Meister Eckharts Mystische Schriften [Meister Eckhart's Mystical Writings]. Berlin: Karl Schnabel, 1903.

Oscar Wilde, *Der Sozialismus und die Seele des Menschen* [The Soul of Man Under Socialism]. With Hedwig Lachmann. Berlin: Karl Schnabel, 1904.

Peter Kropotkin, *Landwirtschaft, Industrie und Handwerk oder Die Vereinigung von Industrie und Landwirtschaft, geistiger und körperlicher Arbeit* [Fields, Factories, and Workshops, or The Union of Industry and Agriculture, Intellectual, and Manual Labor]. With a preface and an afterword. Berlin: S. Calvary and Co., 1904.

Oscar Wilde, *Das Bildnis des Dorian Gray* [The Picture of Dorian Gray]. With Hedwig Lachmann. Leipzig: Insel, 1907.

Oscar Wilde, *Zwei Gespräche von der Kunst und vom Leben*. [Two Conversations on Arts and Life]. With Hedwig Lachmann. Leipzig: Insel, 1907. From Oscar Wilde's *Intentions*.

George Bernard Shaw, *Sozialismus für Millionäre* [Socialism for Millionaires]. Berlin: Concordia, 1907.

Peter Kropotkin, *Gegenseitige Hilfe in der Tier- und Menschenwelt* [Mutual Aid]. Leipzig: Theodor Thomas, 1908.

Peter Kropotkin, *Die Französische Revolution 1789-1793* [The Great French Revolution, 1789-1793]. Two volumes. Leipzig: Theodor Thomas, 1909.

Étienne de La Boétie, *Von der freiwilligen Knechtschaft* [*Discours de la servitude volontaire*] [The Politics of Disobedience: The Discourse of Voluntary Servitude]. *Der Sozialist*, various issues, 1910-1911.

Sir Thomas Malory, *Der Tod Arthurs* [Le Morte d'Arthur]. Three volumes. With Hedwig Lachmann. Leipzig: Insel, 1913.

Rabindranath Tagore, *Das Postamt* [*The Post Office*]. With Hedwig Lachmann. Leipzig: Kurt Wolff, 1918.

Briefe aus der Französischen Revolution [Letters from the French Revolution]. Selected, translated, and annotated by Gustav Landauer. Two volumes. Frankfurt am Main: Rütten und Loening, 1919. Edited posthumously by Martin Buber based on Landauer's plans. Fascinating and extensive overview of the French Revolution along the letters of numerous participants. Landauer writes in the preface: "I know nothing about a work of this kind in France – or in any other nation."

Rabindranath Tagore, *Der König der dunklen Kammer* [*The King of the Dark Chamber*]. With Hedwig Lachmann. Leipzig: Kurt Wolff, 1919.

Walt Whitman, *Der Wundarzt. Briefe, Aufzeichnungen und Gedichte aus dem amerikanischen Sezessionskrieg* [The Surgeon: Letters, Notes, and Poems from the American Civil War]. Poems by Gustav Landauer, prose by Iwan Goll. Zürich: Max Rascher, 1919.

Walt Whitman, *Gesänge und Inschriften* [Songs and Inscriptions]. München: Kurt Wolff, 1921.

Collected Works

SURPRISINGLY, A GERMAN COLLECTED WORKS EDITION OF GUSTAV Landauer has never been compiled. Attempts were made in the 1990s, but none of those came to fruition. The first volume of a planned eight-volume collection appeared with Akademie Verlag in 1997 (*Dichter, Ketzer, Außenseiter. Essays und Reden zu Literatur, Philosophie, Judentum*), but no subsequent volumes have been released.

In 2008, a promising edition was inaugurated by Edition AV Verlag under the editorship of Siegbert Wolf, Germany's principal Landauer scholar. Six volumes are planned. The first two (*Internationalismus* and *Anarchismus*) have been published in 2008 and 2009 respectively. The subsequent ones are to be published in annual succession: *Anti-Politik* (2010), *Antimilitarismus, Krieg und Revolution* [Antimilitarism, War, and Revolution] (2011), *Philosophie und Judentum* [Philosophy and Judaism] (2012), *Literatur* (2013). Additional volumes of Landauer's correspondence might be added. All volumes include extensive biographical and bibliographical references.

Notable publications about Landauer

Braun, Bernhard. *Die Utopie des Geistes. Zur Funktion der Utopie in der politischen Theorie Gustav Landauers* [The Utopia of Spirit: On the Meaning of Utopia in Gustav Landauer's Political Theory]. Idstein: Schulz-Kirchner, 1991. An excellent study of Gustav Landauer's philosophy; includes many biographical details and valuable information on his historical influence.

Delf, Hanna and Gert Mattenklott, eds., *Gustav Landauer im Gespräch. Symposium zum 125. Geburtstag* [Gustav Landauer in Discussion: Symposium for His 125th Birthday]. Tübingen: M. Niemeyer, 1997. Predominantly academic reflections on Landauer's work.

Fiedler, Leonhard M., Renate Heuer, and Annemarie Taeger-Altenhofer, eds., *Gustav Landauer (1870-1919). Eine Bestandsaufnahme zur Rezeption seines Werkes* [Gustav Landauer (1870-1919): His Work in Historical Transmission]. Frankfurt am Main/New York: Campus, 1995. A collection of essays on Gustav Landauer's thought, life, and influence.

Hinz, Thorsten. *Mystik und Anarchie. Meister Eckhart und seine Bedeutung im Denken Gustav Landauers* [Mysticism and Anarchy: The Significance of Meister Eckhart in Gustav Landauer's Thought]. Berlin: Karin Kramer, 2000. Excellent Landauer study with a particular focus on his mysticism.

Kalz, Wolf. *Gustav Landauer. Kultursozialist und Anarchist* [Gustav Landauer: Cultural Socialist and Anarchist]. Meisenheim/Glan: Anton Hain, 1967. Kalz's work was the first extensive study of Landauer in decades. The book provides a good overview, but both structure and tone mainly appeal to academic readers.

Linse, Ulrich, ed., *Gustav Landauer und die Revolutionszeit 1918-1919* [Gustav Landauer and the Revolutionary Period of 1918-1919]. Berlin: Karin Kramer, 1974. Extensive documentation of Gustav Landauer's activities in Munich during the Bavarian Revolution. Inlcudes a comprehensive Landauer bibliography.

Linse, Ulrich. *Organisierter Anarchismus im Deutschen Kaiserreich von 1871* [Organized Anarchism in the German Kaiserreich of 1871]. Berlin: Duncker und Humblot, 1969. A meticulously researched and enormously comprehensive study of anarchism in Germany between 1871 and 1919; the single best source on Gustav Landauer's political activism, on his role within Germany's anarchist movement, and on the organization of *Der Sozialist* and the Socialist Bund.

Matzigkeit, Michael, ed., *"...die beste Sensation ist das Ewige..." Gustav Landauer. Leben, Werk und Wirkung* ["...the Best Sensation of All Is the Eternal...": Gustav Landauer: Life, Work, and Influence]. Düsseldorf: Theatermusem, 1995. Lavishly illustrated documentation of Landauer's life.

Mühsam, Erich, et al. *Gustav Landauer – Worte der Würdigung* [Gustav Landauer – Words of Appreciation]. Darmstadt: Die freie Gesellschaft, 1951. Essays to commemorate Gustav Landauer by Erich Mühsam, Rudolf Rocker, Helmut Rüdiger, and Diego Abad de Santillán.

Pfeiffer, Frank. *"Mir leben die Toten..." Gustav Landauers Programm des libertären Sozialismus* ["For Me, the Dead Are Alive...": Gustav Landauer's Program of a Libertarian Socialism]. Hamburg: Dr.

Kovač, 2005. Extensive overview of Landauer's life and work, with a particular emphasis on Landauer's influence in both politics and arts. Mainly directed towards an academic audience.

Willems, Joachim. *Religiöser Gehalt des Anarchismus und anarchistischer Gehalt der Religion? Die jüdisch-christlich-atheistische Mystik Gustav Landauers zwischen Meister Eckhart und Martin Buber* [Religious Contents of Anarchism and Anarchist Contents of Religion? The Jewish-Christian-Atheist Mysticism of Gustav Landauer between Meister Eckhart and Martin Buber]. Albeck bei Ulm: Ulmer Manuskripte, 2001. An interesting study on the intersections of mysticism and anarchism, as well as the apparently incongruent union of religiousness and atheism in Landauer's thought.

Wolf, Siegbert, ed., *Gustav Landauer Bibliographie*. Grafenau-Döffingen: Trotzdem, 1992. Most comprehensive Landauer bibliography, albeit outdated.

Wolf, Siegbert. *Gustav Landauer zur Einführung* [Gustav Landauer: An Introduction]. Hamburg: Junius, 1988. Most concise and popular introduction to Landauer's life and thought.

LANDAUER'S WORK
IN ENGLISH

"Social Democracy in Germany." London: 127 Ossulston Street, 1896.

"Thoughts on Revolution." Excerpt from *Die Revolution. Anarchy*, no. 54, August 1965.

"Dream and Revolution." Excerpt from *Die Revolution*. Translated by Penelope Rosemont. In *Free Spirits: Annals of the Insurgent Imagination*. Edited by Paul Buhle et. al. San Francisco: City Lights Books, 1982.

"On Communal Settlement and Its Industrialization: An Exchange of Letters between Gustav Landauer and Nachum Goldman." Edited and translated by Avraham Yassour. Haifa: University of Haifa, n.d. [ca. 1995].

For Socialism. Translated by David J. Parent. St. Louis: Telos Press, 1978. Includes the first version of "The Twelve Articles of the Socialist Bund." An excerpt of this edition was reprinted as "Destroying the State by Creating Socialism," in *Anarchism: A Documentary History of Libertarian Ideas*, vol. 1., edited by Robert Graham (Montreal: Black Rose Books, 2005).

Anarchism in Germany and other essays. Translated by Stephen Bender and Gabriel Kuhn. San Francisco: Barbary Coast Publishing Collective, 2005. Contains: "Anarchism in Germany" ("Anarchismus in Deutschland," *Die Zukunft*, January 5, 1895) (reprinted in Graham, ed., *Anarchism: A Documentary History of Libertarian Ideas*, vol. 1); "Walt Whitman" (*Der Sozialist*, Christmas 1913); "Youth's Suicide" ("Selbstmord der Jugend," *Der Sozialist*, April 15, 1911); "The Titanic's Message" ("Die Botschaft der Titanic," *Frankfurter Zeitung*, April 21, 1912, reprinted in *Der Sozialist*, May 1, 1912).

"Anarchic Thoughts on Anarchism." Translated by Jesse Cohn and Gabriel Kuhn. *Perspectives on Anarchist Theory*, vol. 11, no. 1 (Fall 2007). With a translator's note by Jesse Cohn. A revised version of the translation is included in this volume.

About Landauer

Avrich, Paul. "Gustav Landauer." *The Match!*, December 1974.

Avrich, Paul. "The Martyrdom of Gustav Landauer." In *Anarchist Portraits*, Princeton: Princeton University Press, 1988.

Berman, Russell and Tim Luke. "Introduction to *For Socialism*." In *For Socialism* by Gustav Landauer, St. Louis: Telos Press, 1978. Reprinted as "On Gustav Landauer" in *The Radical Papers*, edited by Dimitrios I. Roussopoulos (Montreal: Black Rose, 1987).

Breines, Paul. "The Jew as Revolutionary: The Case of Gustav Landauer." *Leo Baeck Yearbook*, 1967.

C.W. (Colin Ward), "Gustav Landauer." *Anarchy*, no. 54, August 1965.

Esper, Thomas. *The Anarchism of Gustav Landauer*. Chicago: Chicago University Press, 1961.

Gambone, Larry. "For Community: An Introduction to the Communitarian Anarchism of Gustav Landauer." Montreal: Red Lion Press, 2001.

Horrox, James. "Reinventing Resistance: Constructive Activism in Gustav Landauer's Social Philosophy." In *New Perspectives on Anarchism*, edited by Nathan Jun and Shane Wahl. Lanham: Lexington Books, 2009.

Horrox, James. "Socialism and the Soul of Man: Gustav Landauer's Wilde Translations." *Oscholars Special Issue Spring 2010 - The Soul of Man: Oscar Wilde and Socialism*, www.oscholars.com.

Link-Salinger (Hyman), Ruth. *Gustav Landauer: Philosopher of Utopia*. Indianapolis: Hackett Publishing, 1977.

Lunn, Eugene. *Prophet of Community: The Romantic Socialism of Gustav Landauer*. Berkeley: University of California Press, 1973.

Maurer, Charles B. *Call to Revolution: The Mystical Anarchism of Gustav Landauer.* Detroit: Wayne State University Press, 1971.

Werner, Alfred. "A Saintly Revolutionary." *The Jewish Quarterly*, Summer 1959.

Yassour, Avraham. "Gustav Landauer – The Man, the Jew and the Anarchist." *Ya'ad*, no. 2, 1989.

INDEX

About the Authors:

Gabriel Kuhn (born in Innsbruck, Austria, 1972) lives as an independent author and translator in Stockholm, Sweden. He received a Ph.D. in philosophy from the University of Innsbruck in 1996. His publications in German include the award-winning 'Neuer Anarchismus' in den USA: Seattle und die Folgen (2008). His publications with PM Press include Life Under the Jolly Roger: Reflections on Golden Age Piracy (2010), Sober Living for the Revolution: Hardcore Punk, Straight Edge, and Radical Politics (editor, 2010), Soccer vs. The State: Tackling Football And Radical Politics (2011) and Erich Mühsam: Liberating Society from the State and Other Writings (editor/translator, 2011)

Richard J.F. Day is an autonomy-oriented theorist and practitioner, whose work focuses on creating non-statist, non-capitalist, post-colonial, sustainable alternatives to the dominant global order. He works and teaches at Queen's University, and is a founding member of the AKA Autonomous Social Centre, both in Kingston Ontario.

Siegbert Wolf is a German historian based in Frankfurt am Main. He has published extensively on Gustav Landauer and is the editor of a six-volume edition of Landauer's works.

About PM Press:

PM PRESS WAS FOUNDED AT THE END OF 2007 BY A SMALL COLLECTION of folks with decades of publishing, media, and organizing experience. PM co-founder Ramsey Kanaan started AK Press as a young teenager in Scotland almost 30 years ago and, together with his fellow PM Press co-conspirators, has published and distributed hundreds of books, pamphlets, CDs, and DVDs. Members of PM have founded enduring book fairs, spearheaded victorious tenant organizing campaigns, and worked closely with bookstores, academic conferences, and even rock bands to deliver political and challenging ideas to all walks of life. We're old enough to know what we're doing and young enough to know what's at stake.

We seek to create radical and stimulating fiction and non-fiction books, pamphlets, t-shirts, visual and audio materials to entertain, educate and inspire you. We aim to distribute these through every available channel with every available technology - whether that means you are seeing anarchist classics at our bookfair stalls; reading our latest vegan cookbook at the café; downloading geeky fiction e-books; or digging new music and timely videos from our website.

PM Press is always on the lookout for talented and skilled volunteers, artists, activists and writers to work with. If you have a great idea for a project or can contribute in some way, please get in touch.

PM Press
PO Box 23912
Oakland, CA 94623
www.pmpress.org

Friends of PM

THESE ARE INDISPUTABLY MOMENTOUS TIMES — THE FINANCIAL SYSTEM IS melting down globally and the Empire is stumbling. Now more than ever there is a vital need for radical ideas.

In the year since its founding – and on a mere shoestring – PM Press has risen to the formidable challenge of publishing and distributing knowledge and entertainment for the struggles ahead. With over 75 releases to date, we have published an impressive and stimulating array of literature, art, music, politics, and culture. Using every available medium, we've succeeded in connecting those hungry for ideas and information to those putting them into practice.

Friends of PM allows you to directly help impact, amplify, and revitalize the discourse and actions of radical writers, filmmakers, and artists. It provides us with a stable foundation from which we can build upon our early successes and provides a much-needed subsidy for the materials that can't necessarily pay their own way. You can help make that happen--and receive every new title automatically delivered to your door once a month--by joining as a Friend of PM Press. Here are your options:

- **$25 a month:** Get all books and pamphlets plus 50% discount on all webstore purchases
- **$25 a month:** Get all CDs and DVDs plus 50% discount on all webstore purchases
- **$40 a month:** Get all PM Press releases plus 50% discount on all webstore purchases
- **$100 a month:** Sustainer - Everything plus PM merchandise, free downloads, and 50% discount on all webstore purchases

For those who can't afford $25 or more a month, we're introducing Sustainer Rates at $15, $10 and $5. Sustainers get a free PM Press t-shirt and a 50% discount on all purchases from our website.

Your Visa or Mastercard will be billed once a month, until you tell us to stop. Or until our efforts succeed in bringing the revolution around. Or the financial meltdown of Capital makes plastic redundant. Whichever comes first.

LIFE UNDER THE JOLLY ROGER: REFLECTIONS ON GOLDEN AGE PIRACY

by Gabriel Kuhn

Over the last couple of decades an ideological battle has raged over the political legacy and cultural symbolism of the "golden age" pirates who roamed the seas between the Caribbean Islands and the Indian Ocean from 1690 to 1725. They are depicted as romanticized villains on the one hand, and as genuine social rebels on the other. Life Under the Jolly Roger examines the political and cultural significance of these nomadic outlaws by relating historical accounts to a wide range of theoretical concepts--reaching from Marshall Sahlins and Pierre Clastres to Mao-Tse Tung and Eric J. Hobsbawm via Friedrich Nietzsche and Michel Foucault. The meanings of race, gender, sexuality and disability in golden age pirate communities are analyzed and contextualized, as are the pirates' forms of organization, economy and ethics.

While providing an extensive catalog of scholarly references for the academic reader, this delightful and engaging study is directed at a wide audience and demands no other requirements than a love for pirates, daring theoretical speculation and passionate, yet respectful, inquiry.

Product Details:

Written by Gabriel Kuhn
Published by PM Press
ISBN: 978-1-60486-052-8
Pub Date: December 2009
Format: Paperback
Page Count: 272 pages
Size: 9 by 6
Subjects: History, Sociology

Reviews:

"In the golden age of piracy thousands plied the seas in egalitarian and communal alternatives to the piratical age of gold. The last gasps of the hundreds who were hanged and the blood-curdling cries of the thousands traded as slaves inflated the speculative financial bubbles of empire putting an end to these Robin Hoods of the deep seas. In addition to history, Gabriel Kuhn's radical piratology brings philosophy, ethnography, and cultural studies to the stark question of the time: which were the criminals – bankers and brokers or sailors and slaves? By so doing he supplies us with another case where the history isn't dead, it's not even past! Onwards to health-care by eye-patch, peg-leg, and hook!"
 – **Peter Linebaugh, author of *The London Hanged*, co-author of *The Many-Headed Hydra***

"Life Under the Jolly Roger will appeal to anyone interested in pirates and radical practice. It brings the golden age of piracy to life and shows us the link to contemporary radical politics. I recommend this book to those who identify with pirates and seek a well-reasoned analysis of their legacy."
 – **Luis A. Fernandez, author of *Policing Dissent***

"It is rare to find a book that is not only entertaining, but broadens your knowledge as well. More rare even, a book that not only enhances your knowledge but also your perspective: this is the first time the subject of pirates has been analyzed using such a variety of theories, each of which lets you see history and its stories from a different angle. Even if you think you could never be interested in the history of pirates, take a look at this book and you will be."
 – **Nora Räthzel, professor of Sociology at the University of Umeå, Sweden**

LIBERATING SOCIETY FROM THE STATE & OTHER WRITINGS: A POLITICAL READER

Erich Mühsam

Edited and translated by Gabriel Kuhn

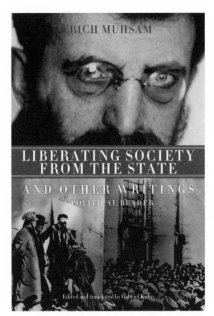

Erich Mühsam (1878-1934), poet, bohe-mian, revolutionary, is one of Germany's most renowned and influential anar-chists. Born into a middle-class Jewish family, he challenged the conventions of bourgeois society at the turn of the century, engaged in heated debates on the rights of women and homosexu-als, and traveled Europe in search of radical communes and artist colonies. He was a pri-mary instigator of the ill-fated Bavarian Council Republic in 1919, and held the libertarian ban-ner high during a Weimar Republic that came under increasing threat by right-wing forces. In 1933, four weeks after Hitler's ascension to power, Mühsam was arrested in his Berlin home. He spent the last sixteen months of his life in detention and died in the Oranienburg Concentration Camp in July 1934.

Mühsam wrote poetry, plays, essays, ar-ticles, and diaries. His work unites a burning desire for individual liberation with anarcho-communist convictions, and bohemian strains with syndicalist tendencies. The body of his writings is immense, yet hardly any English translations exist. This collection presents not only *Liberating the State from Society: What is Communist Anarchism?*, Mühsam's main political pamphlet and one of the key texts in the history of German anarchism, but also some of his best-known poems, unbending defenses of political prisoners, passionate calls for solidarity with the lumpenproletariat, rec-ollections of the utopian community of Monte Verità, debates on the rights of homosexuals and women, excerpts from his journals, and essays contemplating German politics and an-archist theory as much as Jewish identity and the role of intellectuals in the class struggle.

An appendix documents the fate of Ze-nzl Mühsam, who, after her husband's death, escaped to the Soviet Union where she spent wenty years in Gulag camps.

Product Details:

Author: Erich Mühsam
Editor: Gabriel Kuhn
Publisher: PM Press
ISBN: 978-1-60486-055-9
Published: March 2011
Format: Paperback
Page Count: 240
Size: 9 by 6
Subjects: Politics-Anarchism, Philosophy

Praise:

"It has been remarked before how the history of the German libertarian and anarchist movement has yet to be written, and so the project to begin translation of some of the key works of Mühsam – one of the great names of German anarchism, yet virtually unknown in the English-speaking world – is most welcome. The struggles of the German working class in the early 20th century are perhaps some of the most bitter and misunderstood in European history, and it is time they were paid more at-tention. This book is the right place to start."
– Richard Parry, author of
The Bonnot Gang

"We need new ideas. How about studying the ideal for which Erich Mühsam lived, worked, and died?"
--Augustin Souchy, author of Beware Anarchist: A Life for Freedom

DEMANDING THE IMPOSSIBLE: A HISTORY OF ANARCHISM

by Peter Marshall

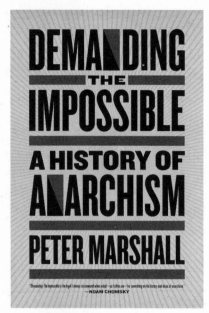

"Demanding The Impossible is the book I always recommend when asked—as I often am—for something on the history and ideas of anarchism."
—NOAM CHOMSKY

Product Details:

Authors: Peter Marshall
Publisher: PM Press
Published: Dec. 2009
ISBN: 978-1-60486-064-1
Format: Paperback
Page Count: 840
Dimensions: 8.5 by 5.5
Subjects: History, Political Science

About the Author:

Peter Marshall is a philosopher, historian, biographer, travel writer and poet. He has written fifteen highly acclaimed books which are being translated into fourteen different languages. His circumnavigation of Africa was made into a 6-part TV series and his voyage around Ireland into a BBC Radio series. He has written articles and reviews for many national newspapers and journals.

Navigating the broad *'river of anarchy'*, from Taoism to Situationism, from Ranters to Punk rockers, from individualists to communists, from anarcho-syndicalists to anarcha-feminists, Demanding the Impossible is an authoritative and lively study of a widely misunderstood subject. It explores the key anarchist concepts of society and the state, freedom and equality, authority and power and investigates the successes and failure of the anarchist movements through-out the world. While remaining sympathetic to anarchism, it presents a balanced and critical account. It covers not only the classic anarchist thinkers, such as Godwin, Proud-hon, Bakunin, Kropotkin, Reclus and Emma Goldman, but also other libertarian figures, such as Nietzsche, Camus, Gandhi, Foucault and Chomsky. No other book on anarchism covers so much so incisively.

In this updated edition, a new epilogue examines the most recent developments, including 'post-anarchism' and 'anarcho-primitivism' as well as the anarchist contribution to the peace, green and 'Global Justice' movements.

Demanding the Impossible is essential reading for anyone wishing to understand what anarchists stand for and what they have achieved. It will also appeal to those who want to discover how anarchism offers an inspiring and original body of ideas and practices which is more relevant than ever in the twenty-first century.

Reviews:

"Demanding the Impossible is the book I always recommend when asked – as I often am – for something on the history and ideas of anarchism."
– Noam Chomsky

"Attractively written and fully referenced...bound to be the standard history."
– Colin Ward, Times Educational Supplement

"Large, labyrinthine, tentative: for me these are all adjectives of praise when applied to works of history, and Demanding the Impossible meets all of them."
– George Woodcock, Independent